THE
7-DAY
MENU
PLANNER

THE 7-DAY MENU PLANNER

Weekly Shopping Lists, Menus, and
Recipes for an Entire Year

Edited by
Cynthia Hizer Jubera

LONGSTREET PRESS
Atlanta, Georgia

Published by LONGSTREET PRESS, INC.
A subsidiary of Cox Newspapers,
A division of Cox Enterprises, Inc.
2140 Newmarket Parkway
Suite 118
Marietta, GA 30067

Printed in the United States of America

1st printing, 1993

Library of Congress Catalog Number 92-84006

ISBN: 1-56352-078-8

This book was printed by R.R. Donnelley & Sons,
    Harrisonburg, Virginia.
The text was set in Goudy.

Cover design by Jill Dible
Book design by Laurie Shock

Acknowledgment: All recipes in this book originally appeared in the *Atlanta Journal and Constitution* and are reprinted here with permission.

Grateful acknowledgment is also due to Dr. Sandra Frank, a dietitian based in Coconut Creek, Florida, and Tom McNees of Decatur, Georgia, a nutritionist and member of the American Dietetic Association, who computed the nutritional analyses for these recipes as they originally appeared in the *Atlanta Journal and Constitution*.

DEDICATION

To my mother, who would stay up all night teaching a little farm girl to bake bread and Coq au Vin, to treat food as the creative life force it is. And to the memory of my father, who, long before it was politically correct, taught me to walk lightly on the earth.

———

To those who have helped me along the way, and without whose help and love, this book would never have happened. To Nathalie Dupree for her friendship, unending guidance and good sense; to Susan Stevenson, who first called me with the column idea; Susan Puckett and Nancy Roquemore, whose editing finesse make this weekly menu planner the success it is; to Karen Sundstrom for her talent with weekly recipe testing; Gretchen Swanger for office help and recipe work; Case Lichtveld of Harry's Farmers Market and Margo Putnam of Sevananda Natural Foods Cooperative for crash courses in everything I ever wanted to know about produce; Mike Hulsey of Inland Seafood for my continuing education in seafood and hands-on cutting tips; to all the produce and meat purveyors, chefs, cooks, farmers and readers who guide me each week; and to my husband, Drew, and my son, Andrew, who, with love and good humor, have tasted more flops than anyone should be subjected to.

INTRODUCTION

This book is for busy people, but busy people who like great food and have families made up of kids, older relatives, vegetarians, fruitarians, picky eaters and those who love cream and those who hate cream.

The dream seemed impossible: to create a weekly menu planner to help busy people shop and cook in an organized way. It's been a challenge, believe me, to develop recipes that would throw a wide net to include all of you out there that need to eat in a hurry, who want to eat healthfully but also want great flavor and an interesting mix of cuisines. It's a weekly jigsaw puzzle, fitting together meals that seem to slide from day to day without creating chaos. Can we go from Mexican to Japanese to rustic American in three days? Can our taste buds take that much havoc after a hard day at the office?

After three years of writing this weekly planner, I hope I've hit most of the bases. Most weeks include some low-fat as well as higher-fat dishes; I figure it will balance out in the end, and you will have the benefit of some great-tasting food. Recipes often call for unsalted butter; many could use margarine instead, if you prefer.

Most weeks are based on a more traditional meat-based diet, again to throw that wide net to include as many of you as possible. For those of you who eat less meat, you can easily cut back or make substitutions; personally, I eat a whole lot more bulgur, miso and greens than the planner reflects. Each week also highlights a produce or fish item that is at its best. And when an item is "in season" it is usually more abundant, of better quality and lower in price. So look through the seasonal highlights included in each month to see what you might best put on your own shopping list. And finally, I want you to look over the bibliography list; it reflects the many talented cookbook authors that have inspired me, and books you might want to add to your own libraries.

It is my goal to show you how to most efficiently fit leftovers into your weekly menus. I love leftovers, as you will soon see. Leftovers are those unheralded blobs that sit in unidentified margarine containers for weeks and eventually get tossed without even a peek inside. But leftovers have a vital role. First of all, they are already peeled, diced and cooked. Secondly, they often taste better after a short stint in the refrigerator. That means you can often cook a quick meal with more intense flavors simply by virtue of letting them be for a day or two. It is my belief that instead of being a nuisance, leftovers should become the backbone of the meals we cook in our busy lives.

The *Menu Planner* attempts to do just that. The beginning of each week generates leftovers; the end of the week uses them. That's the simple grand plan that you will see evolve week after week. Saturday stands on its own, however. Saturday seldom uses leftovers.

After three years, the *Menu Planner* is still evolving, thanks to my many faithful readers who write and call with advice or suggestions. I have personally tested every recipe in this book. For a long time now, my ace recipe tester, Karen Sundstrom, and I would cook every Tuesday (the day before deadline). In the afternoon we would set the table for eight, never knowing who might show up. Some weeks no one came, and we would taste test six or eight dishes alone. Other weeks ten people would show up, some sporting out-of-town guests or children home sick from school. We didn't care! We loved the company and the diversity, and everyone enjoyed being guinea pigs for the *Menu Planner*.

So, if you can't come by next Tuesday, enjoy the book.

Oh, one final note to help use the book: in many of the menus I've included "suggested accompaniments" (marked by an asterisk). Since they're just suggestions, I have neither supplied recipes for preparing them nor included their ingredients in the weekly shopping lists. Now, enjoy.

Cynthia

THE 7-DAY MENU PLANNER

WEEK

1

Meat, poultry, seafood

- ❑ 2 frying chickens, cut up, or 7 to 8 pounds pieces
- ❑ 4 8-ounce pork or veal chops

Produce

- ❑ 3 pounds Yukon Gold or other waxy potatoes
- ❑ 1 3-to 4-pound butternut squash
- ❑ 1 bulb fennel (anise)
- ❑ 1 head loose-leaf lettuce
- ❑ 6 garlic cloves
- ❑ 1 large onion
- ❑ 2 green Vidalia onions or 1 small red onion
- ❑ 2 green bell peppers
- ❑ 2 bunches spinach
- ❑ 1 small bunch kale (optional)
- ❑ 1 head endive
- ❑ 1 pound portabella mushrooms
- ❑ 2 grapefruits

- ❑ 3 navel oranges
- ❑ 1 spicy tart apple
- ❑ 1 pear
- ❑ 1 bunch thyme
- ❑ 1 bunch cilantro

Dairy

- ❑ 2 sticks plus 1 tablespoon unsalted butter
- ❑ 2 eggs
- ❑ 3 ounces low-fat cream cheese

Deli

- ❑ 4 to 6 ounces Gruyere or double creme Brie cheese
- ❑ 1 loaf crusty bread: French, sourdough or other
- ❑ 4 to 8 pita pockets
- ❑ 4 berry muffins
- ❑ 4 to 8 cheddar cheese rolls
- ❑ 1 cup crumbled feta cheese

- ❑ ^{1}/$_4$ to ^{1}/$_3$ cup grated Parmesan cheese
- ❑ 1 10-inch pizza crust
- ❑ 1 lemon cheesecake

Miscellaneous

- ❑ ^{1}/$_2$ cup plus 1 tablespoon orange juice
- ❑ 1 cup chopped walnuts
- ❑ 1 cup semisweet chocolate chips
- ❑ 2 15-ounce cans chickpeas (garbanzos)
- ❑ 2 14 ^{1}/$_2$-ounce cans reduced-sodium chicken broth
- ❑ ^{1}/$_2$ cup pitted black olives
- ❑ 2 to 3 tablespoons pesto
- ❑ ^{1}/$_2$ cup wild rice combination
- ❑ 1 tablespoon Madeira wine

Staples

- ❑ Berry or other fruity vinegar
- ❑ Brown sugar
- ❑ Buttermilk
- ❑ Chili powder
- ❑ Cracked black pepper
- ❑ Dijon mustard
- ❑ Granulated sugar
- ❑ Lemon juice
- ❑ Lime juice
- ❑ Mayonnaise
- ❑ Olive oil
- ❑ Pure vanilla extract
- ❑ Salt
- ❑ Self-rising flour
- ❑ Vegetable oil
- ❑ White wine vinegar

* Suggested accompaniments

** The nutritional analyses accompanying these recipes should be used as general guidelines only.

CHILI ROASTED CHICKEN
BAKED BUTTERNUT SQUASH
WITH GARLIC AND THYME *
ROASTED YUKON
GOLD POTATOES *
BROWN SUGAR TART

This is a good menu for midwinter. Winter squash is still a good bargain and its robust flavor still welcome. The chile-rubbed chicken makes a great Sunday meal and produces plenty of leftovers. Use basil leaves if you can't find cilantro. Save leftover squash and roasted potatoes for later in the week. Cut the tart into small pieces, as it is quite rich.

CHILI ROASTED CHICKEN

Makes 8 servings
Preparation time: 5 minutes
Cooking time: 45 minutes

2 frying chickens cut into 16 pieces, or about 7 pounds parts
2 tablespoons chile powder, or to taste
3 garlic cloves, minced
Salt to taste
$^1/_2$ cup orange juice
$^3/_4$ cup lime juice
$^1/_4$ cup oil
4 teaspoons coarsely ground black pepper
$^1/_4$ cup chopped cilantro

Preheat the oven to 350 degrees. Wash and pat the chicken dry. In the bowl of a food processor, combine the chile powder, garlic, salt, orange juice, lime juice, oil, pepper and cilantro and pulse a few times to make a smooth mixture. Spread the mixture evenly over the skin of the chicken. Place the chicken in a large roasting pan and bake 45 minutes.

Per serving: 535 calories, 33 grams fat, 167 milligrams cholesterol, 178 milligrams sodium.

BROWN SUGAR TART

Makes 8 servings
Preparation time: 10 minutes
Cooking time: 40 minutes

$^3/_4$ cup unsalted butter
2 $^1/_4$ cups firmly packed brown sugar
1 tablespoon pure vanilla extract
2 eggs
2 cups self-rising flour
1 cup chopped pecans
1 cup semisweet chocolate chips, melted

Preheat the oven to 350 degrees. Grease a 10-by-2-inch springform pan. Heat the butter and brown sugar in a medium saucepan about 5 minutes or in the microwave for 1 minute or until the butter is melted. Stir in vanilla and eggs. Add the flour; stir until well blended. Stir in the nuts.

Pour the mixture into the prepared pan and place in the oven. Bake 35 to 45 minutes until golden brown and set in the center, then cool. Drizzle the top of the tart with melted chocolate and cut into wedges.

Per serving: 724 calories, 35 grams fat, 53 milligrams cholesterol, 436 milligrams sodium.

WINTER SALAD
GRUYERE AND

FRENCH BREAD *

Make this refreshing salad — adapted from a wonderful book on fruit *Cooking With Fruit* by Rolce Redard Payne and Dorrit Speyer Senior (Crown, $22)) — while citrus is cheap and at its best quality. Red or white grapefruit will be fine, but the red will add more color. To stand up to the wonderful anise flavor of fennel, choose a rich and full-flavored cheese such as Gruyere, or double creme Brie and a fruity vinegar.

WINTER SALAD

Makes 4 to 6 servings
Preparation time: 10 minutes

2 grapefruits
1 large navel orange
1 fennel bulb (about 1 pound)
1 head loose-leaf lettuce for lining the platter
2 tablespoons fruit vinegar (raspberry, for example)
$^1/_4$ teaspoon Dijon mustard
1 teaspoon granulated sugar
4 tablespoons vegetable oil
Salt and black pepper to taste

Peel the grapefruit and section it. Peel the orange and slice into eighths. Set them aside.

Wash, trim and quarter the fennel bulb, then cut into $^1/_8$-inch thick slices. Place the citrus and fennel in a bowl and toss.

Line a shallow bowl with lettuce and arrange the salad attractively on top. In a small bowl, combine vinegar, mustard, sugar and oil. Whisk until well blended, then season with salt and pepper. Serve the vinaigrette sauce separately, since the salad is also good without any dressing.

Per serving: 139 calories, 10 grams fat, no cholesterol, 13 milligrams sodium.

TUESDAY

CHICKPEAS AND CHICKEN WARM PITA POCKETS *

Leftover chile-flavored chicken and bits of squash add to this delicious bean dish, which is good hot or cold. The recipe makes plenty for another night. Add colored bell peppers if you find them at a bargain.

CHICKPEAS AND CHICKEN

Makes 8 servings
Preparation time: 5 minutes
Cooking time: 15 minutes

2 tablespoons unsalted butter
1 large onion, finely chopped
2 garlic cloves, minced
2 green bell peppers, seeded and chopped
2 15-ounce cans chickpeas (garbanzo beans), drained
2 to 4 roasted chicken pieces, meat and skin cut into large dice, room temperature
1/2 cup cooked butternut squash, cut in squares (optional), room temperature
Salt and pepper to taste

In a large skillet, melt the butter. Add the onion and saute slowly until golden, very soft and sweet. Stir in the garlic and bell pepper and cook for 5 minutes. Stir in the beans, chicken and squash pieces and cook, stirring occasionally, for 5 to 10 minutes, until the ingredients are heated through and fragrant. Add salt

JANUARY

January can bring freezes, floods and wind damage from Florida to California, and produce prices fluctuate along with the weather. Cold weather crops will offer the most value: greens, root vegetables and citrus. Potatoes are at a good price and still good quality, even though they are coming out of storage now. Freezes can cause cracks in carrots, tip burn on lettuce and brown spots on cauliflower.

Apples and pears are coming out of storage but are still very nice, with most of the rest of the fruit available now coming from the tropics. Much of it is very nice, although more expensive than its summer counterparts. Air-freighted fruit will be better tasting and less mealy than fruit that comes by boat. Florida green avocados are a good buy this month.

and pepper to taste. Serve half the dish tonight and reserve half for another night.

Per serving: 373 calories, 16 grams fat, 83 milligrams cholesterol, 389 milligrams sodium.

WEDNESDAY

SPINACH AND ENDIVE SALAD WITH ORANGE BUTTERMILK DRESSING BERRY MUFFINS WITH LOW-FAT CREAM CHEESE *

The dressing recipe makes enough for four servings, but the spinach mixture makes double that, so reserve half to top a pizza later in the week. Both the dressing and the salad ingredients can be prepared ahead of time and held, adding the dressing at serving time. This recipe easily doubles to serve a crowd.

WINTER SPINACH SALAD BOWL

Makes 6 servings
Preparation time: 20 minutes

1 tablespoon orange juice
1/2 tablespoon fruity vinegar
1/4 tablespoon Dijon mustard
1 tablespoon mayonnaise
2 tablespoons vegetable oil
2 tablespoons buttermilk
1 teaspoon grated orange peel
Dash salt and black pepper
2 to 3 bunches (6 to 7 cups washed and dried) spinach leaves, stemmed and torn into bite-size pieces
1 head endive, separated into spears, washed and dried
2 green Vidalia onion bulbs, thinly sliced
1 navel orange, peeled

Whisk together the orange juice, vinegar, mustard and mayonnaise. Whisk the oil and butter-

Price: 4 for $1.00 for small and 2 for $1.00 for larger sizes. Fruit from the Indian River area of Florida, which should be identified with a sticker on the fruit, may be slightly more expensive.

Nutrition: Per half grapefruit: 50 calories, no sodium, an excellent source of vitamin C and a good source of fiber.

Selection: Florida and Texas fruits peak during the fall and early winter and West Coast fruits — from California and Arizona — take over the season in early spring through early summer. Grapefuit should be firm yet springy to the touch and heavy for its size. Minor surface blemishes or a slightly green color does not affect quality, but avoid bad bruises on the peel. Late in the season grapefruit tend to get soft, dry and granular inside. Grapefruit from Florida and Texas have a thinner rind and are juicier inside, while Arizona and California fruit have a thicker rind and less juice.

Storage: Grapefruit will keep at room temperature for a few days, but it will last a week or more if stored in the refrigerator.

Uses: Serve grapefruit fresh and peeled or combine in fruit salads or cooked fruit compotes.

milk together and pour in a thin stream, whisking constantly to make a creamy dressing. Add the orange peel, salt and pepper to taste.

Heap the spinach and endive in a large salad bowl. Add onion slices and toss. Save half this salad mixture for later in the week.

Cut orange into thin crosswise slices, then divide them into small sections and add to the salad. Drizzle dressing over salad and toss just before serving.

Per serving: 144 calories, 10 grams fat, 2 milligrams cholesterol, 185 milligrams sodium.

CHICKPEA AND GREENS SOUP
CHEDDAR CHEESE ROLLS *

Leftovers take a new turn with this comforting soup. If you are lucky enough to have frozen pesto, drop a couple of tablespoons into the soup. Add purchased cheese rolls.

CHICKPEA SOUP

Makes 4 servings
Preparation time: 10 minutes
Cooking time: 15 minutes

3 cups leftover chickpea dish
1 to 2 cups cooked leftover potatoes, cut in large dice
2 to 3 14 1/2-ounce cans reduced-sodium chicken broth
2 to 3 tablespoons pesto
1 to 2 cups kale or spinach, torn into pieces

Place the leftover chickpea combination and potatoes in a large saucepan or heavy skillet. Stir in the broth and pesto and heat through. Just before serving, stir in the greens and turn off the heat. Let the greens heat until just wilted, then serve.

Per serving: 261 calories, 8 grams fat, 1 milligram cholesterol, 496 milligrams sodium.

SPINACH AND FETA PIZZA
FRESH FRUIT SECTIONS *

Leftover salad ingredients can easily go into another salad, but here we have placed them on a pizza for a more filling Friday night meal. Add a platter of fruit — grapefruit, oranges, apple, pear, carambola, and bananas.

SPINACH AND FETA PIZZA

Makes 4 to 6 servings
Preparation time: 5 minutes
Cooking time: 10 minutes

1 10-inch pizza crust
1 cup crumbled feta cheese
3 cups leftover spinach mixture
1/4 to 1/3 cup grated Parmesan cheese

Preheat oven to 400 degrees. On a pizza crust, layer the feta, spinach mixture and top with Parmesan cheese. Bake until bubbly, about 10 minutes.

Per serving: 252 calories, 12 grams fat, 37 milligrams cholesterol, 733 milligrams sodium.

PORK CHOPS WITH RASPBERRY VINEGAR GLAZE
WILD RICE *
SAUTEED PORTABELLA MUSHROOMS
WITH WILTED GREENS
LEMON CHEESECAKE *

Who would think this elegant winter menu could be so easy? Choose center-cut pork or veal chops, depending on which is a better bargain. If you prepare this in a season when berries are available, add a handful to the finished sauce for a few seconds. Both dishes are cooked on the stovetop in minutes; add a rice combination of wild, brown and white rices, available in health food stores and many groceries, and a purchased dessert. Portabella mushrooms are oversized creminis, both brown and robust-tasting. Use creminis if portabellas aren't available, and standard white mushrooms can be used, but will offer less flavor. Any leftover mushrooms make good pizza topping or addition to a soup or stew.

PORK CHOPS WITH RASPBERRY VINEGAR GLAZE

Makes 4 servings
Preparation time: 5 minutes
Marinating time: Overnight
Cooking time: 10 minutes

4 8-ounce pork or veal chops
1 cup berry vinegar
1 tablespoon unsalted butter

Marinate the meat overnight in

a shallow ceramic or glass dish with 1/2 cup of the vinegar.

When ready to cook, heat the butter in a large skillet. Discard the vinegar used as a marinade and brown the chops on both sides. Add the remaining vinegar to the skillet and simmer with the chops until reduced to a syrupy glaze.

Per serving: 313 calories, 22 grams fat, 95 milligrams cholesterol, 85 milligrams sodium.

SAUTEED PORTABELLA MUSHROOMS

Makes 4 servings
Preparation time: 5 minutes
Cooking time: 5 minutes

1 pound large portabella mushrooms, wiped clean and trimmed
4 tablespoons unsalted butter
2 garlic cloves, minced
$^1\!/_2$ teaspoon salt, or to taste
2 tablespoons Madeira or port wine

Melt the butter in a large skillet over moderate to low heat. Add the mushrooms and the garlic and cook, gently stirring until cooked through and softened, 2 to 5 minutes. Season with salt and Madeira and let cook for a few seconds. Serve on a bed of wilted greens: spinach, Swiss chard or dandelion.

Per serving: 111 calories, 10 grams fat, 11 milligrams cholesterol, 301 milligrams sodium.

WEEK 2

SHOPPING LIST

Meat, poultry, seafood

- ❑ 3 pounds sweet Italian sausages
- ❑ 2 to 2 ¹/₂ pounds well-trimmed snapper fillets

Produce

- ❑ 1 head lettuce, any type
- ❑ 4 or 5 large russet potatoes
- ❑ 2 medium potatoes
- ❑ 12 large carrots
- ❑ 11 large garlic cloves
- ❑ 3 large onions
- ❑ 1 sweet onion (Bermuda is good)
- ❑ 1 red bell pepper
- ❑ 3 or 4 ribs celery
- ❑ 2 pounds small mustard greens
- ❑ 1 medium cucumber
- ❑ 3 or 4 ounces spicy, alfalfa or onion sprouts
- ❑ 1 jalapeno chile
- ❑ 1 bunch cilantro
- ❑ 3 or 4 fresh or dried sage leaves
- ❑ 1 small knob ginger

- ❑ 6 large baking apples
- ❑ 1 lemon
- ❑ 3 Key limes
- ❑ 1 orange
- ❑ 2 grapefruit or 1 cup bottled grapefruit sections

Dairy

- ❑ 2 tablespoons margarine
- ❑ 3 tablespoons plus 1 stick unsalted butter
- ❑ 1 ³/₄ cups half and half
- ❑ 1 ¹/₂ cups milk
- ❑ 1 pint vanilla ice cream
- ❑ 1 ¹/₂ cups jalapeno Monterey Jack cheese
- ❑ 8 to 10 ounces feta cheese
- ❑ 3 eggs

Deli

- ❑ 1 quart split pea soup
- ❑ 12 crackers
- ❑ ¹/₂ poundcake
- ❑ 4 pita rounds
- ❑ 1 Key lime pie

Miscellaneous

- ❑ ³/₄ cup bourbon

- ❑ 3 or 4 ounces whole-wheat crackers
- ❑ 3 14 ¹/₂-ounce cans low-sodium chicken broth
- ❑ 1 ¹/₂ cups frozen baby lima beans
- ❑ 1 pint applesauce
- ❑ 1 pound spaghetti
- ❑ 32 ounces crushed or pureed Mexican-style or Italian plum tomatoes
- ❑ 10 to 12 pimento-stuffed green olives
- ❑ 1 cup white basmati or other fragrant rice
- ❑ 3 tablespoons capers
- ❑ 1 16-ounce bag frozen lady peas or other small white beans
- ❑ 2 tablespoons Sambuca liqueur
- ❑ 1 cup chopped pecans
- ❑ 8 ounces crushed pineapple

Staples

- ❑ Allspice
- ❑ Baking Soda
- ❑ Brown sugar

- ❑ Cardamom, pod or ground
- ❑ Cayenne pepper
- ❑ Corn bread mix
- ❑ Cornmeal
- ❑ Curry powder
- ❑ Freshly ground black pepper
- ❑ Granulated sugar
- ❑ Hot pepper jelly
- ❑ Lemon juice
- ❑ Low-fat mayonnaise
- ❑ Nutmeg
- ❑ Olive oil
- ❑ Pure vanilla extract
- ❑ Salt
- ❑ Self-rising flour
- ❑ Stick cinnamon
- ❑ Vegetable shortening
- ❑ Vegetable oil
- ❑ Vinegar
- ❑ Whole cloves
- ❑ Whole wheat flour

* Suggested accompaniments

WHITE BEANS WITH FETA*
ROASTED POTATOES AND
CARROTS WITH
GARLIC AND SAGE
BOURBON-BUTTERSCOTCH
BAKED APPLES

This wintry meal is easy to prepare and offers plenty of fiber and complex carbohydrates. Most of the dishes can bake in the oven at the same time. Quickly saute frozen lady peas or other small white beans with butter, onions and fresh sage, and garnish with crumbles of feta cheese. Make enough for today's meal and reserve 2 to 3 cups to serve later. If you have never roasted vegetables, get ready for an extra-rich flavor, as the sugars in the carrots caramelize. Cook 2 extra potatoes for later in the week, and extra roasted carrots and baked apples adapted from Michael McLaughlin's *The New Ameri-can Kitchen* (Simon & Schuster) will work into other meals during the week.

ROASTED CARROTS WITH GARLIC AND SAGE

Makes 8 servings
Preparation time: 10 minutes
Cooking time: 40 minutes

4 medium potatoes, scrubbed and cut
    in large dice
8 carrots (about 2 pounds) peeled,
    trimmed and sliced lengthwise
    in thin strips
2 tablespoons oil
¼ cup water
10 large garlic cloves, peeled but left
    whole

3 or 4 dried or fresh sage leaves
Salt and black pepper, to taste

Preheat oven to 350 degrees. Arrange the carrots in a large baking dish. Add the oil, water, garlic, sage, salt and pepper. Cover the baking dish with foil and bake until the carrots are tender, about 30 minutes.

Uncover and toss the carrots in the accumulated juices. Raise the oven heat to 450 degrees. Continue baking until they are caramelized, 5 to 10 minutes.
    Per serving: 82 calories, 4 grams fat, no cholesterol, 75 milligrams sodium.

BOURBON-BUTTERSCOTCH BAKED APPLES

Makes 6 servings
Preparation time: 10 minutes
Cooking time: 30 minutes

6 large baking apples, cored
½ cup unsalted butter, cut into
    small pieces
¾ cup brown sugar, firmly packed
¾ cup bourbon
¾ cup light cream
1 tablespoon vanilla
1 tablespoon lemon juice

Preheat the oven to 350 degrees. Remove a thick slice of peel from around the top of each apple with a vegetable peeler. Set the apples upright in a flameproof baking pan. Top the apples with the butter, sprinkle with brown sugar and bourbon. Bake until the apples are puffed and tender, basting them occasionally with the pan juices, 30 to 35 minutes.
    Transfer the apples to a platter and keep warm. Stir the cream into the baking pan and set over high heat. Bring to a boil, then lower the heat to medium high

and cook, stirring frequently, until the sauce is reduced by half and coats a spoon, 7 to 10 minutes. Remove the sauce from the heat and stir in the vanilla and lemon juice. Spoon the sauce onto dessert plates and set an apple in the center of each one and serve immediately.
    Per serving: 302 calories, 10 grams fat, 26 milligrams cholesterol, 7 milligrams sodium.

CURRIED LIMA BEAN
CHOWDER
WHOLE-WHEAT CRACKERS *

Chowder means potatoes in anybody's book, and here, they are teamed with frozen lima beans. This filling soup is delicious and quick to cook, without hours of cooking. This dish makes good use of cooked, leftover potatoes, and speeds cooking time. Save half the recipe to serve later in the week.

CURRIED LIMA BEAN CHOWDER

Makes 8 servings
Preparation time: 15 minutes
Cooking time: 25 minutes

2 tablespoons unsalted butter
1 large onion, chopped
3 to 4 carrots, diced
3 ribs celery, chopped
2 tablespoons curry powder
2 to 3 14 ½-ounce cans (4 cups)
    low-sodium chicken broth
1 ½ cups frozen baby lima beans
2 medium potatoes, cooked, peeled or
    unpeeled, diced
¼ teaspoon nutmeg
A pinch cayenne pepper
1 cup half-and-half (or milk)

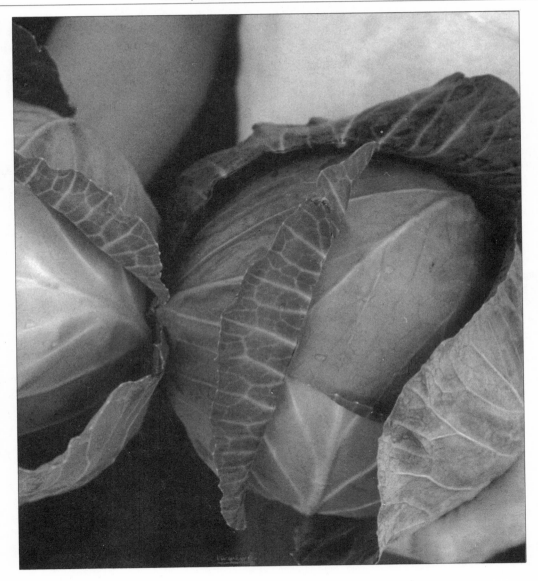

Price: Will average $.28 to $.50 a pound.

Nutrition: Raw cabbage has about 20 calories per cup of shredded cabbage, is rich in vitamin C, has a fair amount of vitamin B1, and is a good source of several minerals and fiber.

Selection: Choose firm heads that feel heavy for their size. Outer leaves should look fresh, have good color and be free of blemishes.

Storage: Refrigerate, unwashed, in a plastic bag for up to 1 week.

Uses: Allow ¼ pound per person. A 1 ½ pound cabbage yields 6 to 8 cups shredded raw cabbage. Use cabbage raw in salads or add to stir-fries or simmered dishes, or use as a wrapping for other foods, such as rice.

Melt the butter in a large saucepan, over moderate heat. Add the onions, carrots and celery; saute 5 to 10 minutes, until onions are soft. Stir in the curry powder and saute for a few more minutes.

Add the chicken stock, beans, potatoes, nutmeg and cayenne. Bring to a boil, then reduce heat to a simmer and cook, uncovered, over low heat until the beans and potatoes are cooked, about 10 minutes. Stir in the half—and—half or milk and bring back to a simmer.

Per serving: 237 calories, 13 grams fat, 41 milligrams cholesterol, 77 milligrams sodium.

TUESDAY

SAUSAGES AND MUSTARD GREENS WITH WHITE BEANS ROASTED CARROTS WITH GARLIC * ICE CREAM WITH WARMED APPLESAUCE *

Sweet Italian sausages go well with the zesty flavor of mustard greens to produce a filling and rustic weeknight dinner. Frozen, chopped mustard greens can be used in place of fresh ones, which will speed up preparation, but the cooked texture of the greens will be softer. Reheat leftover carrots. For dessert, heat applesauce, perhaps with some cider stirred in, and serve over ice cream.

SAUSAGES AND MUSTARD GREENS WITH PASTA

Makes 6 servings
Preparation time: 10 minutes
Cooking time: 30 minutes

2 pounds hot Italian sausage in

casings
2 pounds small mustard greens (rinsed and leaves stripped from stems and roughly chopped)
1 cup water, divided
1/2 teaspoon salt, or to taste
2 cups cooked white beans
2 tablespoons oil
Hot pepper vinegar, to taste

Prick the sausages and place them in a large flameproof casserole. Add half a cup of water, cover and cook over moderately high heat for about 5 minutes, until no longer pink in the middle. (Turn the heat down if necessary.) Uncover and continue cooking over moderate heat, until evenly browned, about 10 minutes. Reserve 1 pound of the cooked sausages for another meal; transfer the remainder to a board.

Add the chopped mustard greens to the casserole and cook over high heat until wilted, a couple of minutes. (If you are using frozen, chopped mustard greens, no need to wilt them.) Add the water and salt and simmer, partly covered, for about 15 minutes, or until tender.

Slice sausages and lay on top of the greens. Continue cooking a few minutes to allow the liquid to evaporate.

Meanwhile, reheat the beans from Sunday and place in a large shallow bowl. Top with the mustard greens and sausages, and season liberally with hot pepper vinegar.

Per serving: 702 calories, 33 grams fat, 83 milligrams cholesterol, 1,217 milligrams sodium.

WEDNESDAY

PITA SANDWICHES WITH FETA

AND AVOCADO CREAM SLICED BAKED APPLES WITH POUNDCAKE *

Stuffed pitas go together quickly and make good use of leftover sausage or beans, paired with avocado and spicy sprouts. Mexican cream is a thick, slightly soured cream available in most large grocery stores in the dairy section; substitute yogurt or sour cream. Spicy sprouts are usually grown from radish seeds and add a wonderful bite to the dish; substitute alfalfa sprouts or equally delicious onion sprouts.

A few slices of poundcake will make a delicious dessert with leftover baked apples, sliced and reheated.

PITA SANDWICHES WITH FETA AND AVOCADO CREAM

Makes 4 servings
Preparation time: 10 minutes
Cooking time: 5 minutes

4 pita rounds, opened but not completely split
2 fresh avocados
1/2 cup Mexican cream
2 tablespoons lime juice
Salt and black pepper, to taste
1/2 cup very thick split pea soup, warmed (optional)
4 to 6 ounces crumbled feta cheese, rinsed
1 medium cucumber, peeled, seeded and sliced into thin rounds
1/2 sweet onion, or 2 green Vidalias, thinly sliced
1 cup spicy sprouts

Turn the oven to 300 degrees. Place the pita breads in the oven just long enough to warm through, 4 or 5 minutes.

Remove the avocado flesh

from the shells. Put the avocado flesh, Mexican cream and lime juice in the work bowl of a food processor and pulse to blend. Add salt and pepper to taste. Divide the puree evenly and spread on the inside of the pita rounds. Layer with other (optional) left-overs, crumbled cheese, cucumber, onion and sprouts and serve. The preheated pita will slightly melt the cheese without wilting the sprouts.

Per serving: 440 calories, 20 grams fat, 58 milligrams cholesterol, 277 milligrams sodium.

THURSDAY

CURRIED LIMA BEAN CHOWDER WITH SAUSAGE *
JALAPENO JACK CHEESE BISCUITS

Leftover bean chowder tastes great with the sausages cooked earlier in the week. These biscuits pack some heat; use a plain Jack cheese if you wish. Save leftover biscuits for tomorrow night's dinner.

JALAPENO CHEESE BISCUITS

Makes 12 biscuits
Preparation time: 5 minutes
Cooking time: 15 minutes

1 cup self-rising flour
$^1/_2$ cup cornmeal
$^1/_4$ teaspoon black pepper
2 tablespoons cold vegetable shortening
$^3/_4$ cup milk
1 $^1/_2$ cups shredded jalapeno Monterey Jack cheese

Preheat oven to 425 degrees.

Spray a baking sheet or use parchment paper.

Place the flour, cornmeal and pepper in the bowl of a food processor and pulse to blend. Add the shortening and pulse just to make a coarse meal. Add the milk and cheese and pulse a few more times, just until combined and dough is sticky.

Drop by spoonfuls about 1 inch apart onto the baking sheet. Bake 12 to 15 minutes or until golden.

Per biscuit: 189 calories, 11 grams fat, 27 milligrams cholesterol, 292 milligrams sodium.

FRIDAY

JALAPENO JACK CHEESE BISCUITS WITH HOT PEPPER JELLY*
AVOCADO AND GRAPEFRUIT SALAD*

Use leftovers to create this easy meal: spread cheese biscuits with hot pepper jelly. Prepare a simple salad of avocado slices and grapefruit sections: place over a bed of lettuce and crumble some feta cheese over, if you wish.

SATURDAY

RED SNAPPER WITH OLIVES AND RED SAUCE
ORANGE BASMATI RICE
SAMBUCA CORN BREAD
PINEAPPLE KEY LIME PIE

Red snapper is delicious in this dish, but look for other, less expensive alternatives, such as other Pacific snapper, even catfish.

If the avocados are perfectly ripe, a simple vinaigrette is all the flavoring they need. Add this rice dish, made with fragrant Basmati rice and finish with a Key lime pie. You may use Indian basmati or American-grown basmati rices, one of which is sold under the Texmati label. Indians usually cook rice with whole spices, such as the cinnamon stick and whole cloves in the following recipe, as they impart more flavor. Simply remove them at the end of cooking.

RED SNAPPER WITH OLIVES AND RED SAUCE

Makes 6 servings
Preparation time: 10 minutes
Cooking time: 20 minutes

2 to 2 $^1/_2$ pounds well-trimmed snapper fillets
2 tablespoons fresh lime juice
Salt and pepper, to taste
3 tablespoons drained capers
1 jalapeno pepper, stemmed, seeded and chopped
1 tablespoon olive oil
1 cup finely chopped onion
1 chopped red bell pepper
2 large garlic cloves, minced
32 ounces canned Mexican-style tomatoes, pureed
10 to 12 drained, pimento-stuffed green olives
$^1/_2$ cup chopped fresh cilantro

Season the fish with lime juice, salt and pepper. Place in a shallow dish with the capers and jalalpeno pepper. Set aside to marinate for 10 to 15 minutes.

Meanwhile, heat the oil in a Dutch oven over medium heat. When hot, add the onion, bell pepper and garlic. Cook, stirring frequently, for 4 minutes. Add tomatoes and olives. Stir to blend, then add the fish, covering the top of the fish with some of the sauce. Bring to a simmer over medium heat, then lower heat and cook 15 minutes or until fish is cooked through. Garnish the fish with cilantro and serve.

Per serving: 353 calories, 11 grams fat, 71 milligrams cholesterol, 771 milligrams sodium.

ORANGE BASMATI RICE

Makes 4 servings
Preparation time: 5 minutes
Cooking time: 20 minutes

2 teaspoons unsalted butter
2 teaspoons orange peel, finely chopped
1 teaspoon granulated sugar
1 cup white basmati or other long-grain fragrant white rice
1 cinnamon stick
1 whole clove
2 star anise pods
2 cups low-sodium chicken broth
Salt, to taste

Heat the butter in a medium (1 1/2 to 2 quart) saucepan over very low heat. Stir in the orange peel and sugar. Cook, stirring, for 1 minute to crystallize the orange peel. Stir in the rice, cinnamon stick, clove and anise pods. Stir to blend. Add the broth and salt.

Stir the rice. Cover and cook over medium heat until the water is absorbed and the rice tender, about 15 minutes. Let stand, uncovered, for 5 minutes. Remove the cinnamon, clove and anise pods before serving.

Per serving: 212 calories, 2 grams fat, 3 milligrams cholesterol, 37 milligrams sodium.

SAMBUCA CORN BREAD

Makes 6 to 8 servings
1 5-ounce package corn bread mix
3/4 cup milk or water
2 tablespoons Sambuca liqueur (or 1 teaspoon anise flavoring)
2 tablespoons melted butter or margarine

Preheat oven to 375 degrees and grease an 8-inch baking dish.

Prepare the corn bread batter according to package directions, adding the liqueur. Pour the batter into the pan and drizzle the top with melted butter. Bake about 25 minutes.

Based on 8 servings, per serving: 119 calories, 6 grams fat, 8 milligrams cholesterol, 124 milligrams sodium.

PINEAPPLE KEY LIME CAKE

Makes 12 servings
Preparation time: 5 minutes
Cooking time: 1 hour

2 cups self-rising flour
1 cup whole-wheat flour
1 teaspoon baking soda
1 teaspoon ground allspice
2 cups granulated sugar
1 cup chopped pecans
1 1/2 cups vegetable oil
3 eggs, beaten
1 8-ounce can crushed pineapple, undrained
Grated peel of 3 Key limes
1/4 cup Key lime juice

Preheat oven to 350 degrees. Butter and sugar the sides of a bundt pan or angel food pan. Set aside.

Sift together flour, soda, all-spice and sugar; add chopped pecans. Mix oil and eggs and fold into flour mixture. Stir in pineapple, lime peel and juice, mixing well. Pour into bundt pan. Bake for 60 minutes or until toothpick inserted in the middle comes out clean. Cover loosely with foil and cool in pan before removing.

Per serving: 567 calories, 36 grams fat, 68 milligrams cholesterol, 285 milligrams sodium.

WEEK

3

SHOPPING LIST

Meats, poultry, seafood

- ❏ 2 chickens, 2 $\frac{1}{2}$ to 3 pounds each, quartered or in pieces
- ❏ 2 ounces ($\frac{1}{4}$ cup) ham
- ❏ 1 pound mahi-mahi, skinned

Produce

- ❏ 1 small head red cabbage
- ❏ 1 small head green cabbage
- ❏ 2 bunches spinach
- ❏ $\frac{1}{2}$ pound snow peas
- ❏ 20 ounces cremini mushrooms
- ❏ 1 bunch bitter greens (dandelion, arugula, watercress)
- ❏ 4 large sweet potatoes
- ❏ 6 medium carrots
- ❏ 1 bunch radishes
- ❏ 6 yellow onions
- ❏ 2 McIntosh apples

- ❏ 1 pint (2 cups) apple cider
- ❏ 2 cooking apples (Golden Delicious or Granny Smith)
- ❏ 1 fresh pineapple (or 1 14 $\frac{1}{2}$-ounce can chunks)

Dairy

- ❏ 3 sticks plus 2 tablespoons butter
- ❏ 1 egg
- ❏ 3 tablespoons sour cream
- ❏ 1 pint vanilla ice cream

Deli

- ❏ 2 loaves French or crusty bread
- ❏ 4 tablespoons grated Cheddar cheese
- ❏ 2 ounces grated Gruyere or Parmesan cheese
- ❏ 1 8-ounce wheel Camembert or

Brie cheese

Miscellaneous

- ❏ $\frac{1}{3}$ cup applejack (apple brandy)
- ❏ 1 8-ounce package mixed dried fruit
- ❏ 10 dried apricots
- ❏ $\frac{1}{2}$ cup orange juice
- ❏ $\frac{1}{4}$ cup Port
- ❏ 3 tablespoons Calvados (apple brandy)
- ❏ 4 cups low-sodium chicken broth
- ❏ 3 14 $\frac{1}{2}$-ounce cans beef broth
- ❏ 2 cups white rice
- ❏ 1 cup walnuts (or almonds or hazelnuts)
- ❏ $\frac{1}{3}$ cup almonds
- ❏ 1 9 $\frac{1}{2}$-ounce jar espresso chocolate sauce
- ❏ 2 tablespoons packaged coconut

Staples

- ❏ Baking powder
- ❏ Baking soda
- ❏ Black pepper
- ❏ Bread, any kind
- ❏ Brown sugar
- ❏ Ground allspice
- ❏ Low-fat mayonnaise
- ❏ Minced garlic in oil
- ❏ Olive oil
- ❏ Paprika
- ❏ Powdered sugar
- ❏ Pure vanilla extract
- ❏ Red wine vinegar
- ❏ Salt
- ❏ Self-rising flour
- ❏ Sugar
- ❏ Vegetable oil
- ❏ Worcestershire sauce

* Suggested accompaniments

BAKED CHICKEN WITH CIDER AND APPLES
GREEN SALAD WITH TOASTED WALNUTS*
BUTTER CAKE WITH WINTER FRUITS

Winter fruits steeped in port and applejack (apple brandy) add deep flavors to this meal. Add a green salad made with bitter greens and toasted walnuts and a vinaigrette made with walnut oil and a fruity vinegar. Be sure to cover the cake as it bakes to prevent burning, then remove the foil for the last few minutes of cooking. A springform pan will make it easier to get the cake out of the pan.

BAKED CHICKEN WITH CIDER AND APPLES

Makes 6 to 8 servings
Preparation time: 10 minutes
Cooking time: 65 minutes

2 chickens (2 ½ to 3 pounds), quartered or in pieces
1 pint (2 cups) apple cider
1 cup all-purpose flour
2 teaspoons ground allspice
Salt and black pepper to taste
3 tablespoons brown sugar
⅓ cup applejack
2 cooking apples (Golden Delicious or Granny Smith), cored and cut into thin wedges

Early in the day, or if possible the day before serving, place the chicken pieces in a shallow dish. Pour the cider over the chicken and marinate in the refrigerator, turning the pieces occasionally. Preheat the oven to 350 degrees.

Remove the chicken from the cider but reserve the cider. Mix the flour, allspice, salt and pepper in a shallow bowl. Dredge the chicken with the flour mixture and place skin side up in a shallow baking pan. Bake 40 minutes.

Meanwhile, combine the reserved cider, brown sugar, applejack and apple slices. Pour the marinade mixture over the chicken and bake 25 minutes more, basting occasionally with the pan juices.

Per serving: 452 calories, 16 grams fat, 117 milligrams cholesterol, 159 milligrams sodium.

BUTTER CAKE WITH WINTER FRUITS

Makes about 10 servings
Preparation time: 10 minutes
Cooking time: 40 minutes

Topping:
1 8-ounce package mixed dried fruit, cut into 1-inch pieces
10 dried apricots, cut in half
½ cup orange juice
¼ cup Port
3 tablespoons unsalted butter
Cake:
1 stick unsalted butter, room temperature
¾ cup sugar, divided
1 large egg
3 tablespoons sour cream
1 teaspoon pure vanilla extract
1 cup self-rising flour
¼ teaspoon baking soda
Powdered sugar (sifted) for garnish

Combine fruit, orange juice, Port and butter in a 4-cup microwave-safe dish and cook uncovered on high about 8 minutes or until fruit is soft and liquid is thick (or cook on the stove about 10 minutes); set aside.

Preheat oven to 350 degrees and spray an 8-inch springform pan with pan spray. In the food processor, process butter, ½ cup sugar, egg, sour cream and vanilla until smooth and fluffy, about 1 minute, stopping to scrape down the sides of work bowl. Blend flour and baking soda in a small bowl, add to butter mixture and process just until combined.

Spread batter in the pan. Top with fruit mixture and sprinkle with remaining sugar. Cover with aluminum foil and bake about 40 minutes, or until cake begins to pull away from the sides of the pan. Cool in the pan 5 minutes before removing. Sift powdered sugar over the top and serve warm or at room temperature.

Per serving: 321 calories, 14 grams fat, 64 milligrams cholesterol, 79 milligrams sodium.

HOT MUSHROOM SANDWICHES
WEDGES OF RED AND GREEN CABBAGE*

HOT MUSHROOM SANDWICHES

Makes 4 to 6 servings
Preparation time: 5-8 minutes
Cooking time: 7-8 minutes

2 cups chopped fresh mushrooms
2 tablespoons butter, softened
⅓ cup low-fat mayonnaise
Salt and pepper, to taste
¼ cup finely diced ham
4 to 6 thick slices French bread

4 tablespoons grated Cheddar
cheese

Preheat oven to 400 degrees. For
the bread slices, trim the ends of
a 14-ounce loaf of French bread
with a serrated knife, cut the
loaf in half lengthwise, then cut
crosswise into 2 or 3 equal portions.

Combine ham, mushrooms,
butter, mayonnaise, salt and
pepper. Spread evenly on the
bread slices. Sprinkle each with
cheddar cheese. Bake until the
cheese is bubbly, about 7 to 8
minutes.

*Per serving (6 servings): 188 calo-
ries, 10 grams fat, 19 milligrams cholesterol, 262 milligrams sodium.*

TUESDAY

TOASTED RICE WITH
CHICKEN AND MUSHROOMS
CARROT STICKS*
HOT BUTTERED TOAST*

A few extra seconds of stirring
turns the rice in this dish toasty
brown and adds a nice crunch.
Brown rice would make a flavorful addition, but add 15 to 20
more minutes to the cooking
time. Add leftover chicken from
earlier in the week, raw carrot
sticks and hot buttered toast for
a comforting touch. Save leftovers to serve later in the week.

TOASTED RICE WITH
CHICKEN AND
MUSHROOMS

Makes 8 servings
Preparation time: 10 minutes
Cooking time: 20 minutes

2 cups rice

6 tablespoons unsalted butter
1 large onion or $^1/_2$ large, chopped
1 tablespoon minced garlic in oil
1 pound cremini mushrooms,
    cleaned and sliced
4 cups low-sodium chicken broth
1 to 2 cups cooked, cubed chicken
1 or 2 cabbage wedges, roughly
    chopped (optional)

Meanwhile, combine the rice
and 3 tablespoons of butter in a
large heavy skillet. Cook over
high heat 3 or 4 minutes, then
add the onion, garlic and mushrooms and continue to cook,
stirring, until the rice is golden,
4 or 5 minutes, and the vegetables softened. Add the broth,
chicken and (optional) cabbage,
and simmer for 10 to 15 minutes. Let the rice stand, covered,
for 5 minutes.

*Per serving: 315 calories, 15 grams
fat, 59 milligrams cholesterol, 465 milligrams sodium.*

WEDNESDAY

ONION SOUP WITH
CHEESE TOAST
SPINACH SALAD*

This onion soup goes together in
minutes with the help of canned
beef broth. Cheese melted on
French bread and floated on top
of the soup is a classic and filling addition — omit the butter
if you are using Gruyere cheese.
Add a spinach salad, and add
any bits of other vegetables you
have on hand, such as radish,
cucumber, mushrooms or snow
peas.

ONION SOUP WITH
CHEESE TOAST

Makes 6 to 8 servings

Preparation time: 10 minutes
Cooking time: 25 minutes

6 tablespoons unsalted butter
4 large yellow onions, thinly
    sliced
$^1/_2$ teaspoon sugar
6 cups beef stock or broth
1 teaspoon Worcestershire sauce
Salt and black pepper to taste
4 to 6 thick slices French bread
4 teaspoons butter or margarine
$^1/_4$ cup (approximately) freshly
    grated Gruyere or Parmesan
    cheese

Heat butter in large saucepan
over medium heat. Add onion
and sugar and saute until gold-
en brown, about 5 minutes. Add
the beef broth and Worcestershire and bring to a boil. Reduce
heat and simmer uncovered 15
to 20 minutes. Add salt and
black pepper to taste.

Meanwhile, toast the slices
of French bread under the broiler for a few seconds, just until
crispy. Spread the untoasted
sides with butter and sprinkle
with the cheese. Return the
bread to the broiler, cheese side
up, until lightly toasted. Ladle
soup into bowls and float the
cheese toast on top.

*Per serving (6 servings; with
canned broth): 261 calories, 14 grams
fat, 31 milligrams cholesterol, 1,250 milligrams sodium.*

THURSDAY

TOASTED RICE WITH
CHICKEN AND MUSHROOMS
WITH PEAS*
WINTER FRUIT CAKE*

Use leftover rice tonight, aug-
mented with frozen peas. If you

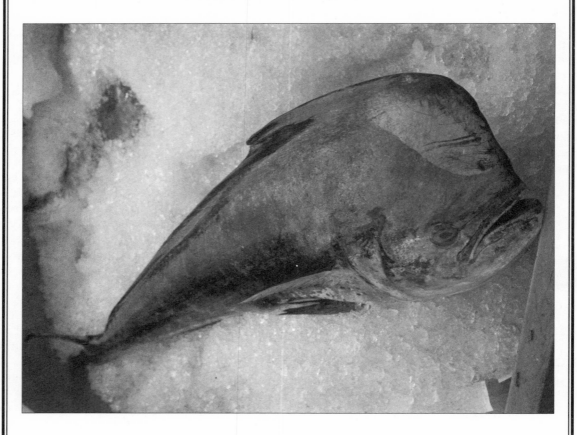

Price: Average $4.99 to $5.99 a pound, with specials at $3.99 a pound.

Nutrition: A 3-ounce portion has 85 calories, no fat, and 73 milligrams cholesterol.

Selection: Look for fillets cut in 6- to 12-ounce portions, about 1-inch thick, and preferably without the tough, inedible skin. Ask the seafood clerk to remove the skin, although it is easy to pull off. The flesh has a small red streak that is edible. If fillets have been stored on top of each other they will likely be discolored from cream-colored to dark red, but the quality will be the same.

Storage: Remove the fish from its store wrapping, rinse it well under cold running water and store in a covered dish in the coldest part of the refrigerator, which is usually the meat keeper. Rinse the fish again before cooking. Cooked, the fish will store another 3 days.

Uses: The dense flesh makes mahi-mahi good for grilling, frying, sauteeing or shish kabob. Serve the fish in whole, skinless fillets, grilled for sandwiches or cut up and sauteed for a warm salad.

have any leftover walnuts, toss them in too. Add slices of cake for dessert.

CAMEMBERT NORMANDE
WITH
MCINTOSH APPLES AND
FRENCH BREAD
RAW VEGETABLES*

This French classic calls for cheese marinated in a fine apple brandy, then heated with a coating of chopped hazelnuts, available at local farmers markets, but here I use walnuts or almonds instead. This winning version is adapted from Sarah Lean Chase's *Cold Weather Cooking* (Workman Publish-ing, $13.95). Sweet-tart McIntosh, Idared, Fuji or Empire apples are my first choice, but Granny Smith would work fine. Serve this at a wintry, simple dinner or as part of a party buffet. When you toast the nuts, add the almonds and coconut for tomorrow night's dinner also.

CAMEMBERT NORMANDE

Makes 4 to 8 servings
Preparation time: 15 minutes
Cooking time: 12 minutes

1 wheel (8 ounces) Camembert
    or Brie
3 to 4 tablespoons Calvados
1 cup walnuts, almonds or skinned
    hazelnuts
1 tablespoon unsalted butter, at
    room temperature
2 crisp McIntosh apples, thinly
    sliced
Sliced French bread

The day before you plan to serve the Camembert, gently scrape the thick white parts of the skin from the cheese but do not remove the rind. Using a fork, poke holes in the surface of the cheese. Place the cheese in a bowl and pour the Calvados over. Allow the cheese to marinate at room temperature for 24 hours, turning occasionally.

To toast the nuts, place them on a baking sheet in the oven at 250 degrees. Watch them and stir them occasionally for about 10 minutes, until they start to turn color and become fragrant. This can be done the day before or the day of serving.

The next day, place the nuts in a food processor and finely chop. Add the butter and pulse until the butter and nuts are blended. Pat the nut mixture evenly over the top and sides of the cheese. Using a spatula, carefully transfer the cheese to a baking dish and refrigerate, covered, for about 1 hour.

When ready to serve, preheat the oven to 400 degrees. Bake the cheese until the nuts are golden brown, about 12 to 15 minutes. Serve at once, spooned onto slices of French bread, with apple slices.

Per serving with one slice bread: 321 calories, 19 grams fat, 24 milligrams cholesterol, 432 milligrams sodium.

WARM MAHI-MAHI SALAD
ON GREENS
GINGER FRIED SWEET
POTATOES
VANILLA ICE CREAM WITH
ESPRESSO CHOCOLATE
SAUCE*

Choose dense and flavorful mahi-mahi fish for this filling salad. The skin of the fish pulls off easily if the seafood clerk hasn't done it for you. The recipe easily doubles to serve more and goes together in minutes. Toast the coconut, wash the spinach and steam the snow peas ahead of time, so the dish will go together while the sweet potatoes are frying.

WARM MAHI-MAHI SALAD

Makes 4 servings
Preparation time: 20 minutes
Cooking time: 10 minutes

2 tablespoons oil
1 pound mahi-mahi
1 medium onion or 1/2 large, sliced
1/4 pound fresh snow peas
1 cup cubed fresh or canned
    pineapple
1/3 cup coarsely chopped toasted
    almonds
Salt to taste
1/2 cup vinaigrette (made with
    olive oil and red wine vinegar)
1 bunch fresh spinach
2 tablespoons toasted coconut

Remove the skin from the fish if necessary, and remove any bones in the flesh. Cut the fish into 1-inch cubes.

In a large skillet, heat the oil, then add the fish and onions and saute 5 to 8 minutes or until the fish is almost cooked throughout. Add snow peas and cook 2 to 3 more minutes. Remove from the heat and place in a large serving bowl. Add pineapple, nuts, salt and vinaigrette. Mix gently but thoroughly. Line serving platter with greens and spoon fish mixture onto the greens. Top with toasted coconut.

Per serving: 377 calories, 23 grams fat, 46 milligrams cholesterol, 237 milligrams sodium.

GINGER FRIED SWEET POTATOES

Makes 4 servings
Preparation time: 15 minutes
Cooking time: 20 minutes

3 large sweet potatoes, peeled
1 quart vegetable oil for frying
Salt and ground ginger
    (or cardamom), to taste

Using a knife or mandoline, cut the sweet potatoes into slices thin as potato chips. Soak them in ice water until ready to use. At the very last minute before serving, heat the oil in a fryer or an electric frying pan to 400 degrees. Blot the sweet potato slices dry and fry them for about 2 minutes or until crisp and golden brown. Remove the chips with a slotted spoon, drain on paper towels and add salt and ground ginger to taste.

Per serving: 525 calories, 35 grams fat, no cholesterol, 470 milligrams sodium.

WEEK 4

SHOPPING LIST

Meat, seafood, poultry

- ❏ 2 3-pound lamb loin roasts or 5 to 6 pounds boneless lamb chunks
- ❏ 4 6-to 8-ounce veal cutlets
- ❏ 1 pound thick-sliced bacon
- ❏ 4 8-ounce boneless, skinless catfish fillets

Produce

- ❏ 2 large yellow onions
- ❏ 14 green onions
- ❏ 2 large garlic cloves
- ❏ 6 shallots
- ❏ 1 pound cremini mushrooms
- ❏ 3 or 4 ounces shiitake mushrooms
- ❏ 1 jicama
- ❏ 1 bunch broccoli raab
- ❏ 1 bunch spinach
- ❏ 3 pounds all-purpose potatoes
- ❏ 1 acorn squash
- ❏ 1 orange
- ❏ 1 fresh pineapple, cored
- ❏ 1 bunch cilantro
- ❏ 1 bunch parsley
- ❏ 2 lemons
- ❏ $^1/_2$ cup apple cider

Dairy

- ❏ 3 sticks plus 4 tablespoons unsalted butter
- ❏ 17 eggs
- ❏ 2 $^1/_4$ cup buttermilk
- ❏ $^1/_2$ cup pepper Jack cheese
- ❏ 2 cups milk

Deli

- ❏ 8 corn or 4 large flour tortillas
- ❏ 2 loaves crusty bread
- ❏ 1 loaf multigrain bread

Miscellaneous

- ❏ $^1/_2$ cup dry white wine
- ❏ 2 tablespoons Triple Sec
- ❏ 1 28-ounce can stewed tomatoes
- ❏ 1 14 $^1/_2$-ounce can low-sodium chicken broth
- ❏ 2 cups English peas, frozen
- ❏ 1 cup frozen or canned corn
- ❏ 1 cup pecan halves
- ❏ $^1/_2$ pound roasted unsalted peanuts, skins removed
- ❏ 4 tablespoons orange juice
- ❏ 1 9-inch partially baked pie crust
- ❏ 1 pound egg noodles

Staples

- ❏ All-purpose flour

- ❏ Almond extract
- ❏ Black pepper
- ❏ Cider vinegar
- ❏ Cinnamon
- ❏ Cornmeal
- ❏ Granulated sugar
- ❏ Hot salsa
- ❏ Lemon juice
- ❏ Olive oil
- ❏ Peanut oil
- ❏ Powdered sugar
- ❏ Pure vanilla extract
- ❏ Red pepper flakes
- ❏ Salt
- ❏ Self-rising flour
- ❏ Sugar
- ❏ Vegetable oil
- ❏ Vegetable shortening

* Suggested accompaniments

ORANGE LAMB STEW
BOILED POTATOES
WITH BUTTER*
BUTTERMILK PECAN PIE

An orange-scented lamb stew is good for a cold winter night, and the following recipe, adapted from *As American as Apple Pie* by Phillip Stephen Schultz (Simon & Schuster, $19.95), makes plenty of leftovers. Pur-chase two lamb loin roasts and cut the meat from the bone to get the necessary amount for the stew (save the bones for a soup stock later). Add boiled potatoes, cut in large dice, and cook 1 extra pound to serve later in the week. Nathalie Dupree's buttermilk pie is a Southern classic; its tangy flavor complements the stew nicely.

ORANGE LAMB STEW

Makes 12 servings
Preparation time: 25 minutes
Cooking time: 40 minutes

5 to 6 pounds of boneless lamb, cut into 1-inch cubes
6 tablespoons all-purpose flour
$^1/_2$ cup vegetable oil
2 large yellow onions, chopped
2 large garlic cloves, minced
$^1/_2$ cup dry white wine
1 28-ounce can stewed tomatoes
1 14$^1/_2$-ounce can low-sodium chicken broth
1 teaspoon salt
$^1/_2$ teaspoon black pepper
1 teaspoon unsalted butter
2 to 3 tablespoons minced orange peel
1 to 2 tablespoons Triple Sec (optional)
2 cups English peas, frozen and thawed

Toss the lamb cubes with the flour to coat. Heat the oil in a large heavy pot over medium heat. Saute the lamb cubes, a few at a time, until well-browned on all sides. Transfer to a bowl.

Add the onions to the pot; cook over medium heat 2 minutes. Add the garlic, cook 3 minutes longer. Stir in the wine, scraping the bottom and sides of the pot with a wooden spoon. Add the tomatoes, chicken broth, salt and pepper. Return the meat to the pot with any accumulated juices. Simmer, covered, 30 to 40 minutes.

Melt the butter in a medium saucepan over medium-low heat. Add the orange peel; cook 4 minutes. Stir in the (optional) Triple Sec and cook on low heat for a minute; then stir into the stew. Add peas and cook until the lamb is tender and the sauce is thickened, about 10 minutes longer.

Per serving: 449 calories, 26 grams fat, 138 milligrams cholesterol, 520 milligrams sodium.

BUTTERMILK PECAN PIE

Makes 8 servings
Preparation time: 10 minutes
Cooking time: 30 minutes

4 eggs
1 $^1/_2$ cups granulated sugar
1 tablespoon flour
$^3/_4$ cup buttermilk
$^1/_2$ cup melted butter
$^1/_2$ teaspoon pure vanilla extract
Dash salt
1 cup pecan halves
1 9-inch partially baked pie crust

Preheat oven to 300 degrees. Beat the eggs and sugar until mixed. Blend in the flour, buttermilk, butter, vanilla and salt; beat until smooth. Add the pecans and pour into the prepared pie shell. Bake about 30 minutes, until set. Cool on a rack a few minutes before cutting, then serve warm or cool.

Per serving: 506 calories, 31 grams fat, 169 milligrams cholesterol, 343 milligrams sodium.

SCRAMBLED EGGS AND CORN IN TORTILLAS
HOT SALSA *
MATCHSTICK JICAMA AND FRESH PINEAPPLE CHUNKS *

Smooth hot salsa over scrambled eggs before tucking them into warmed tortillas. Add crunchy jicama, cut into matchstick pieces, along with fresh pineapple chunks. A sprinkle of lime juice on the jicama and pineapple will add just the right edge.

SCRAMBLED EGGS AND CORN IN TORTILLAS

Makes 4 servings
Preparation time: 15 minutes
Cooking time: 10 minutes

8 corn tortillas or 4 large flour (burrito-size) tortillas
3 tablespoons vegetable oil
6 green onions, white part and some green, chopped
1 cup corn, frozen and thawed or canned and drained
8 eggs, lightly beaten
1 cup water
Salt to taste
10 to 15 cilantro sprigs, chopped
$^1/_2$ cup grated pepper Jack cheese
4 tablespoons chili salsa

Price: 1.99 a bunch

Nutrition: Broccoli rabe is high in vitamins A and C with large amounts of potassium, iron, calcium and fiber.

Selection: Rabe is usually sold in bunches during the cooler months. One or two flowers of the bud tassel may be open, but the flower ends should be green and upright, not curved over, meaning it is overgrown. It may have a few small yellow flowers.

Storage: Wrap in a plastic bag and store in the refrigerator for up to 4 days.

Uses: Broccoli rabe can be cooked quickly or slowly. It is excellent in stir-fries, simmered or tossed in olive oil and cooked briefly. A clear broth of the cooking liquid makes a good antidote for colds and flu symptoms.

This cousin of the better-known broccoli is another member of the cabbage family and just as nutritious. It is prized for its nutritious stems and leaves rather than buds. Look for it in bunches in area specialty stores and farmers markets during the winter months.

Broccoli rabe is to Italians as collards and turnip greens are to Southerners, a slightly bitter green with tender leaves and brisk flavor. After the toughest stems are discarded, the tender stems can be blanched, steamed or stir-fried much like asparagus. It can be used in soup and casserole recipes that call for broccoli. Its seeds are the source of the oil rapeseed.

Preheat the oven to 200 degrees. Warm the tortillas in a dry cast-iron or non-stick pan. Transfer them to a baking pan in a warm oven while the eggs cook.

Melt the oil in a large skillet and add the green onions and corn. Cook for a minute or so, or until the corn is tender.

In a separate bowl, beat the eggs until frothy. Add the water, pour the eggs into the pan over the cooked onions. Cook, gently scrambling with a fork. Add salt to taste. Just as the eggs are finished cooking, add the cilantro. Transfer the warmed tortillas to serving plates and ladle the eggs over them. Sprinkle with cheese and salsa.

Per serving: 533 calories, 32 grams fat, 572 milligrams cholesterol, 501 milligrams sodium.

TUESDAY

HOT BUTTERED NOODLES WITH WINTER MUSHROOM SAUCE SAUTEED BROCCOLI RABE

This is for mushroom lovers. By using a combination of expensive shiitakes, brown creminis are a good choice for this dish brimming over with mushrooms. They resemble the white mushroom in shape, but have a denser texture and stronger flavor and are about the same price. They are available in most grocery stores. Cook extra noodles and set aside for later in the week.

Broccoli rabe (also called "rape" or "rapini"; see In Season) is a favorite, slightly bitter, Italian vegetable. It is quick and delicious when stir-fried in olive oil with red pepper flakes. Cook extra to serve later in the week, tossed with leftover noodles or tucked into an omelet.

HOT BUTTERED NOODLES WITH WINTER MUSHROOM SAUCE

Makes 6 to 8 servings
Preparation time: 10 minutes
Cooking time: 10 minutes

1 pound wide egg noodles
1 pound cremini mushrooms, washed, stemmed and sliced
3 or 4 ounces shiitake mushrooms, washed, stemmed and sliced
8 tablespoons unsalted butter
4 shallots, peeled and thinly sliced
Salt and freshly ground black pepper
3 tablespoons chopped parsley

Cook the egg noodles until al dente. Drain and keep warm. Melt the butter in a large skillet, add the mushrooms and shallots. Saute them slowly over medium heat, 10 minutes. Stir occasionally and add salt and pepper to taste. Pour over noodles and garnish with chopped parsley.

Per serving: 414 calories, 20 grams fat, 99 milligrams cholesterol, 13 milligrams sodium.

SAUTEED BROCCOLI RAAB

Makes 4 to 6 servings
Preparation time: 5 minutes
Cooking time: 5 minutes

2 tablespoons olive oil
1 large bunch broccoli rabe, cut in 2-inch lengths
Salt to taste
1/2 teaspoon crushed red pepper flakes (or to taste)

Heat the olive oil in a large skillet. When hot, add the broccoli rabe and cook, tossing constantly in the hot oil for 5 minutes or until cooked tender-crisp. Add salt and red pepper flakes to taste. Serve hot.

Per serving: 95 calories, 7 grams fat, no cholesterol, 13 milligrams sodium.

WEDNESDAY

SPINACH, POTATO AND BACON SALAD WITH HARD CIDER VINAIGRETTE MULTIGRAIN BREAD AND BUTTER *

Tonight, serve this warming and substantial salad with leftover potatoes, bacon and spinach wilted with a hot bacon and apple cider vinaigrette. The fruity flavor of apple cider goes well with the flavor of smoked bacon. Apple cider that has been stored in the refrigerator a few weeks to turn slightly hard will add an extra kick to the vinaigrette. Add a hearty bread and softened butter.

SPINACH, POTATO AND BACON SALAD WITH HARD CIDER VINAIGRETTE

Makes 6 servings
Preparation time: 10 minutes
Cooking time: 15 minutes

1 pound cooked, diced potatoes, slightly warmed
1/2 cup apple cider, divided, preferably hard
1/2 pound thick-sliced bacon, diced
1/8 cup cider vinegar
1 large bunch fresh spinach, washed and stemmed
Salt and black pepper to taste

Slightly reheat the potatoes, either in the microwave or in boiling water. Place them in a bowl, toss with ¼ cup cider and cover to keep warm.

Meanwhile, in a large skillet, cook the bacon, turning frequently, until crisp, about 10 minutes. Drain bacon and set aside. Set aside 7 tablespoons of the drippings in a small bowl and reserve 2 tablespoons to use later in the week. (If bacon has rendered less than 7 tablespoons, add enough vegetable oil to make up the difference.)

Add the remaining hard cider and vinegar to the skillet and boil until reduced to ⅓ cup, 3 to 5 minutes. Add the spinach to the bowl with the warm potatoes and toss with the warm bacon drippings. Add the hot cider reduction and toss. Taste and season with salt and pepper as needed.

Per serving: 299 calories, 22 grams fat, 25 milligrams cholesterol, 326 milligrams sodium.

THURSDAY

LAMB POT PIE WITH ORANGE PASTRY

Sunday's leftover lamb stew reappears in this delicious pot pie, again inspired by the late Phillip Stephen Schultz's *As American as Apple Pie* (Simon & Schuster, $19.95). If the stew has a lot of liquid, simply cook it down until it evaporates, or spoon enough out so the pastry has a solid base. Have the stew at room temperature before adding the pastry.

LAMB POT PIE WITH ORANGE PASTRY

Makes 4 to 6 servings
Preparation time: 20 minutes
Cooking time: 25 minutes

1 ½ cups all-purpose flour
⅛ teaspoon salt
1 teaspoon finely grated orange peel
½ cup butter-flavored shortening
2 to 4 tablespoons orange juice
4 to 6 cups leftover lamb stew

Combine the flour, salt and orange peel in a large bowl or food processor. Add the shortening with a pastry blender or pulse in the food processor until the dough looks like small peas. Add the orange juice a tablespoon at a time, and mix gently with a fork to form a soft dough. Chill 10 minutes.

Preheat the oven to 400 degrees. Place the leftover stew in a deep-dish pie pan.

Roll out the pastry on a lightly floured board or pastry cloth and cover the stew. Trim the pastry and flute the edges. Cut a slash in the center of the pie. Bake about 25 minutes or until the crust is golden brown.

Per serving (stew and pastry): 744 calories, 47 grams fat, 135 milligrams cholesterol, 606 milligrams sodium.

FRIDAY

HOT BUTTERED NOODLES WITH WARMED SPINACH AND BACON SALAD* LEMON BREAD

The refrigerator should be filled with dabs of leftovers. Serve separately or together, the leftover buttered noodles, topped with any leftover warmed spinach and bacon salad. Save 6 slices lemon bread for tomorrow night's dessert.

LEMON BREAD

Makes 1 large loaf, about 12 slices
Preparation time: 5 minutes
Cooking time: 35 to 45 minutes

⅔ cup unsalted butter, room temperature
1 ⅔ cup sugar
¼ cup lemon juice
3 large eggs
2 ½ cups self-rising flour
½ cup milk

Preheat oven to 350 degrees. Spray a 9-by-5-inch loaf pan with pan spray; set aside.

In the workbowl of a food processor or with a mixer, cream the butter until light, then add sugar and beat until light. Mix in lemon juice, then the eggs, one at a time, beating after each addition. Using a spoon, add the flour to the creamed mixture alternately with the milk. Do not overmix. Spoon the dough into the prepared pan. Bake until golden brown and a knife inserted in the center comes out clean, about 45 minutes.

Per slice: 311 calories, 12 grams fat, 97 milligrams cholesterol, 202 milligrams sodium.

SATURDAY

SCALLOPS WITH WALNUTS
AND SAUTERNES
BAKED KABOCHA SQUASH
WITH CINNAMON *
STEAMED BROCCOLI*
LEMON BREAD PUDDING

Treat yourself to this lovely little meal that is long on nutrition and flavor and short on effort. Bay scallops are lower in price than the larger sea scallops, but either would work for this dish. Kabocha squash is one of the sweetest of the winter squashes, and one will make plenty for 4 people, with leftovers. The lemon bread pudding makes a wonderful finish; next time you make it, double the lemon bread, just to have more lemon bread pudding.

SEARED SCALLOPS WITH WALNUTS AND SAUTERNES

Makes 4 servings
Preparation time: 20 minutes
Cooking time: 10 minutes

$^1/_2$ cup walnut halves, lightly toasted
1 $^1/_2$ tablespoons walnut oil
1 $^1/_4$ pounds fresh bay scallops
2 shallots, minced
$^2/_3$ cup good-quality Sauternes or
    other dessert wine
4 tablespoons unsalted butter,
    chilled, cut into small pieces
Salt and black pepper to taste

Preheat oven to 275 degrees. Toast the walnut halves for 8 to 10 minutes, watching them carefully. When done, turn off the heat.

Meanwhile, heat the oil in a large skillet over medium high heat. Add the scallops and walnuts and saute, shaking the pan to sear the scallops on all sides, just until barely cooked through, 2 to 3 minutes. Remove the scallops and walnuts to a heat-proof pan and keep warm in the oven while preparing the sauce.

To make the sauce, add the shallots to the skillet and cook until softened, 1 minute. Add the wine and boil until reduced to 4 or 5 tablespoons, about 5 minutes. Reduce the heat to the lowest possible setting. Whisk in the butter a little at a time; it should turn into a creamy sauce. Taste for salt and pepper.

Spoon the scallops back into the sauce and coat with the sauce.

Per serving: 390 calories, 25 grams fat, 74 milligrams cholesterol, 364 milligrams sodium.

LEMON BREAD PUDDING

Makes 4 servings
Preparation time: 10 minutes
Cooking time: 40 minutes

6 $^1/_2$-inch-thick slices stale lemon
    bread
1 tablespoon butter or margarine
    (optional)
1 $^1/_2$ cups milk
2 eggs
$^1/_2$ teaspoon pure vanilla extract
$^1/_4$ teaspoon almond extract

Preheat the oven to 350 degrees. If the lemon bread is not stale, heat it under the broiler for just a minute to dry it out. Lightly butter one side of the bread slices; set aside.

Grease a 9-by-5-inch loaf pan with pan spray. Lay the bread slices, buttered sides up, in the bread pan. Beat the eggs slightly and mix with the milk, vanilla and almond extracts. Pour the mixture over the layers of bread and bake for about 40 minutes, until the custard has set around the bread slices and the bits of bread above the custard line are golden brown. Serve with softened vanilla ice cream and a sprinkling of ground cinnamon.

Per serving (doesn't include optional butter or ice cream): 325 calories, 19 grams fat, 246 milligrams cholesterol, 167 milligrams sodium.

WEEK

5

SHOPPING LIST

Meat, poultry, seafood

- ❑ 4 pounds beef short ribs
- ❑ 2 12-ounce packages country ham
- ❑ 4 8-ounce salmon trout

Produce

- ❑ 2 pounds green beans
- ❑ 1 ³/4 pounds rutabagas
- ❑ 1 ¹/2 pounds turnips
- ❑ 6 large russet potatoes
- ❑ 3 onions
- ❑ 2 10-ounce packages fresh pearl onions
- ❑ 1 yellow crockneck squash
- ❑ 1 cup broccoli florets
- ❑ 1 bunch green onions
- ❑ 8 shallots
- ❑ 2 bulbs fennel
- ❑ 2 red bell peppers
- ❑ 1 cup mushrooms
- ❑ 24 stalks asparagus
- ❑ 7 large green apples

- ❑ 2 large pears
- ❑ 2 lemons
- ❑ 1 bunch basil

Dairy

- ❑ 3 sticks plus 3 tablespoons unsalted butter
- ❑ ¹/2 cup whipping cream
- ❑ 6 to 8 ounces white Cheddar cheese
- ❑ 1 egg

Deli

- ❑ 4 pita breads
- ❑ 4 cheesecake brownies

Miscellaneous

- ❑ 4 precooked crepes
- ❑ Corn bread
- ❑ 3 cups couscous, regular or whole wheat
- ❑ 3 cups stone-ground grits
- ❑ 2 16-ounce can garbanzo

beans (chickpeas)
- ❑ 8 ounces frozen turnip greens
- ❑ 1 cup frozen baby okra
- ❑ 1 14 ¹/2-ounce can artichoke hearts
- ❑ ¹/2 cup dried dates
- ❑ 1 orange-rum poundcake
- ❑ 1 cup chicken broth
- ❑ 2 tablespoons Madeira or sherry
- ❑ 1 14 ¹/2-ounce can beef broth
- ❑ 1 cup dried apricots

Staples

- ❑ All-purpose flour
- ❑ Balsamic vinegar
- ❑ Black pepper
- ❑ Brown sugar
- ❑ Chili sauce
- ❑ Coffee
- ❑ Crackers
- ❑ Dried rosemary, thyme or oregano

- ❑ Granulated sugar
- ❑ Ground cinnamon
- ❑ Lemon juice
- ❑ Maple syrup
- ❑ Nutmeg
- ❑ Olive oil
- ❑ Powdered sugar
- ❑ Sage
- ❑ Salt
- ❑ Vanilla beans

* Suggested accompaniments

BRAISED SHORT RIBS *
STEAMED GREEN BEANS *
MASHED RUTABAGAS,
TURNIPS AND POTATOES
APPLE AND PEAR CRUMBLE PIE

This wintry meal takes advantage of inexpensive ingredients that are hearty and satisfying. The mashed root vegetables are surprisingly sweet and a nice switch from mashed potatoes. Reserve leftovers to make into fried patties later in the week. Cook three extra potatoes and extra green beans and reserve for later. The crumb-topped apple and pear pie ends this Sunday dinner perfectly.

MASHED RUTABAGAS, TURNIPS AND POTATOES

Makes 8 servings
Preparation time: 15 minutes
Cooking time: 30 minutes

1 large rutabaga, peeled and
    quartered
2 to 3 large turnips, peeled and
    quartered
2 large or 3 medium russet potatoes,
    peeled and quartered
4 tablespoons unsalted butter,
    melted
1/2 cup milk
Salt and black pepper to taste

Bring a large saucepan or stock pot filled with salted water to boil. Add rutabagas and cook 15 minutes. Add the turnips and potatoes and boil 15 minutes more, or until all the vegetables are tender, then drain.

Using a hand masher or mixer, mash the vegetables together. Mash in butter, milk, and salt and pepper to taste.

Per serving, without added salt: 181 calories, 11 grams fat, 36 milligrams cholesterol, 152 milligrams sodium.

APPLE AND PEAR CRUMBLE PIE

Makes 8 servings
Preparation time: 20 minutes
Cooking time: 1 hour

FILLING:

2/3 cup granulated sugar
1/2 teaspoon ground cinnamon
1/8 teaspoon freshly grated nutmeg
4 large green apples, peeled, cored
    and thinly sliced
2 large pears, peeled, cored and
    thinly sliced
2 to 3 tablespoons lemon juice
TOPPING:
1/2 cup brown sugar
1/2 stick unsalted butter, softened
Finely grated peel of 1 lemon
1 cup all-purpose flour

Preheat oven to 350 degrees. To make the filling: Combine sugar, cinnamon and nutmeg in a large bowl. Sprinkle the apple and pear slices with lemon juice, then toss with the sugar mixture. Place in a 9-inch deep-dish pie pan. Do not add the excess juices.

Place the sugar with the butter and lemon peel in the workbowl of a food processor, pulse until smooth. Add the flour and pulse until mixture is crumbly in texture. Sprinkle the topping over the pie.

Place the pie on a foil-lined baking sheet and bake until golden brown and apples are tender, about 1 hour.

Per serving: 239 calories, 9 grams fat, 23 milligrams cholesterol, 3 milligrams sodium.

VEGETABLE PANCAKES
GREEN BEANS IN LEMON
VINAIGRETTE *
CHEDDAR CHEESE AND
CRACKERS *

Tonight's dinner is composed of leftovers transformed in delicious ways. Make grilled pancakes, similar to potato pancakes, with leftover mashed rutabagas, turnips and potatoes. Add cheese and yesterday's beans with a lemony vinaigrette.

VEGETABLE PANCAKES

Makes 4 servings
Preparation time: 5 minutes
Cooking time: 10 minutes

2 cups mashed rutabagas, turnips
    and potatoes
1 egg
Salt and pepper, to taste
Flour for dredging
4 tablespoons butter

Blend the mashed vegetables with the egg, salt and pepper. Form into patties with your hands and dredge both sides in flour. Set aside or refrigerate until cooking time.

Heat butter in a skillet; when bubbling, add pancakes. Partially cover and cook until crispy on one side, turn and cook other side until crispy and heated through.

Per serving, without added salt: 101 calories, 5 grams fat, 79 milligrams cholesterol, 71 milligrams sodium.

TUESDAY

SCOTT'S COUNTRY HAM WITH RED-EYE GRAVY GRITS *

Atlanta chef Scott Peacock makes the Southern Speciality, country ham with red-eye gravy, that is especially rich and thick because the gravy cooks along with, not after, the ham. This is a fast weeknight supper when you need a comfort boost. The following recipe yields enough country ham to use later in the week for another dinner. Most stores now sell country ham bits in 12- to 16-ounce packages.

Stone-ground grits are available at local farmers markets and have a more pronounced corn flavor and more whole-grain nutrition than the more processed grits available in grocery stores. But cook whatever you can find, they all taste great.

SCOTT'S COUNTRY HAM WITH RED-EYE GRAVY

Makes 8 servings
Preparation time: 10 minutes
Cooking time: 25 minutes

1 tablespoon butter
2 12-ounce packages country ham
2 to 2 1/2 cups black coffee

Heat the butter in a large skillet or two skillets. When the butter is bubbling, add the ham slices in a single layer and cook 2 or 3 minutes until the meat is colored slightly. Turn and cook the other side, about 2 or 3 minutes.

Pour off any excess fat from the skillet and pour the coffee over the meat. Cover and simmer about 20 minutes, until the gravy has thickened. Place the meat on four plates and pour the red-eye gravy over the meat and grits.

Per serving: 140 calories, 8 grams fat, 46 milligrams cholesterol, 1,079 milligrams sodium.

WEDNESDAY

LEMON COUSCOUS WITH STIR-FRIED VEGETABLES CHEESECAKE BROWNIES *

Both instant couscous and whole-wheat couscous, available at health food stores, cooks quickly and makes a delicious meal. Serve it with quickly cooked vegetables, and purchased brownies. Reserve 2 cups cooked couscous to serve later in the week.

LEMON COUSCOUS WITH STIR-FRIED VEGETABLES

Makes 8 servings
Preparation time: 5 minutes
Cooking time: 15 minutes

6 cups water
2 tablespoons butter or margarine
1/2 teaspoon salt
3 cups couscous
1 tablespoon lemon juice
Grated peel of 1 lemon
1/4 cup fresh basil, finely sliced
2 teaspoons olive oil
1 cup broccoli florets fresh, or frozen and thawed
1/2 red bell pepper, cored and cut in thin slivers
1 yellow crookneck squash, sliced
1 cup cooked okra
Salt and black pepper, to taste

In a medium saucepan, bring the water to a boil with the butter and salt. Add the couscous, stir, cover, reduce heat to low and cook for 5 minutes. Remove from the heat, add lemon juice, lemon peel, basil, and fluff the couscous with a fork. Keep covered while cooking the vegetables.

Meanwhile, heat the oil in a skillet. Quickly saute the broccoli, bell peppers and squash; add the okra just long enough to reheat. Add salt and black pepper to taste. Serve over the couscous.

Per serving: 448 calories, 9 grams fat, no cholesterol, 392 milligrams sodium.

THURSDAY

HAM AND APPLE HASH CORN BREAD *

With cooked potatoes and country ham from earlier in the week, this homey dish goes together in minutes. Prepare or purchase corn bread to serve alongside. If you need the dish to serve more than four people, stretch it by adding more potatoes. Regular ham can substitute for country ham if you wish.

HAM AND APPLE HASH

Makes 4 servings
Preparation time: 10 minutes
Cooking time: 20 minutes

3/4 cup chili sauce
3 tablespoons maple syrup
3 tablespoons unsalted butter
1 medium onion, chopped
2 cups diced cooked country ham
1/8 teaspoon ground nutmeg
Salt and black pepper, to taste
Pinch granulated sugar

Price: Will average $.49 a pound.

Nutrition: One cup of cooked, cubed rutabaga has 60 calories and is a good source of vitamin A, niacin and potassium.

Selection: While rutabagas are available year round, their peak season is from October through March.

Choose small to medium-sized rutabagas, 3 to 4 inches in diameter. Look for smooth, firm vegetables that are heavy for their size, lightweight ones may be woody. Organic rutabaga aren't waxed and run smaller in size.

Storage: Rutabagas are usually sold waxed and so will keep for months in the refrigerator. If not waxed, store unwrapped in a cool, dry, dark place with good ventilation for up to 2 months, or in the refrigerator a week or two.

Uses: Allow about $\frac{1}{3}$ pound per serving. Serve boiled and diced, tossed with butter and herbs or mashed. Add quartered rutabagas to soup stocks and stews.

1 apple, diced
3 large potatoes, cooked and cut into
    $^1/_2$-inch dice, room temperature

Combine the chili sauce and maple syrup in a small bowl; set aside. Melt the butter in a 12-inch heavy skillet over medium heat. Add the onion; cook 4 minutes. Add the ham and cook about 3 to 5 minutes, until lightly browned. Reduce the heat. Stir in the nutmeg, salt, pepper, sugar, apple and potatoes. Cook 5 to 10 minutes or until heated through.

Per serving, without added salt: 422 calories, 20 grams fat, 66 milligrams cholesterol, 693 milligrams sodium.

FRIDAY

CHICKPEAS WITH FENNEL AND PEPPERS
TOASTED PITA BREADS*
APPLES AND DATES *

The week's leftovers should taste even better by the end of the week. Stuff chickpeas into pita breads, and offer a platter of winter fruits.

This is a perfect one-dish meal that combines lots of healthy ingredients. Omit the bell peppers if you find they are too expensive. Use spinach or collard greens and add to the dish just long enough to cook them slightly. Use frozen chopped greens if you wish to speed preparation time.

CHICKPEAS WITH FENNEL AND PEPPERS

Makes 6 to 8 servings
Preparation time: 20 minutes
Cooking time: 30 minutes

2 onions, thinly sliced
2 bulbs fennel, thinly sliced bulb only
    (reserve stems for later in the
    week)
1 red bell pepper, thinly sliced
1 tablespoon olive oil
1 tablespoon balsamic vinegar
2 16-ounce cans garbanzo beans
    (chickpeas), drained
4 or 5 dried sage leaves or $^1/_2$
    teaspoon dried rosemary
8 ounces frozen turnip greens, thawed
    and drained well
Salt and black pepper to taste

Heat the oil in a Dutch oven or heavy large saucepan. Add the onions and saute over medium heat until soft and golden, 5 to 10 minutes. Add the vinegar and continue to saute until the onions are brown and wilted, about 5 minutes.

Add the fennel, peppers, and sage to the saucepan. Cover the pan and simmer until the flavors have melded, about 20 minutes. During the last 10 minutes, add the garbanzo beans, then the chopped greens just long enough to heat them through. Add salt and black pepper to taste.

Per serving, without added salt: 210

FEBRUARY

February brings more unsteady weather and produce prices. From Florida frosts to Arizona floods, we can't be sure about domestic produce. Meanwhile, Mexican vegetables are often in full supply and Chilean fruit comes to us in full harvest. You can expect fluctuating prices on most items. Apples have been in storage now for a few months and are higher priced and slightly mealy, but kiwi fruit, pineapples and papaya can be delicious and a bargain. Citrus is still an excellent buy, and this late in the season is at its sweetest.

calories, 5 grams fat, no cholesterol, 635 milligrams sodium.

SATURDAY

POACHED SALMON TROUT WITH FENNEL*
LEMON COUSCOUS WITH LEMON PEEL*
GLAZED PEARL ONIONS AND SHALLOTS
DRIED APRICOTS BAKED WITH VANILLA AND GINGER

Midwinter begs for comfort food, and these rustic dishes fill the bill. A salmon trout is as beautiful as salmon, without the pricetag, and can be poached or cooked in the microwave oven, stuffed with anise-flavored fennel branches (reserved from earlier in the week). Reheat leftover lemon couscous to serve alongside.

Baked apricots offer a delicious and warming dessert, good enough for guests and homey enough for your family. Simply place vanilla beans and ginger slices under the apricots to infuse their flavors, suggests the cookbook author who inspired this recipe, Deborah Madison, in *Savory Way* (Bantam Books, $22.95).

GLAZED PEARL ONIONS AND SHALLOTS

Makes 4 servings
Preparation time: 15 minutes
Cooking time: 10 minutes

2 10-ounce packages fresh pearl
    onions
6 shallots, peeled
2 cups beef broth

To peel fresh pearl onions, place them in a pot of boiling water for 2 minutes, drain and cool. Then cut off the root end and the skins will slide off easily. Trim the root end from the shallots as well. Place onions and shallots in a small, heavy-bottomed saucepan. Pour in just enough beef broth to cover them.

Bring the broth to a boil. Reduce the heat to medium and boil gently until the stock has reduced and formed a glaze.

Per serving: 104 calories, 1 gram fat, no cholesterol, 412 milligrams sodium.

DRIED APRICOTS BAKED WITH VANILLA AND GINGER

Makes 4 servings
Standing time: 15 minutes
Baking time: 1 hour

1 cup dried apricots
1 cup warm water
1 1-inch piece vanilla bean, sliced in
    half lengthwise
3 or 4 slivers of fresh ginger
1 tablespoon sugar
4 precooked crepes
Powdered sugar for garnish

Preheat the oven to 350 degrees. Cover the apricots with warm water and let them stand for 15 to 20 minutes to plump and soften. Drain, reserving the water. Put the water, vanilla bean and ginger in an 8-inch pie plate or baking dish. Scrape out the seeds of the vanilla bean with the tip of a knife and break them up in the water. Lay the apricots over the vanilla beans and ginger and sprinkle them with sugar. Cover with foil and bake until the water is nearly absorbed, about 1 hour. Turn the apricots over in the syrup. Discard the vanilla bean and ginger slices. Keep the apricots warm until serving time.

At serving time, heat the precooked crepes. To serve, place the crepes on four dessert plates, divide the apricots among the crepes, roll and sprinkle with powdered sugar.

Per serving: 194 calories, 3 grams fat, 51 milligrams cholesterol, 148 milligrams sodium.

WEEK

6

SHOPPING LIST

Meat, poultry, seafood

- ❑ 1 3 ¹/₂-to 4-pound pork loin roast (with bone)
- ❑ 4 6-ounce rainbow trout fillets

Produce

- ❑ 1 red or green bell pepper
- ❑ 1 head lettuce, any type
- ❑ 1 jicama
- ❑ 1 bunch broccoli
- ❑ 4 to 6 Yukon Gold potatoes
- ❑ 3 bunches green onions
- ❑ 2 medium onions
- ❑ 4 garlic cloves
- ❑ 2 shallots
- ❑ 3 Granny Smith apples
- ❑ 2 oranges
- ❑ 2 ripe pears
- ❑ 1 pound snow peas

- ❑ 2 or 3 nice radishes
- ❑ 1 large sweet red or 2 hot banana peppers

Dairy

- ❑ 1 ¹/₂ cups plain yogurt
- ❑ 6 large eggs
- ❑ 3 tablespoons butter or margarine
- ❑ 2 to 3 cups vanilla ice cream, ice milk or frozen yogurt

Deli

- ❑ ¹/₄ cup grated Parmesan (or feta) cheese

Miscellaneous

- ❑ 4 cups basmati rice
- ❑ 2 cups frozen green peas
- ❑ 4 to 8 rye crackers

- ❑ 1 14 ¹/₂-ounce can stewed tomatoes
- ❑ 1 14 ¹/₂-ounce can chicken broth
- ❑ 2 8-ounce packages ramen noodles
- ❑ 1 12-ounce bottle Jade or other peanut sauce
- ❑ 5 pistachio nuts (optional)
- ❑ ¹/₂ to 3/4 cup walnuts
- ❑ 1 8-ounce can unsweetened pineapple tidbits
- ❑ 3 tablespoons raisins
- ❑ 2 tablespoons flaked coconut (optional)
- ❑ 2 tablespoons sun-dried tomatoes

Staples

- ❑ Black pepper
- ❑ Brown sugar
- ❑ Cornstarch

- ❑ Curry powder
- ❑ Dried oregano leaves
- ❑ Ground cardamom
- ❑ Ground cinnamon
- ❑ Ground ginger
- ❑ Ground nutmeg
- ❑ Maple syrup
- ❑ Minced garlic in oil
- ❑ Olive oil
- ❑ Oregano
- ❑ Peanut oil
- ❑ Pure vanilla extract
- ❑ Saffron threads
- ❑ Salt
- ❑ Sugar
- ❑ Tamari soy sauce
- ❑ Vegetable oil

* Suggested accompaniments

SPICY PORK ROAST
CURRIED RICE WITH
VEGETABLES
PAN-FRIED APPLE SLICES
WITH MAPLE SYRUP *

Use fragrant Indian basmati rice for the following rice dish, and wait for the house to fill with wonderful popcorn aromas. Both the pork and rice recipes are economical and provide leftovers. The curry dish uses sun-dried tomatoes, a good winter alternative, but if you make this dish in warmer months use some of the wonderful variety of bell peppers. Set aside 1 to 2 cups of the rice for Monday night's soup dinner. For dessert, pan-fry apple slices and walnuts in butter, then drizzle with maple syrup.

SPICY PORK ROAST

Makes 8 servings
Preparation time: 5 minutes
Cooking time: 95 minutes

1 teaspoon dried oregano leaves
1 teaspoon minced garlic
1/4 teaspoon salt
1/4 teaspoon black pepper
1/4 teaspoon ground ginger
1 4-pound pork loin roast
    (with bone)

Preheat the oven to 350 degrees. In a small bowl, mix together the oregano, garlic, salt, black pepper and ginger. Rub the mix over the roast and place it in a roasting pan. You may refrigerate the roast up to 24 hours to develop the flavors of the marinade, or roast immediately. Cook about 20 to 25 minutes per pound, or until a meat thermometer reads 160 degrees. Remove from the oven and let sit 15 minutes before slicing.

Per 3-ounce serving: 213 calories, 12 grams fat, 80 milligrams cholesterol, 125 milligrams sodium.

CURRIED RICE WITH VEGETABLES

Makes 8 to 10 servings
Preparation time: 5 minutes
Cooking time: 45 minutes

2 teaspoons vegetable oil
4 teaspoons minced garlic in oil
2 medium onions, chopped
3 teaspoons good quality curry
    powder
8 cups water
1 teaspoon salt (optional)
4 cups basmati brown rice
2 cups frozen and thawed green peas
2 carrots, sliced into coins
2 tablespoons sun-dried tomatoes,
    diced

In a large saucepan or Dutch oven, heat the oil briefly, add the garlic and onion and saute 4 or 5 minutes, until the onion is softened. Stir in the curry powder and saute 1 minute longer. Add the water and salt and bring the ingredients to a boil. Stir in the rice, reduce the heat to low, cover and simmer for 40 minutes or until the water is almost completely absorbed.

In a separate skillet, saute the peas, carrots and sun-dried tomatoes, then add to the rice and cook 5 minutes longer.

Per serving: 407 calories, 3 grams fat, no cholesterol, 40 milligrams sodium.

MONDAY

TOMATO CURRIED
RICE SOUP
MIXED GREEN SALAD *
RYE CRACKERS *

Dinner menus don't come much easier than this one. Leftover curried rice adds body, flavor and vegetables; substitute other vegetables or plain cooked rice if you wish. Crumbled feta cheese would make a wonderful substitute for parmesan.

TOMATO CURRIED RICE SOUP

Makes 4 servings
Preparation time: 5 minutes
Cooking time: 5 minutes

1 14 1/2-ounce can stewed tomatoes
1 14 1/2-ounce can chicken broth
1 to 2 cups leftover curried rice with
    peas and peppers
1/4 cup Parmesan cheese

In a medium saucepan, place the tomatoes and juice, chicken broth and rice mixture and bring to a boil. Lower heat and simmer for 3 or 4 minutes. Ladle into soup bowls and sprinkle with cheese.

Per serving: 164 calories, 3 grams fat, 5 milligrams cholesterol, 761 milligrams sodium.

TUESDAY

RAMEN NOODLES WITH PORK
AND PEANUT SAUCE *
GARLICKY SNOW PEAS SAUTE

Ramen noodles, available in the soup section of the grocery store, can be quickly boiled (discard the flavor packet) and drained, then tossed with leftover chopped pork and a spicy Szechuan sauce made from peanuts, ginger, garlic and vinegar — a wonderful version under the Jade label can be ordered from Williams-Sonoma (1-800-541-2233). Remember to drain the yogurt for tomorrow's dinner. Save any leftover snow peas for a later meal. Prepare 2 packs of ramen noodles and leftovers can be reheated with extra snow peas for Friday night's meal if you don't want to order carryout Mexican food.

Price: Small ones will run 5 for $1.00 and larger ones will run 3 for $1.00.

Nutrition: A medium-sized tangerine has about 60 calories and provides a full day's supply of vitamin C.

Selection: Tangerines, like other citrus, do not develop more flavor or sweetness after harvest. Choose fruit that is heavy for its size, and avoid soft or decayed spots or mushy interior flesh. Surface brusing of the peel will make no different to the interior quality. Unlike other citrus fruit, the interior flesh of the honey tangerine doesn't get dry and granular as it ages; it merely turns mushy.

Storage: Store tangerines in the refrigerator for about 2

weeks.

Uses: The honey tangerine is best used fresh for fruit salads or eating out of hand. It makes a rich, sweet juice.

Even though we usually think of tangerines at Christmas time, late winter is the best season for this aromatic fruit. The Florida citrus crop is in and looking good, so look for plenty of supplies in local grocery stores through the end of the month.

SNOW PEAS WITH GARLIC

Makes 4 to 6 servings
Preparation time: 10 minutes
Cooking time: 5 minutes

1 tablespoon peanut oil
2 or 3 cloves garlic, minced
4 green onions, chopped
1 large sweet red or 2 hot banana peppers, diced
1 pound fresh snow peas, trimmed
2 or 3 nice radishes, thinly sliced
1 teaspoon tamari soy sauce

Heat oil in a wok or deep skillet. Add garlic, onions and pepper and saute until the onion is softened and fragrant, about 1 minute. Add the snow peas and saute until tender-crisp, 2 or 3 minutes. Toss in radishes and toss with soy sauce.

Per serving (1/6 recipe): 80 calories, 5 grams fat, no cholesterol, 119 milligrams sodium.

WEDNESDAY

INDIAN RICE WITH PEAS
AND PEPPERS *
YOGURT AND
SAFFRON CREAM
FRUIT PLATTER *

Serve leftover Indian rice tonight and offer a plate of assorted fruits to dip in saffron-flavored yogurt. A full-fat yogurt makes a thicker cream.

YOGURT AND SAFFRON CREAM

Makes 4 servings
Preparation time: 10 minutes
Draining time: overnight

1 ¹/₂ cups plain yogurt
¹/₂ cup shelled pistachio nuts (optional)
¹/₄ to ¹/₃ cup sugar
¹/₂ teaspoon ground cardamom
1 teaspoon saffron threads soaked in

4 teaspoons warm milk

Line a sieve with cheesecloth or a thin towel. Spoon in the yogurt and leave to drain, refrigerated, overnight. Peel the pistachio nuts, then chop into slivers.

Put the drained yogurt into the workbowl of a food processor with the sugar and process for 30 or more seconds to fully blend. Stir in the ground cardamom and saffron. Chill before serving. Spoon the yogurt onto a platter, garnish with (optional) pistachio nuts, and surround with a fruit platter of sliced apples, oranges and pears.

Per serving (with lowfat yogurt): 136 calories, 2 grams fat, 6 milligrams cholesterol, 62 milligrams sodium.

THURSDAY

FRITTATA WITH PORK
STEAMED BROCCOLI *

Here's a quick answer to that seemingly scattered supply of leftovers taking up space in the refrigerator.

FRITTATA WITH PORK

Makes 4 servings
Preparation time: 5 minutes
Cooking time: 8 minutes

6 large eggs
Salt and ground black pepper to taste
3 tablespoons butter, margarine or vegetable oil
3 green onions, chopped
1 cup cooked, diced pork
1/2 cup chopped, cooked vegetables (peas or snow peas)

Preheat broiler. In a medium bowl, beat eggs with salt and pepper. Set aside.

In a 10-inch skillet over low heat, melt the butter or oil and saute green onions until tender. Stir in the meat and vegetables and cook just until heated through. Turn down heat to lowest setting. Add egg mixture and cook about 5 minutes, or until egg is set and only top surface is runny.

Broil 30 to 60 seconds, or until top surface is cooked but not brown.

Per serving: 293 calories, 22 grams fat, 468 milligrams cholesterol, 225 milligrams sodium.

FRIDAY

BEAN AND CHEESE BURRITOS *
CHIPS AND SALSA *
GREEN SALAD WITH SLICED JICAMA *

If you have leftover ramen noodles and sauteed snow peas, stir them together for a simple supper. Otherwise, order the supreme burritos from your favorite Mexican carryout store. Add a salad of greens and sliced jicama.

SATURDAY

RAINBOW TROUT WITH WALNUTS AND OREGANO
STEAMED YUKON GOLD POTATOES AND PEAS *
WARM PINEAPPLE SUNDAES

This company dinner goes together in minutes. Use fresh oregano in the rainbow trout dish if you have it, but dried adds plenty of flavor. Chop the shallots and walnuts in a food processor to speed preparation. Yukon Gold potatoes have a rich buttery flesh — look for them at Big Star grocery stores and Harry's Farmers Market. If you have any pineapple topping left after dessert, freeze it to use on another occasion.

RAINBOW TROUT WITH WALNUTS AND OREGANO

Makes 4 servings
Preparation time: 5 minutes
Cooking time: 10 minutes

1 tablespoon vegetable oil
1 large shallot, minced
4 6-ounce rainbow trout fillets
Salt and black pepper to taste
1/4 to 1/2 cup finely chopped walnuts
2 green onions or 1 green Vidalia, chopped
1 teaspoon dried oregano, or 1 tablespoon fresh

In a large skillet, heat vegetable oil. Add the shallots and saute a few seconds, just until they are softened and fragrant. Add the trout and saute, flesh-side down, on top of the shallots for 4 minutes. Turn and cook 1 or 2 minutes longer; place on a platter and keep warm.

Meanwhile, saute the walnuts, green onion and oregano for 2 minutes. Top the trout with the walnut mixture, and serve.

Per serving: 284 calories, 13 grams fat, 103 milligrams cholesterol 49 milligrams sodium.

WARM PINEAPPLE SUNDAES

Makes 4 to 6 servings
Preparation time: 10 minutes
Cooking time: 10 minutes

1 8-ounce can unsweetened pineapple tidbits, undrained
2 tablespoons flaked coconut, toasted (optional)
2 tablespoons brown sugar
1 tablespoon water
2 teaspoons cornstarch
3 tablespoons raisins
1 1/2 teaspoons margarine
1 1/2 teaspoons ground cinnamon
1/8 teaspoon ground nutmeg
1/2 teaspoon pure vanilla extract
2 to 3 cups vanilla ice cream, ice milk or frozen yogurt

Preheat the oven to 250 degrees. Place the coconut on a baking sheet and toast it while gathering the other items.

Meanwhile, drain the pineapple, reserving juice, and set the pineapple aside. Combine the reserved juice, brown sugar, water and cornstarch in a small non-aluminum saucepan. Cook over medium heat, stirring until thickened, 3 to 5 minutes. Stir in pineapple, raisins, margarine, cinnamon and nutmeg. Cook over low heat, stirring frequently, until warm. Stir in vanilla.

Serve over ice cream or frozen yogurt.

Per serving, sauce only (6 servings): 56 calories, less than 1 gram fat, no cholesterol, 3 milligrams sodium.

WEEK

7

SHOPPING LIST

Meat, poultry, seafood

- ❏ 1 3-pound turkey breast half
- ❏ 4 6-ounce whole rainbow trout

Produce

- ❏ 1 head lettuce, any type
- ❏ 1 head nappa cabbage
- ❏ 3 pounds all-purpose potatoes
- ❏ 6 russet baking potatoes
- ❏ 1 pound pencil-thin asparagus
- ❏ 2 shallots
- ❏ 1 yellow onion
- ❏ 1 red bell pepper
- ❏ 1 bunch broccoli
- ❏ 2 cups snow peas
- ❏ 1 large cucumber
- ❏ 3 fennel bulbs
- ❏ 1/2 cup mushrooms
- ❏ 1 15-ounce package spicy or alfalfa sprouts
- ❏ 5 lemons
- ❏ 2 oranges
- ❏ 6 large pears
- ❏ 1 pint strawberries
- ❏ 1 small knob ginger root
- ❏ 1 bunch rosemary
- ❏ 1 bunch parsley
- ❏ 1 bunch cilantro
- ❏ 1 cup firm tofu
- ❏ 2 green onions
- ❏ 4 garlic cloves

Dairy

- ❏ 1 stick plus 1 tablespoon butter or margarine

Deli

- ❏ 8 ounces Parmesan cheese
- ❏ 4 blueberry muffins
- ❏ 4 hard rolls

- ❏ 4 slices carrot cake

Miscellaneous

- ❏ 1 1/2 cups pecans
- ❏ 1 pound dried pasta
- ❏ 1/3 cup Marsala or dry sherry
- ❏ 3/4 cup long-grain rice
- ❏ 2 teaspoons sesame seeds
- ❏ 4 tablespoons sliced black olives
- ❏ 1 ounce bittersweet chocolate

Staples

- ❏ All-purpose flour
- ❏ Black pepper
- ❏ Brown sugar
- ❏ Fat-free vinaigrette
- ❏ Light soy sauce
- ❏ Minced garlic in oil
- ❏ Olive oil
- ❏ Prepared hot mustard

- ❏ Rice vinegar
- ❏ Salt
- ❏ Vegetable cooking spray
- ❏ Vegetable oil

* Suggested accompaniments

BAKED TURKEY BREAST WITH HOT MUSTARD
MASHED POTATOES WITH SOUR CREAM, GARLIC AND PARMESAN CHEESE *
STEAMED PENCIL-THIN ASPARAGUS WITH FRESH BASIL *
DUTCH-TOPPED PEAR CRISP

Turkey breast offers lean meat at affordable prices. Choose one that is large enough to provide for more than one meal. Add mashed potatoes (mixed with sour cream) and a steamed vegetable as side dishes, and the following delicious dessert, based on a similar dessert from *Jane Brody's Good Food Gourmet*. Cook plenty of mashed potatoes to serve later in the week. Toss the asparagus with a couple of tablespoons of basil and reserve the rest for Friday night's dinner.

BAKED TURKEY BREAST WITH HOT MUSTARD

Makes 8 servings
Preparation time: 5 minutes
Cooking time: 1 hour

1 teaspoon coarse salt
$1/2$ teaspoon coarse-ground black pepper
2 tablespoons prepared hot mustard
1 3-pound turkey breast half, skin removed

Preheat the oven to 350 degrees. Combine the salt, pepper and mustard; mix well.

Remove the skin from the turkey and spread the mustard mixture evenly over the meat. Place the meat in a roasting pan and bake 1 hour or longer, basting occasionally with pan juices. When meat juices run clear, the meat is cooked. Remove from the

oven and let the meat stand 10 to 15 minutes before carving, so the meat doesn't crumble.

Per serving: 207 calories, 5 grams fat, 111 milligrams cholesterol, 407 milligrams sodium.

DUTCH-TOPPED PEAR CRISP

Makes 6 servings
Preparation time: 20 minutes
Cooking time: 30 minutes

1 cup all-purpose flour
$1/2$ cup firmly packed brown sugar
1 tablespoon grated orange peel (optional)
3 to 4 tablespoons unsalted butter
1 cup finely chopped pecans
6 large firm-ripe pears

Preheat the oven to 350 degrees. Grease an 8-inch-square baking pan with pan spray.

Place the flour and brown sugar in the workbowl of a food processor. Pulse until blended. Add the (optional) orange peel and butter and pulse until it forms small pebbles. Stir in the pecans with a spoon.

Peel, core and slice the pears lengthwise into thin slices. Spread the slices evenly in the pan, then sprinkle the flour-butter mixture evenly over the pears. Bake for 30 minutes. Serve warm or at room temperature.

Per serving: 386 calories, 19 grams fat, no cholesterol, 83 milligrams sodium.

PASTA WITH VEGETABLES AND CREAMY PECAN SAUCE
BLUEBERRY MUFFINS *

This delicious pasta dish is creamy and still low in fat, and parsley offers the extra benefit of lots of vitamin C. Look at the price of red bell peppers; if too high, substitute nappa cabbage or carrots.

Many stores sell broccoli florets already cut; this will speed preparation. The recipe makes enough for two meals during the week.

PASTA WITH VEGETABLES AND CREAMY PECAN SAUCE

Makes 8 servings
Preparation time: 15 minutes
Cooking time: 20 minutes

1 pound dried pasta
1 cup broccoli florets
1 tablespoon olive oil
2 shallots, finely chopped
2 teaspoons minced garlic in oil
1 red bell pepper, cored and cut in thin slices (optional)
1 cup snow peas, ends and strings removed
2 to 4 tablespoons dry sherry
$1/2$ cup pecans, chopped
$1/3$ cup grated Parmesan cheese
1 cup parsley, finely chopped

Bring a large pot of salted water to a boil, then add the pasta. In a couple of minutes, add the broccoli; both should finish cooking at the same time. When cooked, drain (reserving $1/2$ cup of the pasta water), and place the pasta and broccoli in a large, shallow pasta dish.

Meanwhile, put the oil in a skillet. When hot, saute the shallots over medium heat until soft and fragrant, 1 or 2 minutes. Add the garlic, (optional) red pepper and snow peas and saute until tender, 2 or 3 minutes. Pour in the sherry and return to a boil, then spoon the contents of the pan over the pasta and toss.

Chop the pecans in the workbowl of a food processor, then add the Parmesan cheese and parsley and pulse to blend. Add $1/2$ cup of the pasta water to the workbowl and puree several seconds until smooth. Toss the pasta and vegetables with the cheese sauce.

Per serving: 381 calories, 12 grams fat, 13 milligrams cholesterol, 311 milligrams sodium.

In Season • Fennel

Price: May be sold by the bunch or the pound. Prices range from $.99 to $1.69 a bunch or an average of $1.59 a pound.

Nutrition: Fennel has 30 calories per cup and is a fair source of vitamin A, calcium, potassium and niacin.

Selection: Fennel is at its best from October through April. Look for firm, squat, white bulbs with a pearly sheen and no signs of dryness. The stalks and feathery leaves should be bright green and crisp, not limp.

Storage: Fennel stalks and leaves do not store well, only 3 or 4 days; after that, they dry out or rot and lose their flavor. Store the stalks and leaves separately: Cut the stalks from the wide bases, wrap in plastic and set in the coldest part of the refrigerator. The bulbs will store this well for a week or more.

Uses: Allow about half of a 4-inch bulb per serving. Serve raw in salads with apples, nuts, tomatoes or sweet peppers, sauteed or stir-fried, added to rice dishes, pilafs and cooked with onion for stuffings. Add to soups or braise or bake with cheese.

TUESDAY

RICE SAUTE WITH SNOW PEAS
AND SPICY SPROUTS
CUCUMBER SLICES WITH
RICE VINEGAR *

This dish is also delicious made with brown rice, but expect the rice to take about 20 minutes longer to cook. Spicy sprouts (alfalfa sprouts combined with radish sprouts) are available in most local stores. Add a simple salad of sliced cucumbers sprinkled with rice wine vinegar. Reserve some fresh cilantro to serve later in the week.

RICE SAUTE WITH SNOW PEAS AND SPICY SPROUTS

Makes 4 servings
Preparation time: 10 minutes
Cooking time: 20 minutes

³/₄ cup long-grain rice
1 tablespoon olive oil
1 yellow onion, diced
1 cup cubed firm tofu
1 cup snow peas, ends and strings removed
2 teaspoons sesame seeds
¹/₂ cup spicy sprouts
1 tablespoon light soy sauce
2 tablespoons fresh cilantro leaves, roughly chopped

Put the rice in a saucepan and cover with salted water by ¹/₄ inch. Bring to a boil over high heat, then lower the heat. Cook, covered until the water is absorbed, about 20 minutes.

Meanwhile, heat the oil in a frying pan and saute the onion until golden brown or even a bit burned, about 8 minutes. Add the tofu and snow peas to the onions and saute briefly until the tofu is heated through and the peas slightly cooked. Remove from the heat, sprinkle with sesame seeds, sprouts, soy sauce and cilantro leaves and toss with the rice. Serve immediately.

Per serving: 290 calories, 10 grams fat, no cholesterol, 134 milligrams sodium.

WEDNESDAY

HOT TURKEY SALAD

MASHED POTATO PANCAKES *
HARD ROLLS *
CARROT CAKE *

Use leftover turkey for tonight's salad dinner and use leftover potatoes to form and cook potato pancakes. Add hard rolls and a purchased carrot cake for dessert.

HOT TURKEY SALAD

Makes 4 servings
Preparation time: 10 minutes
Cooking time: 10 minutes

1 to 2 cups cooked, sliced turkey
¹/₂ head lettuce, any type
1 to 2 cups shredded nappa cabbage
¹/₂ cup mushrooms, sliced
4 tablespoons sliced black olives
2 green onions, thinly sliced
3 tablespoons fat-free vinaigrette
4 teaspoons low-fat sour cream
Cilantro leaves for garnish (optional)

Heat the oven to 350 degrees. Cut the turkey into julienne slices and put in a baking pan. Place in the oven for 10 minutes or until heated through and crisp.
Meanwhile, make t
Tear the lettuce leaves
size pieces, shred the cab

put in a large salad bowl. Add the mushrooms, black olives, green onions and vinaigrette and toss.

Place the salad ingredients on four dinner plates, top with the warmed turkey and a teaspoon of low-fat sour cream. Garnish with cilantro leaves, if desired, or left-over spicy or alfalfa sprouts.

Per serving: 158 calories, 6 grams fat, 54 milligrams cholesterol, 118 milligrams sodium.

THURSDAY

RICH AND CREAMY PASTA IN PARSLEY NUT SAUCE *
ORANGE AND FENNEL SALAD

Leftover pasta goes well with a refreshing pairing of anise-flavored fennel and late-season oranges. This salad is adapted from Biba Caggiano's *Modern Italian Cooking* (Simon & Schuster, $14). Fennel is a good winter vegetable to take advantage of for another month, and Florida oranges are a good value now.

ORANGE AND FENNEL SALAD

Makes 4 servings
Preparation time: 15 minutes

1 large fennel bulb, thinly sliced
2 navel oranges, peeled and thinly sliced
Salt and freshly ground black pepper
3 or 4 tablespoons vinaigrette

Remove the long stalks and bruised outer leaves of the fennel. Slice off the root ends of each bulb. Wash and dry the fennel bulbs thoroughly and cut them into quarters, then cut each quarter into thin slices.

Layer the fennel and orange slices in a salad bowl and season with salt and pepper, and drizzle with vinaigrette.

Per serving: 184 calories, 14 grams

fat, no cholesterol, 5 milligrams sodium.

FRIDAY

MEDITERRANEAN TROUT GRILLED WITH FENNEL
ITALIAN ROSEMARY POTATOES
STEAMED BROCCOLI *
STRAWBERRIES WITH SHAVED CHOCOLATE *

Make this Valentine's meal tantalizing with wonderful aromas. Trout stuffed with anise-flavored fennel is a dish you will want to make over and over. The baked potatoes are crispy on the outside and creamy inside; organic russet potatoes have a particularly velvety texture; look for them at health food stores and some grocery stores.

MEDITERRANEAN TROUT GRILLED WITH FENNEL

Makes 4 servings
Preparation time: 5 minutes
Cooking time: 10 minutes

2 bunches fresh fennel with leaves and stalks
4 6-ounce whole rainbow trout
4 lemons, halved
1/4 cup unsalted butter, melted

Prepare a charcoal fire in the grill. The coals are ready when they are covered with a fine layer of white ash.

Place a thick bed of fresh fennel on one side of a hinged fish grill. Place the fish on top and cover with another layer of fresh fennel. Close the grill. Set the grill over the hot coals and cook the fish for 10 minutes per inch, turning often. When the fish is done, remove it to a platter, discard the fennel and serve accompanied with lemon halves and melted butter.

Per serving: 315 calories, 17 grams fat, 134 milligrams cholesterol, 164 milligrams sodium.

ROSEMARY POTATOES

Makes 8 servings
Preparation time: 10 minutes
Standing time: 30 minutes
Cooking time: 45 minutes

6 large russet potatoes, each cut in 8 wedges
1/3 cup olive oil
4 large cloves garlic, peeled and cut in thin slivers
Salt and freshly ground black pepper, to taste
4 tablespoons chopped fresh rosemary, divided in half
3 or 4 tablespoons grated Parmesan cheese

Put the potatoes in a mixing bowl and toss with the olive oil, garlic, salt, pepper and half the rosemary. Let marinate at room temperature 30 minutes.

Preheat the oven to 350 degrees. Put the potatoes in a roasting pan and bake 45 minutes, tossing them occasionally for even browning. Half way through the baking, sprinkle with the remaining rosemary and the cheese; continue roasting until the potatoes are crusty and golden brown.

SATURDAY

CUBAN SANDWICHES *
ROSEMARY POTATOES*
COLESLAW *
FRESH FRUIT SALAD *

After last night's big splash, look to your favorite take-out deli for dinner. A Cuban sandwich is built with roast pork, Swiss cheese and mojo sauce on Cuban bread. Add leftover rosemary potatoes from last night's meal.

WEEK 8

SHOPPING LIST

Meat, poultry, seafood

- ❑ 2 pound boneless pork loin, whole or large cubes
- ❑ 6 skinless, boneless chicken breast halves
- ❑ 4 to 8 ounces crab meat, back fin fine

Produce

- ❑ 2 pounds carrots
- ❑ 1 zucchini
- ❑ 4 garlic cloves
- ❑ 7 green onions
- ❑ 2 to 3 ounces mushrooms
- ❑ 1 large onion
- ❑ 2 leeks
- ❑ 1 head lettuce, any type
- ❑ 5 pounds new potatoes, large size
- ❑ 1 bunch arugula or other spicy green

- ❑ 1 bunch chives
- ❑ 1 large bunch parsley
- ❑ 2 large bunch watercress
- ❑ 2 lemons
- ❑ 1 orange
- ❑ 1 apple

Dairy

- ❑ 1 cup low-fat sour cream
- ❑ 6 tablespoons unsalted butter

Deli

- ❑ 1 apple cobbler
- ❑ 4 multigrain muffins
- ❑ 1 loaf crusty bread
- ❑ 4 to 6 ounces Swiss cheese
- ❑ 20 slices party-size bread
- ❑ 4 to 8 flour tortillas
- ❑ 4 ounces plain Havarti cheese

Miscellaneous

- ❑ 2 pounds sauerkraut
- ❑ 1 cup pearled barley
- ❑ 2 cups rice
- ❑ 3 14 $^1/_2$-ounce cans low-sodium chicken broth
- ❑ $^1/_2$ cup white wine
- ❑ $^1/_2$ cup currants (or raisins)
- ❑ 1 cup refried beans

Staples

- ❑ Black pepper
- ❑ Cayenne pepper
- ❑ Dijon mustard
- ❑ Flour
- ❑ Ground cumin
- ❑ Lard
- ❑ Lemon juice
- ❑ Mayonnaise
- ❑ Minced garlic in oil
- ❑ Molasses

- ❑ Olive oil
- ❑ Salt
- ❑ Vegetable oil

BARLEY SOUP WITH PORK AND SAUERKRAUT
SPICY RICE
STEAMED VEGETABLES WITH LEMON PEEL*
APPLE COBBLER*

Choose a hearty pork and sauerkraut recipe while the weather is still blustery. This dish, adapted from *Heartland* by Marcia Adams (Clarkson Potter, $30.00) adds healthy barley for a dish, uses both economical ingredients and provides energy in cold weather. The leftovers will taste even better after a day or two in the refrigerator. Add a flavorful rice dish and steamed vegetables, both of which will generate leftovers.

BARLEY SOUP WITH PORK AND SAUERKRAUT

Makes 6 to 8 servings
Preparation time: 5 minutes
Cooking time: 2 1/2 hours

2 pounds coarse-cut sauerkraut
1 1/2 to 2 pounds pork loin or shoulder, in large cubes
1 large apple, peeled, cored and diced
1 cup regular pearled barley
2 tablespoons molasses
Black pepper, to taste

Place the sauerkraut in a large sieve, rinse and drain well. Place the pork in the bottom of a 4- to 5-quart Dutch oven. Add the drained sauerkraut, apple and barley. Add enough water to cover the kraut by 1/4 inch. Add the molasses and pepper and bring to a boil; reduce the heat and simmer, covered, until the pork is very tender, about 2 hours. It will take longer if you use a tougher cut of meat. Add water as need-

ed. Serve hot with lots of broth.

SPICY RICE

Makes 10 servings
Preparation time: 5 minutes
Cooking time: 30 minutes

2 tablespoons olive oil
2 garlic cloves, crushed
1 star anise
2 cups rice
2 cups low-sodium chicken stock
2 cups water
6 green onions, minced
1/4 cup chopped fresh cilantro

In a large saucepan, heat the oil. Add the garlic and star anise and saute 3 or 4 minutes. Add the rice and saute 3 minutes. Add the stock and water and bring to a boil. Reduce the heat to low, cover and cook 20 minutes. Turn off the heat, and let the rice sit 5 or 10 minutes. Remove the star anise before serving. Serve garnished with green onions and cilantro.

WATERCRESS AND MUSHROOM CREPES
MULTIGRAIN MUFFINS*

Purchased crepes from the produce section of the grocery store will do nicely for this meal, or make your own homemade crepes. Save the flavorful watercress stems and add to your next stir-fry.

WATERCRESS AND MUSHROOM CREPES

Makes 4 servings
Preparation time: 10 minutes
Cooking time: 10 minutes

1 teaspoon oil
1 cup sliced mushrooms

1 cup low-fat sour cream
1 tablespoon lemon juice
1/2 cup watercress leaves
Salt and pepper, to taste

Preheat the oven to 350 degrees. In a medium skillet, heat 1 teaspoon of oil. Saute the mushrooms a couple of minutes. Meanwhile, beat the sour cream with the lemon juice until light. Add the mushrooms, watercress, salt and pepper and mix well.

Spoon about 2 tablespoons of the mixture in each crepe and roll each up. Place the rolled crepes in a lightly buttered shallow baking dish. Heat the crepes for 10 minutes and serve.

SAUTEED MIDEAST CHICKEN
SPICY RICE*

This quick recipe should become a regular in your recipe file, inspired by *Sweet Onions & Sour Cherries* by Jeannette Ferrary and Louise Fiszer (Simon & Schuster, $25.00). The vegetables form a rich-tasting sauce for the chicken, and the dish is wonderful the day after, hot or cold. Boneless chicken breasts offer the most ease at serving time, but choose any chicken pieces on sale. Double the recipe for a party, and chicken could be cut in bite-size pieces for a buffet. Reserve leftovers to serve later in the week. Reheat leftover rice.

SAUTEED MIDEAST CHICKEN

Makes 6 servings
Preparation time: 10 minutes
Cooking time: 20 minutes

3 tablespoons oil
Salt and pepper to taste

Flour for dredging
6 skinless, boneless chicken breast
  halves
1 tablespoon minced garlic in oil
1 large onion, chopped
4 large carrots, peeled and coarsely
  grated
$^1/_2$ cup white wine
$^1/_2$ cup chicken broth
1 teaspoon ground cumin
$^1/_2$ cup raisins
Fresh parsley or cilantro for garnish

Put the oil in a large skillet over medium heat. While the oil is heating, place the salt, pepper and flour in a paper bag and dredge the chicken pieces in flour. Place in the hot fat and cook for about 5 minutes on each side, or until golden-brown. (If you use other chicken pieces, or pieces with bone, the cooking times will be longer.) Move the cooked chicken to a platter and keep warm.

In the same pan, cook the garlic in oil, onion and carrots until tender, 3 or 4 minutes. Stir in the wine and broth and raise the heat. Scrape up any bits of cooked food on the bottom of the pan. Add the cumin, raisins and reserved chicken. Lower the heat back to a simmer, cover and cook another 8 to 10 minutes. Serve the chicken pieces with plenty of sauce, and garnish with chopped parsley or cilantro.

WEDNESDAY

GARLIC CHIVE NEW
POTATOES
OPEN-FACED CHEESE
SANDWICHES*
GREEN SALAD*

Garlic and chives make a great flavor combination with new potatoes. Use the two herbs or look for garlic chives, also called flat-leaf Chinese chives. Cook the full recipe and reserve half the potatoes to use later in the week.

GARLIC CHIVE NEW POTATOES

Makes 4 servings plus leftovers
Preparation time: 5 minutes
Cooking time: 25 minutes

4 pounds new potatoes (size A),
  half of them quartered
$^1/_4$ cup unsalted butter, melted
2 tablespoons chopped fresh chives
  or garlic chives
1 teaspoon finely minced garlic
  (optional)

Heat several inches of water to boiling in a large saucepan and add the potatoes. Cover and bring to a boil, then reduce heat to

IN SEASON ❁ WATERCRESS

Price: Look for bunches to range from $.49 to $.89 a bunch. Watercress sprouts average $1.49 to $1.69 a cup.

Nutrition: One cup of raw watercress has 7 calories and is high in fiber and a good source of vitamin A, C and iron.

Selection: Watercress is available year round, but like other salad greens, the peak seasons for availability and good prices are spring and fall. Choose greens with small, supple stems, and avoid those that are woody or broken or have yellowing leaves.

Storage: Rinse with cold water, shake off excess and dry well. Watercress has a short shelf life and must be kept moist and very cold. Wrap in paper towels and refrigerate in a plastic bag in the coldest part of the refrigerator for no more than 2 days.

Uses: Allow $^1/_2$ bunch per serving if a main component of a salad or soup; but as a garnish, one bunch will serve 4 to 6. The peppery flavor of raw watercress is important in salads and sandwiches, to garnish sea-food or served in soups. The stems are wonderful stir-fried. The delicate lobed leaves of watercress looks as innocous as any salad green loafing in the produce bin. One bite tells a different tale: the flavor is as peppery as its cousin, the mustard green. It is a welcome addition to blander lettuces or vegetables. Look for excellent supplies of watercress in most stores.

medium. Boil 20 to 25 minutes or until tender, then drain. Reserve 5 large potatoes for Saturday night.

Meanwhile, melt the butter in the microwave or stove top. Drizzle over the potatoes, and sprinkle with garlic chives or chives and minced garlic.

Per serving: 235 calories, 6 grams fat, 15 milligrams cholesterol, 11 milligrams sodium.

THURSDAY

GRILLED PORK AND SAUERKRAUT SANDWICHES
DILL PICKLES*

This take-off from the standard corned beef and sauerkraut sandwich uses leftover pork and sauerkraut from earlier in the week.

GRILLED PORK AND SAUERKRAUT SANDWICHES

Makes 4 servings
Preparation time: 5 minutes
Cooking time: 5 minutes

8 slices firm white bread
2 tablespoons Dijon mustard
4 to 6 ounces thinly sliced Swiss cheese
4 to 6 ounces thinly sliced pork
4 to 8 tablespoons sauerkraut, room temperature

Preheat the broiler.

Spread mustard on 4 slices of bread, then layer the cheese, sauerkraut and pork. Mash the sandwiches down slightly with your hand to make sure they hold together. Brush both outsides of the sandwiches with butter and place on the baking sheet. Broil until golden brown on the bottom, about 1 1/2 minutes, then turn and broil until golden brown on the second side, 20 to 30 seconds.

FRIDAY

CHICKEN TACOS*
REFRIED BEANS AND CHIPS*

Leftover chicken, soft flour tortillas and your favorite hot sauce will make a wonderful Friday night meal. Don't forget to scoop up the flavorful carrot and onion sauce around the chicken pieces.

SATURDAY

LEMON-PEELED CRAB BITES
POTATO AND LEEK ROSTI
WATERCRESS SALAD*

Three appetizers quickly add up to a full meal, and these three do as well at a stand-up party as they do at a sit-down meal.

Use good-quality crab for the first appetizer, and to speed up the crab puff dish, use purchased crackers or party-size breads. Swiss potato cake, called rosti, is made of potatoes and leeks and bits of leftover cooked pork from earlier in the week, grated and fried in lard, butter or oil until crisp. This recipe uses cooked potatoes to speed up the process. Serve it cut into wedges, with a big dinner salad of watercress and other piquant winter greens.

LEMON-PEELED CRAB BITES

Makes 4 servings
Preparation time: 10 minutes
Cooking time: 10 minutes

2 tablespoons mayonnais
1/2 cup packed grated plain Havarti cheese
1/2 cup packed crab meat
2 tablespoons chives, minced
1 teaspoon lemon juice

1/8 teaspoon grated lemon peel
Salt to taste
20 slices party-size bread
2 tablespoons chives

Combine the mayonnaise, cheese, crab meat, chives, lemon juice and peel in a mixing bowl and blend well. Add salt to taste. Cover and refrigerate until ready to serve.

When ready to bake, preheat oven to 350 degrees.

Spread each bread with one or two teaspoons of the crab mixture. Place on a baking sheet and bake until the cheese has melted and the filling is golden, about 10 minutes. Remove from the oven and sprinkle with chives or parsley. Serve warm.

POTATO AND LEEK ROSTI

Makes 4 to 6 servings
Preparation time: 10 minutes
Cooking time: 15 minutes

2 large leeks, trimmed of all but 2 inches of green
4 to 6 tablespoons lard, unsalted butter or oil
2 or 3 tablespoons cooked, shredded pork
Salt and freshly ground pepper
3 large red potatoes cooked, cooled, peeled and grated

Cut the leeks crosswise and wash, then cut into 1-inch pieces and then into fine julienne.

In a heavy 10-inch skillet, melt half the butter over medium-low heat. Add the leeks and saute 3 or 4 minutes. Season with salt and pepper, then add the pork and grated potatoes. Press the mixture firmly with a spatula.

Cook the rosti uncovered for 7 to 10 minutes, adding the remaining butter or lard if necessary. Turn up the heat to crisp the bottom. Cut the cooked rosti into wedges and serve hot.

WEEK

9

SHOPPING LIST

Meat, poultry, seafood

- ❑ 2 pounds smoked turkey breast
- ❑ 4 boneless pork loin chops (about 2 pounds)
- ❑ $^1/_2$ pound bacon

Produce

- ❑ 3 bunches red Swiss chard
- ❑ 1 pound mustard greens (or 1 10-ounce package frozen)
- ❑ 1 bunch spinach
- ❑ 1 large onion
- ❑ 1 large red onion
- ❑ 12 new potatoes (B size)
- ❑ 5 leeks
- ❑ 12 large garlic cloves
- ❑ 12 ounces white mushrooms (4 may be shiitake)
- ❑ 3 or 4 large carrots
- ❑ 3 apples

- ❑ 7 large ripe but firm pears
- ❑ 1 ripe avocado
- ❑ 1 lemon
- ❑ 1 bunch rosemary

Dairy

- ❑ 1 pint frozen yogurt
- ❑ 1 stick unsalted butter
- ❑ $^3/_4$ cup half-and-half

Deli

- ❑ 1 loaf crusty bread
- ❑ $^3/_4$ cup grated Parmesan cheese
- ❑ 10 ounces Jack cheese, sliced
- ❑ 1 12-inch Boboli or other pizza crust

Miscellaneous

- ❑ 2 to 4 ounces whole-wheat crackers

- ❑ 2 cups millet
- ❑ 2 $^1/_2$ cups short-grain brown or Italian Arborio rice
- ❑ 3 14 $^1/_2$ ounce cans low-sodium chicken broth, or 6 chicken or vegetable bouillon cubes
- ❑ 1 cup dry white wine
- ❑ dry mustard
- ❑ salt
- ❑ black pepper
- ❑ coarse salt (optional)
- ❑ 2 tablespoons dried tomatoes
- ❑ $^3/_4$ cup dried sour cherries
- ❑ $^1/_2$ cup orange juice
- ❑ 2 9-inch pastry shells
- ❑ 8 slices whole wheat bread
- ❑ 4 metal or wooden skewers

Staples

- ❑ Bread crumbs
- ❑ Cornmeal
- ❑ Cornstarch
- ❑ Lemon juice
- ❑ Minced garlic in oil
- ❑ Olive oil
- ❑ Sesame seeds
- ❑ Sugar
- ❑ Tamari sauce
- ❑ Vegetable pan spray

**WINTER RISOTTO WITH
MUSHROOMS AND DRIED
TOMATOES
WARM SPINACH SALAD*
CRUSTY BREAD*
PEAR PIE WITH SOUR
CHERRIES**

Enjoy these wintry dishes while the weather still warrants hearty food. Creamy risotto can be made stove-top or in the microwave; either way don't forget to stir it to make it creamy.

A pie crust made with whole-grains would taste great with the pears, and port would make a flavorful substitute for orange juice if you wish. Save leftovers of risotto, bread and pie for later in the week.

Dried cherries are available at local farmers markets, but the dried cherries from Michigan, usually sold under the American Spoon label, are sour and the most delicious. Look for them at Williams-Sonoma, and other specialty stores.

WINTER RISOTTO WITH MUSHROOMS AND DRIED TOMATOES

Makes 8 to 10 servings
Preparation time: 10 minutes
Cooking time: 30 minutes

1 tablespoon olive oil
2 large leeks, cut in fine julienne
4 large garlic cloves, minced
2 1/2 cups short-grain brown rice or Italian Arborio rice
6 cups vegetable or chicken broth
3/4 to 1 cup dry white wine
1 teaspoon dry mustard
1/2 teaspoon coarsely-ground black pepper
Salt to taste
1/2 to 3/4 pound cremini mushrooms, stemmed and sliced
2 tablespoons sun-dried tomatoes, chopped, with 1 teaspoon oil from the bottle
1/2 cup grated Parmesan cheese

Heat oil in a large soup pot, then saute the leeks and garlic for 5 minutes. Stir in the rice and saute for another 5 minutes or until the rice browns slightly. Pour in the broth, wine, mustard, pepper and salt.

Cook at a simmer, uncovered, on the stovetop for 30 to 45 minutes, stirring about every 10 minutes. Remove the pot from the oven and beat the rice with a wooden spoon a few times.

Meanwhile, saute the mushrooms and dried tomatoes in the teaspoon of oil from the tomatoes until soft and fragrant, about 5 minutes. Stir into the rice, along with the grated cheese. Add salt and pepper to taste and serve.

Per serving: 355 calories, 5 grams fat, 4 milligrams cholesterol, 687 milligrams sodium.

PEAR PIE WITH SOUR CHERRIES

Makes 8 servings
Preparation time: 20 minutes plus standing time for cherries
Cooking time: 50 minutes

1 cup dried sour cherries
1/2 cup orange juice or port
5 ripe but firm pears
1/2 cup sugar
Dash salt
2 tablespoons lemon juice
2 tablespoons cornstarch
Pastry for 2 pie shells

Preheat the oven to 425 degrees. Combine the dried cherries and juice in a small bowl. Cover and set aside for a couple of hours to soften the cherries.

Peel, core, and slice the pears, then combine them in a large bowl with the sugar, salt, lemon juice and cornstarch. Using a slotted spoon, add the cherries to the filling, then measure and add 1/4 cup of the juice in which they had been soaking. Roll out the two pastry shells. Place one in a 9-inch pie pan. Turn the filling into the shell. Lay the top pastry over the filling. Trim off all but 1 inch of the overhang, then turn it under the bottomcrust. Crimp into an attractive edge. Poke several steam vents in the crust, then bake for 20 minutes. Lower the oven temperature to 375 and bake another 30 minutes or until any visible juices bubble thickly. Cool the pie on a rack and serve barely warm or at room temperature.

Per serving: 389 calories, 16 grams fat, 14 milligrams cholesterol, 305 milligrams sodium.

**SMOKED TURKEY, JACK
CHEESE AND AVOCADO
SANDWICHES*
WILTED RED CHARD
WITH TAMARI**

The red stalks and veins of red chard make this wilted vegetable beautiful to look at (see In Season, page 46). Serve the chard on the side, or even on the sandwich. Tamari soy sauce has the most intense flavor, but others will do fine. Leftovers work beautifully into tomorrow night's millet dish.

WILTED RED CHARD WITH TAMARI

Makes 8 servings
Preparation time: 5 minutes
Cooking time: 5 to 8 minutes

2 large bunches red Swiss chard
1 to 2 tablespoons tamari or other soy
    sauce
2 tablespoons sesame seeds

Wash the chard well and shake off the water, leaving some water on the leaves. Tear the leaves from the stems and cut the chard in large pieces. Place the oil in a skillet, and when hot, add the chard. Toss the chard; it will wilt almost immediately. Remove from the heat in a minute or so and toss with tamari. Sprinkle with sesame seeds and serve.

Per serving: 81 calories, 8 grams fat, no cholesterol, 208 milligrams sodium.

TUESDAY

LEMON MILLET WITH RED SWISS CHARD AND TAMARI PEAR PIE WITH SOUR CHERRIES*

Millet is a healthy whole grain available in health food stores that cooks quickly and serves as a great variation from rice.

Here, it is paired with leftover cooked Swiss chard from last night's meal, already cooked and wonderfully seasoned. The millet has a strong lemon flavor, cut it back if you wish. I didn't add salt to the dish, since tamari from last night's dish is quite salty. Save leftovers to serve later in the week.

LEMON MILLET WITH RED SWISS CHARD

Makes 8 servings
Preparation time: 5 to 10 minutes
Cooking time: 20 to 30 minutes

8 cups water
1 bunch red Swiss chard, wilted
2 tablespoons olive oil
2 cups millet, picked over and
    rinsed
2 leeks, white and green parts,
    thoroughly rinsed and thinly
    sliced, or 2 onions, coarsely
    chopped
8 to 10 garlic cloves, minced
1 tablespoon oregano
1 tablespoon grated lemon peel
Freshly ground black pepper
2 to 3 tablespoons lemon juice

Bring the water to boil in a large saucepan. Add the chard and cook uncovered, 1 minute. Drain in a colander set over a large measuring cup to catch the cooking liquid, then run the cooked chard under cold running water to stop the cooking. You will need 6 cups cooking liquid, add more water if necessary. Heat the oil in the saucepan. Add the millet and toast, stirring frequently, until the grains begin to turn brown and pop, 3 or 4 minutes. Stir in the leeks and garlic and continue to saute for 2 minutes, stirring frequently. Add the chard cooking liquid. Bring to a boil, then lower the heat to a simmer and cook for 20 minutes. Stir in the cooked chard, lemon peel, pepper and just enough lemon juice to perk up the flavors.

Per serving: 279 calories, 5 grams fat, no cholesterol, 626 milligrams sodium.

WEDNESDAY

SOUTHERN MUSTARD GREENS AND GARLIC PIZZA FROZEN YOGURT*

This pizza is delicious on its own, but tonight might be a good time to clean out your refrigerator. Add other ingredients to the topping that you may have: black olives, half a red or green bell pepper. Swiss chard works as well on the pizza as mustard greens, and you might have fun trying the dish with bits of country ham instead of bacon.

SOUTHERN MUSTARD GREENS AND GARLIC PIZZA

Makes 6 to 8 servings
Preparation time: 10 minutes
Cooking time: 25 minutes

2 to 3 tablespoons cornmeal
    (for baking pan)
1 12-inch Boboli or other pizza
    bread
1 pound fresh young mustard
    greens, trimmed of stems and
    roughly chopped or 10-ounce
    package mustard or other frozen
    chopped greens
1/4 pound bacon
1 medium onion, chopped
1 teaspoon minced garlic in oil
1/2 cup half-and-half
Pinch black pepper and salt to taste
3 to 4 tablespoons grated Parmesan
    cheese

Preheat oven to 500 degrees. Sprinkle a large baking sheet with cornmeal, and place pizza bread over. To make the topping: Bring a large pot of salted water to boil and add the fresh greens; cook 5 to 10 minutes, until just tender. Drain well, squeeze to press out

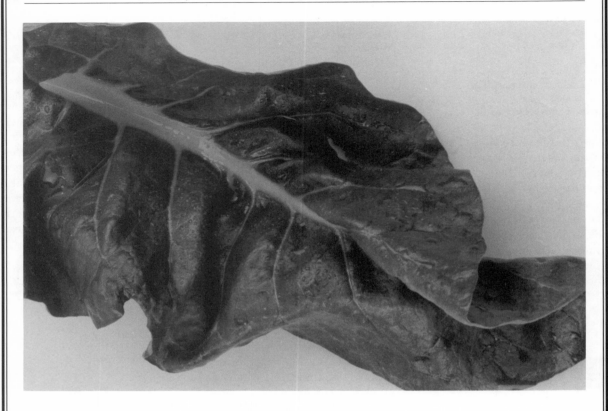

Price: Red Swiss chard is sold by the bunch and by the pound and will range from $.69 to $1.69 a bunch or about $.69 to $1.29 a pound. Look for organic supplies to run about $1.29 a pound.

Nutrition: Chard averages 30 calories for a 3 ¹/₂-ounce cooked portion. Like other greens, it is an excellent source of calcium and potassium and vitamins A and C.

Selection: Look for glossy leaves with heavy red stems that are free of blemishes or deep cuts.

Storage: Wrap chard in paper towels and enclose in plastic wrap. Refrigerate for 3 or 4 days. Red Swiss chard seems to store several days longer than green Swiss chard.

Uses: Allow ¹/₃ to ¹/₂ pound greens per person. Add to soups, wrap it around fish or quickly saute or wilt, just as you would spinach. Small tender leaves can be used in salads.

As a member of the beet family, Swiss chard isn't really a first cousin to spinach, but it is often called spinach beet, for its look-alike leaves. The flavor is similar, with just a bit more bite. And of course, then there are the beautiful red stems and veins that look so lovely when red chard is just wilted. Look for chard during the winter months of the year, when other greens are available.

Chard's stems and leaves are best cooked separately. Pull the leafy part from the tougher stem. The stems can then be steamed or stir-fried much like asparagus.

Recipes with spinach often call for a pinch of nutmeg, and it works as a flavor enhancer for chard as well. Other foods that bring out chard's flavor are garlic, oregano or tarragon.

moisture (or cook the frozen greens according to package directions, then drain and press out moisture).

Meanwhile, in a large skillet cook the bacon until crisp. Drain, crumble and reserve. Add the onion and minced garlic to the bacon drippings and saute about 4 minutes, until soft and fragrant. Stir in the greens, half-and-half, pepper and grated cheese. Add salt to taste. Spoon the filling on the pizza bread and sprinkle with bacon. Bake 10 to 12 minutes.

Per serving: 223 calories, 10 grams fat, 20 milligrams cholesterol, 481 milligrams sodium.

THURSDAY

SMOKED TURKEY AND RISOTTO SOUP
STEAMED CARROTS*
WHOLE GRAIN CRACKERS*

Leftover risotto lends rich flavors and creaminess to this turkey soup. Smoked turkey is a delicious addition, but plain cooked turkey or chicken would also be good choices. Add a simple steamed vegetable and crackers.

SMOKED TURKEY AND RISOTTO SOUP

Makes 4 servings
Preparation time: 5 minutes
Cooking time: 15 minutes

1 tablespoon oil
1/2 large onion, chopped
4 to 6 cups chicken broth
2 to 3 cups cooked risotto
1 cup smoked turkey, cut into large dices
Salt and pepper to taste

In a large saucepan, heat the oil and saute the onion 5 minutes or until fragrant. Add the chicken broth, risotto and turkey and heat to a simmer. Add salt and pepper to taste, and serve.

Per serving: 279 calories, 9 grams fat, 22 milligrams cholesterol, 1,279 milligrams sodium.

FRIDAY

GRATIN OF LEMON MILLET*
CHEESE AND FRUIT*

Turn leftover millet into an enticing gratin by spooning the leftovers into a greased baking dish and top with buttered bread crumbs. Heat until bubbling, about 10 minutes, then finish under the broiler for a minute to brown the top. Add a soft cheese and apples and pears.

SATURDAY

PORK WITH MUSHROOM CREAM SAUCE
ON A BED OF WILTED SWISS CHARD*
GRILLED YELLOW FINN NEW POTATOES AND RED ONIONS
FRESH FRUIT*

Wilt red chard, as you did earlier in the week, to make a beautiful presentation for the pork chops and mushroom sauce. Shiitake or other mushrooms would make a wonderful dish; otherwise use white mushrooms. Choose small, B-size potatoes, Yellow Fins or Yukon Golds, or new red potatoes, especially Red Bliss, if you can find them. Serve the pota-

toes and onions on the skewers or off; either way, this is a very pretty dish.

PORK WITH MUSHROOM CREAM SAUCE

Makes 4 servings
Preparation time: 5 minutes
Cooking time: 15 minutes

4 boneless pork loin chops (about 2 pounds)
1/4 cup unsalted butter
1 large leek, washed and finely julienned
Salt and pepper, to taste
4 ounces mushrooms, sliced
1/4 cup half-and-half

Melt butter in a 10-inch skillet over medium-high heat and add pork chops. Cook for 10 minutes, turning once, until chops are done. Remove them and keep warm. In the skillet, stir in the leek and saute until soft and fragrant, 3 or 4 minutes. Stir in salt, pepper and mushrooms; cook over medium heat about 5 minutes or until tender. Stir in half-and-half; cook 1 minute until slightly reduced.

Make mounds of the wilted chard on each plate; place a pork chop and drizzle sauce over each.

Per serving (not including chard): 455 calories, 32 grams fat, 155 milligrms cholesterol, 103 milligrams sodium.

GRILLED YELLOW FINN POTATOES AND RED ONIONS

Makes 4 servings
Preparation time: 5 minutes
Cooking time: 25 minutes

6 or 8-inch skewers, wooden or metal
1 red onion, peeled, halved and cut into wedges

12 new potatoes, size B, unpeeled
2 tablespoons unsalted butter,
    melted
1 to 2 tablespoons herbs de Provence
Salt, to taste
Vegetable pan spray

If using wooden skewers, soak them in water for 30 minutes before using. Preheat oven to 375 degrees.

To thread the skewers, thread a wedge of onion, then a potato, then another wedge of onion and potato on the four skewers, with the vegetables evenly divided. Brush the vegetables with melted butter and sprinkle with herbs de Provence and salt. Spray a large heavy baking pan generously with pan spray; arrange the skewers in the pan. The skewers can be assembled 1 to 2 hours ahead and left at cool room temperature.

Bake 10 minutes and turn the skewers over. Continue baking another 10 to 15 minutes, or until the potatoes are tender when pierced with a knife. Remove and cool about 5 minutes. Serve hot or at room temperature.

Per serving: 199 calories, 6 grams fat, 15 milligrams cholesterol, 12 milligrams sodium.

WEEK

10

SHOPPING LIST

Meat, Poultry, Seafood

- ❑ 2 frying chickens
- ❑ 1 pound lean ground lamb
- ❑ 1 pound large shrimp

Produce

- ❑ 1 bunch watercress
- ❑ 1 bunch bok choy
- ❑ 1 head nappa cabbage
- ❑ ¹/₂ pound snow peas
- ❑ 1 red bell pepper
- ❑ 1 bunch red Swiss chard
- ❑ 3 green onions (or 1 green Vidalia)
- ❑ 1 onion
- ❑ 2 carrots
- ❑ 4 stalks celery
- ❑ 1 pound asparagus
- ❑ 2 green Vidalias (or ¹/₂ red onion)
- ❑ 5 garlic cloves
- ❑ 1 bunch spinach
- ❑ 1 lemon

- ❑ 2 kiwi fruit
- ❑ 1 navel orange
- ❑ 3 juice oranges
- ❑ 4 tangerines
- ❑ 2 large bunches mint

Dairy

- ❑ 1 stick plus 2 tablespoons unsalted butter
- ❑ 3 eggs
- ❑ 3 ounces low-fat cream cheese
- ❑ 2 tablespoons milk

Deli

- ❑ 4 to 8 cheddar cheese bread sticks
- ❑ 4 ounces feta cheese
- ❑ 1 loaf crusty bread
- ❑ 4 pita breads

Miscellaneous

- ❑ 3 cups dried aromatic

rice
- ❑ ¹/₄ cup dry sherry
- ❑ ¹/₄ cup chopped macadamia nuts
- ❑ 2 tablespoons white wine
- ❑ 1 pound fettucine noodles
- ❑ 3 14 ¹/₂-ounce cans beef broth
- ❑ 8 slices multigrain bread

Staples

- ❑ All-purpose flour
- ❑ Black pepper
- ❑ Chili-flavored sesame oil
- ❑ Chinese five-spice
- ❑ Cornstarch
- ❑ Ground allspice
- ❑ Ground cumin
- ❑ Lemon juice
- ❑ Low-fat mayonnaise
- ❑ Minced garlic in oil
- ❑ Olive oil
- ❑ Peanut oil
- ❑ Poppyseeds

- ❑ Powdered sugar
- ❑ Red wine vinegar
- ❑ Salt
- ❑ Sesame oil
- ❑ Soy sauce
- ❑ Star anise
- ❑ Sugar

FIVE-SPICE ROAST CHICKEN
WITH JUICE ORANGES
STEAMED AROMATIC RICE*
STEAMED ORIENTAL
VEGETABLES*
LEMON-MACADAMIA BARS

This easy chicken dish, a take-off of a similar dish from Lou Seibert Pappas and Jane Horn, roasts to a fragrant and mahogany crust. Florida oranges are at their sweetest now, and Hawaiian papayas are good and inexpensive. In fact, any tropical fruit (mango or papaya) would lend a wonderful flavor to the dish. The entire meal provides leftovers for the week, so make enough rice and vegetables to serve a second time. (If saving rice for Saturday night, put 3 cups cooked in the freezer to keep it fresher.) Steam baby bok choy, nappa cabbage and choy sum or Chinese long beans. Lemon bars add a refreshing flavor to the meal; substitute another nut if you wish. Cut the cookie recipe in half if you need to, but they do go fast.

FIVE-SPICE ROAST CHICKEN WITH JUICE ORANGES

Makes 8 servings
Preparation time: 10 minutes
Cooking time: 1 hour 15 minutes

2 broiler-fryer chickens
Salt and black pepper to taste
2 teaspoons Chinese five-spice
$^1/_4$ cup soy sauce
$^1/_4$ cup dry sherry
The juice of 1 orange
2 teaspoons minced garlic in oil
2 oranges, peeled, divided into sections, and seeded

Preheat oven to 425 degrees.

Rub the chickens with salt, pepper and five spice and place on a rack in a baking pan. Roast 15 minutes.

Meanwhile, in a small bowl, combine the soy sauce, sherry, orange juice and minced garlic; brush some of the baste over the birds. Reduce heat to 375 degrees and roast 1 hour longer, or until drumsticks move easily, basting with remaining sauce. During the last few minutes of roasting, place fruit slices in pan juices and heat until hot throughout. Transfer birds to a platter, carve and serve with fruit alongside.

LEMON-MACADAMIA BARS

Makes 24 bars
Preparation time: 10 minutes
Cooking time: 40 minutes

Crust:
2 tablespoons macadamia nuts
1 cup all-purpose flour
$^1/_4$ cup confectioners' sugar
Pinch salt
$^1/_2$ cup butter slightly soft

Filling:
1 cup sugar
2 tablespoons flour
Juice of 1 lemon (at least 3 tablespoons)
Rind of 1 lemon
2 eggs
Confectioners' sugar (for topping)

Preheat oven to 350 degrees. Put the nuts in the workbowl of a food processor and pulse a few times to chop them. Add the flour, confectioners' sugar and salt and pulse to blend. Add the butter with a few pulses until the dough looks like small peas. Spoon the dough into an ungreased 9-by-13-inch baking pan and pat down well. Bake 20

minutes, until crust is golden. Remove from the oven.

Prepare the filling after the crust has been baked. In the food processor or by hand, mix together the sugar, flour, lemon juice and rind and eggs and beat well. Immediately pour over the hot crust and return to oven. Bake 20 minutes.

Remove to a rack, then sprinkle with powdered sugar and cut into squares.

Per bar: 92 calories, 4 grams fat, 33 milligrams cholesterol, 55 milligrams sodium.

KIWI FRUIT, ORANGE AND
WATERCRESS SALAD*
FETA SALAD DRESSING
CHEDDAR CHEESE
BREAD STICKS*

Kiwi fruit are at a low price now and can work their way into myriad dishes, such as this fruit salad. Instead of a blander lettuce, watercress provides a peppery counterpart, and the feta salad dressing pulls it all together. Add a sliced cucumber if you wish. Save leftover salad dressing to use later in the week.

FETA SALAD DRESSING

Makes 8 servings
Preparation time: 5 minutes

$^1/_4$ cup red wine vinegar
2 tablespoons white wine
4 ounces ($^3/_4$ cup) feta cheese, rinsed and crumbled
$^1/_2$ cup olive oil
Salt and black pepper to taste

In a bowl combine vinegar, wine

and cheese. Add the oil in a thin stream, whisking until it is blended. Add salt and pepper to taste. Reserve half the dressing for later in the week, and drizzle the remainder over the salad.

TUESDAY

**SAUTEED MEATBALLS
POPPYSEED NOODLES*
STIR-FRIED CHINESE
VEGETABLES***

This menu both uses and generates leftovers. Chinese vegetables steamed earlier in the week can be stir-fried tonight. Prepare fettucine noodles, then toss with butter and poppyseeds, and cook enough to have leftovers for another meal. Look for ground lamb at most grocery stores. Half of the meatball recipe, adapted from Lou Seibert Pappas and Jane Horn's *The New Harvest* (101 Productions, $9.95), can be cooked tonight, and the remainder dropped into a warming soup tomorrow night.

SAUTEED MEATBALLS

*Makes 8 servings
Preparation time: 10 minutes
Cooking time: 10 minutes*

1 pound lean ground lamb
3 tablespoons cornstarch
1 egg
$^1/_4$ cup minced fresh mint
$^1/_4$ teaspoon ground allspice
2 garlic cloves, minced

Combine the ingredients in a large bowl. Shape into 3/4-inch balls and refrigerate until ready to use. Reserve one-third of the balls for tomorrow night's meal.

MARCH

Vegetable prices have stabilized. Broccoli, carrots, bell peppers and summer squashes are more affordable than in earlier weeks. With the end of the winter season, artichoke supplies are higher priced, but the spring crop will be coming in a few weeks. Asparagus is still at a good price and looking wonderful. Tomatoes are coming down in price, and winter squash supplies are getting tight.

Look for great prices on spinach and Florida tomatoes. Green beans are coming down in price, while onions are slightly higher. Look carefully at onions — especially the reds — for soft spots and molding. Potatoes are steady, with Florida potatoes beautiful and a good price. California reds are more expensive, and organic yellow Finns are beautiful now.

Rainy spring weather has produce looking good. Spinach is a bit dirty but very nice; Vidalia onions are in from Georgia fields; asparagus is still very cheap, but artichokes and yellow squash have gone up in price. Sugar snap and snowpeas are coming down in price with the spring weather, and greens are looking wonderful. Some stores are carrying white Chilean asparagus.

Celery is still especially high, potatoes are up, and the new, white, tiny creamers are just in from Florida.

Pineapples have taken a turn for the worse; the flavor of both Hawaiian and Honduran supplies is fine for cooking but less desirable for fresh eating. Florida avocados are tight since that season is ending. Although California Hass avocados are in good supply, their prices probably won't drop much with the tightening supplies of Florida avocados. Chilean fruit is still abundant; look for air-shipped and tree-ripened for the best flavor. Look for the Kent variety of Mexican mangoes; they are creamy and almost stringless and very sweet.

Florida strawberries are fragrant and very flavorful. California supplies are less so, with more white on the crown, but they will be better next month. Kiwi fruit are still a great buy everywhere in town. Grapefruit have finally gotten sweet, and California navels are in. Watch tangerines closely for softness, especially organic supplies, which have not been sprayed with mold inhibitors.

Look for nice rhubarb now, and California strawberries are quite sweet. Florida grapefruit are really on their last leg now, soft and sweet.

Florida strawberries and kumquats are in their prime. Some stores still have a good selection of apples and pears. Several stores are carrying a wide variety of specialty bananas. Valencia oranges are coming in nicely, and don't miss the sweetest tangerine of the season, the Honey. It is seedier and harder to peel, but worth the effort.

To cook, heat a heavy skillet and saute the meatballs until thoroughly cooked, about 10 minutes. Season with salt and pepper to taste. Toss with cooked poppyseed noodles and serve.

WEDNESDAY

MOROCCAN CHARD AND
MEATBALL SOUP
CRUSTY BREAD*
PLATTER OF TANGERINES
AND KUMQUATS*

Lamb meatballs add more flavor than meat to this mostly-vegetable soup. It is a first cousin to the Italian stratatelle, a hearty soup made with meat balls and spinach. Serve with plenty of crusty bread for dipping. Get the best of the season's tangerines and kumquats; they are very sweet and inexpensive now. The late-season Honey tangerine is seedier and harder to peel, but the flavor makes it worth the work.

MOROCCAN CHARD AND MEATBALL SOUP

Makes 4 to 6 servings
Preparation time: 10 minutes
Cooking time: 20 minutes

1 bunch red Swiss chard
1 tablespoon olive oil
1 onion, chopped
2 carrots, shredded
2 stalks celery, chopped
$1/2$ teaspoon each ground cumin and
    black pepper
1 $1/2$ quarts beef stock
1 star anise
2 tablespoons chopped mint

Remove ribs from Swiss chard; slice thinly. Chop leaves separately; set aside.

In a large soup pot, heat the oil. Saute the chard ribs, onion, carrot and celery until fragrant, 3 or 4 minutes. Add cumin, pepper, beef stock and star anise; bring to a boil. Add meatballs, cover and simmer 5 minutes. Add chopped chard leaves into the hot broth, simmer 5 minutes longer. Season with salt and mint and ladle into bowls.

THURSDAY

CHICKEN SALAD WITH
TANGERINES AND RED
ONIONS
MULTIGRAIN BREAD*
STEAMED ASPARAGUS*

Leftover five-spice chicken tastes great paired with citrus and spring sweet onions; be sure to include some of the flavorful crust. Substitute $1/2$ a red onion for green Vidalias if you wish. It tastes even better after a day in the refrigerator.

CHICKEN SALAD WITH TANGERINES AND GREEN VIDALIAS

Makes 6 servings
Preparation time: 10 minutes

2 tangerines
2 cups cooked chicken, coarsely
    chopped
$1/2$ cup chopped celery
2 green Vidalias, chopped
$1/4$ cup chopped mint (or parsley)

DRESSING:
3 ounces low-fat cream cheese, room
    temperature
$1/2$ cup lite mayonnaise
2 tablespoons milk
Salt and pepper to taste
Several pieces spinach

Using a zester, remove the peel from the tangerines to make 1 to 2 tablespoons and reserve, then peel the tangerines.

Cut the tangerines into large dice, then remove seeds and pith. Place the sections in a bowl with the chicken, celery, onion and mint.

To make the dressing, combine all the ingredients in the workbowl of a food processor or blender and pulse until combined.

Gently toss the chicken mixture with the dressing. Chill until ready to serve. Serve with spinach (or lettuce) and bread.

FRIDAY

POPPY SEED NOODLES,
ASPARAGUS AND FETA SALAD
DRESSING*
WARMED PITA BREADS*

Make this delicious dinner by combining leftover noodles, asparagus and salad dressing, and you can serve it cold or warm. If serving cold, slightly reheat the noodles and asparagus before combining with the salad dressing. Any leftover chicken salad makes this pasta dish good enough to serve company.

SATURDAY

STIR-FRIED SPICY SHRIMP,
LEMON RICE AND SPINACH
FRUIT SALAD OF BURRO, RED
AND MANZANO BANANAS
WITH SWEETENED YOGURT*

Don't let the list of ingredients, which are mostly seasonings,

Price: Will average $.70 to $.99 a pound.

Nutrition: Specialty bananas range in calories from 85 to 118 for a 3.5 ounce serving. They are low in sodium and high in vitamin A and potassium.

Selection: Choose bananas when they are not fully ripe to use in cooking, but for dessert uses, let them ripen fully.

Burro: A squarish yellow banana but smaller than the Cavendish, with a lemony flavor. When fully ripe the yellow skin has black spots.

Red: These come to the stores with a green-ruby peel, turning to dark purple or maroon when ripe. The flesh is orange-tinted or even pink. It is sweeter and more fragrant than the Cavendish, with flavor over- tones of raspberry and strawber- ry. It's a favorite choice. The peels are often thicker than the Cavendish.

Manzano: Also called the apple or finger banana, these 3- or 4-inch stubs are cute and a favorite of children. It ripens from green to completely black. The uglier and blacker the peel, the sweeter the fruit. It has the usual banana flavor with over- tones of strawberry and apple. It can be quite astringent when not fully ripe.

Cavendish: The main com- mercial variety of banana. Like other dessert bananas.

Storage: Store bananas at 56 to 58 degrees, but not at refrigerator temperatures, as this will kill the delicate flavor. Let them ripen at room temperature, which, depending on the variety, will take up to a week. Bananas produce ethylene gas and should not be stored in a closed bag with other fruits unless you want them to ripen quickly. Bananas will store for several days and will be black or speckled black when ripe.

Uses: If unripe these bananas need to be cooked to be edible. When fully ripe, serve them raw as other bananas.

We don't settle for just one apple variety, so why should we settle for only one banana vari- ety? The standard yellow Cavendish banana is a fine fruit, but it is only one of dozens. And like apples, the flavors, textures and cooking properties of bananas widely differ.

scare you away from this fabulous meal — dishes don't get much better than this. (Add more preparation time if you don't buy shelled shrimp.) Swiss chard could be substituted for the spinach, for a slightly stronger flavor. Ripe red, burro and the stubby little manzano bananas (see In Season, page 53), sliced together make a wonderful fruit salad. Serve them with with other fruits, such as kiwi fruit, and serve with a sweetened yogurt dressing.

STIR-FRIED SPICY SHRIMP, LEMON RICE AND SPINACH

Makes 4 servings
Preparation time: 30 minutes
Standing time: 30 minutes
Cooking time: 15 minutes

3 tablespoons soy sauce
2 teaspooons chile-flavored
    sesame oil
2 teaspoons minced garlic in oil,
    divided
2 teaspoons gingerroot, grated
$^1/_2$ teaspoon red pepper flakes
1 pound large shrimp, shelled
The peel of 1 lemon, grated
3 green onions, trimmed and cut
    lengthwise into thin pieces
1 bunch washed, trimmed and torn
    spinach leaves
3 cups cooked long-grain white or
    brown rice
Cilantro leaves for garnish (optional)

To make the marinade, combine 2 tablespoons soy sauce, hot sesame oil, half of the minced garlic in oil and 1 teaspoon ginger in a large bowl. Add the shrimp and toss to coat. Cover and marinate for 30 minutes at room temperature, or 1 hour or longer in the refrigerator.

When ready to serve, heat a wok or large nonstick skillet over medium-high heat until hot enough to make a drop of water dance. Add peanut oil and then the shrimp a few at a time. Stir-fry just until lightly browned on both sides, 5 to 8 minutes, then remove to a platter and keep warm. Scrape the pan drippings over the shrimp, leaving the barest amount of oil in the pan.

Get the pan hot again. Add the remaining minced garlic in oil, lemon peel and ginger and stir-fry 20 seconds. Add the green onions and spinach and stir-fry 10 seconds.

Add the rice and reserved shrimp and stir-fry over high heat 2 or 3 minutes. Sprinkle with the remaining tablespoon of soy sauce and toss. Sprinkle with cilantro and serve.

WEEK

11

SHOPPING LIST

Meat, Poultry, Seafood

- ❑ ¹/₄ pound salt pork
- ❑ ¹/₂ pound boneless lamb shoulder
- ❑ 6 to 8 ounces kielbasa
- ❑ 4 slices bacon
- ❑ 1 2 ¹/₂-pound sea bass or red snapper, cleaned with head and tail on

Produce

- ❑ 1 large onion
- ❑ 9 garlic cloves
- ❑ 5 green onions
- ❑ 2 zucchini
- ❑ 2 baby bok choy
- ❑ 1 head romaine lettuce
- ❑ 1 or 2 heads Bibb or Boston lettuce
- ❑ 5 medium green bell peppers
- ❑ 4 ounces shiitake mushrooms
- ❑ 4 ounces cremini (or white) mushrooms
- ❑ 1 package (3 to 4 ounces) enoki mushrooms
- ❑ 8 ounces white mushrooms
- ❑ 1 small knob fresh ginger
- ❑ 1 bunch Italian parsley
- ❑ 1 bunch parsley
- ❑ 1 bunch dill
- ❑ 1 bunch sage leaves
- ❑ 2 or 3 sprigs rosemary
- ❑ 1 bunch mint
- ❑ 1 bunch basil
- ❑ 1 cored and peeled pineapple
- ❑ 1 ripe pear

Dairy

- ❑ ³/₄ cup (3 ounces) shredded sharp Cheddar cheese
- ❑ 2 eggs
- ❑ 3 extra-large eggs
- ❑ 1 stick unsalted butter
- ❑ 4 tablespoons raspberry yogurt

Deli

- ❑ ¹/₂ lemon poundcake
- ❑ 2 cups cheese crackers

Miscellaneous

- ❑ 1 1-pound bag dried navy beans
- ❑ 1 14 ¹/₂-ounce can crushed tomatoes
- ❑ ¹/₂ cup light rum
- ❑ ¹/₂ cup walnut halves
- ❑ ¹/₂ cup dried cherries
- ❑ 3 cups dried rice
- ❑ 1 10-ounce package frozen raspberries
- ❑ 2 cups frozen corn
- ❑ 8 ounces buckwheat (soba) noodles
- ❑ 8 ounces linguine
- ❑ 1 ¹/₂ cups roasted peanuts, skins removed
- ❑ 1 ¹/₂ cups pecans
- ❑ 2 ounces unsweetened chocolate

Staples

- ❑ Bay leaves
- ❑ Black pepper
- ❑ Bread crumbs (optional)
- ❑ Brown sugar
- ❑ Cayenne pepper
- ❑ Chili sesame oil
- ❑ Coarse salt
- ❑ Dry sherry
- ❑ Dried thyme, savory or herbs de Provence
- ❑ Dry white wine
- ❑ Granulated sugar
- ❑ Hot pepper vinegar
- ❑ Light corn syrup
- ❑ Light soy sauce
- ❑ Nutmeg
- ❑ Peanut oil
- ❑ Salt
- ❑ Vanilla
- ❑ Vinaigrette
- ❑ Vegetable oil

* Suggested accompaniments

INDIANA CASSOULET
DRIED CHERRY AND WALNUT SALAD WITH RASPBERRY YOGURT

The famous French dish called cassoulet has another name in the Midwest: ham and beans. It's a dense, delicious and filling dish made with inexpensive ingredients; its only requirement is a few hours of slow cooking. Cooking times may vary, depending on the age of the beans or even the hardness of the cooking water. Frozen beans would cut the cooking time by an hour, but they will be softer.

The French version uses lamb, roasted duck or goose and several days' labor; this version is simpler. Don't omit the lamb for its intense flavor or the salt pork — it provides the smoothness that is the mark of a good cassoulet. The entire dish can be combined several days in advance and refrigerated. Leftovers taste better than the newly-made dish.

Add a salad with dried cherries, available at farmers markets and specialty stores. Michigan cherries, sold under the American Spoon label, are the tartest and tastiest. Substitute other dried fruit if necessary.

INDIANA CASSOULET

Makes 10 1-cup servings
Preparation time: 10 minutes
Standing time: 1 hour
Cooking time: 1 1/2 hours

1 pound dried navy beans (or 2 pounds frozen)
2 bay leaves
Big handful of parsley sprigs
1/4 pound salt pork, rind removed, finely cubed
1/2 pound boneless lamb shoulder, cut in 2-inch pieces
1 large onion, chopped
3 garlic cloves, minced
6 to 8 ounces fully cooked kielbasa, cut in 1-inch pieces
1 14 1/2-ounce can crushed tomatoes
1/2 cup dry white wine
2 tablespoons parsley, chopped
1 teaspoon dried herbs — thyme, savory or herbs de Provence
Salt and black pepper to taste
1/4 cup dry bread crumbs (optional)
1 tablespoon minced parsley (optional)

In a large pot, bring the beans and water to a boil. Remove from heat and let sit for 1 hour. Drain the beans and cover with fresh water. Add the bay leaves and parsley; cover and bring to a boil. Lower the heat to a simmer, partially covered for 30 minutes. Drain, reserving the cooking liquid.

Meanwhile, in a large skillet, combine the cubed salt pork and lamb and brown over medium heat. Add the onion and garlic and cook 3 to 5 minutes or until the onion starts to brown. Add the meat mixture and the kielbasa to the beans.

Add the tomatoes, wine, parsley, dried seasonings and salt and pepper to the bean mixture. Add enough of the reserved cooking liquid to come within 1 inch of the top of the beans (about 1 cup). Bake uncovered for about 1 hour. (Do not let the beans get mushy. Add more of the cooking liquid if necessary.) About 20 minutes before the beans are done, combine the bread crumbs and parsley and sprinkle over the beans and press them down into the cooking liquid to thicken the juices. Bake for 20 minutes until the crumbs are brown and crusted on top. Serve hot.

Per serving: 378 calories, 20 grams fat, 41 milligrams cholesterol, 498 milligrams sodium.

DRIED CHERRY WALNUT SALAD WITH RASPBERRY YOGURT

Makes 4 servings
Preparation time: 10 minutes

1 or 2 heads soft lettuce such as Bibb or Boston, depending on size
1 ripe pear, peeled and sliced
1/2 cup walnut halves
1/2 cup dried cherries
4 tablespoons raspberry yogurt

Arrange lettuce leaves on four salad plates. Top with slices of pear, walnuts and cherries. Puree the yogurt in the food processor to thin it slightly, then spoon it over each salad.

Per serving: 173 calories, 10 grams fat, no cholesterol, 7 milligrams sodium.

STIR-FRIED BABY BOK CHOY AND SQUASH
STEAMED RICE *

This simple stir-fry employs only a couple of vegetables and simple seasonings, yet it is delicious and elegant. Baby bok choy is a delicious cabbage (see In Season). Add squares of tofu or strips of fresh basil if you wish. Cook extra rice for Thursday's dinner.

STIR-FRIED BABY BOK CHOY AND SQUASH

Makes 4 servings
Preparation time: 5 minutes
Cooking time: 10 minutes

1 tablespoon peanut oil
2 cloves garlic, minced

2 green onions, sliced
2 baby bok choy, sliced ½-inch thick, stems separated from greens
2 zucchini, sliced and halved
3 tablespoons dry sherry
Mint leaves
1 tablespoon light soy sauce
2 teaspoons chili sesame oil

Heat a wok or large skillet until hot, then add the oil and garlic. Stir-fry for 30 seconds. Add the sliced green onions and bok choy stems and stir-fry for 3 or 4 minutes. Add the zucchini and stir-fry 2 more minutes. Add bok choy greens and cook 1 minute. Turn off the heat and toss with sherry and soy sauce and sesame oil. Serve at once with hot rice.

Per serving: 81 calories, 6 grams fat, no cholesterol, 146 milligrams sodium.

TUESDAY

CASSOULET-STUFFED PEPPERS LEMON POUNDCAKE WITH RASPBERRY PUREE *

Leftover cassoulet comes in handy for this stuffed pepper dish. Substitute 2 cups of canned red beans if necessary. Add purchased lemon poundcake for dessert. To puree frozen raspberries, pulse them in the food processor a few times; strain out the seeds if you wish.

CASSOULET-STUFFED PEPPERS

Makes 4 servings
Preparation time: 5 minutes
Cooking time: 10 minutes

4 medium green bell peppers
2 cups corn kernels (canned or frozen)
1 ½ to 2 cups cooked cassoulet beans and meat

¾ cup shredded sharp Cheddar (about 3 ounces)
Freshly ground black pepper to taste
A few shakes of cayenne pepper, or to taste

Preheat the oven to 375 degrees. Bring a saucepan of water to a boil.

Cut off the tops of the peppers and remove the seeds and inner ribs. Immerse the peppers in the boiling water and cook them for 5 minutes. With tongs, remove the peppers and place them on towels, hole side down, to drain and cool. In a medium bowl, combine the corn, cassoulet, cheese, pepper and cayenne. Divide the filling among the cooled peppers. Place the filled peppers in a baking dish cut side up in a baking dish, and pour a little water into the dish. Place the dish in the hot oven and bake, uncovered, for about 20 minutes.

Per serving: 360 calories, 18 grams fat, 43 milligrams cholesterol, 651 milligrams sodium.

WEDNESDAY

WILD MUSHROOMS WITH BACON, GARLIC AND MINT BUCKWHEAT NOODLES *

Don't let "wild" scare you away. This mushroom and pasta dish is delicious. Buckwheat noodles, or soba noodles, are hearty enough to stand up to the various mushroom flavors — look for them at farmers' markets, health-food or Japanese grocery stores. Substitute egg noodles or linguine if you wish. The dish is rustic and would make a wonderful company dish, but the family will appreciate it too.

WILD MUSHROOMS WITH BACON, GARLIC AND MINT

Makes 4 servings
Preparation time: 5 minutes
Cooking time: 10 minutes

1 teaspoon peanut oil
4 slices bacon, diced
2 cloves garlic, minced
4 ounces shiitake mushrooms, stemmed and quartered
4 ounces cremini (or white) mushrooms, stemmed and sliced
4 ounces enoki mushrooms
2 tablespoons minced mint
Salt and black pepper to taste

In a wok or skillet, heat the peanut oil over high heat until hot. Lower the heat and add the bacon and cook, stirring occasionally until golden, 6 to 7 minutes. Transfer the bacon to paper towels to drain.

Pour off all but 3 tablespoons of the fat. Add the garlic and stir-fry for 20 seconds; do not let it burn. Add the shiitakes and cremini and stir-fry for 2 minutes. Add the enokis and stir-fry another 2 minutes or until all the mushrooms are tender and softened. Just before serving, stir in the mint, salt, pepper and bacon.

Per serving: 70 calories, 5 grams fat, 5 milligrams cholesterol, 105 milligrams sodium.

THURSDAY

FRIED RICE WITH VEGETABLES FRESH PINEAPPLE RINGS *

A few minutes of cooking will turn leftovers into a filling dinner. Leftover vegetables — bok choy, mushrooms, onions and peppers — are all fair game for

Price: Will average $.99 a pound.

Nutrition: Low in calories and high in vitamins A and C. One cup of cooked bok choy has as much calcium as 1 cup of milk.

Selection: Although it is available all year, the quality is the best during the cooler months of spring and fall. Bok choy heads vary in size depending on season and maturity. Look for crisp, green leaves and stems that are not flabby or shriveled. Avoid heads with slippery brown spots on leaves, this indicates overchilling, which robs the vegetable of flavor.

Storage: Store in the crisper in the refrigerator for 1 week.

Uses: Allow $1/4$ to $1/3$ pound per serving. The tender hearts can be served raw; but stems and leaves are delicious steamed or stir-fried. Also used to make the famous Korean pickled vegetable kimchi.

Another cabbage family vegetable offers delicious steaming and stir-frying possibilities. Regular bok choy has become a stir-fry staple, but baby bok choy, also called chanchai bok choy, has special attributes.

The 5 to 6-inch-long cabbage is more tender and finer-textured than its larger version, and has a refreshing cucumber taste. Its stalks are green and small, rather than the larger, white stalks of regular bok choy. It may have an especially delicate and tender center of yellow flowers called sum, which is usually labeled bok choy sum or choy sum. Sometime this tender center is sold separately.

The tougher stalks should be added to a stir-fry first and cooked before the more tender and spicy-flavored leaves are added.

Be sure to thoroughly wash the vegetable before using; because it grows so close to the ground, sand readily hides in between the stalks.

this dish. Start with cold cooked rice; hot rice will stick together.

FRIED RICE WITH VEGETABLES

Makes 4 servings
Preparation time: 10 minutes
Cooking time: 10 minutes

2 tablespoons peanut oil
1 egg
2 cloves garlic, minced
2 teaspoons grated fresh ginger
2 or 3 green onions, sliced
1 bell pepper, cut into thin slivers
1 cup mushrooms, sliced
2 tablespoons light soy sauce
3 cups cooked rice

In a wok or large skillet, heat 1 tablespoon of oil on medium heat. Add the egg, stirring occasionally, until soft curds form. Remove the egg from the wok and set aside. Increase the heat to medium-high and add remaining oil. When hot, add garlic, ginger and onions and stir-fry for 1 minute. Add the bell pepper and mushrooms and continue to stir-fry a couple of minutes, until the vegetables are tender-crisp. Toss in the soy sauce and rice and continue to cook until the rice is heated through and slightly crisped. Stir in eggs, toss gently and serve hot.

Per serving: 275 calories, 9 grams fat, 68 milligrams cholesterol, 261 milligrams sodium.

FRIDAY

TOMATO SOUP *
CHEESE CRACKERS *
GREEN SALAD *

Several local restaurants have excellent tomato soup: Order it for takeout. Add cheese crackers, available in many grocery store delis, a green salad with the green tops of bok choy, and fruit for dessert.

SATURDAY

RED SNAPPER FLAMED WITH
FRESH HERBS
BUTTERED LEMON ANGEL
HAIR LINGUINE *
CAESAR SALAD *
GEORGIA PEANUT-PECAN
CHOCOLATE TORTE

Don't miss this fragrant and impressive fish dish for Saturday night company, especially with red snapper at its lowest price this month. It is easily baked in an aluminim or parchment bag, then opened and covered with herbs. Only fresh herbs will do, and be sure the rum is warmed before pouring it over the fish. Use long-handled matches if possible, and stand back while flaming. Elizabeth Terry, Savannah chef-owner of Elizabeth's makes this wonderful chocolate torte with Georgia ingredients, and it shouldn't be missed.

RED SNAPPER FLAMED WITH FRESH HERBS

Makes 4 servings
Standing time: 30 minutes
Cooking time: 35 minutes

1 sea bass or red snapper, about 2 ½ pounds, cleaned with head and tail on
Coarse salt, to taste
Black pepper, to taste
15 sprigs Italian parsley
1 bunch dill
10 fresh sage leaves
2 or 3 sprigs fresh rosemary
5 or 6 sprigs fresh mint
3 large bay leaves
2 or 3 large stems fresh basil leaves
½ cup light rum

Wash the fish well, then put it in a shallow bowl of salted water to soak and season it for 30 minutes.

Preheat the oven to 375 degrees.

Drain the fish and pat dry inside and out with paper towels. Put a large sheet of aluminum foil on a board shiny side up. Sprinkle the foil with a little salt and pepper and lay the fish on the foil. Wrap the fish completely in the foil and put in a baking dish. Bake for 15 minutes; turn the fish over and bake for 15 minutes longer.

Unwrap the fish and transfer to a large heat-proof serving platter, adding the juices collected in the foil. Place the herbs over the fish.

In a small saucepan, warm the rum over low heat. Pour the rum over the fish, then stand away and light the rum with a match. As soon as the flames die down, serve the fish with some of the charred and fragrant herbs.

Per serving: 256 calories, 5 grams fat, 93 milligrams cholesterol, 155 milligrams sodium.

GEORGIA PEANUT-PECAN CHOCOLATE TORTE

Makes 10 servings
Preparation time: 20 minutes
Cooking time: 40 minutes

CRUST:
1 cup peanuts, toasted, skin removed
1 cup pecans, toasted and chopped
1 cup brown sugar
¼ teaspoon grated nutmeg
2 ounces (½ stick) chilled unsalted butter, cubed

FILLING:
2 ounces unsweetened chocolate
1 ½ ounces unsalted butter, scant
   ½ stick
¾ cup granulated sugar
1 cup light corn syrup
3 extra-large eggs
2 teaspoons vanilla
½ cup peanuts, chopped
½ cup pecans, chopped

Preheat oven to 300 degrees.

To make the shell, process in a food processor the peanuts, pecans, brown sugar, nutmeg and 2 ounces butter until the mixture holds together in small crumbs. Press the dough into the bottom and up the sides of a 10-inch springform pan. Set aside. To make the filling, melt the chocolate and butter in a small bowl over warm water, or in the microwave on medium (50 percent) power for 2 minutes. Set aside.

Combine the sugar and corn syrup in a saucepan and bring to a boil while stirring with a wooden spoon. Boil about 2 minutes to completely dissolve the sugar. Set aside to cool. Beat the eggs into the bowl of a mixer about 5 minutes until very fluffy. Slowly add the cooled corn syrup mixture and the melted chocolate. Add the vanilla and nuts and pour into the springform pan. Bake for 40 minutes.

Per serving: 599 calories, 33 grams fat, 131 milligrams cholesterol, 59 milligrams sodium.

WEEK

12

SHOPPING LIST

Meat, poultry, seafood

- ❑ 3 pounds lamb shoulder, cut into chunks
- ❑ 1 $\frac{1}{2}$ to 2 pounds ham slices
- ❑ 4 slices bacon
- ❑ 4 swordfish steaks

Produce

- ❑ 4 onions
- ❑ 10 to 12 medium to large all-purpose (not russet) potatoes
- ❑ 3 green bell peppers
- ❑ 6 green onions
- ❑ 2 heads romaine
- ❑ 8 to 10 cherry tomatoes
- ❑ 3 carrots
- ❑ 3 garlic cloves
- ❑ 1 avocado
- ❑ 1 orange

- ❑ 1 pint strawberries
- ❑ 2 ripe pears
- ❑ 1 bunch Italian parsley

Dairy

- ❑ 1 $\frac{1}{2}$ sticks unsalted butter
- ❑ $\frac{1}{2}$ cup sour cream
- ❑ 2 large eggs
- ❑ 1 pint ice cream

Deli

- ❑ 10 to 16 whole grain crackers
- ❑ 4 corned beef sandwiches
- ❑ 1 pint coleslaw
- ❑ 4 to 8 oatmeal cookies
- ❑ 1 loaf crusty bread
- ❑ $\frac{3}{4}$ cup Parmesan cheese
- ❑ 1 pint Italian ice cream

Miscellaneous

- ❑ 1 pound frozen black-eyed peas
- ❑ 2 cups dry aromatic white rice
- ❑ 1 10-ounce package refrigerator biscuits (or homemade)

Staples

- ❑ Baking soda
- ❑ Bread crumbs
- ❑ Cayenne pepper
- ❑ Honey mustard
- ❑ Olive oil
- ❑ Pepper
- ❑ Rice wine vinegar
- ❑ Rosemary
- ❑ Salt
- ❑ Self-rising flour
- ❑ Sugar

- ❑ Vegetable oil
- ❑ White miso
- ❑ Worcestershire sauce

LUCK OF THE IRISH STEW
CITRUSY SOUR CREAM
POUND CAKE

Start the week of St. Patrick's with this easy lamb stew. Unlike most braises, it doesn't require a first step of browning the meat. Serve the stew with Irish soda bread, available in delis around the St. Patrick holiday. Sour cream cake recipes are plentiful, I even made one for my wedding. This wonderful version is adapted from Marion Cunningham's *The Supper Book* (Knopf, $22.00). Bake it in a loaf pan or bundt cake pan. It will be slightly lighter if you separate the egg and fold in the whites after the sour cream.

LUCK OF THE IRISH STEW

Makes 8 servings
Preparation time: 15 minutes
Cooking time: 2 1/2 hours

3 pounds lamb shoulder, cut into
    large chunks
Salt and pepper to taste
5 large onions, sliced
5 medium boiling potatoes, cut in
    thick slices or chunks
2 tablespoons dried rosemary,
    crushed
3 cups water

Preheat the oven to 350 degrees.

In a large Dutch oven, place a layer of lamb pieces. Salt and pepper the pieces, then add a layer of onions and pototes, and sprinkle with rosemary. Salt and pepper each layer, then repeat the layers. Add the water, cover and bake for 2 1/2 hours or until the meat is very tender.

CITRUSY SOUR CREAM POUND CAKE

Makes 1 loaf
Preparation time: 10 minutes
Cooking time: 40 minutes

1 stick unsalted butter at room
    temperature
3/4 cup sugar
2 large eggs
1 tablespoon orange juice
1 tablespoon grated orange peel
1 cup self-rising flour
1/2 teaspoon baking soda
1/2 cup sour cream
1/2 cup finely chopped pecans

Preheat the oven to 325 degrees. Grease and lightly flour a loaf pan (pan spray is fine).

Beat the butter and sugar together with a mixer or in the food processor until light and fluffy. Add the eggs, orange juice and peel and continue to beat another minute. Add the flour and baking soda and pulse just until blended, then, with a spoon, stir in the sour cream. Stir in the nuts and spoon into the prepared pan.

Bake for 40 minutes or until a toothpick comes out clean. Cool on a cake rack about 10 minutes before slicing.

STEAMED AROMATIC RICE
WITH PARMESAN CHEESE*
WINTER GREEN SALAD*
HONEY MUSTARD
VINAIGRETTE
WHOLE GRAIN CRACKERS*

Make a big dinner salad with lettuces, tomato, avocado and bacon strips, then top it with this different salad dressing. One of the best honey mustards on the market is Montego, which uses honey (many "honey mustards" use corn syrup). Reserve the remaining vinaigrette to serve later in the week. Serve hearty portions of steamed fragrant rice topped with parmesan cheese as a first course before the salad; cook enough rice to have 1 cup leftover for later in the week.

HONEY MUSTARD VINAIGRETTE

Makes 1 cup
Preparation time: 1 minute

1/2 cup vegetable oil
4 tablespoons rice wine vinegar
4 tablespoons honey mustard
1 teaspoon Worcestershire sauce
Salt to taste

Combine the ingredients in a blender or food processor and pulse for 10 or 15 seconds. Drizzle 3 or 4 tablespoons vinaigrette over the composed salad and refrigerate the remainder to use later in the week.

SAUTEED HAM SLICES*
SOUTHERN SPICY
BLACK-EYED PEAS
CITRUSY SOUR CREAM POUND
CAKE WITH ICE CREAM*

A traditional Southern meal gets some extra zip with this black-eyed pea recipe. It makes plenty to have leftovers to use later in the week. Chopped basil or mint would make a good garnish, but don't cook these herbs as you cook the parsley, or they will lose all their fragrance. Hot pepper vinegar is found everywhere in the South, a natural accompaniment to beans, peas and cooked greens. (Try this dish in the summer when banana peppers are in season.) Save about 4 ounces ham for later, too. Serve leftover cake with ice cream.

SOUTHERN SPICY BLACK-EYED PEAS

Makes 8 servings
Preparation time: 10 minutes
Cooking time: 20 minutes

1 pound frozen black-eyed peas
3 cups water or low-sodium
    chicken broth
$^1/_2$ teaspoon salt
1 tablespoon fresh Italian parsley
1 tablespoon vegetable oil
1 bell pepper, seeded and diced
Hot pepper vinegar, to taste

Place the peas, stock, salt and parsley in a large saucepan, bring to a boil. Lower the heat to a simmer and cook, uncovered, for 20 minutes, or until the peas are tender but not mushy. (Allow less time if the peas are thawed.) Drain the peas and set aside.

Meanwhile, heat the oil over medium-high heat in a large skillet. Add the diced bell pepper to the hot oil and saute 5 minutes. Fold in the peas, being careful not to mash them. Sprinkle with hot pepper vinegar.

WEDNESDAY

CORN BEEF SANDWICHES*
COLE SLAW*
SOUR CREAM POTATO CHIPS *
OATMEAL COOKIES*

You can celebrate St. Patrick's day without cooking an Irish meal.

Look to local delis for corn beef sandwiches and good cole slaw. Sour cream potato chips and oatmeal cookies complete the picture.

THURSDAY

HOPPIN' JOHN SALAD
CRUSTY BREAD*

Use the vinaigrette reserved from Monday night's meal to toss with the following salad, a take-off of the traditional Low Country black-eyed pea and rice dish, and a great way to use leftovers, inspired by Sharon Tyler Herbst in her book, *Cooking Smart* (Harper Collins, $25.00).

HOPPIN' JOHN SALAD

Makes 4 servings
Preparation time: 15 minutes
Standing time: up to 3 hours

2 $^1/_2$ to 3 cups cooked black-eyed
    peas
1 cup cooked white rice
1 green bell pepper, diced
4 ounces ham, diced
6 green onions (to make $^1/_2$ cup plus
2 tablespoons), white and
    green parts
$^1/_2$ cup Honey Mustard Vinaigrette
Salt and cayenne to taste
1 bunch salad greens (optional)

In a medium bowl, combine the peas, rice, green pepper, red pepper, ham, $^1/_2$ cup of green onions and the vinaigrette. Cover and refrigerate as long as 3 hours.

To serve, season with salt and cayenne to taste. Serve on a bed of salad greens, garnished with remaining green onions. (May be covered and refrigerated up to 3 days.)

FRIDAY

IRELAND'S IRISH
STEW POT PIE*
STEAMED CARROT STICKS*

Leftover stew can transform instantly into a luscious pot pie. Reheat the stew for 15 minutes in the oven, then top with homemade or refrigerated biscuits and put back in the oven for about 10 minutes, or until the biscuits are golden brown.

SATURDAY

SWORDFISH STEAKS WITH
SWEET ONIONS AND
WHITE MISO
ROASTED GARLIC
POTATO CAKE
MIXED GREEN SALAD*
FRESH FRUIT WITH
ITALIAN ICE CREAM*

Use Vidalia onions if you see them in stores yet, or other sweet onions, such as red onions, would be delicious. White miso, made from soybeans, is protein-rich, sweet-salty and adds a haunting flavor to the onion sauce. It is available at health food stores, Oriental stores and local farmers markets that carry ethnic foods.

Some potato cakes are sauteed in oil; this wonderful one, full of garlic and cheese, is roasted in the oven. For this rustic meal, cook the potato dish and turn off the oven before starting the swordfish dish; the residual oven heat will be enough to complete the fish. Let the onions cook slowly to bring out their natural sweetness. The sweet rice wine

Price: Will average $.49 to $.79 a pound, with creamer size at the high end of the scale.

Nutrition: 1/2 cup of potatoes has about 70 calories, is a good source of potassium, vitamin C, complex carbohydrates and fiber, and is low in fat and sodium.

Selection: New potatoes will be available for 4 to 6 weeks. Choose potatoes that look firm and plump with no eyes or cuts. The skin should be thin and tender so that it can be rubbed off with your fingernail. Size A potatoes are the size of a small orange, size B are the size of golf balls.

Storage: Thin-skinned new potatoes don't store as well as older or thick-skinned ones. Store new potatoes in a dark, cool (50 degrees), well-ventilated place for 1 to 2 weeks.

Uses: Allow about 6 ounces of potatoes per serving. New potatoes are best boiled and served with a cream sauce or butter and herbs, baked or roasted or served cold in a salad.

vinegar will complement them beautifully. Add a green salad and a selection of fresh fruit: strawberries and ripe pears with a purchased Italian ice cream or creme sauce.

SWORDFISH STEAKS WITH SWEET ONIONS AND WHITE MISO

Makes 4 servings
Preparation time: 5 minutes
Cooking time: 15 minutes

2 tablespoons olive oil
4 swordfish steaks
2 medium sweet onions, thinly sliced
3 to 4 tablespoons rice wine vinegar
1 teaspoon white miso, or to taste

Heat the oil in a large skillet over medium heat. Add steaks and cook until golden, about 2 or 3 minutes. Turn the steaks and cook 2 minutes longer on the other side. (Check the fish to see if it flakes; do not overcook.) Transfer the steaks to a heatproof platter and reserve in a heated oven that has been turned off.

Add the onions to the skillet. Cook over medium to medium-low heat, stirring, until the onions are soft and fragrant and golden, 5 to 10 minutes. Add the vinegar and miso and deglaze the pan by scraping up any bits of food and stirring into the vinegar. Cook until the vinegar is almost all reduced and the onions are shiny and glazy, 1 to 2 minutes. To serve, spoon the onion sauce over the steaks and serve.

ROASTED GARLIC POTATO CAKE

Makes 4 to 6 servings
Preparation time: 15 minutes
Cooking time: 30 minutes

2 pounds all-purpose potatoes, cut into 1/4-inch-thick rounds

Salt and pepper to taste
2 or 3 cloves garlic, finely minced
1/4 cup chopped fresh Italian parsley
1/4 freshly grated parmesan cheese
1/4 cup bread crumbs
4 tablespoons unsalted butter, cut in small pieces

Preheat the oven to 350 degrees. Butter or grease a baking pan. Chop the garlic, parsley, cheese and bread crumbs in a food processor to speed up preparation.

Place the potatoes in the baking pan in one overlapping layer. Season with salt and pepper and top with garlic, parsley, Parmesan cheese and bread crumbs. Dot with the butter. Bake until potatoes are golden brown, about 30 minutes.

WEEK

13

SHOPPING LIST

Meat, poultry, seafood

- ❑ 1 6-to 8-pound smoked ham
- ❑ 3 strips bacon
- ❑ 16 chicken thighs

Produce

- ❑ 3 pounds new red potatoes
- ❑ 3 medium potatoes
- ❑ 1 medium carrot
- ❑ 1 small bunch collard greens
- ❑ 2 pounds asparagus
- ❑ 1 bunch watercress
- ❑ 2 Belgian endives
- ❑ 1 head radicchio
- ❑ 1 small jicama
- ❑ 2 red or green bell peppers
- ❑ 1 head romaine lettuce
- ❑ 2 apples
- ❑ 1 orange
- ❑ 1 lemon
- ❑ 1 to 2 pints strawberries

- ❑ 1 bunch cilantro
- ❑ 1 bunch mint
- ❑ 1 knob fresh ginger
- ❑ 1 4.5-ounce jar minced garlic
- ❑ 2 garlic cloves

Dairy

- ❑ 1/4 cup plain non-fat yogurt
- ❑ 5 eggs
- ❑ 2 cups whole milk or half-and-half
- ❑ 5 tablespoons butter
- ❑ 2 1/2 cups milk
- ❑ 6 to 8 ounces medium-sharp Cheddar cheese, grated
- ❑ 6 ounces rindless goat cheese
- ❑ 1 pint chocolate frozen yogurt

Deli

- ❑ 1 loaf French bread

- ❑ 4 ounces Saga or other blue cheese
- ❑ 1/4 cup Parmesan cheese
- ❑ 8 sugar cookies
- ❑ 4 corn muffins
- ❑ 4 brownies
- ❑ 1 package (of 10) large flour tortillas (fajita size)

Miscellaneous

- ❑ 1 cup pecans
- ❑ 3/4 cup walnuts
- ❑ 1/4 cup maple syrup
- ❑ 1 cup lentils
- ❑ 1/2 cup walnut oil
- ❑ 1 6-ounce package rice noodles (rice sticks)
- ❑ 1 16-ounce Boboli pizza crust
- ❑ 1 or 2 6-ounce cans of clams
- ❑ 1 pound spiral pasta
- ❑ 1 8-ounce can pineapple tidbits

Staples

- ❑ All-purpose flour
- ❑ Black pepper
- ❑ Cayenne pepper
- ❑ Cornmeal
- ❑ Curry powder
- ❑ Dijon mustard
- ❑ Dried oregano
- ❑ Grated nutmeg
- ❑ Ground cinnamon
- ❑ Hoisin sauce
- ❑ Honey
- ❑ Olive oil
- ❑ Oriental sesame oil
- ❑ Peanut or vegetable oil
- ❑ Red wine vinegar
- ❑ Rice vinegar
- ❑ Salt
- ❑ Soy sauce
- ❑ Sugar
- ❑ Tabasco pepper sauce
- ❑ Turmeric
- ❑ Wheat germ

* Suggested accompaniments

SUNDAY

HONEY-BAKED HAM *
ASPARAGUS WITH GINGER-
ORANGE DRESSING
ROASTED NEW POTATOES
WITH MINT *
BAKED MAPLE-ALMOND
CUSTARD WITH
STRAWBERRIES*

Easter Sunday wouldn't be complete without a baked ham, asparagus and new potatoes garnished with fresh mint. Choose a partially baked ham and cook to an internal temperature of 160 degrees. Glaze it with honey and bourbon. Take advantage of the dishes that can be baked at the same time — the ham, potatoes and the custard — or bake the custard earlier in the day and refrigerate it until serving time. Boil an extra pound of asparagus to serve in salads and dinner later in the week. The children at your holiday table may not like asparagus, but they will like the custard dessert. Everything yields leftovers for the week.

ASPARAGUS WITH GINGER-ORANGE DRESSING

Makes 4 servings
Preparation time: 5 minutes
Cooking time: 5 minutes

1 pound asparagus
2 tablespoons rice vinegar
2 teaspoons Dijon mustard
1 teaspoon soy sauce
1 teaspoon peeled grated fresh ginger
2 or 3 teaspoons minced orange peel
1 teaspoon garlic, finely minced
1/4 cup peanut or other vegetable oil
1 tablespoon Oriental sesame oil
Salt and black pepper to taste

Cook asparagus in a large pot of boiling salted water until tender-crisp, about 5 minutes. Drain and run under cold water to cool. Drain and pat dry.

In a food processor or bowl, whisk together the vinegar, mustard, soy sauce, ginger, orange peel and garlic. Add the peanut and sesame oils in a slow stream, with the food processor running. Season to taste with salt and pepper. Arrange asparagus on plates and spoon vinaigrette over.

Per serving: 122 calories, 11 grams fat, no cholesterol, 124 milligrams sodium.

BAKED MAPLE-ALMOND CUSTARD

Makes 8 servings
Preparation time: 10 minutes
Cooking time: 35 to 40 minutes

1 cup almonds
1/3 cup sugar
Pinch salt
1/4 cup good-quality maple syrup
4 large egg yolks
1 large egg
2 cups whole milk or half-and-half, scalded

Preheat oven to 350 degrees.

In a food processor or blender, process almonds until quite fine. Add sugar and salt until blended, then add maple syrup and process until a thick paste forms.

Meanwhile, scald the milk on the stove or heat in the microwave 1 1/2 to 2 minutes.

In a large bowl, beat together the yolks and whole egg. With the food processor running, pour in the eggs, then the hot milk. Pour mixture into eight 6-ounce custard cups or souffle dishes. Place cups in a shallow baking dish and pour enough water into the baking dish to reach halfway up the sides of the custard cups. Bake 35 minutes or until set. Serve at room temperature or lightly chilled.

Per serving: 233 calories, 15 grams fat, 178 milligrams cholesterol, 93 milligrams sodium.

MONDAY ·

LENTILS WITH OLIVE OIL
AND HERBS *
BITTER GREENS AND
SAGA BLUE SALAD
FRENCH BREAD AND BUTTER *

Lentils can be simmered in salted water for 20 minutes, drained and tossed with fresh herbs and your best quality (heated) olive oil for a fragrant and wonderfully simple dinner. Add the following classic salad and French bread and butter. It is intensely walnutty and delicious. While you are toasting walnuts for tonight, toast more for Saturday night's salad.

BITTER GREENS AND SAGA BLUE SALAD

Makes 4 servings
Preparation time: 15 minutes

1/2 cup walnuts, toasted
2 tablespoons red wine vinegar
1 tablespoon Dijon mustard
Salt and freshly ground black pepper
6 to 8 tablespoons walnut oil
1 bunch arugula, washed and patted dry
2 Belgian endives, cored and julienned
1 head radicchio or other red chicory
4 ounces Saga blue or other blue cheese, crumbled

To toast the walnuts, heat the oven to 250 degrees. Place the nuts on a baking sheet and place in the oven for 10 to 15 minutes. Watch them carefully, turning every few minutes, to prevent burning.

In the workbowl of a food processor (or in a small bowl), pulse together the vinegar, mustard, a pinch of salt and plenty of freshly ground black pepper. With the machine running, add the walnut oil in a thin, steady stream. Add more salt or pepper if needed.

In a large salad bowl, toss together the lettuces. Add the dressing and toss again. Put the salad on four salad plates and garnish with the cheese and walnuts.

Per serving: 275 calories, 26 grams fat, 21 milligrams cholesterol, 465 milligrams sodium.

TUESDAY

THAI GRILLED CHICKEN
RICE NOODLES *
STIR-FRIED PEPPERS, JICAMA
AND ASPARAGUS *

This chicken dish is pungent, to say the least. Green curry paste, sold under the Thai Kitchen label, will speed kitchen preparation, but you could easily make your own sauce using ground tumeric, curry powder and fish or hoisin sauce. Make this in the oven, but it is also great on the grill. For baking, place the chicken pieces far enough apart in the baking dishes so they don't touch — as the pan juices evaporate, the chicken skin will become extra crisp. Boil delicate rice noodles, also called rice sticks, available in the Oriental section of the grocery store, and stir-fry bell peppers with jicama and leftover asparagus.

THAI GRILLED CHICKEN

Makes 8 servings
Preparation time: 5 minutes
Cooking time: 30 to 40 minutes

$^1/_4$ cup minced garlic in oil
$^1/_4$ cup finely chopped cilantro
1 teaspoon sugar
2 to 4 teaspoons green curry paste
16 chicken thighs (about 6 pounds)

Place the garlic, cilantro, sugar and curry paste in the workbowl of a food processor and process to a paste. Rub over the chicken pieces and refrigerate 4 hours or overnight.

Preheat the oven to 400 degrees. Lift the chicken from the marinade and arrange in baking pans. Bake uncovered for 30 to 40 minutes, until the meat is no longer pink near the bone.

Per serving: 253 calories, 15 grams fat, 98 milligrams cholesterol, 92 milligrams sodium.

WEDNESDAY

WHITE SURPRISE PIZZA
GREEN SALAD *
BAKED MAPLE-PECAN
CUSTARD AND SUGAR
COOKIES *

Weeknight pizza can go together in minutes with the help of a premade pizza crust, available in most grocery stores. Serve leftover custard with purchased sugar cookies.

WHITE SURPRISE PIZZA

Makes 4 servings
Preparation time: 10 minutes
Cooking time: 15 minutes

1 16-ounce Boboli pizza crust
2 tablespoons cornmeal
1 or 2 6-ounce cans of clams, drained
3 teaspoons minced garlic in oil
3 strips cooked bacon, crumbled
2 tablespoons Parmesan cheese
2 teaspoons dried oregano
$^1/_2$ teaspoon Tabasco pepper sauce

Preheat oven to 450 degrees.

Dust the pizza crust with cornmeal. Sprinkle the clams evenly over the dough; add garlic, bacon, cheese and oregano. Drizzle with Tabasco sauce and bake for 15 minutes, or until the crust is golden brown.

Per serving: 415 calories, 7 grams fat, 33 milligrams cholesterol, 725 milligrams sodium.

THURSDAY

PORTUGUESE COLLARD SOUP
CORN MUFFINS *

Use some Easter ham for tonight's healthy and filling soup, a take-off of a classic, but fattier soup. Kale is a healthy green, smaller but similar to collards. Purchase or prepare corn muffins to dunk in the soup, and add sugar cookies for dessert.

PORTUGUESE KALE SOUP

Makes 6 servings
Preparation time: 10 minutes
Cooking time: 20 minutes

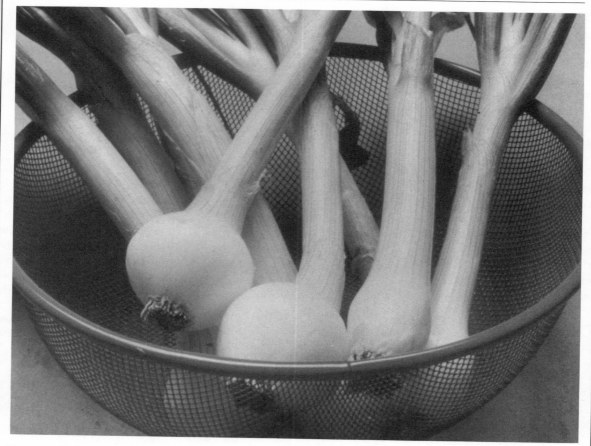

Price: Will average $.75 a bunch, with 3 to 4 onions in a bunch.

Nutrition: One tablespoon of chopped green onion has 2 calories, and is a fair source of vitamin A.

Selection: Choose onions that have crisp, fresh-looking tops and clean, white bottoms.

Storage: Refrigerate the whole onions, unwashed, in a plastic bag for up to 1 week. Just as the dry Vidalias are more delicate and susceptible to bruising and have a shorter shelf life, so do the green vidalia onions.

Their higher sugar and water content may cause them to go bad faster.

Uses: To use, rinse and pat the onions dry, then trim root ends and strip off and discard any wilted outer leaves. Leave whole or sliced into rounds. Serve whole onions raw, grilled, or as part of a shish kabob, or slice the bulbs to saute or add to salads or sandwiches.

While it's too early in the season to enjoy the dry Vidalia onions that have made Georgia famous, the early green Vidalia Onions are being harvested

now. They have a similar sweet flavor and tender bulbs just smaller than the size of golf balls.

Most Georgia farmers have only been harvesting and marketing the green Vidalias for a few years, according to the Vidalia Onion Committee. The onions will be in local grocery stores and farmers markets until April or May. They are also available by mail order. For more information call the Vidalia Onion Committee at 912-537-1918.

3 medium potatoes, diced
1 medium carrot, cut in thinly sliced
4 to 5 cups water
1 to 2 large handfuls kale leaves,
    washed and roughly chopped
4 ounces ham, cut into ¹/₂-inch
    chunks
1 tablespoon olive oil
1 teaspoon salt

In a saucepan, combine potatoes, carrot and water and simmer over medium heat until fork-tender, about 10 minutes. Transfer the potatoes and carrots to a food processor (leave the cooking water in the pan) and blend until smooth; return potato mixture to pan with cooking liquid and stir together.

Add chopped kale and ham to the soup and simmer, uncovered, for 10 minutes. Add oil and salt. If soup is too thick, add more water.

Per serving: 143 calories, 4 grams fat, 12 milligrams cholesterol, 723 milligrams sodium.

FRIDAY

CHICKEN TORTILLAS *
POTATOES AND
STIR-FRIED
VEGETABLES *
CHOCOLATE FROZEN
YOGURT *

For tonight's low-key dinner, pull your leftovers from the refrigerator — barbecued chicken, roasted potatoes, asparagus, lettuce, bell peppers and cilantro and fold them into heated flour tortillas.

SATURDAY

COMPANY MACARONI
AND CHEESE
APPLE AND ROMAINE SALAD
BROWNIES *

This macaroni and cheese, adapted from Michael McLaughlin's *The New Ameri-can Kitchen* (Simon & Schuster, $24.95), will please young children as well as dinner guests ready for a hearty meal. Sometimes you can find a good-quality prepared white sauce in speciality stores; if so, you can omit the sauce-making steps below. Add the yogurt-laced apple salad, similar to a Waldorf salad, and purchased brownies for a dinner of family favorites.

COMPANY MACARONI AND CHEESE

Makes 6 to 8 servings
Preparation time: 15 minutes
Cooking time: 40 minutes

1 pound spiral pasta
3 tablespoons butter
2 medium garlic cloves, minced
3 tablespoons all-purpose flour
2 ¹/₂ cups milk
¹/₂ teaspoon salt
Pinch grated nutmeg and cayenne
    pepper
6 to 8 ounces medium-sharp Cheddar
    cheese, grated
6 ounces mild rindless goat cheese,
    crumbled
Freshly ground black pepper
2 cups baked ham cut in thin slices
¹/₄ cup toasted wheat germ
2 to 4 tablespoons Parmesan cheese

Preheat the oven to 400 degrees. Cook the pasta in boiling salted water until just tender, about 8 minutes. Drain and rinse under cold water.

Meanwhile, in a heavy saucepan over low heat, melt the butter, stir in the garlic, then whisk in the flour. Gradually whisk in the milk and add salt, nutmeg and pepper. Stir as it thickens. Whisk in the cheeses and stir until smooth.

Spray a 3-quart baking dish with vegetable spray. In a large bowl, combine the cheese sauce, pepper and pasta. Spoon the mixture into the prepared baking dish, then tuck ham slices in between the pasta. In a small bowl, combine the wheat germ and grated Parmesan, then sprinkle over the pasta. Bake 30 to 40 minutes or until the top is lightly browned and the pasta is bubbling. Let the dish stand 5 minutes before serving.

Per serving: 382 calories, 21 grams fat, 74 milligrams cholesterol, 1,012 milligrams sodium.

APPLE AND ROMAINE SALAD

Makes 6 servings
Preparation time: 10 minutes

2 apples, thinly sliced
2 tablespoons lemon juice
1 cup water
1/4 cup julienned jicama
1 pineapple, cored, sliced and cut
    into chunks
¹/₄ cup toasted walnuts, coarsely
    chopped
¹/₄ cup plain low-fat yogurt
1 teaspoon honey
¹/₂ teaspoon cinnamon
4 Romaine lettuce leaves
¹/₂ cup mint sprigs for garnish
    (optional)

Place sliced apples in mixture of lemon juice and water. Refrigerate until serving time.

Meanwhile, toast the walnuts. Heat the oven to 250 degrees and place the nuts on a baking sheet. Bake, tossing, until they are brown and fragrant, but don't let them burn.

Drain the apples and pat dry. Combine the apples, jicama, pineapple and walnuts in a large bowl. Combine the yogurt, honey and cinnamon and toss with the other salad ingredients. Serve on a bed of lettuce

Per serving: 68 calories, 2 grams fat, less than 1 milligram cholesterol, 20 milligrams sodium.

WEEK

14

SHOPPING LIST

Meat, poultry, seafood

- ❑ 8 chicken breast halves
- ❑ 1 ¼ pounds orange roughy fillets

Produce

- ❑ 1 bunch green Vidalia onions (about 1 pound)
- ❑ 2 pounds asparagus
- ❑ 3 pounds new red potatoes
- ❑ 1 medium yellow onion
- ❑ 1 pound baby carrots
- ❑ ½ pound mushrooms
- ❑ 2 oranges
- ❑ 9 kiwi fruit
- ❑ 3 lemons
- ❑ 1 head garlic
- ❑ 1 bunch tarragon
- ❑ 1 bunch chives (optional)
- ❑ 1 bunch sorrel leaves (or fresh spinach)
- ❑ 1 small knob fresh ginger

Dairy

- ❑ 16 ounces part-skim ricotta cheese
- ❑ 2 sticks unsalted butter
- ❑ 1 cup buttermilk
- ❑ 2 tablespoons cream
- ❑ 4 eggs
- ❑ 6 ounces (¾ cup) plain non-fat yogurt
- ❑ ¼ cup light mayonnaise

Deli

- ❑ 6 ounces provolone cheese, sliced
- ❑ 6 ounces Jarlsburg (or other Swiss) cheese, sliced
- ❑ ¼ cup grated Parmesan cheese
- ❑ ½ cup blue cheese
- ❑ Coleslaw
- ❑ 1 loaf crusty French or Italian bread
- ❑ 4 jumbo oatmeal-pecan (or other) cookies

Miscellaneous

- ❑ 2 ounces unsweetened chocolate
- ❑ 2 1-pound loaves frozen bread dough
- ❑ 8 3-inch tartlet shells
- ❑ 2 ½ cups dry fragrant rice (such as jasmine or Texmati)
- ❑ ⅔ cup shredded coconut
- ❑ ⅓ cup coarsely chopped almonds
- ❑ ¼ cup chicken broth
- ❑ ½ cup frozen peas
- ❑ ¼ cup clam juice or dry vermouth

Staples

- ❑ Black pepper
- ❑ Confectioners' sugar
- ❑ Dried oregano
- ❑ Dried rosemary
- ❑ Granulated sugar
- ❑ Honey (optional)
- ❑ Light soy sauce

- ❑ Olive oil
- ❑ Oriental sesame oil
- ❑ Peanut oil
- ❑ Pure vanilla extract
- ❑ Red wine vinegar
- ❑ Salt
- ❑ Self-rising flour

* Suggested accompaniments

CHEESE-FILLED FOCACCIA
GREEN SALAD*
KIWI TARTLETS

Choose this hearty bread for an informal Sunday dinner. The secret ingredient is slices of baby green Vidalia onions. A month before mature sweet Vidalias hit the stores, the green onions appear with bulbs the size of golf balls and as sweet as the grown-up onions themselves. They lend themselves to quick sautees and other tender recipes in which a mature onion would take longer cooking (see In Season, page 68). The recipe offers plenty of left-overs to serve later in the week (or freeze extras). Thaw the bread dough in the microwave on defrost setting for 15 minutes (or in the refrigerator overnight). While a filling of pastry cream is standard for kiwi tarts, this lower-fat version is just as delicious and is easy to prepare.

CHEESE-FILLED FOCACCIA

Makes 12 servings
Preparation time (not including thawing time): 25 minutes
Cooking time: 30 minutes

2 1-pound loaves frozen bread dough, thawed
2 tablespoons olive oil
6 ounces sliced provolone cheese
6 ounces sliced Jarlsburg (or other Swiss) cheese
1 teaspoon dried oregano
1 teaspoon dried rosemary
1 teaspoon minced garlic
4 tablespoons grated Parmesan cheese
1 or 2 bulbs green Vidalia onions, thinly sliced (white part only)

On a lightly floured surface, roll one thawed bread loaf into a 15-by-10-inch rectangle. If dough shrinks back after rolling, let the dough rest for a few minutes, then continue rolling.

With vegetable spray, grease a jelly-roll pan and press the dough to fit into the corners of the pan. Brush dough with half the olive oil and cover with provolone and Jarlsburg cheese, oregano, rosemary and garlic.

Roll out the second thawed bread loaf to the same size as the first half and place it on top of the cheese and herbs. Pinch together the edges of the bottom and top crusts to seal. Brush the top with remaining olive oil, sprinkle with Parmesan and green Vidalia onion slices and let rise until double, about 15 minutes. Brush the Vidalia onions with a little olive oil to keep them from burning in the oven.

Preheat the oven to 375 degrees.

Bake for 25 minutes or until golden brown, then move to cool on a wire rack. Slice and serve warm, cut into strips or squares.

Per serving: 346 calories, 13 grams fat, 25 milligrams cholesterol, 618 milligrams sodium.

KIWI TARTLETS

Makes 8 servings
Preparation time: 10 minutes
Cooking time: 15 minutes

8 3-inch tart shells
2 cups part-skim ricotta cheese
2 tablespoons grated lemon peel
1/4 cup granulated sugar
6 kiwis, peeled and sliced
Confectioners' sugar

Preheat oven to 400 degrees. Bake tart shells for 8 to 10 minutes; set aside. Whisk together ricotta cheese, lemon peel and sugar in a medium-size bowl. Spoon into tart shells. Arrange sliced kiwis over filling, pressing lightly. Dust with confectioners' sugar.

Per tartlet: 291 calories, 14 grams fat, 19 milligrams cholesterol, 339 milligrams sodium.

BROILED CHICKEN BREASTS*
FRAGRANT RICE*
PAN-STEAMED ASPARAGUS

For extra flavor, marinate chicken breasts in lemon juice and any fresh herbs you have on hand. Cook extras of everything to use in later meals. Look for fragrant rice, such as jasmine, at ethnic markets and some grocery stores.

PAN-STEAMED ASPARAGUS

Makes 6 servings
Preparation time: 5 minutes
Cooking time: 8 minutes

2 pounds fresh asparagus, ends snapped off
2 tablespoons unsalted butter
Salt to taste
Lemon wedges

Wash asparagus. In a wide skillet or saucepan, melt the butter over moderate heat. Add asparagus spears with just the water left from washing. Cover and cook for 5 to 6 minutes, shaking occasionally. (Watch carefully, don't let the asparagus burn.) Cook 2 or 3 more minutes, or until asparagus is tender-crisp. Add salt to taste and serve with lemon wedges.

Per serving: 51 calories, 2 grams fat, 5 milligrams cholesterol, 6 milligrams sodium.

TUESDAY

ASPARAGUS AND POTATOES WITH BUTTERMILK BLUE CHEESE DRESSING CRUSTY BREAD*

Use leftover asparagus for tonight's delicious dinner and cook new potatoes, reserving extras to make roasted potatoes later in the week. The buttermilk dressing (without boiled eggs) is lower in fat than many salad dressings.

ASPARAGUS AND POTATOES WITH BUTTERMILK BLUE CHEESE DRESSING

Makes 6 servings
Preparation time: 10 minutes
Cooking time: 15 minutes for potatoes

2 pounds new red potatoes, quartered
1 cup fresh buttermilk
$^{1}/_{2}$ cup crumbled blue cheese
3 to 4 tablespoons good quality
    vinaigrette
$^{1}/_{2}$ cup chopped chives (or green
    onion)
Salt and black pepper to taste
1 pound cooked asparagus
2 hard-boiled eggs, chopped
    (optional)

Boil or microwave the potatoes until tender (about 10 minutes).

Whisk together the buttermilk, cheese, vinaigrette, chives, salt and pepper, mashing the bits of cheese with the back of a spoon.

Place asparagus, potatoes and (optional) eggs on a serving

APRIL

Citrus are barely hanging on, with oranges and grapefruit still in the stores. Small limes are a good bargain but larger limes are quite expensive. Hawaiian pineapple have sweetened up from a few weeks ago, but look for them to get even sweeter as we approach summer. Honeydew melon has only fair flavor right now, but Costa Rican cantaloupe is very sweet. Costa Rica is the first of the South American countries to bathe melons in a chlorine bath to rid them of any trace of salmonella or cholera organisms.

Mexican cantaloupes will be a good value, and Chilean white grapes are still a good value in most stores. Other Chilean fruit — peaches and plums — are high in price and flavor is only so-so. Florida strawberries are medium sized, beautiful and moderately priced.

Start watching for soft spots on the citrus. Tangelos are very nice now, along with California navels and grapefruit; tangerines are quite soft. Storage apples are more expensive than winter supplies, and storage pears from Washington state are being sold alongside fresh Chile pears. Asparagus and artichokes are a great buy right now. Most lettuces have improved in quality with the end of California rains, although head lettuce still has minor problems. Look for good new potatoes, both red, white and Yukon Gold or Yellow Finn — all the new potato supplies are very tasty. Snow peas and bok choy and baby bok choy are cheap and plentiful now. Sweet corn is getting cheaper and will start to head down in price in the next few weeks.

If you see high prices this month, it is because of heavy rains in the production areas of Florida and California which prevents growers from getting seed into the ground. All beans, squash and peppers will continue to be sky-high unless the produce comes from Mexico, then it may be lower. Larger yellow squash are gone and smaller sizes are scarce. We are starting to see the first of the Florida new red potato crop, which is one of the tastiest potatoes in the country. Sweet potatoes are still delicious and a good buy, as are winter greens.

Cool weather vegetables — cabbages, collards, snow peas and lettuces are a good value. Prices are slowly dropping and availability is getting better. Lettuce prices should stabilize shortly, and spinach continues to be a great bargain. Grab the last of winter squash, although sweet potatoes continue to look good.

Price: Will range from $1.29 to $1.99 a pound. Some stores may feature Easter specials for $.99 a pound.

Nutrition: One cup cooked asparagus has 35 calories and is high in vitamin A, vitamin C, folic acid and iron, and low in sodium.

Selection: The season for West coast asparagus peaks March through June, then imported asparagus begins through the summer and fall. Choose firm, brittle spears that are bright green with tightly closed tips. Medium-sized stalks, one size up from pencil size have the most flavor and tenderness and least waste, while the pencil size has less flavor and more fiber. Spears that have tips that have spread out will be astringent-tasting from overmaturity. The very first harvest of an asparagus bed produces thick stalks, low in fiber and high in sugar. As the season progresses, stalks get increasingly thin and fibrous.

Storage: Most sources advise to wrap ends in a damp paper towel and refrigerate, unwashed, in a plastic bag up to 4 days. Other sources recommend that if asparagus is submerged in water during storage, it won't last longer but will be of higher quality and flavor than if it has been stored out of water.

Uses: Allow $1/3$ to $1/2$ pound per person. Asparagus is best boiled, steamed, grilled or stir-fried until tender-crisp. It can be served hot or cold, with a sauce or folded into omelets and salads.

Asparagus is a traditional favorite for the Easter table. "There is never enough asparagus for Easter," said one California grower.

platter and pour dressing over.

Per serving: 194 calories, 10 grams fat, 12 milligrams cholesterol, 260 milligrams sodium.

WEDNESDAY

CHEESE-FILLED FOCACCIA*
BABY CARROTS WITH
FRENCH DIP
KIWI TARTLETS*

The following tarragon and garlic-flavored dip benefits from standing time to develop flavors, but the anise flavor of fresh tarragon comes through even if you must make the dip at the last minute. Fresh tarragon really accents this dish. If you find beautiful, tiny carrots with the greens still on, try to leave them on. Save leftovers for tomorrow night.

BABY CARROTS WITH FRENCH DIP

Makes 6 to 8 servings
Preparation time: 5-10 minutes
Cooking time: 10 minutes

1 to 1 $^1/_2$ pound baby carrots, cleaned
$^1/_2$ cup plain non-fat yogurt
$^1/_4$ cup light mayonnaise
1 large clove garlic, mashed
1 tablespoon freshly chopped tarragon leaves (or 1 teaspoon dried)
$^1/_8$ teaspoon salt
1 tablespoon red wine vinegar

Steam, boil or microwave the carrots for 1 or 2 minutes, drain and cool. Set aside. In a food processor, pulse together the yogurt, mayonnaise, garlic, tarragon, salt, vinegar and sugar. If possible,

allow to stand for 30 minutes to blend flavors. Arrange vegetables on a serving platter, then drizzle with some of the dip. Place remaining dip in a small bowl and serve alongside.

Per serving: 31 calories, 1 gram fat, 2 milligrams cholesterol, 37 milligrams sodium.

THURSDAY

COCONUT AND CHICKEN
FRIED RICE
BABY CARROTS WITH
FRENCH DIP*
FRESH ORANGE SLICES
AND KIWI HALVES*

Try this delicious variation of fried rice with the added sweetness of toasted coconut. Stir in leftover carrots from last night's dinner, or serve them alone, as you did last night. For dessert, simply cut unpeeled kiwis into halves and scoop out the ambrosial fruit with a spoon — children especially love to eat kiwis this way.

COCONUT AND CHICKEN FRIED RICE

Makes 4 to 6 servings
Preparation time: 5 minutes
Cooking time: 15 minutes

$^1/_3$ cup shredded coconut
$^1/_3$ cup coarsely chopped almonds
$^1/_4$ cup chicken broth
2 tablespoons light soy sauce
2 teaspoons Oriental sesame oil
2 tablespoons peanut oil
1 teaspoon minced fresh ginger
2 green onions, chopped
3 cups cooked rice
1 cup diced cooked chicken
$^1/_2$ to 1 cup cooked carrots, thinly sliced

Preheat oven to 300 degrees. Spread almonds in a shallow pan and toast until golden, 9 to 10 minutes. Meanwhile, spread coconut in a second pan and toast it in the oven, watching carefully to prevent it from burning, 3 or 4 minutes. Set almonds and coconut aside.

To make the sauce, stir together the chicken broth, soy sauce and sesame oil and set aside.

Place a wok or frying pan over high heat until hot. Add the peanut oil. When hot, add ginger and green onion and cook, stirring, until onion is soft, about 1 minute. Reduce heat and stir in the rice, chicken, carrots. Stir-fry for a couple of minutes, until everything is cooked through. Add the reserved sauce and cook another minute. Serve, garnished with coconut and almonds.

Per serving: 386 calories, 16 grams fat, 18 milligrams cholesterol, 396 milligrams sodium.

FRIDAY

COCONUT AND CHICKEN
FRIED RICE* WITH
STIR-FRIED RADISH,
CARROT, GREEN VIDALIAS
AND ASPARAGUS*

Even small amounts of the week's leftovers go together in a simple stir-fry. Use leftover coconut and chicken fried rice as a base and add to it small amounts of vegetables. Add a scrambled egg to make the dish go a little further if you wish.

ORANGE ROUGHY WITH
SORREL AND MUSHROOMS
ROASTED FLORIDA
NEW POTATOES*
COCONUT BROWNIES

Orange roughy often is served simply broiled, but this recipe pairs it with an elegant butter sauce, laced with lemon-flavored sorrel leaves (available in many produce sections and health food stores). If sorrel is unavailable, substitute spinach leaves and a teaspoon of lemon juice. Specialty mushrooms, such as shiitake or cremini, would offer additional flavor to this simple and elegant dish. Add roasted new potatoes, tossed with butter and any leftover herbs, and brownies. Frozen coconut offers a fresher flavor than packaged, but you will need to defrost it and pat it dry to remove excess moisture.

ORANGE ROUGHY WITH SORREL AND MUSHROOMS

Makes 4 servings
Preparation time: 10 minutes
Cooking time: 20 minutes

1 to 1 $\frac{1}{2}$ pounds orange roughy
    fillets
$\frac{1}{4}$ cup clam juice or dry vermouth
1 stick butter, cut in pieces
10 sorrel leaves, finely chopped
$\frac{1}{2}$ pound mushrooms, sliced
2 tablespoons heavy cream
Few drops lemon juice (optional)
Salt to taste

Microwave or poach the fish fillets in a little of the clam broth until they flake, 5 to 10 minutes. Remove to a platter, cover and keep warm.

In a medium saucepan, bring the clam broth or vermouth to a boil over medium heat. Continue to cook until reduced by half. Lower the heat and whisk in the butter, piece by piece, to make a thick, creamy sauce. Add the sorrel and mushrooms; cook for another 3 or 4 minutes until softened. Stir in the cream and (optional) lemon juice; add salt to taste. Spoon some sauce onto each plate and top with the fish.

Per serving (using vermouth): 503 calories, 36 grams fat, 139 milligrams cholesterol, 319 milligrams sodium.

COCONUT BROWNIES

Makes 16 brownies
Preparation time: 15 minutes
Cooking time: 17 minutes

6 tablespoons unsalted butter
2 ounces unsweetened chocolate,
    roughly chopped
1 cup sugar
2 eggs
1 teaspoon pure vanilla extract
1 cup self-rising flour
$\frac{1}{4}$ cup shredded coconut

Preheat the oven to 375 degrees. Grease an 8-by-11-inch baking dish with pan spray.

To melt the butter and chocolate, place the butter and chocolate in a 1 $\frac{1}{2}$-quart microwave-safe dish and microwave, covered, on high heat, 3 to 4 minutes, stirring once or twice. Stir in the sugar. Beat in eggs one at a time, then stir in the vanilla. Add flour to the chocolate mixture all at once and mix until incorporated. Stir in coconut.

Scrape batter into prepared pan and smooth the surface. Bake for about 17 minutes, or until a knife inserted in the middle comes out clean (do not over bake or they will be dry). Put the pan on a rack to cool, then cut brownies into bars.

Per brownie: 189 calories, 9 grams fat, 60 milligrams cholesterol, 85 milligrams sodium.

WEEK

15

SHOPPING LIST

Meat, poultry, seafood

- ❑ 3 pounds center-cut beef filet, trimmed and tied
- ❑ 4 slices bacon
- ❑ 4 bratwurst
- ❑ 2 pounds large shrimp, unpeeled

Produce

- ❑ 4 medium artichokes (10 ounces each)
- ❑ 16 garlic cloves
- ❑ 2 medium shallots
- ❑ 6 leeks
- ❑ 1 large onion
- ❑ 3 large potatoes
- ❑ 2 pounds broccoli rabe
- ❑ 1 bunch celery
- ❑ 1 bunch sage
- ❑ 1 bunch Italian flat-leaf parsley

- ❑ 1 bunch sorrel leaves
- ❑ 1 quart strawberries
- ❑ 5 lemons
- ❑ 1 pound fresh asparagus

Dairy

- ❑ 8 ounces Cheddar cheese
- ❑ 1 8-ounce container lemon yogurt
- ❑ 2 eggs
- ❑ 1 stick ($^1/_2$ cup) butter or margarine

Deli

- ❑ 1 Sacher torte or other chocolate cake
- ❑ 1 broccoli quiche
- ❑ 8 ounces ($^1/_2$ cup) pro-sciutto
- ❑ 1 loaf crusty bread

Miscellaneous

- ❑ 3 tablespoons cognac or brandy
- ❑ 3 14 $^1/_2$-ounce cans chicken broth
- ❑ 1 10-ounce bag frozen lima beans
- ❑ 2 tablespoons pine nuts
- ❑ 1 pound lemon angel-hair pasta
- ❑ $^1/_4$ cup sun-dried toma-toes in oil

Staples

- ❑ All-purpose flour
- ❑ Apple cider vinegar
- ❑ Black pepper
- ❑ Bread
- ❑ Coarse-grained salt
- ❑ Dijon mustard
- ❑ Dried thyme leaves

- ❑ Granulated sugar
- ❑ Lemon juice
- ❑ Olive oil
- ❑ Powdered sugar
- ❑ Salt
- ❑ Vegetable oil

* Suggested accompaniments

FILET OF BEEF WITH BRANDY
AND WALNUT OIL
PARCHMENT-BAKED
ARTICHOKES WITH FRESH
SAGE LEAVES
SACHER TORTE *

Start the week off with an entree of roast beef and artichokes that will stand up to the most demanding of your dinner guests. Filet of beef is a first-class meat, the home of filet mignon and Chateaubriand. Save leftovers for sandwiches or soup later in the week. The first-of-the-season artichokes (see In Season, page 80), redolent of sage and garlic, are adapted from Sally Schneider's stylist dish in *The Art of Low-Calorie Cooking* (Stewart, Tabori & Chang, $35). She says the steaming-in-parchment method creates "meltingly tender vegetables with a concentrated flavor." See for yourselves with this elegant dish. Purchase Sacher torte (chocolate-raspberry cake) for dessert.

FILET OF BEEF WITH BRANDY AND WALNUT OIL

Makes 6 to 8 servings
Preparation time: 10 minutes
Marinating time: Overnight
Cooking time: 30 to 35 minutes

2 garlic cloves, minced
2 large shallots, minced
1 teaspoon herbs de Provence
$1/2$ teaspoon salt
$1/4$ cup brandy
$1/3$ cup walnut oil, divided
$2 1/2$ to 3 pounds aged center-cut beef filet, trimmed of fat and sinew and tied

Put the garlic and shallots in the workbowl of a food processor and pulse to mince, add the herbs de Provence and pulse again. Place in a shallow ceramic dish large enough to hold the meat and marinade. Add the garlic mixture, salt, brandy, oil and meat. Turn the meat to cover it completely. Cover the dish, refrigerate and marinate several hours or overnight.

Adjust oven rack to the lowest position. Preheat the oven to 450 degrees.

Remove meat from the marinade and pat dry. Put in a roasting pan and place in the oven. Immediately turn the oven to 350 degrees, turning to sear on all sides. Roast 20 minutes or until an instant-read thermometer reads 130-140 degrees for medium-rare when inserted into the thickest area. Remove from the oven and cover loosely with foil and let sit for 10 minutes, then remove the strings and slice the beef into 1/4-inch-thick slices. Serve the pan juices in a gravy boat.

Per serving: 418 calories, 28 grams fat, 114 milligrams cholesterol, 83 milligrams sodium.

PARCHMENT-BAKED ARTICHOKES WITH FRESH SAGE LEAVES

Makes 4 servings
Preparation time: 10 minutes
Cooking time: 25 minutes

4 medium artichokes (about 10 ounces each)
1 tablespoon plus 2 teaspoons olive oil
8 garlic cloves, peeled
12 fresh sage leaves
Salt and freshly ground black pepper to taste

Preheat oven to 450 degrees.

Cut the stems off the artichokes and pull off any brown or tough outer leaves. Slice the artichokes in half lengthwise, then slice each half lengthwise, making $1/2$-inch-thick slices. Cut out the furry chokes and discard.

Place a 14-by-26-inch piece of heavy-duty aluminum foil or parchment paper on a baking sheet. Brush artichoke slices on both sides with the olive oil. Arrange the slices on half of the foil, then scatter the garlic cloves over the artichokes and tuck the sage leaves under and between the slices. Sprinkle with salt and pepper to taste. Fold the other half of the foil over the artichokes and seal the edges together.

Bake for 10 minutes, then flip the package over and bake 15 minutes longer. Remove from the oven and let stand 5 to 8 minutes without opening. Cut through the foil and gently peel off, taking care not to expose your fingers to hot steam. Transfer the vegetables to a serving dish. Serve hot or at room temperature, or let cool, cover, refrigerate and serve chilled.

Per serving: 129 calories, 6 grams fat, no cholesterol, 252 milligrams sodium.

LEEK AND POTATO SOUP
GRILLED CHEESE
SANDWICHES *

My friend Ann Brewer makes this soup on chilly days in December at her Christmas tree farm in Covington, Georgia. The soup can be on the table in the 20 minutes it takes to cook the potatoes, but a longer cooking time will blend flavors and make the kitchen smell wonderful.

LEEK AND POTATO SOUP

Makes 8 servings
Preparation time: 15 minutes
Cooking time: 30 minutes

4 slices bacon
6 leeks, trimmed, washed and
    thinly sliced
1 large onion, chopped
2 tablespoons all-purpose flour
3 14 ¹/₂-ounce cans chicken broth
3 large potatoes, peeled and
    thinly sliced
4 tablespoons chopped fresh parsley
    (optional)

Cook the bacon in a Dutch oven or other large pot over medium heat for 5 minutes. Add the leeks and onion and saute for 5 minutes. Reduce heat to low, add flour and stir until smooth. Cook 1 minute, stirring constantly until thickened. Gradually stir in the broth, cook over medium heat. Add the sliced potatoes and parsley, cover and simmer 30 to 45 minutes. Garnish with parsley, if desired, before serving.
    Per serving: 161 calories, 3 grams fat, 3 milligrams cholesterol, 121 milligrams sodium.

TUESDAY

GRILLED BRATWURST *
LIMA BEANS WITH FRESH SAGE
LEMON YOGURT WITH
STRAWBERRIES *

A mere handful of fresh sage leaves is a powerful flavoring ingredient: It will add character and fragrance to frozen lima beans. The beans offer both a filling starchy vegetable and a nutritious line-up of vitamins and minerals. Add bratwurst and a dessert of lemon yogurt and strawberries, which should be at a good price now.

LIMA BEANS WITH FRESH SAGE

Makes 4 servings
Preparation time: 5 minutes
Cooking time: 8 minutes

1 tablespoon olive oil
1 10-ounce bag frozen lima beans,
    thawed
8 to 10 fresh sage leaves
Salt and pepper to taste

Heat the oil over moderate heat in a large skillet, then add the lima beans and toss. Add the sage leaves, salt and pepper, and cook, stirring constantly, for about 5 minutes, or until the beans are thoroughly heated and the sage leaves are fragrant.
    Per serving: 124 calories, 4 grams fat, no cholesterol, 37 milligrams sodium.

WEDNESDAY

BROCCOLI QUICHE *
SAUTE OF BROCCOLI RABE
WITH PROSCIUTTO
AND PINE NUTS

This is a flavorful midweek dinner that could easily double for company fare. Broccoli rabe is similar to broccoli (see In Season, page 21), but more like a tender Southern green. Its long stems lend themselves to sauteing, but kale, mustard greens or Swiss chard could be used with excellent results. Give this dish a different character by substituting bacon for the prosciutto. If you do, discard most of the grease, or the dish will taste heavier and fattier. Serve a purchased quiche or make your own.

BROCCOLI SAUTE WITH PROSCIUTTO AND PINE NUTS

Makes 4 to 6 servings
Preparation: 5 minutes
Cooking time: 5 minutes

2 pounds broccoli rabe or kale(see
    In Season, page 21)
Salt, to taste
4 tablespoons combination olive and
    walnut or pecan oil, divided
2 tablespoons pine nuts
¹/₂ cup finely diced prosciutto
Salt and freshly ground black pepper
    to taste

Remove the tough stems from the broccoli and some of the large leaves. Slice the broccoli into 1-inch pieces. Cook in the microwave on high (100 percent power) 1 minute or in boiling water for 2 or 3 minutes. Immediately drain under cold water and set aside.
    In a large skillet, heat 1 tablespoon of oil over low heat, add the pine nuts and saute until lightly browned, shaking the skillet to prevent them from burning. Remove the pine nuts from the skillet and reserve.
    Heat the remaining oil over low heat. Add the prosciutto and saute for 30 seconds. Add the broccoli, season with salt and pepper and cook for a few seconds, tossing until heated through. Add the reserved nuts.
    Per serving: 304 calories, 24 grams fat, 22 milligrams cholesterol, 323 milligrams sodium.

Price: Will vary from $.69 to $1.29 a piece, depending on size.

Nutrition: One average artichoke has about 45 calories, is high in potassium, phosphorus and vitamins A and C, and high in sodium.

Selection: Right now the artichokes coming to market have purple or brown spots, affectionately termed "winter kissed." This coloring caused by frost does not affect quality. Artichoke aficionados think these are the sweetest and best artichokes of the year. The peak season for California artichokes is spring, with 50 percent of the year's crop coming from March through May. Choose tight, compact heads with fresh-looking leaves that feel heavy for their size.

Storage: Refrigerate, unwashed, in a plastic bag for up to 1 week.

Uses: Allow one medium artichoke per person. Whole artichokes are most often served as an appetizer with a dipping sauce, or the heart is removed and used in salads, antipasto plates, in pizzas and frittatas, or sauteed with olive oil and herbs.

Across the Mediterranean, artichokes come almond-flavored and lavender-colored, to a mild variety that is blanched perfectly white. Some varieties are so small and tender they are simply sliced, piled on a plate and eaten raw.

But in the U.S. the old reliable, and usually large, globe artichoke is the standard variety. The bulk of the harvest comes in two seasons, spring and fall, with smaller and continuing harvests the rest of the year. Late winter brings to market the "winter-kissed" sweet chokes that aren't necessarily smaller or more tender, but have an intense nutty flavor.

Beginning in March, the artichokes will come to market fully green, larger, and because of the larger harvest, prices will likely drop.

THURSDAY

POTATO AND LIMA BEAN SOUP *
ROAST BEEF SANDWICHES*
LEMON BARS

Serve leftover roast beef sandwiches, or stir leftover sliced roast beef and lima beans into the potato soup before reheating; they will add protein, a hearty starch and requisite green vegetable vitamins. For dessert, try light lemon bars, a perennial favorite.

LEMON BARS

Makes 16 bars
Preparation time: 15 minutes
Cooking time: 35 minutes

$^1/_4$ cup powdered sugar
$^1/_2$ cup butter or margarine, softened
1 cup all-purpose flour
$^1/_4$ teaspoon salt
2 eggs
1 cup granulated sugar
2 tablespoons fresh lemon juice
Rind of 1 lemon, grated
2 tablespoons all-purpose flour

Preheat oven to 350 degrees.
Cream powdered sugar with butter until fluffy. Add flour and salt. Mix well. Press mixture into the bottom of a greased 9-inch-square baking pan. Bake 15 minutes. In mixing bowl, beat eggs. Add granulated sugar, lemon juice, lemon rind and flour. Pour mixture over baked crust. Bake 20 minutes more.
Per serving: 148 calories, 7 grams fat, 34 milligrams cholesterol, 124 milligrams sodium.

FRIDAY

STUFFED SHELLS *
MIXED GREEN SALAD *
LEMON BARS *

Look to your nearest Italian restaurant or deli takeout for tomato sauce covered pasta shells. Add a green salad and leftover lemon bars from last night's dinner.

SATURDAY

SHRIMP SALAD WITH FRESH SORREL
ASPARAGUS IN LEMON AND CAPER VINAIGRETTE
LEMON ANGEL-HAIR PASTA TOSSED WITH SUN-DRIED TOMATOES*
CRUSTY BREAD *

This is an evening of elegant, light salads. Shrimp salads are always popular but usually mayonnaise is included. Here, shrimp are combined with fresh lemony sorrel leaves, a perfect companion for spring, then seasoned with oil and fresh herbs (or substitute mint or basil leaves). The shrimp are always cooked in the shells for best flavor; devein them if you wish.

SHRIMP SALAD WITH FRESH SORREL

Makes 6 servings
Preparation time: 25 minutes
Cooking time: 3 minutes
Standing time: 30 minutes

2 pounds large shrimp, unshelled
Coarse-grained salt
1 bunch celery, tender inner
stalks only
3 lemons, divided
1 tablespoon apple cider vinegar
$^1/_2$ cup olive oil
Salt and freshly ground black pepper
15 sprigs Italian parsley leaves
5 to 8 whole fresh sorrel leaves

Wash the shrimp well and put them in a bowl of cold water with coarse-grained salt and let them soak for 15 minutes.
Put the water and shrimp and vinegar in a medium-size saucepan and bring to a boil. Cook for 3 minutes, then drain. When cool enough to handle, shell and set aside.
Meanwhile, wash the celery and reserve the outer stalks for another use. Cut the inner stalks lengthwise into matchstick pieces. Place the celery in a bowl of cold water and the juice of 1 lemon and let stand a few minutes.
Place the shrimp, olive oil, salt and pepper in a glass bowl. Drain the celery and add it and juice of remaining 2 lemons; cover and refrigerate for 30 minutes. Coarsely chop the parsley and sorrel and sprinkle the leaves over the salad.
Per serving: 307 calories, 17 grams fat, 230 milligrams cholesterol, 262 milligrams sodium.

ASPARAGUS IN LEMON AND CAPER VINAIGRETTE

Makes 4 servings
Preparation time: 10 minutes
Cooking time: 3-4 minutes

1 pound fresh asparagus, tough ends broken off
Salted water
2 tablespoons lemon juice
1 teaspoon Dijon mustard
1 clove garlic, crushed
1 tablespoon minced Italian parsley

$^1/_2$ cup vegetable oil
Salt, to taste
2 to 3 tablespoons capers, drained

Place salted water in a skillet to a depth of 1 inch. Add the asparagus, covered, and cook until crisp-tender, about 3 to 4 minutes. Drain and place on a serving platter.

Meanwhile, in the workbowl of a food processor or in a small bowl, place the lemon juice, mustard, garlic and parsley. With the processor running, pour in the oil in a steady stream, or whisk together. Add salt to taste. Pour over asparagus and sprinkle capers over. Cover and chill. Serve at room temperature.

Per serving: 149 calories, 14 grams fat, no cholesterol, 85 milligrams sodium.

WEEK

16

Meat, poultry, seafood

- ❑ 5 to 6 pounds fresh ham, boned, rolled and tied
- ❑ 7 boneless, skinless chicken breast halves

Produce

- ❑ 3 to 3 ¹/₂ pounds Yukon Gold potatoes
- ❑ 4 heads baby bok choy
- ❑ 1 ¹/₂ to 2 pounds asparagus
- ❑ 1 head soft lettuce
- ❑ 1 cup variety lettuce: chicory, arugula, dandelion greens
- ❑ 1 avocado
- ❑ ¹/₂ pint (1 cup) cherry tomatoes
- ❑ 1 small knob ginger
- ❑ 8 garlic cloves
- ❑ 8 green onions
- ❑ 1 bunch dill
- ❑ 1 bunch Italian parsley
- ❑ 1 bunch mint, orange or chocolate mint
- ❑ 2 ¹/₂ pints strawberries
- ❑ 1 lemon
- ❑ 6 large, firm pears
- ❑ 1 orange

Dairy

- ❑ 2 tablespoons unsalted butter
- ❑ 6 ounces Cheddar cheese, grated
- ❑ 3 eggs
- ❑ 4 ounces Swiss cheese
- ❑ 1 pint vanilla ice cream

Deli

- ❑ 4 corn muffins
- ❑ 1 loaf pesto bread
- ❑ 1 loaf crusty bread
- ❑ 3 tablespoons freshly grated Parmesan cheese
- ❑ 4 to 6 ounces mascarpone or full-fat cream cheese

Miscellaneous

- ❑ ¹/₃ cup Campari
- ❑ ¹/₂ cup orange juice
- ❑ ¹/₂ cup low-sodium chicken broth
- ❑ 1 cup semisweet chocolate pieces
- ❑ 4 tablespoons Triple Sec or other orange liqueur
- ❑ 3 tablespoons sherry
- ❑ 1 cup red wine
- ❑ 2 cups dry white wine
- ❑ 1 9-inch pie crust
- ❑ 4 cups frozen lima beans
- ❑ 3 cups dry rice
- ❑ ¹/₂ cup bread and butter pickles
- ❑ 2 14-ounce cans artichoke hearts
- ❑ ¹/₂ pound lemon fettucine or angel-hair pasta
- ❑ 1 5-ounce can pitted black olives
- ❑ ¹/₂ cup pistachio nuts

Staples

- ❑ Allspice berries
- ❑ Black pepper
- ❑ Capers
- ❑ Confectioners' sugar
- ❑ Granulated sugar
- ❑ Honey mustard
- ❑ Lemon juice
- ❑ Low-fat mayonnaise
- ❑ Olive oil
- ❑ Oriental sesame oil
- ❑ Red currant jelly
- ❑ Salt
- ❑ Sesame seeds
- ❑ Star anise
- ❑ Vinaigrette
- ❑ White wine vinegar
- ❑ Worcestershire sauce
- ❑ Walnut oil

* Suggested accompaniments

ROAST FRESH HAM WITH
CAMPARI-ORANGE GLAZE
ROASTED YUKON GOLD
POTATOES WITH GARLIC
AND WALNUT OIL**
GINGERED ASPARAGUS *
CHOCOLATE TART WITH
STRAWBERRIES

Campari — the bright red, licorice-flavored Italian aperitif — creates a handsome lacquered crust and helps cut the sweetness of this ham. Purchase a bone-in ham and have the butcher bone and tie it. The rustic flavors of garlic and walnut oil turn simple roasted Yukon Gold potatoes into a first-class dish, and wait till you smell the kitchen. Add steamed asparagus tossed in vinaigrette and grated ginger. Cook plenty of both to serve later. The strawberry tart is a personal favorite, adapted from *The Silver Palate Cookbook* by Julee Rosso and Sheila Lukins (Workman, $9.95). For the mint garnish, perhaps you can find one of the new interesting mint varieties available, such as orange or chocolate mint. (Buy the plants from a local nursery and start them in your yard for a nonstop supply.)

ROAST FRESH HAM WITH CAMPARI-ORANGE GLAZE

Makes 8 servings
Preparation time: 10 minutes
Cooking time: 3 hours

¹/₄ cup finely minced Italian parsley
2 tablespoons minced orange peel
2 garlic cloves, finely minced
¹/₂ fresh ham (5 to 6 pounds) rolled and tied
Salt and black pepper
¹/₃ cup Campari
¹/₂ cup orange juice
¹/₂ cup low-sodium chicken broth

Preheat oven to 350 degrees and position a rack in the lower third of the oven. In a small bowl, stir together parsley, orange peel and garlic. Untie roast. Season inside surfaces of ham lightly with salt and generously with pepper, then with the parsley mixture. Retie roast.

Set in a shallow baking dish just large enough to hold it and bake about 30 minutes per pound, about 2 ¹/₂ hours, occasionally removing juices from the pan and reserving them.

Add Campari and orange juice to pan; bake ham another 30 minutes, basting often. The ham is done when an instant-read thermometer inserted in thickest part registers 170 degrees.

Transfer to a cutting board and cover with a foil tent. Degrease reserved roasting juices and add enough chicken broth to total 1 cup. Add mixture to liquid in baking dish and bring to a boil, stirring to deglaze dish and reduce and thicken the sauce. Add salt and pepper to taste. Carve roast; pass the sauce at the table. From *The New American Kitchen* by Michael McLaughlin (Simon & Schuster, $24.95).

Per serving: 465 calories, 30 grams fat, 111 milligrams cholesterol, 1,619 milligrams sodium.

CHOCOLATE TART WITH STRAWBERRIES

Makes 8 servings
Cooking time: 5 minutes
Chilling time: 2 hours

1 cup semisweet chocolate pieces
2 tablespoons unsalted butter
2 tablespoons Triple Sec or other orange liqueur
¹/₄ cup confectioners' sugar, sifted
1 tablespoon water
1 9-inch prebaked pie crust
3 cups (1 ¹/₂ pints) strawberries, washed, stemmed and dried
3 tablespoons red currant jelly
2 tablespoons Triple Sec or other orange liqueur
Sprigs of fresh mint, orange or chocolate mint for garnish

Place chocolate and butter in a microwave-safe dish and heat on medium (50 percent power) for 2 to 4 minutes, until melted. Whisk in the liqueur, then the confectioners' sugar and water, until mixture is thoroughly smooth. While warm, pour it into the tart shell. It should be about 1/8-inch thick. Place berries, tips up, in warm chocolate filling in a circular pattern, working from outside in until surface is covered.

Place jelly and 1 tablespoon liqueur in a microwave-safe bowl, stir, and heat on medium 30 seconds. Brush glaze over berries. Refrigerate tart 2 hours, remove 45 minutes before serving. Garnish with mint.

Per serving: 304 calories, 18 grams fat, 8 milligrams cholesterol, 139 milligrams sodium.

LIMA BEANS AND
GRATED CHEDDAR
CORN MUFFINS *

A filling and simple meal is called for after the Easter feast. Serve lima beans drizzled with cheese and onions and add purchased corn muffins.

LIMA BEANS AND GRATED CHEDDAR

Makes 4 servings
Preparation time: 5 minutes
Cooking time: 15 minutes

4 cups frozen lima beans, thawed
8 green onions, chopped
6 ounces Cheddar cheese,
    finely grated
4 tablespoons olive oil
3 tablespoons white wine vinegar
2 teaspoons Worcestershire sauce

Place the lima beans in a saucepan of boiling water, in a steamer basket or in a microwave-safe dish and cook for 5 minutes, or until the beans are cooked. Drain and place in a baking dish or microwave-proof dish.

Chop the green onions, reserving the green tops for garnish. Toss the green onions, cheese, olive oil, vinegar and Worcestershire sauce and sprinkle over the limas. Either cook in the microwave oven on medium (50 percent power) for 2 minutes, or in the oven (preheated to 350 degrees) for 8 to 10 minutes, until cheese is melted.

Per serving: 522 calories, 28 grams fat, 45 milligrams cholesterol, 375 milligrams sodium.

TUESDAY

**BROILED OR GRILLED
CHICKEN BREASTS WITH
HONEY MUSTARD AND
SESAME SEEDS ***
STIR-FRIED BABY BOK CHOY
STEAMED RICE *

Baby bok choy is a delicate vegetable with a flavor similar to Swiss chard. Lee Chadwick, owner of Camerron, an Atlanta special events facility, cooked this dish for a group of Atlantans she recently guided to the Hong Kong Food Festival. Her executive chef, Randy Harris, uses tamari, a wheat-free Japanese soy sauce, but any soy sauce is fine. Brush chicken with prepared honey mustard before broiling; sprinkle with sesame seeds at the end of cooking so the seeds won't burn. Cook 3 extra halves to serve later in the week, and if you choose to grill the chicken, the smokey flavor will add to the dish for Saturday night. Cook extra rice to serve later also.

STIR-FRIED BABY BOK CHOY

Makes 4 servings
Preparation time: 5 minutes
Cooking time: 2 minutes

1 tablespoon Oriental sesame oil
1 tablespoon grated fresh ginger
2 garlic cloves, minced
3 tablespoons sherry
1 tablespoon water
2 tablespoons tamari or other
    soy sauce
4 heads baby bok choy, split
    lengthwise

Heat a wok or skillet. When hot, add the sesame oil, ginger and garlic. When the ginger and garlic are fragrant, in 20 to 30 seconds, add the sherry, water, tamari and bok choy. Braise, uncovered, over high heat for 1 minute, until the vegetables are tender-crisp. Serve at once over hot rice.

Per serving: 88 calories, 4 grams fat, no cholesterol, 580 milligrams sodium.

WEDNESDAY

**ASPARAGUS POTATO SALAD
PESTO BREAD ***
**FRESH STRAWBERRIES
STEEPED IN RED WINE ***

Use leftover asparagus and roasted potatoes for tonight's dinner salad. Before dinner, place strawberries in wine goblets, cover with red wine and stir in a teaspoon of honey if you wish. Serve for dessert.

ASPARAGUS POTATO SALAD

Makes 4 servings
Preparation time: 10 minutes

1 head soft lettuce
1 cup variety lettuce: chicory,
    arugula, dandelion greens
1/2 pound cooked asparagus
1 to 1 1/2 pounds cooked potatoes,
    sliced, room temperature
2 tablespoons capers
1/4 to 1/2 cup vinaigrette
1 boiled egg, grated

Clean and pat dry the lettuces; arrange on four plates. In a large bowl, toss asparagus, potatoes, capers and vinaigrette and arrange over lettuce. Sprinkle each salad with egg and serve.

Per serving: 191 calories, 6 grams fat, 102 milligrams cholesterol, 185 milligrams sodium.

THURSDAY

**ARTICHOKE, HAM AND SWISS
CHEESE SANDWICHES
BREAD AND BUTTER PICKLES ***

Canned artichokes hold a respected position in any busy

Price: Will range from $1.50 a pint to $1.50 a quart.

Nutrition: Strawberries have about 55 calories a cup and are an excellent source of vitamin C, a significant source of folacin, with no fat or sodium.

Selection: Choose firm, plump berries that are fully-colored. Avoid bruises or soft spots.

Storage: Store in vegetable drawers at the bottom of the refrigerator, which is the coldest part of the refrigerator with the highest humidity. Store strawberries for 2 to 4 days. To freeze, bag them, unwashed, and freeze. If washed before freezing, the berries will turn to mush.

Uses: One pound of berries yields about 4 cups sliced berries. Serve berries fresh on breakfast cereal, yogurt or ice cream, fruit salads, or fresh strawberry pie, or add to rhubarb and bake in a pie.

You can forget that June used to be THE month for strawberry shortcake and pie; with the help of modern agriculture, strawberries are now in season every month of the year. Florida berries start early in the month, in plenty of time for Easter in fact. Sometimes these berries are beautiful and delicious, some years they are only beautiful — in recent years Florida rains have taken their toll on the berries' flavor.

California berries come in season right on the heels of Florida's harvest. Prices and availability are at a peak this month, and if bad weather holds back, strawberries should be widely available. Throughout the year, berries also come from Mexico, Costa Rica, Brazil, New Zealand and Guatamala to fill in the winter season.

Many of the berries advertised will be the Driscoll brand, a high-quality patented variety grown in California. They are of excellent quality and have a superior flavor.

Avoid berries that have come through a rain storm, as they will be soggy and watery-tasting and will be damaged with pits.

person's kitchen. Here, they turn a plain grilled cheese sandwich into something memorable.

ARTICHOKE, HAM AND SWISS CHEESE SANDWICHES

Makes 4 servings
Preparation time: 10 minutes
Cooking time: 10 minutes

1 12-to 14-inch baguette (crusty French bread)
1 14-ounce can artichoke hearts, drained and coarsely chopped
$^1/_4$ cup low-fat mayonnaise
3 tablespoons freshly grated Parmesan cheese
Black pepper
4 ounces Swiss cheese, thinly sliced
8 ounces cooked fresh ham, thinly sliced, room temperature

Preheat oven to 350 degrees. Cut bread in half horizontally. In a bowl, mix together artichoke hearts, mayonnaise, Parmesan cheese and pepper. Layer Swiss cheese, ham and artichokes, ending with a thin layer of cheese. Place top of baguette on cheese and cut into four portions. Place sandwiches on a baking sheet and bake until cheese has melted and bread is crisp.

Per serving: 477 calories, 18 grams fat, 72 milligrams cholesterol, 1,460 milligrams sodium.

FRIDAY

FRIED RICE *
STRAWBERRY SUNDAES *

Turn leftover rice and vegetables — asparagus, bok choy — into a fried rice meal-in-one. Two scrambled eggs are plenty to serve four; garnish with chopped green onions. Add ice cream and fresh strawberries for dessert.

SATURDAY

FETTUCCINE WITH CHICKEN, ARTICHOKES AND DILL
POACHED PEARS AND PISTACHIO NUTS
STUFFED WITH MASCARPONE

Serve this pasta dish, hot or cold, for Saturday night company. If you grilled the chicken earlier in the week, it will add a wonderful smokey flavor and complement the artichokes. Add elegant wine-simmered pears, stuffed with rich Italian cream cheese, for dessert. This time of year look for d'Anjou pears. They are still excellent, coming out of winter storage and cook beautifully.

FETTUCCINE WITH CHICKEN, ARTICHOKES AND DILL

Makes 4 servings
Preparation time: 25 minutes
Marinating time: 2 hours
Cooking time: 20 minutes

$^1/_4$ cup packed dill leaves
1 garlic clove
$^3/_4$ cup vinaigrette
Salt and black pepper to taste
1 14-ounce can artichoke hearts, drained, rinsed, quartered
1 medium avocado, peeled, pitted, rinsed, cut in $^3/_4$-inch dice
$^1/_2$ pound lemon fettucine or angel-hair pasta
2 or 3 halves skinned chicken breasts, cooked, sliced in thin strips
1 cup cherry tomatoes, halved
1 5-ounce can pitted black olives, chopped and drained

To make dressing, put the dill in the workbowl of a food processor and pulse to mince. Add garlic and pulse to mince. With the machine running, pour in vinaigrette, stop and add salt and pepper to taste. Put the dressing into a large serving bowl; add artichokes and cubes of ripe avocado. Let marinate in the refrigerator for a couple of hours. Before serving, bring artichoke mixture to room temperature.

Bring a pot of salted water to a boil and cook the pasta until al dente, about 8 to 10 minutes. Drain and toss with the artichoke mixture. Fold in chicken strips, tomatoes and olives. Add salt and pepper to taste.

Per serving: 886 calories, 49 grams fat, 121 milligrams cholesterol, 410 milligrams sodium.

POACHED PEARS AND PISTACHIO NUTS STUFFED WITH MASCARPONE

Makes 6 servings
Preparation time: 20 minutes
Cooking time: 20 minutes

2 cups dry white wine
$^1/_2$ cup granulated sugar
5 or 6 allspice berries
1 or 2 star anise
6 large, firm wide-based pears, about $^1/_2$-pound each
4 to 6 ounces mascarpone (or full-fat cream cheese), at room temperature
$^2/_3$ to $^1/_2$ cup coarsely chopped pistachio nuts, toasted

In a wide skillet with a non-reacting coating, add the wine and sugar over moderate heat. Stir until the sugar is dissolved. Add allspice and star anise. Bring to a boil, reduce heat and cook for 5 minutes.

Meanwhile, peel the pears, leaving stems intact. Cut a thin slice off bottom of each so the pears stand up, then set them upright in the simmering wine. Cover pot tightly and cook over low heat, basting occasionally, for 15 minutes or until pears are tender but slightly firm. Remove the pears from the skillet with a slotted spoon; place on paper towels to drain and cool. Bring liquid to a boil and reduce to 2/3 cup, then remove and discard allspice berries and star anise. Pour the syrup into a bowl and refrigerate for 15 minutes or until thickened.

While syrup is cooling, with a melon baller, make a round cavity in the bottom of each pear. Mash the cheese with a fork and press cheese in to fill each pear cavity. Place the pears on serving plates, brush them with some of the syrup, spoon remaining syrup around the pears and sprinkle toasted nuts around.

Per serving: 380 calories, 15 grams fat, 28 milligrams cholesterol, 10 milligrams sodium.

WEEK

17

SHOPPING LIST

Meat, poultry, seafood

- ❏ 1 5-pound roasting chicken
- ❏ 1 pound bratwurst
- ❏ 4 pork chops
- ❏ 4 slices bacon
- ❏ 1 pound swordfish

Produce

- ❏ 3 pounds tiny new "creamer" potatoes (or new red potatoes, size B)
- ❏ 1 1/2 cups frozen English peas
- ❏ 8 green onions
- ❏ 2 medium yellow onions
- ❏ 1 cucumber
- ❏ 1 small jicama
- ❏ 1 1/2 pounds brussels sprouts
- ❏ 7 sweet potatoes
- ❏ 1/2 pound escarole, Belgian endive or chicory

- ❏ 2 cloves garlic
- ❏ 1 large grapefruit
- ❏ 2 medium navel oranges
- ❏ 1 avocado
- ❏ 3 apples
- ❏ 2 bunches grapes
- ❏ 2 bananas
- ❏ 2 kiwi fruit
- ❏ 3 lemons
- ❏ 1 bunch cilantro
- ❏ 1 tiny chili pepper, such as serrano

Dairy

- ❏ 6 tablespoons unsalted butter
- ❏ 4 tablespoons margarine
- ❏ 2 eggs
- ❏ 1 cup vanilla low-fat yogurt
- ❏ 1 pint ice cream, any flavor
- ❏ 2 cups milk (or 1 cup milk and 1 cup half-and-half)

Deli

- ❏ 4 corn muffins

Miscellaneous

- ❏ 1 pound spinach linguine
- ❏ 1 pound silken-firm tofu
- ❏ 1 cup commercial Sichuan peanut sauce, such as Jade
- ❏ 1/2 cup roasted peanuts
- ❏ 1 cup cornmeal, preferably stone-ground
- ❏ 2 cups frozen raspberries
- ❏ 2 or 3 tablespoons sesame seeds
- ❏ Applesauce

Staples

- ❏ All-purpose flour
- ❏ Bay leaves
- ❏ Black pepper
- ❏ Cinnamon
- ❏ Honey

- ❏ Olive oil
- ❏ Chile-garlic sesame oil
- ❏ Rice vinegar
- ❏ Salt
- ❏ Sugar

* Suggested accompaniments

ROAST CHICKEN *
CREAMERS AND PEAS
LEMON PUDDING CAKE

The season of tiny brand-new potatoes is finally here, with a peel delicate enough to brush off with your fingers. Look for them at Harry's Farmers Market and Dekalb Farmers Market for the next month. My signature spring dish is barely boiled creamers and fresh English peas tossed in a light cream sauce. If you can't find the tiniest new potatoes, choose the B size, about the size of a golf ball, and cut them in half. Choose a 5-pound roasting chicken to provide leftovers for the week.

CREAMERS AND PEAS

Makes 4 servings
Preparation time: 5 minutes
Cooking time: 10 minutes

1 pound whole tiny new potatoes, scrubbed
2 tablespoons butter
2 green onions, (white part only) chopped
2 tablespoons all-purpose flour
Salt and black pepper to taste
1 cup milk or half-and-half
1 1/2 cups frozen English peas, thawed

Cook the potatoes in a small amount of boiling salted water about 10 minutes or until cooked through. Drain.

Meanwhile, over low heat, melt butter in a saucepan, and saute green onion 2 minutes. Whisk in flour, salt and pepper, then gradually whisk in the

milk. Cook until thickened and bubbly. Stir in potatoes and peas; heat through.

Per serving: 249 calories, 8 grams fat, 24 milligrams cholesterol, 146 milligrams sodium.

LEMON PUDDING CAKE

Makes 4 servings
Preparation time: 15-20 minutes
Cooking time: 40 minutes

1/3 cup sugar
3 tablespoons all-purpose flour
1 teaspoon grated lemon peel
3 tablespoons lemon juice
2 tablespoons unsalted butter, melted
2 slightly beaten egg yolks
1 cup milk
2 egg whites

Preheat oven to 350 degrees.

In a mixing bowl, combine the sugar and flour. Stir in lemon peel, juice and melted margarine. Combine yolks and milk, add to flour mixture and stir just till combined.

Beat egg whites until stiff peaks form, then gently fold into lemon batter. Transfer to a 1-quart casserole and place casserole in a larger pan. Place in the oven and add hot water to the larger pan to a depth of 1/2 inch. Bake about 40 minutes or until golden and top springs back.

Per serving: 208 calories, 11 grams fat, 146 milligrams cholesterol, 131 milligrams sodium.

SPINACH NOODLES WITH
SILKEN TOFU AND
PEANUT SAUCE

SLICED CUCUMBERS
AND JICAMA WITH
SESAME SEEDS AND
RICE VINEGAR *

Spinach linguine makes this dish particularly pretty, and commercial Sichuan peanut sauce pulls it together in minutes. Serve it hot or cold and save plenty of leftovers to serve later in the week. Look for the Jade brand at Williams-Sonoma. Look for chile-garlic sesame oil or paste (or just chile sesame oil) in ethnic grocery stores, farmers markets, or the oriental section of some grocery stores.

SPINACH NOODLES WITH SILKEN TOFU AND PEANUT SAUCE

Makes 8 to 9 servings
Preparation time: 5 to 10 minutes
Cooking time: 10 minutes

1 pound spinach linguine
Salt
1 cup commercial peanut sauce, such as Jade
2 tablespoons chile-garlic sesame oil
2 or 3 tablespoons rice vinegar
1/2 cup chopped cilantro leaves
4 or 5 green onions, thinly sliced on the diagonal
1 pound silken-firm tofu, cut into small cubes
1/4 cup chopped, roasted peanuts

Cook noodles in boiling, salted water until al dente, about 8 minutes. Drain and rinse (in cold water if you want to serve the noodles cold, warm if you want to serve them warm). Toss with the peanut sauce, sesame oil and rice vinegar, then fold in cilantro, green onions and tofu. Cover and refrigerate if not serv-

Price: Will range from $.99 to $1.99 a pound.

Nutrition: Peas are an excellent source of fiber and provide vitamins A and C. A 4-ounce serving has 60 calories.

Selection: Look for the best value on snow peas from February through June. Choose the tiniest, firmest, most crisp, bright green pods with a minimum of rust. Discard large, woody pods or ones that are frayed along the edges.

Storage: Store peas in the refrigerator, unwashed and wrapped in a plastic bag, for about 3 days.

Uses: Allow about ¼ pound of snow peas per serving. Snow peas are delicious briefly microwaved, steamed, stir-fried, served alone or added to salad, fruit salad or meat dishes. Raw, they also make a good appetizer served with a dip.

The status of snow peas has tumbled from exotic to every-day, and that is good news for vegetable lovers. The flat edible pods, also called sugar peas or Chinese pea pods, contain 4 or 5 tiny peas the size of pepper-corns and are eaten in their entirety. They are delicious, nutritious and cook quickly to enhance myriad last-minute dishes. While snow peas are available year round in most markets, this cool-weather crop is a particularly good bargain right now.

Edible pea pods differ from English peas in that the edible pods do not develop a tough, supportive lining called a parch-ment. While snow peas are asso-ciated with Chinese cooking, it is likely they were first cultivat-ed in Europe. They have been popular in French cooking since the seventeenth century.

The sugars in peas quickly turn to starch when they are picked, so try to purchase the peas close to when you plan to cook them. To use edible pea pods, break off the tips and pull backward to remove the strings. While they can be served raw, a brief cooking enhances their fla-vor, color and sweetness.

The peas cook very quickly, so be careful not to overcook. A standard ingredient in stir-fried dishes, snow peas are also deli-cious quickly sauteed with other vegetables in a little butter or tossed in pasta dishes.

ing immediately. At serving time, toss with peanut sauce and garnish with peanuts and cilantro sprigs. Adapted from *The Savory Way* by Deborah Madison (Bantam Books, $22.95).

Per serving: 317 calories, 16 grams fat, no cholesterol, 68 milligrams sodium.

TUESDAY

GRILLED BRATWURST *
GARLIC CORNMEAL MUSH
STEAMED BRUSSELS
SPROUTS *
APPLES AND GRAPES *

Garlic adds punch to this comforting Southern cornmeal dish, and the entire dinner can be cooked in 20 minutes. Look for freshly made bratwurst, a German sausage made of ground pork and veal and seasoned with ginger, nutmeg and coriander or caraway, in the meat case at many grocery stores. Look for stone-ground grits for incomparable flavor and whole-grain nutrition. Leftover mush can be refrigerated, sliced and sauteed for another meal.

GARLIC CORNMEAL MUSH

Makes 4 to 6 servings

4 cups salted water
1 cup stone-ground yellow cornmeal
2 large cloves garlic, minced
4 tablespoons unsalted butter or
    more to taste

In a large, heavy saucepan, bring salted water to a boil. Add cornmeal very slowly while whisking to avoid lumps. Cook 18 to 20 minutes uncovered over low heat (mixture should bubble gently), whisking or stirring occasionally to keep it from burning. Mush is done when it pulls away from the sides of the pot as you stir.

Meanwhile, prepare garlic butter: in a small skillet or saucepan cook garlic in butter over low heat 3 or 4 minutes or until garlic just releases its fragrance and is a pale gold color. Drizzle the garlic butter over the cooked grits.

Per serving: 141 calories, 8 grams fat, 21 milligrams cholesterol, 350 milligrams sodium.

WEDNESDAY

ROASTED CHICKEN PIECES *
BAKED SWEET POTATOES
WITH BUTTER AND
CINNAMON *
FRUIT FONDUE

Leftover chicken legs or wings will make a good side dish to tonight's stuffed baked sweet potatoes. Cook the potatoes in the microwave oven if you are pressed for time, and cook 3 additional ones for tomorrow night's dinner. If you have an hour to spare, they will turn sweeter when baked at 350 degrees in the oven. Add fruit and the raspberry dipping sauce for a delicious dessert fondue.

FRUIT FONDUE

Makes 4 servings

2 cups assorted fruit, such as banana
    slices, apple slices, kiwi chunks,
    grapes
2 cups frozen raspberries
1 cup vanilla low-fat yogurt
4 teaspoons sugar (optional)

In a blender or food processor, whip together the raspberries, yogurt and (optional) sugar. Serve with cut-up fruit.

Per serving: 129 calories, 1 gram fat, 2 milligrams cholesterol, 31 milligrams sodium.

THURSDAY

PORK CHOPS *
SWEET POTATO HASH
BROWNS WITH BACON
AND ONIONS
APPLESAUCE *

Here is another homey meal that your family will love. Add pork chops — any cut that is on sale — and commercial applesauce made from Granny Smith apples.

SWEET POTATO HASH BROWNS WITH BACON AND ONIONS

Makes 4 servings

4 slices bacon, diced
1 medium yellow onion, sliced
3 medium sweet potatoes, cooked,
    peeled and diced
Salt and black pepper to taste

On medium heat, cook the bacon pieces until brown; add sliced onions and cook until they are golden brown, about 7 minutes. Remove the bacon and onions from the skillet.

Pour off enough bacon grease to leave ¹/₄ cup in the skillet. Add potato chunks and pan fry about 7 to 8 minutes, turning occasionally. Remove the pan from the heat, add bacon and onion and season with salt and pepper. Adapted from *Thrill of the Grill* by Chris Schlesinger and John Willoughby (William Morrow, $24.95).

Per serving: 236 calories, 14 grams fat, 16 milligrams cholesterol, 11 milligrams sodium.

FRIDAY

COLD NOODLE SALAD WITH TOFU AND CUCUMBERS JICAMA WITH SESAME SEEDS AND RICE VINEGAR*

Take advantage of leftover noodles and cucumbers, which should taste better after a day or two in the refrigerator. Fold in leftover cucumber salad and sprinkle the top with more chopped peanuts and cilantro.

SATURDAY

BROILED MARINATED SWORDFISH CITRUS AND AVOCADO SALAD WITH INDIA JOSE CILANTRO DRESSING CORN MUFFINS *

The first swordfish specials of the season are here, and if it is warm outside, outdoor grilling can't be far behind. These swordfish chunks grill to a fragrant turn, tucked between bay leaves and onion and lemon slices. If you are using wood skewers, soak them in water for 30 minutes before using. Take advantage of in-season Hass avocados and end-of-the-season grapefruit to make the following refreshing fruit salad. If time is a big factor, bottled citrus slices, available in the produce section, could be substituted. Make the dressing at the last minute for the freshest flavor.

GRILLED SWORDFISH

Makes 6 servings

1 medium onion
8 whole bay leaves
¹/₄ cup olive oil
¹/₄ cup lemon juice
³/₄ teaspoon salt
1 pound swordfish steak, cut in
    ³/₄-inch chunks
2 lemons, cut in wedges

Peel and halve the onions, then cut each half into 4 or 5 wedges and separate the layers. Place the onion pieces in a large bowl, lay bay leaves across. Stir in the olive oil, lemon juice and salt. Place swordfish chunks in the marinade and turn to coat. Cover and marinate at least 30 minutes or up to 2 hours refrigerated.

Thread 4 skewers, starting with an onion, then a bay leaf, then a chunk of swordfish and a lemon wedge. Continue in the same fashion until all the pieces have been threaded. Place the skewers under the broiler for about 10 minutes, turning once, until the fish is cooked through and the onions are tender.

Per serving: 169 calories, 8 grams fat, 38 milligrams cholesterol, 354 milligrams sodium.

CITRUS AND AVOCADO SALAD WITH INDIA JOSE CILANTRO DRESSING

Makes 6 servings

¹/₂ pound escarole, Belgian
    endive or chicory
1 large grapefruit
2 medium navel oranges
1 medium-large, very ripe avocado,
    pitted, peeled and cut in
    ¹/₂- inch dice

DRESSING:

¹/₃ to ¹/₂ cup coarsely chopped
    cilantro leaves, not packed
3 tablespoons lemon juice
4 tablespoons peanut oil
1 tablespoon honey
1/4 teaspoon salt, or to taste
1 very small ice cube
1 tiny chili pepper, such as serrano,
    seeded and minced (optional)

Rinse escarole and dry thoroughly. Cut in bite-size pieces; wrap and chill if you have time. Peel and remove white pith from grapefruit, then remove sections from the membranes. Peel and remove pith from oranges, cut in half and cut sections in thin slices.

To serve, arrange escarole on serving dish or platter. Arrange grapefruit and oranges over and top with avocado dice.

To make the dressing, combine cilantro, lemon juice, oil, honey, salt and ice in food processor and puree. Add minced hot pepper and pour over salad. Adapted from

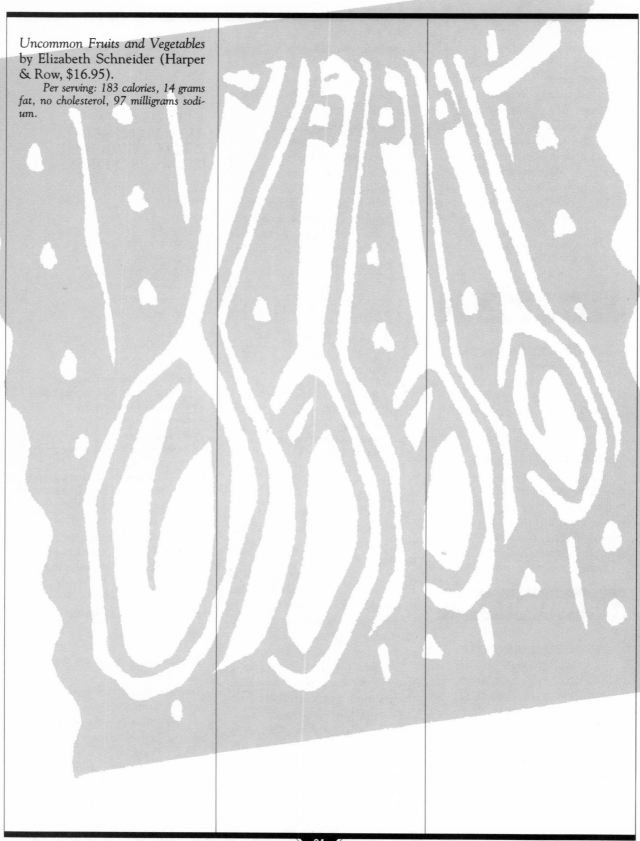

Uncommon Fruits and Vegetables by Elizabeth Schneider (Harper & Row, $16.95).

Per serving: 183 calories, 14 grams fat, no cholesterol, 97 milligrams sodium.

WEEK

18

SHOPPING LIST

Meat, poultry, seafood

- ❑ 1 5- to 7-pound turkey breast
- ❑ 12 to 16 ounces lean ground beef
- ❑ 4 slices bacon
- ❑ 2 pounds halibut steaks

Produce

- ❑ 1 ¹/₂ pounds brussels sprouts
- ❑ 1 ¹/₂ pounds all-purpose potatoes
- ❑ 1 pound small turnips
- ❑ 2 large Vidalia onions
- ❑ 8 green onions
- ❑ 2 large shallots
- ❑ 6 carrots
- ❑ 1 rib celery
- ❑ 1 red bell pepper
- ❑ 1 head lettuce, any type
- ❑ 1 pound spinach
- ❑ 1 pint cherry tomatoes

- ❑ 2 apples
- ❑ 1 lemon
- ❑ 2 oranges
- ❑ 1 bunch thyme leaves
- ❑ 1 bunch tarragon (optional)

Dairy

- ❑ 1 ¹/₂ sticks butter
- ❑ 2 cups cream or half-and-half
- ❑ 1 cup plain non-fat yogurt
- ❑ 5 eggs
- ❑ 1 ¹/₄ cups milk

Deli

- ❑ 6 ounces hard cheese, such as Cheddar or blue
- ❑ 1 loaf crusty bread
- ❑ Tuna salad
- ❑ Pita bread rounds
- ❑ Greek Salad

- ❑ Vanilla pudding

Miscellaneous

- ❑ 1 ²/₃ cups chocolate chips
- ❑ ¹/₂ cup chopped nuts (pecans or walnuts)
- ❑ 3 tablespoons almonds
- ❑ 8 slices white bread
- ❑ 1 10-ounce package frozen chopped spinach
- ❑ 1 19-ounce can garbanzo beans
- ❑ 6 ounces dried peaches (or apricots)
- ❑ ¹/₃ cup shredded coconut
- ❑ 1 tablespoon orange juice
- ❑ 1 16-ounce can cranberry sauce
- ❑ 1 cup wild rice
- ❑ 1 tablespoon light corn syrup

Staples

- ❑ Baking powder
- ❑ Baking soda
- ❑ Brown sugar
- ❑ Fennel or anise seed
- ❑ Granulated sugar
- ❑ Ground black pepper
- ❑ Ground cinnamon
- ❑ Kosher salt
- ❑ Light mayonnaise
- ❑ Minced garlic in oil
- ❑ Olive oil
- ❑ Pure vanilla extract
- ❑ Salt
- ❑ Self-rising flour
- ❑ Vegetable shortening
- ❑ Vinaigrette

*Suggested accompaniments

ROASTED TURKEY BREAST *
SCALLOPED TURNIPS
AND POTATOES
STEAMED BRUSSELS SPROUTS *
FUDGY-CHIP CAKE

A large turkey breast will provide sandwiches and another dinner, extra brussels sprouts can be served cold, and the Fudgy-Chip Cake will find its way into lunch boxes and be eaten as snacks. Smaller turnips are not as hot or woody as larger ones; fresh ones picked each day are available at local farmers markets. The turnips and potatoes are especially delicate and sweet made with new potatoes and sweet new turnips. In the winter, when rutabagas are in season, substitute them for the turnips.

SCALLOPED TURNIPS AND POTATOES

Makes 8 to 10 servings
Preparation time: 10 minutes
Cooking time: 45 minutes

1 tablespoon minced garlic in oil
2 tablespoons butter
2 new potatoes, cut into $^1/_2$-inch slices
2 pounds new baby turnips, scrubbed and cut into $^1/_2$-inch slices
2 cups heavy cream or half-and-half
1 teaspoon fresh or dry thyme leaves
2 teaspoons salt
$^1/_2$ teaspoon freshly ground black pepper

Preheat oven to 350 degrees. Grease a 9-inch-square baking dish with the chopped garlic and butter and set aside.

Mix the potatoes and turnips together and spread them evenly in the baking dish. Sprinkle thyme leaves, salt and pepper over. Heat the cream or half-and-half to boiling either in the microwave oven or on the stove top, then pour over the potatoes and turnips. Cover loosely with aluminum foil and bake 30 minutes. Remove foil and bake 15 more minutes, or until golden brown.

Per serving (if 4 servings): 312 calories, 18 grams fat, 52 milligrams cholesterol, 672 milligrams sodium.

FUDGY-CHIP CAKE

Makes 12 servings
Preparation time: 10 minutes
Cooking time: 40 minutes

2 cups self-rising flour
1 cup brown sugar (packed)
$^1/_2$ cup granulated sugar
$^1/_2$ cup vegetable shortening
1 $^1/_4$ cups milk
3 eggs
$^1/_2$ cup semisweet chocolate pieces, finely chopped
1 $^1/_2$ teaspoons pure vanilla extract

GLAZE:
$^1/_2$ cup semisweet chocolate pieces
2 tablespoons butter
1 tablespoon light corn syrup

Preheat oven to 350 degrees. Grease and flour a 9-by-12-inch cake pan and set aside.

In a large mixing bowl add the flour, both sugars, shortening, milk, eggs, chocolate pieces and vanilla. With an electric mixer, beat 30 seconds on low speed, scraping the bowl to keep the batter together, then beat 3 minutes on high speed, scraping the bowl. Pour the batter into the prepared cake pan.

Bake 35 to 40 minutes or until a knife inserted in the center comes out clean. Cool the cake on a rack.

Meanwhile, prepare the glaze. Heat the chocolate pieces, butter and corn syrup over low heat, stirring constantly, until melted. Cool slightly and spread over the cooled cake.

Per serving: 337 calories, 15 grams fat, 75 milligrams cholesterol, 281 milligrams sodium.

VIDALIA ONION SANDWICH
BRUSSELS SPROUTS IN LEMON
VINAIGRETTE *
CHEESE AND SLICED APPLES *

Celebrate spring as Georgians do best, with an onion sandwich made with the sweetest onions in the land. We've added spinach and cherry tomatoes, but true onion aficionados don't bother with these extras. Toss cooked Brussels sprouts with a vinaigrette made with lemon juice and add sprigs of any fresh herbs you may have.

VIDALIA ONION SANDWICH

Makes 4 servings
Preparation time: 5 minutes
Chilling time: 30 minutes

1 large Vidalia onion, unpeeled
4 tablespoons light mayonnaise
8 slices white or whole wheat bread
4 to 8 spinach leaves
4 to 6 cherry tomatoes, sliced

Place one unpeeled Vidalia onion in the refrigerator and chill for about 1 hour before serving. (Or, peel and cut into slices and place the slices in a bowl of ice water for about 30 minutes.) Drain on paper towels. Either method will help bring out a sweeter flavor for raw eating.

Slice the onion into ¼-inch slices, or drain the slices if you used the second method. Spread mayonnaise on two slices of bread and add a thick slice of Vidalia onion, spinach leaves and tomato slices.

Per serving: 193 calories, 6 grams fat, 5 milligrams cholesterol, 271 milligrams sodium.

TUESDAY

VEGGIE-BEEF BURGERS
BOILED POTATOES *

Tonight, serve hamburgers that have an added healthy twist — quickly pureed beans and spinach. If you use frozen spinach, thaw it, then squeeze out the liquid before adding to the meat mixture. The burgers are a bit too crumbly to serve in a bun, but are delicious served alone or with a flavorful sauce such as a tomato or mango chutney, available at many grocery stores.

Cook about 3 pounds of potatoes, and reserve half for a later dinner.

VEGGIE-BEEF BURGERS

Makes 4 servings
Preparation time: 10 minutes
Cooking time: 10 minutes

12 to 16 ounces lean ground beef
1 cup finely chopped spinach
½ to ¾ cup cooked garbanzo
    beans, mashed
½ medium onion, minced
1 teaspoon salt
Freshly ground black pepper to taste
4 buns

M<small>AY</small>

Florida and South Georgia vegetables are in the market now — green bell peppers, summer squashes, celery, sweet corn, eggplant, tomatoes and cabbage are all good values now. California grape harvests have begun but prices are high for now. Beware of cheap cantaloupe in the market, some of it has little sugar and little flavor. Both Mexican and Florida watermelon are available.

New potatoes from Idaho, Colorado and Maine will continue until late May or early June, and new red potatoes coming from Arizona are of excellent quality. Lettuce supplies are a bit tight, which may raise prices this week. Sweet potatoes will continue to be an excellent buy for several weeks.

In produce departments, cabbage, sweet corn and delicious watermelon, tomatoes and Vidalia onions are plentiful. Georgia snap beans, yellow crookneck squash and purple hull peas are available at the Farmers Market. California peaches, plums and nectarines are in good quantity, and Georgia field peaches are a good buy. (Field peaches are not graded for uniform size and appearance, but the flavor may be better.) Brought to market straight from the field and not precooled, they are left on the tree for ripening as long as possible.

The earliest Georgia peaches, such as June Gold, will be starting this week and will be available in small supply at the State Farmers Market. Other peach varieties that are larger and sweeter will be coming in another 3 weeks.

Florida limes are dropping in price, and the smaller sizes are very reasonably priced. Florida Valencia oranges have good interior quality, so don't let the scarred appearance stop you from buying them. Chilean grapes prices are low and continue to be stable in price. California strawberries are in good supply at good prices, and many grocery stores will be running promotions.

Cold-storage apples and pears are higher in price than before Christmas. Hot-house rhubarb is in many stores and a welcome respite from milder-tasting fruit. Pineapples are sweeter again, and there are good prices on California Hass avocados.

Grapefruit season is officially finished, and the first cherries of the season — the red Burlats from California — are at Harry's Farmers Market. The red Bing and yellow Ranier cherries will be ready in a couple of weeks. Melons are coming from Texas and California and are looking increasingly better each week, but watermelons will likely be expensive for the Memorial weekend. Sweet red mangoes are in season now, and banana prices are returning to normal.

Preheat the broiler.

Combine all the ingredients in a bowl and mix until well blended. Shape the mixture into four 4-inch patties. Broil the patties 5 minutes per side. Serve open-faced on buns.

Per serving (not including bun): 308 calories, 10 grams fat, 63 milligrams cholesterol, 955 milligrams sodium.

WEDNESDAY

HASH BROWN POTATOES, ONIONS AND CHEESE *
CARROT STICKS *
DRIED PEACH NUGGETS

Cooked potatoes can be transformed into a great meal in minutes. Dice the potatoes and saute them along with sliced onions, until crispy and cooked through. Sprinkle with grated Cheddar cheese and serve as the cheese melts. Add the following easy dessert, a healthy lunch box treat for your children.

DRIED PEACH NUGGETS

Makes 2 dozen nuggets
Preparation time: 10 minutes
Chilling time: 15 minutes

3 to 6 tablespoons finely chopped pecans
1 cup (6 ounces) dried but soft apricots
6 tablespoons shredded (packaged, not frozen) coconut
1 tablespoon apple juice

Process the nuts in the workbowl of a food processor until finely chopped. Set aside.

Process the peaches until finely chopped. Add the coconut and apple juice. Process

several more seconds, scraping the bowl, to make a fairly smooth paste. Divide into 4 equal portions and wrap each in plastic wrap and refrigerate to chill, about 15 minutes.

Roll each portion back and forth on a smooth surface to form a narrow rope. Sprinkle the chopped nuts on a piece of waxed paper and roll each fruit roll over the nuts to coat. Slice each rope into 12 inch slices.

Per nugget: 29 calories, 1 gram fat, no cholesterol, 4 milligrams sodium.

THURSDAY

WILTED SPINACH AND ORANGE SALAD
SLICED TURKEY AND CRANBERRY SANDWICHES *

The fastest, and perhaps favorite, way to serve leftover turkey is in turkey sandwiches, complete with canned cranberry sauce, on crusty bread. Add a big salad, full of fruit and the anise flavor of fresh fennel — it's a winner. Use fresh tarragon leaves, instead, if you wish.

WILTED SPINACH AND ORANGE SALAD

Makes 4 to 6 servings
Preparation time: 15 minutes
Cooking time: 15 minutes

4 slices bacon
½ pound fresh spinach, washed, dried and stemmed
4 green onions, diced
1 to 2 tablespoons bacon drippings (or vegetable oil)
1 tablespoon lemon juice
½ teaspoon sugar
Salt and coarsely-ground black pepper to taste

½ teaspoon fennel or anise seed (or 1 teaspoon tarragon leaves, optional)
2 oranges, peeled and cut into bite-size pieces

In a medium-size skillet, fry bacon, drain and crumble, reserving drippings. Set bacon aside.

Tear spinach leaves into bite-sized pieces. In a salad bowl, toss spinach, green onions and orange pieces; set aside. Mix together the bacon drippings (or vegetable oil), lemon juice, sugar, salt and fennel seed in a small saucepan. Bring to a boil and pour over the spinach mixture. Garnish with bacon crumbles and serve.

Per serving (if 4 servings): 127 calories, 8 grams fat, 10 milligrams cholesterol, 279 milligrams sodium.

FRIDAY

TUNA SALAD IN PITA POCKETS*
TURNIP AND POTATO GRATIN*
VANILLA PUDDING *

The grocery store should be able to provide the salad and dessert for tonight's dinner; all you need to do is heat pita breads for 5 minutes, slice them in half and stuff with tuna salad, and reheat the potato gratin from Sunday's meal.

SATURDAY

GRILLED HALIBUT AND CHARRED VEGETABLE SALAD
STEAMED WILD RICE *
YOGURT COFFEE CAKE

On the first spring night

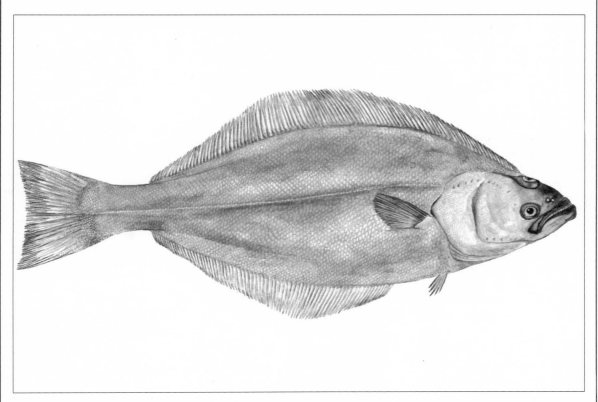

Price: Will range from $4.99 to $6.99 a pound, which is $1.00 cheaper than the frozen halibut available year round. The fish will be arriving in local grocery stores May 9 or 10th and will be available approximately through May 18.

Nutrition: Pacific halibut is a low-fat fish. A 3 ^{1}/$_2$-ounce portion contains 110 calories and 32 milligrams cholesterol.

Selection: Pacific halibut steaks come in a rectangular shape about 6 inches thick and will range from 6 to 16 inches long, depending on the part of the fish from which they were cut. A large steak can be divided into four boneless quarters

which makes attractive servings. Choose steaks that are firm and fresh-looking.

Storage: Store the fish in its store package in the coldest part of the refrigerator for 2 or 3 days.

Uses: Allow two pounds of fish to amply serve 4 people, as the skin and center bone are to be removed after cooking. Halibut is a versatile fish that is excellent grilled, broiled, sauteed or poached, and makes good sandwiches.

Official halibut fishing "season" will open in Alaska on May 7 and will finish 24 hours later, surely the shortest fishing season of them all. For a couple

of weeks, grocery stores across the country will be flooded with fresh, high-quality and low-priced Pacific halibut, a sweet and flaky fish from the flounder family.

In that short period, millions of pounds of fish will be caught, which will provide the majority of the year's income for many fishermen. Due to over fishing and a natural decline in numbers of fish ready to harvest, Alaska has turned to three 24-hour seasons in May, June and September, while Canada allows seasonal quotas, which can be caught between May and November.

warm enough to sit outside, serve grilled halibut on a bed of crunchy vegetables. For extra flavor, toss the vegetables, cold or hot, with tarragon; its anise flavor is a perfect partner for fish. The vegetables are especially good with this dish when slightly charred, so grill or saute them for just a minute before serving. Use a vegetable grill pan, available at many stores, to hold the cut vegetables over the fire. Cook the cake earlier in the day. This one may become one of your favorites.

GRILLED HALIBUT AND CHARRED VEGETABLE SALAD

Makes 4 servings
Preparation time: 15 to 20 minutes
Cooking time: 10 minutes

2 pounds halibut steaks, 1-inch thick
$^1/_2$ cup olive oil
2 large shallots, finely minced
2 carrots, julienned or shredded
1 red bell pepper, slivered
$^1/_4$ cup thinly sliced green onions, green and white parts
2 or 3 tablespoons rice wine vinegar
1 to 2 tablespoons fresh tarragon leaves (optional)
Few drops lemon juice

Preheat a grill or broiler.

If the halibut steaks are large, cut them into 4 serving pieces. Whisk together the olive oil and shallots and brush the steaks with 2 to 3 tablespoons of the mixture (reserve the remainder for the salad), then add salt and pepper to taste. Grill the steaks 3 to 4 minutes, turn and brush second side and grill 3 or 4 more minutes. (Estimate 10 minutes of cooking for 1-inch steaks.)

To serve the vegetables cold, toss the carrots, bell pepper, green onions, vinegar and tarragon with the remaining oil mixture. Divide evenly among four serving plates. To serve the vegetables warm, grill or saute them in a hot wok or skillet until just softened, 2 or 3 minutes. Spoon the vegetables on serving plates and top with grilled halibut steaks. Sprinkle the steaks with lemon juice and serve.

Per serving: 579 calories, 34 grams fat, 93 milligrams cholesterol, 171 milligrams sodium.

BUTTERSCOTCH YOGURT COFFEE CAKE

Makes 12 servings
Preparation time: 15 minutes
Cooking time: 45 minutes

1 cup plain non-fat yogurt
1 teaspoon baking soda
$^1/_2$ cup unsalted butter, room temperature
1 $^1/_4$ cups sugar
2 eggs, beaten
1 $^3/_4$ cups self-rising flour
$^2/_3$ cup butterscotch chips (optional)
$^1/_2$ cup chopped nuts
1 teaspoon cinnamon
$^1/_2$ cup (packed) brown sugar

Preheat oven to 350 degrees. Grease a 9-by-13-inch pan with pan spray.

Mix together the yogurt and soda in a mixing bowl; set aside. In the workbowl of a food processor or with an electric mixer, cream together the butter, sugar and eggs until fluffy. Add the flour and pulse just until it is combined. Add the butter mixture and pulse, then the yogurt mixture and pulse.

Pour the batter into the prepared cake pan and sprinkle with (optional) chips. Combine the topping ingredients and sprinkle over the top. Bake 40 to 45 minutes.

Per serving: 345 calories, 15 grams fat, 66 milligrams cholesterol, 225 milligrams sodium.

WEEK

19

SHOPPING LIST

Meat, poultry, seafood

- ☐ 1 pound ground chuck or
- ☐ 1 4-pound lamb roast with bone (shoulder or leg)
- ☐ 4 6- to 8-ounce center-cut pork chops
- ☐ 4 6- to 8-ounce salmon steaks

Produce

- ☐ 2 pounds new red potatoes
- ☐ 2 pounds asparagus
- ☐ 1 pound green beans
- ☐ 1 10-ounce package pearl onions
- ☐ 1 medium yellow onion
- ☐ 1 small turnip
- ☐ 1 small head nappa cabbage
- ☐ 1 small red onion
- ☐ 1 large shallot
- ☐ 2 medium carrots

- ☐ 1 cup snow peas
- ☐ 12 large stalks rhubarb
- ☐ 1 1/2 pints strawberries
- ☐ 1 bunch tarragon
- ☐ 1 bunch mint
- ☐ 1 bunch chives
- ☐ 1 small jar minced garlic
- ☐ 1 small knob fresh ginger
- ☐ 1 bunch dill

Dairy

- ☐ 1 cup milk
- ☐ 3 ounces (3/4 cup) grated Cheddar cheese
- ☐ 2 tablespoons butter or margarine
- ☐ 2 sticks butter

Deli

- ☐ 1/2 cup grated Parmesan cheese
- ☐ 2 ounces feta cheese
- ☐ 2 to 4 whole wheat pita breads

Miscellaneous

- ☐ 1 14 1/2-ounce can whole peeled tomatoes
- ☐ 1 cup rice
- ☐ 2 cups bulgur
- ☐ 8 ounces wide egg noodles
- ☐ 1/4 cup orange juice
- ☐ 2 4-ounce packages ramen noodles (any flavor)
- ☐ 1/3 cup dry tawny port (or other port)
- ☐ 1 14 1/2-ounce can chicken or beef broth plus 1/4 cup beef broth
- ☐ 1 cup slivered almonds
- ☐ Low-fat ranch-style dressing
- ☐ Stir-fry or pepper-orange dressing
- ☐ 1 pint vanilla ice cream

Staples

- ☐ All-purpose flour
- ☐ Brown sugar
- ☐ Cornstarch
- ☐ Dried herbs de Provence or Italian seasoning
- ☐ Granulated sugar
- ☐ Ground black pepper
- ☐ Hazelnut or walnut oil
- ☐ Honey (optional)
- ☐ Olive oil
- ☐ Peanut oil
- ☐ Salt
- ☐ Self-rising flour
- ☐ Vegetable shortening

* Suggested accompaniments

SUNDAY

OVEN-ROASTED LAMB
AND POTATOES
STEAMED ASPARAGUS*
CHEDDAR AND CHIVE
BISCUITS

When it comes to flavor and ease, this one-pot meal is a winner. Choose whichever lamb roast you find on sale, just make sure it is big enough to yield leftovers. If garlic chives, sometimes called Chinese chives, are in the stores, by all means use them for an additional garlic boost that enhances these biscuits.

OVEN-ROASTED LAMB AND POTATOES

Makes 6 servings
Preparation time: 10 minutes
Cooking time: 1 hour

1 10-ounce package pearl onions, peeled
4 pounds lamb, with bone (shoulder or leg)
3 tablespoons olive oil
1 tablespoon dried herbs de Provence (or Italian seasoning)
2 pounds new red potatoes, cut in halves
1 14 1/2-ounce can whole tomatoes, drained
1/2 cup grated Parmesan cheese
Salt and freshly ground black pepper

Preheat the oven to 350 degrees. To peel the onions, bring 2 cups of water to a boil in the microwave or saucepan, add the onions and boil for 30 seconds. Remove onions from water with slotted spoon, rinse under cold water and remove peels; set aside.

Cut the lamb into bite-sized chunks, reserving the bone. Heat the oil in a deep skillet or Dutch oven; add the remaining ingredients, including the reserved bone,

and stir well. Bake, uncovered, for 1 hour, stirring occasionally.

Per serving: 637 calories, 27 grams fat, 196 milligrams cholesterol, 407 milligrams sodium.

CHEDDAR AND CHIVE BISCUITS

Makes 2 dozen biscuits
Preparation time: 10 minutes
Cooking time: 10 to 12 minutes

2 cups self-rising flour
1/4 cup vegetable shortening
3/4 cup grated Cheddar or other sharp cheese
1/4 cup chopped fresh chives
1 cup milk

Preheat oven to 450 degrees.

Put the flour in the workbowl of a food processor. Add the shortening and pulse until the mixture resembles coarse crumbs. Stir in the grated cheese and chives. Add the milk and pulse just until the mixture forms a soft dough that pulls away from the sides of the bowl.

Turn the dough out onto a lightly floured surface, knead 5 or 6 times to mix the dough, then roll out until 1/2 inch thick. Cut biscuits with a floured biscuit cutter and place on an ungreased cookie sheet. Bake until golden brown, 10 to 12 minutes.

Per serving (2 biscuits): 150 calories, 7 grams fat, 9 milligrams cholesterol, 279 milligrams sodium.

MONDAY

BULGUR RICE PILAF
WITH ONIONS AND CARROTS*

Bulgur and rice served together make a delicious, nutty-flavored dish, and the addition of fresh vegetables make it a complete, healthy meal. Reserve any leftovers for tomorrow night's dinner.

Use fresh dill if you can find it.

BULGUR RICE PILAF WITH ONIONS AND CARROTS

Makes 8 servings
Preparation time: 20 minutes
Cooking time: 20 minutes

1 cup rice
2 tablespoons olive oil
1 large onion, finely diced
2 or 3 carrots, grated
1 new turnips, scrubbed and finely chopped
2 or 3 tablespoons fresh dill
1 1/2 teaspoons salt
2 cups bulgur (cracked wheat)
2 cups nappa cabbage, chopped

Place rice and 2 cups water in a saucepan. Bring it to a boil, cover, lower heat and cook until soft, about 18 minutes.

Meanwhile, place the oil in a skillet. Add the onions, carrots, and turnip saute for 5 minutes. Add dill, 1 teaspoon salt and bulgur; toss to coat the bulgur with the oil and vegetables. Add 4 cups water, cover and cook until the water has evaporated, 10 minutes. Add the cabbage and cook 5 minutes. Add the cooked rice and stir together and serve.

Per serving: 194 calories, 4 grams fat, no cholesterol, 578 milligrams sodium.

TUESDAY

PITA POCKETS WITH LAMB,
BULGUR AND MINT
FRESH ORANGE SLICES
WITH CRYSTALLIZED
GINGER*

Take advantage of the growing supply of leftovers to make tonight's delicious dinner.

Price: Will range from $.99 to $2.00 a pound.

Nutrition: One cup of diced fruit has about 20 calories and is a good source of vitamin C, calcium and potassium.

Selection: In season from February through June and peaking in May, rhubarb is sold ripe and ready to use. Choose firm stalks, red or red-green striped, and avoid stalks that are flabby or badly bruised. Field-grown rhubarb has large, thick stalks that are streaked dark red and green and are very tart. Hothouse rhubarb will be very light pink, have few strings and a blander flavor.

Storage: Refrigerate, unwashed, and store in the refrigerator in a plastic bag up to 1 week.

Uses: One pound of rhubarb yields about 3 cups sliced. Rhubarb must be cooked to soften. It is tart and must be cooked with sugar, fruit juice or sweet fruit. Stew it with a tiny amount of water and sugar to use as a fruit sauce, or use in pies and cobblers.

PITA POCKETS WITH LAMB, BULGUR AND MINT

Makes 4 servings
Preparation time: 10 minutes
Cooking time: 5 minutes

2 to 4 whole wheat pita breads, cut in half
1 cup cooked, diced lamb
1 to 2 cups cooked bulgur and rice mixture
2 ounces feta cheese, rinsed, drained and crumbled
1/2 small red onion, peeled and sliced
2 tablespoons fresh mint leaves, roughly chopped
4 tablespoons low-fat ranch-style salad dressing

Turn the oven to 350 degrees and place pita breads on a cookie sheet. Heat in the oven about 5 minutes, just until warm.

Meanwhile, in a medium-size mixing bowl, combine the lamb, bulgur and rice, cheese, onion, mint leaves and salad dressing. Spoon the mixture into the pita breads and serve.

Per serving: 222 calories, 7 grams fat, 46 milligrams cholesterol, 467 milligrams sodium.

WEDNESDAY

PORK CHOPS WITH RHUBARB SAUCE BUTTERED NOODLES*

MIXED GREEN SALAD* CHEESE-CHIVE BISCUITS*

A sweet-tart rhubarb sauce makes the perfect counterpoint to pork, and this recipe gets high marks in the lean department, too. Cook a couple of extra pork chops to use for tomorrow night's dinner.

PORK CHOPS WITH RHUBARB SAUCE

Makes 4 servings
Preparation time: 5 minutes
Cooking time: 20 minutes

4 6- to 8-ounce rib or loin pork chops
1 teaspoon rosemary
Salt and pepper to taste
2 cups chopped rhubarb (about 6 medium stalks)
1/4 cup orange juice
1 tablespoon brown sugar honey
1 tablespoon cornstarch
2 tablespoons cold water

Preheat the broiler.

Combine the rosemary, salt and pepper and rub over the chops. Place chops on a broiler rack sprayed with vegetable oil. Broil the meat about 10 minutes; then turn and broil other side, 5 to 10 minutes longer, or until they are cooked through.

Meanwhile, combine rhubarb, apple juice and brown sugar in a medium saucepan and heat to boiling. Reduce heat, cover and simmer until rhubarb is tender, about 10 minutes. In a small bowl, mix the cornstarch and water; stir into rhubarb. Heat to boiling; stir until thickened, about 1 minute. Serve the sauce over the pork chops.

Per serving: 441 calories, 24 grams fat, 151 milligrams cholesterol, 438 milligrams sodium.

THURSDAY

RAMEN NOODLES WITH PORK ASPARAGUS IN VINAIGRETTE*

Ramen noodles and leftover pork chops make a fast dinner. For the best flavor, discard the flavor packet that comes with the noodles and add flavor with any number of stir-fry or Oriental sauces available commercially. Most stores carry a few versions of stir-fry sauce in the Oriental section. The pepper-orange dressing made by Honeycup is especially nice. Leftover nappa cabbage would make a good addition.

RAMEN NOODLES WITH PORK

Makes 4 to 6 servings
Preparation time: 10 minutes
Cooking time: 8 to 10 minutes

1 tablespoon peanut oil
1 teaspoon fresh ginger, peeled and grated

1 teaspoon minced garlic in oil
1 cup snow peas, trimmed
2 4-ounce packages ramen noodles
1 14 1/2-ounce can chicken or beef
   broth
1/2 to 1 cup cooked pork, cut into
   chunks
2 tablespoons stir-fry or pepper-
   orange dressing

In a wok or deep skillet, heat the peanut oil. Saute the ginger, garlic and snow peas for 1 minute. Add the noodles, broth and pork, cover and cook 5 to 8 minutes, until the noodles are soft and have absorbed most of the liquid. Remove from the heat and stir in the sauce.

Per serving: 162 calories, 9 grams fat, 16 milligrams cholesterol, 958 milligrams sodium.

FRIDAY

MACARONI AND CHEESE*
COLESLAW*
OATMEAL COOKIES*

Tonight's dinner is waiting at the deli counter in your grocery store. Choose from an array of pasta dishes, such as macaroni and cheese, that the kids will enjoy as much as you.

SATURDAY

GRILLED SALMON WITH
PORT-TARRAGON
BUTTER SAUCE
ROASTED POTATOES
AND GREEN BEANS*
STRAWBERRY-RHUBARB CRISP

This wonderful meal says spring, from the robust port sauce to the divine rhubarb crisp that ends the meal. Roast potatoes (prefer-

ably Yukon Gold), along with green beans, a little olive oil, salt and pepper. These beans are so good they may not make it to the table.

GRILLED SALMON WITH PORT-TARRAGON BUTTER SAUCE

Makes 4 servings
Preparation time: 15 minutes
Cooking time: 10 minutes

4 6- to 8-ounce salmon steaks,
   cut 1 inch thick
Salt and black pepper to taste
1/3 cup dry port
1/4 cup (tightly packed)
   fresh tarragon
1 large shallot, minced
1/4 cup beef broth
1 stick cold butter, cut into
   tablespoons
1 teaspoon hazelnut or walnut oil
   (or olive oil)
Extra tarragon sprigs for garnish

Light a grill or preheat the broiler. Season the salmon steaks well with salt and pepper and set aside.

To prepare the sauce, combine the port, tarragon, shallot and beef broth in a small saucepan. Bring to a boil over high heat, skimming off any foam that rises to the surface. Boil until the liquid is reduced to 2 tablespoons, about 5 minutes. Remove from the heat and whisk in the cold butter, 1 tablespoon at a time, until the sauce is smooth and thickened.

Rub the salmon steaks with the hazelnut or walnut oil and grill, turning once, until crusty brown on the outside and rosy-pink inside, about 10 minutes total (or broil the steaks 5 minutes per side).

Reheat the sauce, stirring constantly, over very low heat,

but don't let it boil. Serve the steaks with the sauce napped over and garnish with extra tarragon sprigs.

Per serving: 611 calories, 39 grams fat, 160 milligrams cholesterol, 403 milligrams sodium.

STRAWBERRY-RHUBARB CRISP

Makes 6 to 8 servings
Preparation time: 15 minutes
Cooking time: 1 hour

1 cup slivered almonds
1 cup all-purpose flour
1 cup (packed) brown sugar
1 teaspoon salt
1 stick cold, unsalted butter, cut
   into pieces
8 stalks rhubarb, ends trimmed
1 pint strawberries, washed, hulled
   and halved
1/3 to 1/4 cup sugar
2 tablespoons all-purpose flour

Preheat the oven to 350 degrees. Toast the almonds in the oven until slightly browned, 6 to 8 minutes. Cool and chop coarsely.

In a food processor, process together the flour, brown sugar, salt and almonds. Add the cold butter pieces and pulse until it makes crumbs the size of coarse meal.

Toss fruit with the sugar and flour until evenly coated, then transfer to a 8-by 8-inch baking pan. Sprinkle the top with the almond mixture. Bake for 1 hour or until bubbly and crisp on top. Serve warm with (optional) ice cream.

Per serving (6 servings): 544 calories, 26 grams fat, 41 milligrams cholesterol, 96 milligrams sodium.

WEEK 20

SHOPPING LIST

Meat, poultry, seafood

- ❏ 4 8-to 10-ounce steaks
- ❏ 4 ounces country ham pieces
- ❏ 4 6-to 8-ounce grouper fillets, all bones removed
- ❏ $^{1}/_{2}$ ounce caviar (optional)

Produce

- ❏ 12 large ears sweet corn (or substitute 4 cups frozen corn for 4-5 ears of the fresh)
- ❏ 1 pound large carrots
- ❏ 1 clove garlic
- ❏ 2 yellow onions
- ❏ 1 large Vidalia onion
- ❏ 4 cups (packed) bitter greens (arugula, turnip, mustard or dandelion)
- ❏ 3 $^{1}/_{2}$ pounds new potatoes
- ❏ 1 hot chili pepper
- ❏ 1 head romaine lettuce

- ❏ 1 large tomato
- ❏ 2 lemons
- ❏ 1 bunch basil
- ❏ 1 bunch mint
- ❏ 2 bunches chives

Dairy

- ❏ $^{1}/_{3}$ cup light sour cream or creme fraiche
- ❏ 4 ounces cream cheese
- ❏ 3 sticks plus 3 tablespoons unsalted butter
- ❏ 17 eggs
- ❏ 1 pint black cherry frozen yogurt
- ❏ 1/2 cup milk

Deli

- ❏ 8 to 10 ounces assorted cheeses
- ❏ 4 ounces pepper-covered cheese
- ❏ 1 cup freshly grated Parmesan cheese
- ❏ 4 sesame seed buns

- ❏ 1 loaf cheese bread
- ❏ 2 loaves crusty bread

Miscellaneous

- ❏ $^{3}/_{4}$ pound sturdy pasta, such as fusilli, shells or penne
- ❏ 4 anchovy fillets (for Caesar salad)
- ❏ 4 ounces unsweetened chocolate
- ❏ 1 cup walnut pieces
- ❏ 1 cup raspberry preserves
- ❏ 8 slices sandwich bread

Staples

- ❏ All-purpose flour
- ❏ Black pepper, freshly ground
- ❏ Cornmeal
- ❏ Dijon mustard
- ❏ Dried red pepper flakes
- ❏ Granulated sugar
- ❏ Olive oil
- ❏ Peanut oil

- ❏ Pure vanilla extract
- ❏ Salt
- ❏ Self-rising flour
- ❏ Tartar sauce
- ❏ Walnut oil
- ❏ Wine vinegar, herb-infused

* Suggested accompaniments

SUNDAY

GRILLED STEAKS *
PICNIC CARROTS WITH WALNUT VINAIGRETTE
SWEET CORN GRILLED IN THE HUSK *
LEMON CREAM CHEESE POUNDCAKE

If you plan your holiday cookout today, this menu will provide the perfect feast. Soak the corn in salt-water 30 minutes before cooking, then dot the cooked corn with basil or fresh mint leaves. Cook extra corn for later in the week. Grease the cake pan with butter or shortening rather than pan spray; because butter is thicker, it will hold more sugar to the sides of the cake pan. Because the cake is so moist, it will stay moist for days.

PICNIC CARROTS WITH WALNUT VINAIGRETTE

Makes 8 servings
Preparation time: 30 minutes

2 tablespoons fruity vinegar, such as raspberry
1 tablespoon Dijon mustard
$^1/_4$ teaspoon granulated sugar
$^1/_4$ teaspoon salt
1 garlic clove, finely minced
2 tablespoons walnut oil
$^1/_4$ cup peanut oil
10 to 12 baby carrots, scrubbed and cut into julienne
$^1/_4$ cup finely chopped fresh basil or mint

Put the vinegar, mustard, sugar, salt and garlic in the workbowl of a food processor. With the machine running, slowly pour in the walnut and peanut oils until the dressing turns creamy. Place carrots and basil or mint in a medium-sized bowl. Set aside. Pour the vinaigrette over the carrots and toss. Chill slightly before serving.

Per serving: 118 calories, 10 grams fat, no cholesterol, 119 milligrams sodium.

LEMON CREAM CHEESE POUNDCAKE

Makes 10 servings
Preparation time: 20 minutes
Cooking time: 1 hour

1 cup granulated sugar
$^1/_4$ cup (2 ounces) cream cheese, at room temperature
$^1/_4$ cup (4 tablespoons) unsalted butter, room temperature
3 eggs
Peel of 1 lemon, Juice of 1 lemon
Pinch of salt
1 cup all-purpose flour
$^2/_3$ cup granulated sugar
$^2/_3$ cup water

Preheat oven to 350 degrees. Grease a 10-inch tube or bundt pan. Add a few tablespoons of sugar to the pan and rotate until a thick coat of sugar adheres to the sides, then tap out the excess.

Blend the cream cheese and butter with a mixer and cream until fluffy. Gradually add sugar and continue beating. Beat the mixture for 5 minutes. Add eggs one at a time and beat for 1 minute after each addition. Add the lemon peel, 1 tablespoon of lemon juice and salt. By hand, stir flour. Pour the batter into the pan and bake for 1 hour or until a knife inserted in the middle comes out dry.

Remove cake from oven and let rest 10 minutes, then remove from the cake pan and place on a serving plate. Poke holes in the cake with a toothpick. Drizzle the lemon syrup over the holes and let it absorb.

Per serving: 238 calories, 8 grams fat, 87 milligrams cholesterol, 93 milligrams sodium.

MONDAY

PASTA WITH SPRING GREENS AND FETA
CRUSTY BREAD *
LEMON CREAM CHEESE POUNDCAKE *

Pasta with a creamy bite — this is a great dish and an excellent spring tonic. Use the bitter green of your choice — arugula, dandelion, turnip, spinach, mustard or wonderful beet greens. (Collards will take too long for this dish.) Use good quality goat and Parmesan cheeses; they make a difference. Use miso for a salty flavor, found in Oriental markets and health food stores.

PASTA WITH SPRING GREENS AND FETA

Makes 4 servings
Preparation time: 10 minutes
Cooking time: 15 minutes

2 to 3 tablespoons olive oil
2 yellow onions, chopped (about 2 cups)
$^3/_4$ pound large, sturdy pasta, such as fusilli, shells or penne
4 cups (packed) bitter greens, washed, dried and coarsely chopped
Miso or salt to taste
4 ounces pepper-covered goat cheese, crumbled
Freshly grated Parmesan cheese, to taste
Freshly ground black pepper

Heat the oil in a deep skillet or wok over medium heat. Add the onions and cook until soft and fragrant, about 10 minutes. Meanwhile, cook the pasta until al dente.

Add the chopped greens to the skillet, and a teaspoon of miso or lightly salt. Stir-fry the greens just until they begin to wilt, less than 5 minutes, depending on the greens used, then add the crumbled cheese. Drain the cooked pasta and stir into the mixture in the skillet. Mix the ingredients and cook for a few more minutes on low heat. Sprinkle each serving with Parmesan cheese and black pepper.

Per serving: 397 calories, 14 grams fat, 25 milligrams cholesterol, 362 milligrams sodium.

TUESDAY

POTATO SALAD WITH COUNTRY HAM
FRIED EGG SANDWICHES*
CARROT STICKS*

Serve this homey meal when comfort food is at the top of your wish list. The potato salad is best served warm; almost as good at room temperature. Add chopped green onions if you wish. Most grocery stores now sell small packages, about a half-pound, of country ham bits, and they are perfect for seasoning potato salad or simmering with grits. Reserve any leftover country ham in the freezer to flavor later dishes.

POTATO SALAD WITH COUNTRY HAM

Makes 8 servings
Preparation time: 5 minutes
Cooking time: 15 minutes

3 1/2 pounds new potatoes, sliced
    1/4-inch thick, unpeeled
Salt
1/4 pound thin country ham pieces,
    cut in 1-inch pieces
2 to 3 tablespoons wine vinegar,
    herb-infused if possible
2 to 3 tablespoons olive oil
Black pepper, to taste

Bring a large pot of water to a boil. Add the potatoes and salt; return to boil and cook about 15 minutes or until the potatoes are soft but still hold together. When cooked, drain the potatoes, place them back in the pot and turn the heat on low just long enough to evaporate the water still on the potatoes.

Meanwhile, in a small skillet, fry the country ham. Set aside.

Spoon the cooked ham and drippings onto the potatoes and toss. Drizzle with vinegar and olive oil, and pepper to taste.

Per serving: 236 calories, 6 grams fat, 4 milligrams cholesterol, 171 milligrams sodium.

WEDNESDAY

FRIED GROUPER SANDWICH
POTATO SALAD WITH COUNTRY HAM*
BLACK CHERRY FROZEN YOGURT*

For tonight's summery meal, toss any leftover potato salad with leftover vegetables: broccoli, sprouts or celery. Grouper is a great fish on the grill, but you can also pan-fry or broil it. Serve with lettuce, tomatoes and tartar sauce on a sesame seed bun. Finish with black cherry frozen yogurt.

FRIED GROUPER SANDWICH

Makes 4 servings
Preparation time: 5 minutes
Cooking time: 10 minutes

4 6- to 8-ounce grouper fillets with
    all bones removed
2 tablespoons olive or vegetable oil
Salt and black pepper to taste
4 sesame seed buns
Lettuce, tomato slices, tartar sauce

Preheat the grill or broiler. Pat the fish fillets dry, then brush each with a little of the oil. Season to taste with salt and pepper. Cook on one side 4 to 5 minutes, then turn and cook on the other 4 or 5 minutes or until the flesh flakes. Serve immediately on buns with lettuce, tomato slices and tartar sauce.

Per serving: 336 calories, 11 grams fat, 65 milligrams cholesterol, 292 milligrams sodium.

THURSDAY

FRIED CORN
CARROTS WITH WALNUT VINAIGRETTE*
TOASTED CHEESE BREAD*

Take advantage of low prices on delicious Florida sweet corn this week. Fried corn, which is really

barely sauteed, tastes as good as it sounds, and makes a perfect supper dish. Use fresh or frozen corn. Add leftover carrot salad and cheese bread from the supermarket bakery.

FRIED CORN

Makes 4 servings
Preparation time: 10 minutes
Cooking time: 5-8 minutes

4 cups fresh or frozen and thawed
    corn kernels
1 large sweet Vidalia onion, sliced
    into thin rings
2 to 3 tablespoons unsalted butter
Salt and ground pepper to taste
Dried red pepper flakes or seeded and
    minced hot fresh chili pepper to
    taste
2 or 3 tablespoons fresh basil or mint,
    minced

Melt the butter in a large skillet and add the onions. Cook until soft and fragrant, about 5 minutes. Add the corn, salt and pepper to taste and red pepper flakes or hot chili pepper and fry just until the corn is hot and gives up a bit of its liquid, 3 or 4 minutes. Toss with the herbs and serve.

Per serving: 211 calories, 7 grams fat, 15 milligrams cholesterol, 7 milligrams sodium.

FRIDAY

VEGETABLE SOUP *
SESAME CRACKERS *
LEMON CREAM CHEESE POUNDCAKE *

Try your grocery store's salad bar for tonight's quick pickup soup. Add crackers and leftover cake from earlier in the week.

SATURDAY

SCOTT'S CORNCAKES
CAESAR SALAD *
CHEESE PLATTER *
CRUSTY BREAD *
RASPBERRY BROWNIES

Price: Prices range from $6.99 to $7.99 a pound.

Nutrition: Grouper is a low-fat fish with 92 calories, 1 gram fat, 37 milligrams cholesterol, and 247 milligrams Omega-3 fatty acids per 3 1/2-ounce serving.

Selection: Fillets range in size from 12 ounces to one pound and are thicker than red snapper fillets, which increases cooking time.

Storage: Store in the coldest part of the refrigerator for 2 or 3 days.

Uses: It is good in chowders, fried, microwaved or grilled and makes a good replacement in recipes calling for cod, haddock, porgy, snapper, halibut or chicken breast.

Red Grouper, a member of the sea bass family and first cousin to red snapper, is plentiful now and waiting for the frying pan. Although grouper is available year-round, it is at its best quality and lowest prices starting now through the warmer months. From early spring through fall, grouper comes fresh from Florida; after that, the fish migrate south, and we get more expensive imports from Central and South America.

Grouper is a lean fish with firm white meat and mild flavor. While it can be prepared in sophisticated dishes, my personal favorite is fried and served in a sandwich, and preferably in a beach shack on some warm, sunny Florida coast.

Chef Scott Peacock's delicate corncakes make a delicious light dinner course. Topped with sour cream and caviar, they could also be impressive finger fare for parties. Delicate Georgia sturgeon caviar is delicious and a fraction of the cost of Beluga caviar. It is being harvested off the Georgia coast now, and is available in 24 hours by special request at most grocery store seafood counters. Any available caviar will do, however. The corncakes should be fried in a hot skillet, and are best cooked in clarified butter to prevent the milk solids from burning. It's easy to clarify butter in the microwave: Melt 4 tablespoons and scoop the bubbling milk solids off the top. Don't miss these brownies; they are perfect for this meal, but also pack into picnics and lunch boxes.

SCOTT'S CORNCAKES

Makes 8 servings
Preparation time: 5 minutes
Standing time: Up to an hour
Cooking time: 10 minutes

1 cup cooked corn, pureed (3 large ears)
2 eggs
2 egg yolks
1/2 cup milk
1/4 cup unsalted butter, melted and cooled, plus clarified butter for frying
1/3 cup all-purpose flour
1/3 cup cornmeal
1 teaspoon salt
1/4 teaspoon black pepper
2 tablespoons chopped chives
1/4 cup chopped chives for garnish
1/3 cup light sour cream (or creme fraiche)
1/2 ounce caviar (optional)

To puree the corn, cut cooked corn from the cobs and pulse in a food processor. Stir in the eggs, egg yolks, milk and cooled, melted butter. In a separate bowl combine the flour, cornmeal, salt and black pepper. Stir the two mixtures together and refrigerate the batter for up to one hour.

Just before cooking, stir in the 2 tablespoons of chopped chives. In a hot skillet with small amounts of clarified butter, fry silver-dollar-sized pancakes. Cook 1 minute or until bubbles appear on the tops of the pancakes, turn and cook 1 minute on the other side. Remove from the pan.

To serve, dollop each corncake with a teaspoon of sour cream and a tiny amount of caviar. Place on a large serving platter and snip chives over the top.

Per serving: 174 calories, 11 grams fat, 154 milligrams cholesterol, 336 milligrams sodium.

RASPBERRY BROWNIES

Makes 16 brownies
Preparation time: 20 minutes
Freezing time: 30 minutes
Cooking time: 45 minutes

4 ounces unsweetened chocolate
1 stick (8 ounces) unsalted butter
1 teaspoon pure vanilla extract
2 cups granulated sugar
4 eggs
1 cup self-rising flour
1 cup walnut pieces
1 cup raspberry preserves

Grease a 9-by-13-inch baking pan.

Put the chocolate in a microwave-safe dish, cover and microwave on high (100 percent power) for 1 1/2 minutes; add the butter, re-cover and microwave on high for 30 seconds more. Add the salt, vanilla and sugar and mix well. Add the eggs one at a time, mixing after each one. Add the flour and beat until smooth. Stir in the walnut pieces.

Pour half the batter into the prepared baking pan and smooth it into an even surface with a spatula. Put the pan in the freezer for 30 minutes to firm the batter.

Preheat the oven. Remove the batter from the freezer and spread the preserves over the batter in an even layer. Pour the remaining batter over the preserves and gently smooth it level.

Bake for 40 to 45 minutes. Cook the brownies for 10 minutes before cutting, then cut and cool on a wire rack.

Per serving: 384 calories, 20 grams fat, 99 milligrams cholesterol, 171 milligrams sodium.

WEEK

21

SHOPPING LIST

Meat, poultry, seafood

- ❑ 8 soft-shell crabs, pre-cleaned
- ❑ 2 pounds (approximately) chicken leg quarters
- ❑ 1 ½ pounds catfish fillets

Produce

- ❑ 2 heads red leaf lettuce
- ❑ 2 bunches broccoli
- ❑ 1 medium zucchini
- ❑ 4 medium yellow onions
- ❑ 4 ounces mushrooms
- ❑ 1 bunch fresh spinach
- ❑ 3 pounds green beans
- ❑ 1 pound asparagus
- ❑ 1 pound jicama
- ❑ 1 pint cherry tomatoes
- ❑ 1 12-ounce package baby carrots
- ❑ 3 large carrots
- ❑ 1 medium rutabaga, about ³/₄ pound
- ❑ 1 bell pepper, green or

red
- ❑ 3 cloves garlic
- ❑ 1 bunch Italian parsley
- ❑ 1 bunch tarragon
- ❑ 2 lemons

Dairy

- ❑ 1 stick margarine
- ❑ 1 stick plus 5 tablespoons butter
- ❑ 1 pint (2 cups) part-skim ricotta cheese
- ❑ 6 ounces shredded Cheddar cheese
- ❑ ¹/₄ cup grated Parmesan cheese
- ❑ 10 eggs

Deli

- ❑ 2 loaves crusty bread
- ❑ 4 bran muffins
- ❑ 4 brownies
- ❑ 1 pound sliced roast beef

Miscellaneous

- ❑ 1 pound lasagna noodles
- ❑ 2 cups rice
- ❑ 1 quart jar marinara sauce, such as Prego
- ❑ 1 12-ounce can beer
- ❑ 8 slices thick-sliced bread
- ❑ 2 cups mayonnaise
- ❑ 1 tablespoon capers
- ❑ ¹/₄ cup beef broth
- ❑ 1 10-ounce can water chestnuts
- ❑ ¹/₄ cup pecans
- ❑ 1 or 2 tablespoons dark miso (optional)

Staples

- ❑ All-purpose flour
- ❑ Baking powder
- ❑ Balsamic vinegar
- ❑ Black pepper
- ❑ Confectioners' sugar
- ❑ Dill pickles
- ❑ Dried basil

- ❑ Dried oregano
- ❑ Dried thyme
- ❑ Granulated sugar
- ❑ Ground cayenne pepper
- ❑ Honey mustard
- ❑ Olive oil
- ❑ Paprika
- ❑ Prepared mustard
- ❑ Salt
- ❑ Vegetable oil
- ❑ Wine vinegar

* Suggested accompaniments

SUNDAY

VEGETABLE LASAGNA
MIXED GREEN SALAD *
CRUSTY BREAD *

Try this delicious vegetable lasagna as it is served at the American Roadhouse in Atlanta. Cook the pasta until very soft, beyond al dente, and the resulting dish will be tender enough to melt in your mouth. Serve the pasta with a green salad tossed with onion and any extra herbs, and crusty bread. Save extra portions of lasagna to serve later in the week.

VEGETABLE LASAGNA

Makes 8 servings
Preparation time: 20 minutes
Cooking time: 45 minutes

1/2 pound lasagna noodles
1/2 stick (4 tablespoons) margarine
1/2 stick (4 tablespoons) unsalted butter
1 large stalk broccoli, cut into florets
1 medium zucchini, sliced
1 medium yellow onion, chopped
1/4 cup sliced mushrooms, chopped
1/2 teaspoon each salt, dried basil, thyme, oregano
3 cups to 1 quart marinara (tomato) sauce, such as Prego
1 cup fresh spinach, deribbed and roughly chopped
2 cups part-skim ricotta cheese
2 cups part-skim mozzarella
1/4 cup grated Parmesan cheese

Bring a pot of water to a boil; add 1 tablespoon vegetable oil. Add the noodles and cook until soft, about 10 minutes. Drain and rinse the noodles under cold water and set aside.

Melt the margarine and but-ter in a large skillet and add the broccoli, zucchini, onion and mushrooms. Sprinkle the salt and dried seasonings over the vegetables and saute until crisp-tender, about 5 minutes. Remove the vegetables from the margarine with a slotted spoon and set aside.

To make the lasagna layers: spoon 1/2 cup marinara sauce into the bottom of a 9-by-13-inch baking pan and spread it evenly. Sprinkle 1/4 cup mozzarella cheese over the marinara sauce. Place one layer of noodles side-by-side over the cheese. Sprinkle half the cooked vegetables and half the (uncooked) spinach over noodles in an even layer, then spread 1/2 cup ricotta and 1 more cup marinara sauce. Sprinkle on 1/2 cup mozzarella cheese, cover with lasagna noodles. Repeat the layers with 1 cup ricotta, 1/2 cup marinara, 1/4 cup mozzarella, 1/4 cup Parmesan cheese, and the remaining vegetables, spinach and ricotta. Sprinkle remaining mozzarella over all. Bake at 325 degrees for 30 minutes.

Per serving: 324 calories, 21 grams fat, 49 milligrams cholesterol, 495 milligrams sodium.

MONDAY

BEER BATTERED AND FRIED
SOFT SHELL CRABS ON
TEXAS TOAST
HOT TARTAR SAUCE
FRIED ONION RINGS *
STEAMED GREEN BEANS
AND ASPARAGUS *

Just the thing to open the sum-mer season this Memorial Day: soft shell crabs, sweet and newly in-season. Most local grocery stores are now carrying pre-cleaned crabs, and they make an effortless and special meal. The following recipe dips the crabs in a tangy beer batter. In fact, dip the onion rings in the remaining batter to fry them, too. Don't forget to make the accompanying tartar sauce to serve with the crabs. Microwave 1 pound of asparagus and 2 pounds of green beans to have plenty for tomorrow night's dinner.

BEER BATTERED AND FRIED SOFT SHELL CRABS ON TEXAS TOAST

Makes 4 servings
Preparation time: 5 minutes
Cooking time: 20 minutes

1 1/4 cups all-purpose flour (lightly spoon into cup)
2 teaspoons salt
1 teaspoon paprika
1/2 teaspoon baking powder
1 12-ounce can warm beer
Vegetable oil
All-purpose flour
8 soft shell crabs, patted dry
8 slices thick-sliced white bread

To make the batter, stir together the flour, salt, paprika and baking powder, then whisk in the beer. Make the batter at least 1 to 2 hours in advance, as it will thicken as it stands.

Heat vegetable oil in a deep iron skillet or other frying pan to 375 degrees. Dust the crabs lightly with additional flour, then dip in the batter. Lay the crabs in the pan in a single layer and fry the crab 2 to 5 minutes, until golden brown. Drain well.

Price: Will range from $2.39 to $2.99 each.

Nutrition: A 3 1/2-ounce raw portion has 81 calories and 1 gram fat.

Selection: Choose plump, fresh, unfrozen crabs. For convenience, choose crabs with the lungs, mouth, eyes and spongy gill tissue removed. Crabs that have been precleaned will have a shelf life of 4 to 5 days, a couple of days longer than crabs you might buy that have not been precleaned.

Storage: Place crabs in a covered dish or plastic container and cover with moist paper towels. Add a couple of ice cubes before replacing the lid. Store in the coldest part of the refrigerator, such as the meat drawer.

Uses: Soft shell crabs can be grilled, sauteed, fried or broiled, and are served alone with a tartar sauce or, for a more informal dinner, in a sandwich. Microwaving is not recommended. Plan on serving two small or one large crab per person in a sandwich or as an entree.

Soft shell crabs are a sign of the season. The sweet and juicy crabs are a favorite spring dish that Easterners look forward to all winter long. The crunchy soft crabs are cooked, often pan-fried, and eaten whole. The peak season for soft shell crabs is May, when the waters of the Chesapeake Bay warm. Soft shell crabs can come from up and down the Atlantic ocean and the Gulf of Mexico, but eighty percent still come from the Chesapeake Bay.

Meanwhile, toast the bread until golden brown and serve at once with crabs and tartar sauce.

Per serving: 422 calories, 14 grams fat, 82 milligrams cholesterol, 1,252 milligrams sodium.

HOT TARTAR SAUCE

Makes 1 cup
Preparation time: 10 minutes

1 cup prepared mayonnaise
1 teaspoon chopped Italian parsley
2 tablespoons minced dill pickle
1 tablespoon drained capers, minced
1 tablespoon onion, minced
1 clove garlic, minced
Dash cayenne pepper
Salt and black pepper to taste

Put the parsley, dill pickle, capers, onion and garlic in the workbowl of a food processor and pulse until the ingredients are minced. Stir in the mayonnaise, cayenne, and salt and pepper. Refrigerated, this will keep for a week.

Per 1 tablespoon serving: 101 calories, 11 grams fat, 8 milligrams cholesterol, 98 milligrams sodium.

TUESDAY

GREEN BEAN AND JICAMA SALAD
DEVILED EGGS *
BRAN MUFFINS *

Fresh green beans and crunchy jicama make a good salad combination and an easy weeknight dinner. Save the leftovers for a meal later in the week. Add deviled eggs, or simply boiled eggs if that is all you have time to prepare, along with purchased bran muffins.

GREEN BEAN AND JICAMA SALAD

Makes 8 servings
Preparation time: 10 minutes

VINAIGRETTE:
1/4 teaspoon salt
1/8 teaspoon black pepper
3 tablespoons balsamic vinegar
1 tablespoon lemon juice
3 3/4 cup vegetable or olive oil

SALAD:
2 pounds green beans, trimmed and cooked
1 pound jicama, pared and cut in julienne strips
1 pint cherry tomatoes, halved
1 head red leaf lettuce

To make vinaigrette, combine salt, pepper, vinegar and lemon juice in a food processor. With motor running, pour in oil in a thin, steady stream.

Place green beans in a large bowl. Add jicama, tomatoes and toss together. Put lettuce leaves on salad plates and spoon bean mixture over.

Per serving (assuming 2/3 of dressing used): 159 calories, 13 grams fat, no cholesterol, 97 milligrams sodium.

WEDNESDAY

GRILLED CHICKEN LEG QUARTERS WITH HONEY MUSTARD*
STEAMED RICE*
BUTTERY BROCCOLI STIR-FRY

Prepare the broccoli stir-fry with beef broth, or substitute a tablespoon of dark miso and a cup of water. Miso is a fermented soybean paste, available in health food stores and Oriental markets.

It tastes remarkably like beef without the meat. Substitute jicama for the water chestnuts if you prefer. Cook extra rice for dinner Saturday night.

BUTTERY BROCCOLI STIR-FRY

Makes 8 servings
Preparation time: 15 minutes
Cooking time: 15 minutes

1/4 cup butter or margarine
1 tablespoon sugar
1 teaspoon salt
1/4 cup beef broth or dark miso
1 12-ounce package baby carrots, scrubbed
3/4 pound fresh rutabaga, pared and diced
1 large bunch broccoli, stems peeled and diced and florets cut in small pieces
1 10-ounce can water chestnuts, drained and rinsed
1 bell pepper, red or green, cut into 1-inch squares

In a large skillet, melt the butter. Add sugar and salt; stir to dissolve the sugar. Add broth, carrots and rutabagas; bring to a boil, turn heat down to a simmer and cook 4 minutes.

Add the broccoli, chestnuts and peppers and continue to cook, covered, for 5 to 7 minutes or until the vegetables are tender-crisp. Remove the lid and boil 2 more minutes to reduce the liquid, if necessary.

Per serving: 118 calories, 6 grams fat, 15 milligrams cholesterol, 391 milligrams sodium.

THURSDAY

VEGETABLE LASAGNA *
GARLIC BREAD
BROWNIES *

Serve the remaining portions of vegetable lasagna tonight, along with homemade garlic bread and purchased brownies. The garlic bread tastes even better when cooked on the outdoor grill.

GARLIC BREAD

Makes 8 servings
Preparation time: 10 minutes
Cooking time: 10 minutes

1 pound loaf Italian bread,
　　unsliced
1/4 cup good quality olive oil
1/4 cup (packed) Italian parsley
2 cloves garlic, finely minced
1/4 teaspoon salt (optional)

Preheat oven to 400 degrees.
　　Put the garlic in the workbowl of a food processor and process until finely minced. Add the olive oil, parsley and salt and pulse again.
　　Split the loaf in half lengthwise and spread both halves with the mixture. Place the halves back together and wrap in aluminum foil. Place on baking sheet and bake for 10 to 15 minutes or until heated through.
　　Per serving: 221 calories, 7 grams fat, no cholesterol, 288 milligrams sodium.

FRIDAY

ROAST BEEF SANDWICHES *
GLAZED BROCCOLI MELANGE*
GREEN BEAN AND

JICAMA SALAD *

Pick up the makings for roast beef sandwiches from the deli section of the grocery store, and add leftover salads from the refrigerator.

SATURDAY

SAUTEED CATFISH FILLETS *
TARRAGON-SCENTED
CARROTS
STIR-FRIED RICE WITH
PECANS AND PARSLEY *
BLUEBERRY AND LEMON
CHEESE PIE

Catfish fillets can be sauteed while the carrots cook and leftover rice from Wednesday's dinner reheats with chopped pecans and parsley. Add the following Blueberry and Lemon Cheese pie, compliments of cookbook author and friend Nathalie Dupree. Also called lemon conserve, lemon curd is available at some grocery stores and all specialty stores, or you can use the recipe below to make your own.

TARRAGON-SCENTED CARROTS

Makes 4 servings
Preparation time: 5 minutes
Cooking time: 12 minutes

3 large carrots, thinly sliced (2 cups)
1/2 Vidalia onion, thinly sliced into
　　rings
1 tablespoon fresh tarragon
2 tablespoons water
Salt and freshly ground black pepper
1 teaspoon butter

Heat a medium non-stick skillet.

Place carrots and onion in the dish; sprinkle with tarragon, water and pepper to taste. Cover and microwave on high (100 percent power) for 10 to 12 minutes, or until tender. Stir in butter and salt to taste.
　　Per serving: 83 calories, 6 grams fat, 15 milligrams cholesterol, 78 milligrams sodium.

BLUEBERRY AND LEMON CHEESE PIE

Makes 6 to 8 servings
Preparation time: 5 minutes

2 cups heavy cream
1 9-inch prebaked pie crust
1/2 pint blueberries
2 cups lemon curd or lemon cheese
　　(see recipe below)

Whip the cream and set aside. Fill the prebaked pie crust with the blueberries. Mix the lemon cheese with the whipped cream and top the blueberries with the mixture. Serve within a few hours or freeze.
　　Per serving (one-eighth of pie): 486 calories, 38 grams fat, 188 milligrams cholesterol, 299 milligrams sodium.

LEMON CHEESE

Makes 2 1/2 cups
Preparation time: 10 minutes
Cooking time: 10 minutes

1 cup sugar
1/2 cup butter
Grated rind and strained juice of 3
　　lemons (3 tablespoons rind and
　　1/2 cup juice)
3 eggs, beaten to mix

Place the sugar, butter, lemon rind and juice, and eggs in a heavy saucepan and cook gently over low heat until the mixture is thick but still falls easily from a spoon, 8 to 10 minutes. Do not boil or the mixture will separate.

Remove from the heat and cool. Store in the refrigerator in a tightly covered jar or freeze. Because of the high acidity, the mixture will keep indefinitely in the refrigerator.

WEEK

22

SHOPPING LIST

Meat, poultry, chicken

- ❏ 2 3-pound chickens
- ❏ 2 large ham steaks
- ❏ 5 squid bodies (about ⅓ to ½ pound)

Produce

- ❏ 3 pounds new potatoes
- ❏ 1 pound carrots
- ❏ 4 ripe tomatoes
- ❏ 2 large yellow (or red) tomatoes
- ❏ 1 pound green beans
- ❏ 1 cup cauliflower florets
- ❏ 1 Vidalia onion
- ❏ 2 ribs celery (or lovage)
- ❏ 1 bunch green onions
- ❏ 1 red bell pepper
- ❏ 2 zucchini
- ❏ 1 cup mushrooms
- ❏ 2 lemons
- ❏ 1 bunch fresh parsley
- ❏ 1 bunch basil
- ❏ 1 shallot

- ❏ 2 garlic cloves
- ❏ 2 tablespoons tarragon
- ❏ 3 to 3 ½ pounds fresh Bing cherries, stems attached
- ❏ 1 pint blackberries

Dairy

- ❏ 3 ¼ cups buttermilk
- ❏ ¼ cup butter
- ❏ 3 ¼ cups buttermilk
- ❏ ¾ cup low-fat plain yogurt
- ❏ ¼ cup low-fat milk
- ❏ 2 ½ cups whole milk or half-and-half
- ❏ 3 eggs
- ❏ ½ pint (1 cup) sour cream

Deli

- ❏ 1 loaf crusty bread
- ❏ 2 ounces shredded mozzarella cheese

- ❏ 2 to 3 tablespoons grated Parmesan cheese

Miscellaneous

- ❏ 2 cups long-grain white rice
- ❏ 1 4-ounce can pitted black olives
- ❏ ½ cup corn kernels, canned or frozen
- ❏ 3 to 4 tablespoons amaretto liqueur
- ❏ 2 tablespoons slivered almonds
- ❏ 3 tablespoons Kirsch
- ❏ 8 to 10 ounces dry spaghetti
- ❏ 8 ounces dry lemon fettucine
- ❏ 1 tablespoon crystallized ginger

Staples

- ❏ All-purpose flour

- ❏ Black pepper
- ❏ Confectioners' sugar
- ❏ Granulated sugar
- ❏ Ground cloves
- ❏ Lemon juice
- ❏ Minced garlic
- ❏ Olive oil
- ❏ Raspberry vinegar
- ❏ Salt
- ❏ Sugar
- ❏ Vegetable oil
- ❏ Vinaigrette

* Suggested accompaniments

SUNDAY

BUTTERMILK CHICKEN
STEAMED RICE*
STEAMED ZUCCHINI*
CHERRY FLAN

A buttermilk marinade makes chicken tender, and the following recipe provides leftovers. Add simple side dishes — steamed rice (cook 2 extra cups to use later in the week), and a classic summer dessert when cherries are in season, a French clafouti or cherry flan. It's not necessary to pit the cherries for this dessert, but do alert your guests to their presence.

BUTTERMILK CHICKEN

Makes 8 servings
Preparation time: 20 minutes
Cooking time: 1 hour

2 3-pound chickens, cut in pieces
3 cups buttermilk
1 cup all-purpose flour
2 teaspoons salt
Black pepper, to taste
1/4 cup fresh parsley, roughly
    chopped
1/4 cup vegetable oil
1/4 cup butter

Put chicken pieces in a large dish and pour buttermilk over. Refrigerate 2 to 3 hours or longer, and turn a couple of times if you can.
    Preheat oven to 350 degrees.
    Put flour, salt, pepper and parsley in a paper bag or shallow dish and dredge chicken pieces in the mixture.
    Heat oil and butter in a heavy skillet and brown the chicken pieces. Place the browned chicken pieces in a large, flat baking dish, pour the remaining buttermilk over the chicken and bake for 1 hour.
    Per serving: 671 calories, 37 grams fat, 195 milligrams cholesterol, 789 milligrams sodium.

CHERRY FLAN

Makes 6 to 8 servings
Preparation time: 10 minutes
Cooking time: 35 to 45 minutes

3/4 cup all-purpose flour
1/2 cup granulated sugar
1/8 teaspoon salt
3 large eggs
3 tablespoons Kirsch
2 cups whole milk or half-and-half
1 pound fresh cherries, stemmed
Confectioners' sugar for sprinkling

Preheat oven to 400 degrees. Grease or butter a deep-dish pie pan or 8-by-8-inch baking dish.
    In a mixing bowl, combine the flour, sugar and salt. Gradually beat in the eggs one at a time. Add the Kirsch and milk and beat vigorously until the mixture is smooth.
    Spread out the cherries in the buttered pie pan. Pour on the batter and place in the oven. Lower oven heat to 350 degrees. Bake for 35 to 45 minutes or until the flan is browned and crusty around the edges but still soft in the center. Cool on a rack until lukewarm, then serve, sprinkled with confectioners' sugar.
    Per serving: 265 calories, 6 grams fat, 148 milligrams cholesterol, 127 milligrams sodium.

MONDAY

VEGETABLE PASTA SALAD WITH LEMON VINAIGRETTE

CRUSTY BREAD*

Dinner in the summertime cries for cold food. Start the work week with this flavorful one. The citrus vinaigrette adds a cooling relief from the hot weather. Accompany the salad with a simple French, Italian or sourdough bread.

VEGETABLE PASTA SALAD WITH LEMON VINAIGRETTE

Makes 8 servings
Preparation time: 15 minutes
Cooking time: 8 minutes

1 pound green beans, cut in 1-inch
    pieces
1 cup cauliflower florets
1/2 Vidalia or other sweet onion,
    thinly sliced
3 or 4 large (1 to 2 cups sliced) ripe
    tomatoes
8 to 10 ounces dry spaghetti

LEMON VINAIGRETTE:
1/3 cup vegetable oil
2 tablespoons lemon juice
1 garlic clove, minced
1 teaspoon sugar
3 or tablespoons chopped fresh basil
Salt and black pepper to taste

Steam or microwave the green beans and cauliflower 5 to 8 minutes or until tender-crisp. Run them under cold water to stop the cooking. Cook the pasta in a large pot of salted water until al dente; then drain.
    Meanwhile, make the vinaigrette. Whisk together oil, lemon juice, garlic, sugar, salt and pepper to taste. In a large serving bowl, combine beans, cauliflower, onion, tomatoes, cooked pasta and lemon vinaigrette. Toss with basil; mix well and chill for several hours, if possible, before serving.

Per serving: 167 calories, 12 grams fat, no cholesterol, 6 milligrams sodium.

TUESDAY

BUTTERMILK TARRAGON CHICKEN SALAD STEAMED ZUCCHINI* CHERRY FLAN*

This chicken salad recipe is an eternal favorite, but no one knows the secret ingredient is the bite of buttermilk. If you have creme fraiche, its tangy flavor and creamy texture would make an excellent substitute for buttermilk. If you grow lovage in your garden, or see it in farmers markets, snap it up in place of the celery. It looks and grows just like celery, and its anise flavor complements the tarragon and really makes this a memorable dish. Serve the salad wrapped in lettuce leaves or in a traditional sandwich. Add leftover flan for dessert.

BUTTERMILK TARRAGON CHICKEN SALAD

Makes 4 to 6 servings
Preparation time: 15 minutes

4 chicken breast halves, cooked
$^1/_4$ cup buttermilk or creme fraiche
$^3/_4$ cup low-fat plain yogurt
2 celery ribs, cut into 1-inch long pencil strips
2 tablespoons slivered almonds
2 tablespoons fresh tarragon leaves
Salt and black pepper to taste

Shred chicken into bite-size pieces and place in a bowl. Whisk together the buttermilk and mayonnaise and pour over chicken. Add the celery,

JUNE

High summer is here, and with it comes a bounty of foods that we haven't seen since last season: cherries, early peaches, local shrimp. Florida produce is on the wane and produce harvests have started moving up both the Eastern and Western seaboards. Cucumbers, bell peppers, tomatoes and squash prices are fluctuating as growing areas all over the country change, moving from Florida to areas up the Eastern seaboard, and with similar movement on the Western coast. Potatoes are high now, except for new red potatoes. Some California long whites, a summer all-purpose potato with wonderful flavor, have started arriving. Blueberry prices have been exceptionally low and are now fluctuating up and down. The Carolina berries may be gone in just a couple of weeks. California white Perlette grapes are still sour this early in the season, but some Red Flame grapes now coming in are very tasty. A few end-of-the-season Vidalia onions are around, the rest put in storage to sell through the summer and fall.

Driscoll strawberries will be featured in several stores; their flavor is considered the best of commercial strawberries. Also look for Driscoll raspberries and blackberries.

almonds, tarragon, salt and pepper and toss well. Refrigerate, covered, for a few hours, if possible, to develop the tarragon flavor.

Per serving: 199 calories, 11 grams fat, 58 milligrams cholesterol, 76 milligrams sodium.

WEDNESDAY

HAM STEAK WITH CHERRIES NEW POTATOES WITH HERB BUTTER * CARROTS TOSSED WITH RASPBERRY VINEGAR*

This savory dish is a wonderful way to serve cherries. The sweet bite of the fruit and crystallized ginger matches perfectly with ham. Although cherries are in season and wonderful now, this dish can be made with canned cherries also. Look for crystallized ginger in the spice section of the grocery store. Toss roasted or microwaved potatoes with butter and minced chives. Cook 2 or 3 extra potatoes to serve later in the week.

HAM STEAK WITH CHERRIES

Makes 6 servings
Preparation time: 10 minutes
Cooking time: 15 minutes

2 large ham steaks, about $^1/_2$-inch thick
2 cups (about 1 pound unpitted) Bing cherries, pitted and diced
1 tablespoon chopped crystallized ginger

1 tablespoon granulated sugar
Dash ground cloves
1 tablespoon flour
$^1/_2$ cup water

In a large skillet, over medium heat, saute the ham slices 2 or 3 minutes on each side, until cooked through and slightly crisp. Remove and keep warm.

Meanwhile, pit the cherries and dice. Add them to the skillet with the ginger, sugar and cloves. Stir the flour into a small amount of water to form a paste, then whisk in remaining water. Add this mixture to pan. Cook, stirring, until the cherries cook down slightly and sauce thickens, about 7 to 10 minutes. Add more water if necessary. Serve sauce over ham.

Per serving: 329 calories, 14 grams fat, 84 milligrams cholesterol, 1530 milligrams sodium.

THURSDAY

DAN'S DINNER NUMBER ONE FRESH BLACKBERRIES AND CREAM*

It's easy to feed hungry people when you have a few set recipes, ones you can prepare automatically. This quick dinner, from my friend, Dan Papineau, adjusts easily to the number of people you want to feed and the contents of your refrigerator. Summer squash, celery, cucumbers, fresh basil or cilantro can also be tossed into the salad if you have them available. Reserve a couple of tablespoons chopped olives for Saturday night's dinner. Serve fresh berries — local fruit is available now and delicious served simply with cream or out-of-hand.

DAN'S DINNER NUMBER ONE

Makes 4 servings
Preparation time: 10 minutes

2 cups cooked and chilled rice
1 4-ounce can pitted black olives, drained
$^1/_2$ cup corn kernels, fresh or canned and drained
1 carrot, scrubbed and sliced thin
1 cup mushrooms, scrubbed and sliced
1 medium or large ripe red tomato, cut into sections
$^1/_4$ to $^1/_3$ cup vinaigrette
2 to 3 tablespoons grated Parmesan cheese

In a large bowl, combine rice, olives, corn, carrot, mushrooms, tomato and vinaigrette. Sprinkle the cheese over salad and serve.

Per serving: 237 calories, 14 grams fat, 2 milligrams cholesterol, 198 milligrams sodium.

FRIDAY

VEGETABLE PASTA SALAD*
CARROTS WITH RASPBERRY VINEGAR*
TARRAGON CHICKEN SALAD*

This week's leftovers may be the best yet. Bits of chicken salad and ham steak with cherries can be scooped up with lettuce leaves, and the carrots can be mixed with the pasta salad.

SATURDAY

LEMON FETTUCINE WITH CALAMARI, YELLOW TOMATOES AND GARLIC FOCACCIA*

CHERRIES DIPPED IN AMARETTO SOUR CREAM

Lemon fettucine adds a special tang to this already wonderful dish. Yellow tomatoes are widely available now, so take advantage of their mild flavor and low acid, but don't hesitate to substitute red tomatoes if necessary. Squid toughens if cooked too long, so keep that 1-minute cooking time firmly in mind. Pick up a focaccia — flat bread strewn with herbs before baking — at a local bakery or farmers' market. This simple cherry dessert does strawberries and sour cream one better: serve it while the fruits are at their best this month.

LEMON FETTUCINE WITH CALAMARI, YELLOW TOMATOES AND GARLIC

Makes 4 servings
Preparation time: 10 minutes
Cooking time: 15 minutes

1 tablespoon olive oil
2 cloves garlic, chopped
1 shallot, chopped
2 large yellow tomatoes, diced and dried on paper towels
$^1/_4$ cup or more fresh basil leaves, roughly chopped
Crushed red pepper flakes
Salt and black pepper to taste
8 ounces dried lemon fettuccine
5 squid bodies (about $^3/_4$ pound), cut into thin rings
2 to 3 tablespoons chopped black olives

Heat the olive oil in a deep skillet over medium heat. Add the garlic and shallots and saute 2 minutes. Add the tomatoes, basil and a pinch of crushed red pepper flakes. Add salt and pepper to taste and simmer a few minutes.

Meanwhile, cook the pasta.

Price: $1.99 a pound.

Nutrition: A four-ounce serving has 80 calories and is a good source of vitamin C.

Selection: Choose plump golden cherries with a red blush that are not bruised or broken.

Storage: Store cherries in the refrigerator, covered or uncovered, and eat within a day or two.

Uses: Eat Ranier cherries fresh, out of hand or in fruit salads.

Both the red Bing, black Lambert and golden Ranier cherry are in season and will be in farmers markets and some stores a few short weeks. The Ranier come later than the Bings and are sweeter and more delicate than the Bing or Lambert, and shouldn't be missed. They should be eaten fresh rather than in cooking. Look for sporadic supplies of sour cherries, usually coming from Michigan in late June. They aren't always available nationally, but are unexcelled for pies.

The delicate Ranier cherry is more expensive than red cherries. They aren't as risky to grow as other cherries, but require four or five successive picks from each tree and skilled pickers that won't exert too much pressure on each cherry as it is picked. Also, because the Ranier has more sugar content than other cherries, it is more perishable.

Bring a pot of salted water to a boil and add the pasta. Cook about 10 minutes or until al dente. Drain and add to the tomato sauce in the skillet.

Cut the squid into rings with scissors. Put the remaining tablespoon olive oil in a skillet and heat over high heat. Add the squid, season with salt and pepper and saute 1 minute. If the squid are large and thick-walled, they will take a few seconds longer to cook, but if you overcook them, they will turn rubbery. Immediately stir them into the tomato sauce. Serve immediately, garnished with the black olives.

Per serving: 333 calories, 8 grams fat, 89 milligrams cholesterol, 127 milligrams sodium.

CHERRIES WITH AMARETTO SOUR CREAM AND ALMONDS

Makes 4 servings
Preparation time: 10-15 minutes
Cooking time: 4 minutes

1 to 1 1/2 pounds fresh cherries
1 cup low-fat sour cream
2 to 3 tablespoons amaretto (almond) liqueur
1/4 cup slivered almonds, lightly toasted

Heat the oven to 250 degrees. To toast the almonds, place them in a single layer in a baking pan and bake about 10 minutes or until they start to turn golden and get very fragrant. Stir or shake the pan several times to let them cook evenly. Remove from the oven and place in the food processor. Pulse a few times to coarsely chop.

Meanwhile, rinse the cherries and let them dry. Place them in a shallow serving bowl. Stir the sour cream and amaretto together and put in a small serving bowl, then sprinkle with the reserved toasted almonds. Let guests serve themselves by dipping a cherry in the sour cream mixture.

Per serving: 344 calories, 16 grams fat, 26 milligrams cholesterol, 32 milligrams sodium.

WEEK

23

SHOPPING LIST

Meat, poultry, seafood

- ❑ 12 rib lamb chops (2 $\frac{1}{2}$ pounds)
- ❑ 4 6- to 8-ounce halibut steaks

Produce

- ❑ 2 yellow onions
- ❑ 1 Vidalia onion
- ❑ 1 red bell pepper
- ❑ 1 pound mustard greens
- ❑ 1 pound new red potatoes
- ❑ 3 yellow squash
- ❑ 1 pound asparagus
- ❑ 8 ounces mushrooms
- ❑ 4 large Idaho potatoes
- ❑ 2 heads red leaf lettuce
- ❑ 1 cup ($\frac{1}{2}$ pint) black (or red) cherries
- ❑ 1 cup ($\frac{1}{2}$ pint) black grapes

- ❑ $\frac{1}{2}$ cup blueberries
- ❑ 2 ripe peaches
- ❑ 1 cup strawberries
- ❑ 1 lemon
- ❑ 1 bunch fresh mint sprigs
- ❑ 1 bunch rosemary

Dairy

- ❑ 4 sticks unsalted butter
- ❑ $\frac{3}{4}$ cup heavy cream
- ❑ 1 cup low-fat sour cream
- ❑ 1 pint ice cream
- ❑ 6 to 8 ounces white Cheddar cheese

Deli

- ❑ 4 bratwurst
- ❑ 1 loaf crusty bread
- ❑ 4 pita breads
- ❑ 1 2-ounce block Parmesan cheese

Miscellaneous

- ❑ $\frac{1}{2}$ cup raisins
- ❑ 2 19-ounce cans garbanzo beans
- ❑ 2 tablespoons Triple Sec orange liqueur
- ❑ 1 cup chopped pecans
- ❑ $\frac{1}{2}$ cup chopped walnuts
- ❑ 3 tablespoons pine nuts
- ❑ 2 $\frac{1}{2}$ cups raw white rice

Staples

- ❑ All-purpose flour
- ❑ Balsamic vinegar
- ❑ Black pepper
- ❑ Brown sugar
- ❑ Dried thyme
- ❑ Olive oil
- ❑ Pure vanilla extract
- ❑ Salt
- ❑ Sugar
- ❑ Vegetable oil

- ❑ Walnut oil
- ❑ White or red wine vinegar

* Suggested accompaniments

MARINATED GARBANZO
SALAD
WARM PITA BREADS*
SUMMER PECAN PIE

This hearty bean salad is filling enough for big appetites, yet light enough for a hot summer evening. It is especially nice served on a large platter with other summery salads. The recipe makes plenty for leftovers, and the salad just gets tastier with every passing day. The step of pouring vinegar over the hot vegetables makes them more flavorful. Add warm pita breads and stuff the salad in the centers of the breads. The pecan pie is unlike any you have had before, and you might like this version better. Save portions to serve later in the week. Use a purchased pie shell if you wish. If you think of it, toast the pecans for today's dessert and walnuts for Tuesday's meal together, to save time later in the week.

MARINATED GARBANZO SALAD

Makes 8 servings
Preparation time: 5 minutes
Cooking time: 25 minutes

$^1/_2$ cup olive oil
1 large onion, diced
1 tablespoon dried thyme or 2 tablespoons fresh
1 large bell pepper, red or green, chopped
$^1/_2$ cup raisins
2 19-ounce cans garbanzos, drained and rinsed
$^1/_2$ teaspoon salt
$^1/_2$ cup rice wine vinegar

1 head red leaf lettuce

Put the olive oil in a large, heavy saucepan. Add the onions and thyme and cook over low heat, covered, until onions are meltingly tender and lightly colored, about 15 minutes. (They can cook another 10 minutes if you have the time.)

Stir in the red pepper and cook for another 5 minutes. Add raisins, garbanzos and salt, and cook for another 5 minutes, stirring occasionally. Do not overcook.

Put the mixture in a large heat-proof bowl and pour the vinegar over, and toss. Let the salad cool to room temperature, then cover and refrigerate for several hours or overnight before serving. The salad is best served at room temperature, but you can serve it hot or cold. Just before serving, separate the lettuce leaves and clean and dry them. Serve the salad on the lettuce leaves.

SUMMER PECAN PIE

Makes 8 servings
Preparation time: 20 minutes
Cooking time: 1 hour

1 9-inch pie shell
$^1/_2$ cup sugar
1 to 2 tablespoons orange liqueur or kirsch
$^3/_4$ cup heavy cream
1 cup chopped pecans, lightly toasted

Preheat the oven to 350 degrees. If the pie dough is not frozen, put it in the freezer for 15 minutes to firm it before baking. Place the frozen shell in the oven and bake 15 to 20 minutes until lightly browned. While the pie crust is baking, toast the

pecans for about 10 minutes. Stir them to keep them from burning, and watch them carefully, and remove as soon as they are browned and fragrant. Remove the pie shell from the oven and let cool completely before adding the filling.

Heat the oven to 400 degrees.

Put the sugar, Triple Sec, cream and nuts in a large bowl and stir well to combine. Pour into the pie shell. Place a cookie sheet under the tart pan to catch any drips. Bake for 45 to 50 minutes until caramelized and deep brown.

GRILLED BRATWURST*
MIXED GREEN SALAD*
BLUEBERRY FRUIT SALAD

Keep tonight's dinner easy with quick-grilled sausages and two salads. If black grapes and cherries aren't available, don't hesitate to use red ones — only the look will change. If you are short on 2-hour spans of time to let the salad flavors merge, serve it anyway, it will still be delicious.

BLUEBERRY FRUIT SALAD

Makes 4 servings
Preparation time: 5 minutes
Standing time: 2 hours

1 cup black cherries, pitted
1 cup black grapes
2 fresh ripe peaches, peeled and sliced
1 cup blueberries
$^1/_4$ cup brown sugar

Price: Peaches range from $.49 to $.99 per pound in local grocery stores and farmers markets.

Nutrition: A medium peach has about 40 calories, less than 1 gram fat and no sodium, and is a good source of vitamin C, vitamin A and phosphorus.

Selection: Choose peaches with a creamy or yellow undercolor; a red blush is a characteristic of the variety rather than a guarantee of good quality. Ripe peaches give to gentle pressure; avoid green, extrahard and badly bruised fruit. Peaches don't become any sweeter after they're picked, but ripening makes mature fruit softer and juicier.

Storage: Ripen firm-ripe fruit at room temperature in a loosely closed paper bag. Refrigerate ripe fruit, unwashed, in the same bag for up to 3 days. Most commercial peaches have been defuzzed and rubbed with a very light coat of paraffin wax to prolong shelf life.

Uses: One pound of peaches (3 medium or 2 large) yields 1 1/2 to 2 cups sliced fruit. Serve out-of-hand or sliced into fruit or poultry salads, over pancakes or breakfast cereal. Gently poach or bake into pies and cobblers, or add to homemade ice cream. You may use peaches in recipes calling for nectarines, but take into consideration that peaches will be juicier.

Late June through July is the best time to buy or pick a Georgia peach, with earlier cling-stone varieties passed and the easier to eat free-stone varieties widely available at local grocery stores and farm stands. A few farms offer U-pick opportunities, and it is here that you will get the best quality fruit and the variety you prefer.

Juice of 1 lemon
$1/2$ cup low-fat sour cream
Sprinkling of brown sugar
    for garnish
Fresh mint sprigs

Combine the cherries, grapes, blueberries and peaches in a large bowl. Sprinkle with the brown sugar and lemon juice. Let stand 2 hours, tossing several times. Juices will collect in the bottom of the bowl.

Lift the fruit out with a slotted spoon and put in large goblets. Stir the remaining fruit juices into the sour cream and place a spoonful over the fruit. Sprinkle with brown sugar and garnish with mint sprigs.

TUESDAY

MUSTARD GREENS WITH WALNUT VINAIGRETTE MARINATED GARBANZO SALAD* CRUSTY BREAD*

Enjoy the pungent flavor of young mustard greens only gently cooked in the following green dish. If the greens are especially young and tender, omit the blanching stage. To toast walnuts, turn the oven to 350 degrees. Place the walnuts on a cookie sheet and heat them until lightly browned, about 10 minutes.

Add leftover garbanzo salad, especially delicious now that the flavors have had a day or two to develop, and crusty bread.

MUSTARD GREENS WITH WALNUT VINAIGRETTE

Makes 4 servings
Preparation time: 10 minutes
Cooking time: 10 minutes

1 pound fresh mustard greens, washed
2 tablespoons walnut oil
1 tablespoon red wine vinegar
Salt and black pepper, to taste
$1/2$ cup chopped walnuts, lightly toasted

Drop greens into a large pot of boiling, salted water and blanch uncovered 1 or 2 minutes to remove some of the natural bitterness in the leaves.

Drain the greens in a colander or sieve and press with the back of a wooden spoon to release water. Chop the greens coarsely and place in a heat-proof serving bowl.

In a large skillet, heat the oil over low heat until just warm. Whisk in the vinegar, and salt and pepper to taste. Pour the warm vinaigrette over the greens in the bowl. Garnish with nuts and serve.

WEDNESDAY

HALIBUT STEAKS WITH GRILLED VEGETABLES ICE CREAM AND STRAWBERRIES*

These grilled vegetables will hopefully become a standard recipe for you, and make the full recipe to use leftovers later in the week. Watch them closely, however, as they cook quickly and can burn in an instant.

Cook and serve them together with Alaskan halibut steaks, still in season and delicious. This dish is also absolutely lovely baked in parchment, but the result will be steamed fish and vegetables rather than the crispier texture and color of grilled. Save 2 cups leftover grilled vegetables for tomorrow night's meal.

HALIBUT STEAKS WITH GRILLED VEGETABLES

Makes 6 servings
Preparation time: 15 minutes
Cooking time: 5 to 8 minutes

4 6- to 8-ounce halibut steaks
1 pound new red potatoes, unpeeled and sliced $1/4$-inch thick
3 yellow squash, sliced $1/2$-inch thick on the diagonal
8 ounces mushrooms, cleaned and cut in half
5 to 6 tablespoons olive oil
5 to 6 tablespoons balsamic vinegar or red wine vinegar
$1/4$ cup fresh herbs, roughly chopped
Salt and pepper to taste

Preheat the broiler or grill.

Add the olive oil, vinegar, herbs and pepper in a food processor or blender and blend (or use a prepared vinaigrette). Brush the vinaigrette liberally over the steaks and toss the vegetables with all but 2 tablespoons of the vinaigrette. Place the steaks and vegetables on a broiling pan.

Broil about 5 minutes and check the vegetables to make sure they aren't burning. Turn the steaks over, then turn the vegetables over, brushing them with the remaining vinaigrette and broil another 3 to 5 minutes, until cooked.

THURSDAY

BAKED POTATOES WITH GRILLED VEGETABLES AND WHITE CHEDDAR CHEESE
SUMMER PECAN PIE*

Baked potatoes with the fixings make a hearty and delicious dinner. Idaho potatoes offer the driest, most crumbly texture that most of us prefer for a baked potato. Cut the leftover vegetables into slivers and reheat in a dry skillet to keep their texture intact. Serve leftover tart for dessert.

BAKED POTATOES WITH GRILLED VEGETABLES AND WHITE CHEDDAR CHEESE

Makes 4 servings
Preparation time: 5 minutes
Cooking time: 50 minutes

4 large Idaho baking potatoes
4 teaspoons vegetable oil
2 to 3 cups grilled vegetables, leftover
6 to 8 ounces white Cheddar cheese, grated

Preheat the oven to 350 degrees. Rub the skins of the potatoes with a teaspoon of vegetable oil and salt them lightly. Bake the potatoes for 45 minutes or until cooked through. Leave the oven turned on.

Meanwhile, reheat the grilled vegetables left from last night's dinner. Cut open the potatoes and squeeze them lightly to make a cavity, and set them on a cookie sheet. Fill the cavities with the vegetables. Sprinkle with the cheese and place the potatoes in the oven just until the cheese has melted.

FRIDAY

HOT AND SOUR SOUP*
COLD SESAME NOODLES*
FRESH LYCHEES IN SEASON*
FORTUNE COOKIES*

Dinner is as close as your favorite Chinese restaurant: call and order dinner and pick up the fixings on your way home from work. Order this flavorful soup and our always-favorite sesame noodles, and be sure they tuck in some fortune cookies for dessert with the fragrant and fragile lychees, in season for just a few weeks.

SATURDAY

GRILLED LAMB CHOPS WITH SWEET ONION BUTTER
STEAMED RICE*
ASPARAGUS WITH PARMESAN SLIVERS*
ROSEMARY SHORTBREAD COOKIES

Tonight's dinner is packed with our favorite flavors, from mint and sweet onions to sweet golden cherries. The flavored butter can be made with almost any herb, from thyme to chives to cilantro. Freeze the logs and pull out a slice or two as you need them. Grill the chops to cut fat to a minimum. If you choose to saute them, use a large skillet to pre-vent overcrowding and uneven cooking. The rosemary cookies, adapted from Geraldene Holt's *Recipes from a French Herb Garden*, are sensational, and an unusual use for rosemary which usually gets put in savory dishes. Pulse the sugar in the food processor a couple of times to "make" it super fine — it will make a cookie with a finer crumb.

GRILLED LAMB CHOPS WITH SWEET ONION BUTTER

Makes 4 servings
Preparation time: 5 minutes plus 15 minutes freezing time
Cooking time: 8 minutes

1/4 cup closely packed, fresh, clean mint leaves
1/2 cup sweet onions, minced
Salt, to taste
1 stick unsalted butter, room temperature, in large chunks
1 tablespoon sesame or walnut oil
12 rib lamb chops (about 2 1/2 pounds)
Salt and black pepper to taste

Heat the grill.

Meanwhile, put the mint, onions and salt in the workbowl of a food processor and process until finely chopped. Add butter chunks and process until well combined, pulsing and stirring as necessary. Roll the mixture into a log shape and wrap in aluminum foil. Chill 1 hour or freeze 15 minutes to make it hard enough to slice into 1/4-inch rounds.

Grill the chops 3 to 5 minutes on each side, until still rosy pink inside and browned on the outside. Keep warm and serve immediately, topped with a thin slice of the mint butter.

ROSEMARY SHORTBREAD COOKIES

Makes 30 cookies
Preparation time: 10 minutes
Cooking time: 8 to 12 minutes

1 stick salted or unsalted butter
1/4 cup sugar
1 1/3 cups all-purpose flour
2 to 3 tablespoons fresh rosemary
    leaves, finely chopped (stems
    discarded)
A little extra sugar for garnish

Preheat the oven to 325 degrees.
Put the sugar in the work-bowl of a food processor and process to make it extra-fine. Add the butter and continue to process until the mixture is smooth. Add the flour and rosemary and continue to process and pulse to make a soft dough. Remove the dough from the bowl and shape it into a ball.

Roll out the dough on a floured board to 1/4-inch thickness. Cut lines 1 inch apart, then cut lines in the other direction to form diamond shapes. Bake (on parchment paper preferably) for 8 to 12 minutes, or until the shortbread is just changing color — but watch carefully or it will burn quickly. Transfer to a rack and sprinkle with the extra sugar while still warm.

WEEK

24

SHOPPING LIST

Meat, poultry, seafood

- ❏ 2 chickens in leg quarters or pieces, 2 ¹/₂ pounds each
- ❏ 1 pound ham steaks
- ❏ 1 ¹/₂ pounds large or jumbo shrimp

Produce

- ❏ 2 pounds broccoli
- ❏ 3 pounds new red potatoes
- ❏ 1 head lettuce, any type
- ❏ 2 large Vidalia or other sweet onions
- ❏ 1 bunch green Vidalia onions
- ❏ 3 small yellow crookneck squash
- ❏ 3 small zucchini squash
- ❏ 4 medium sweet potatoes
- ❏ 1 small green bell pepper
- ❏ 1 pineapple, peeled and cored

- ❏ 2 large limes
- ❏ 3 mangoes
- ❏ 4 garlic cloves
- ❏ 1 bunch cilantro
- ❏ 1 bunch oregano
- ❏ 1 bunch parsley
- ❏ 1 bunch sage
- ❏ 1 bunch basil

Dairy

- ❏ 1 8-ounce container whipped cream cheese
- ❏ 3 eggs
- ❏ 2 sticks unsalted butter
- ❏ 1 ¹/₂ cups plain non-fat yogurt
- ❏ 1 large scoop vanilla ice cream, sherbet or frozen yogurt

Deli

- ❏ 4 pita breads, white or whole-wheat
- ❏ 1 8-ounce package short-

bread cookies

Miscellaneous

- ❏ ¹/₂ cup dried tomatoes
- ❏ ¹/₄ cup green olives stuffed with garlic or pimento
- ❏ ¹/₄ cup capers
- ❏ ¹/₂ cup dry white wine
- ❏ 3 ounces unsweetened chocolate
- ❏ 1 1-pound box confectioners' sugar
- ❏ 8 ounces wheel-shaped pasta
- ❏ 2 to 2 ¹/₂ cups dry rice
- ❏ 2 ¹/₂ cups tropical blend fruit juice
- ❏ ¹/₂ cup dark rum
- ❏ ¹/₂ cup Key lime juice

Staples

- ❏ Balsamic vinegar (optional)

- ❏ Bay leaves
- ❏ Brown sugar
- ❏ Cocoa powder
- ❏ Herbs de Provence
- ❏ Coarsely ground black pepper
- ❏ Dried sage (optional)
- ❏ Minced garlic in oil
- ❏ Olive oil
- ❏ Pure vanilla extract
- ❏ Red wine vinegar
- ❏ Salt
- ❏ Self-rising flour
- ❏ Sugar

* Suggested accompaniments

PICNIC CHICKEN
BOILED NEW RED
POTATOES *
STEAMED BROCCOLI *
CHOCOLATE PUDDING CAKE

This chicken dish tastes great hot or cold and makes excellent pool or picnic fare. The secret of its intense flavor is an overnight marinade, but if you are out of time, cook it anyway for a delicious dish. Put this chocolate cake recipe on your can't-live-without list. It is adapted from a recipe from Judith Olney's *The Farm Market Cookbook* (Doubleday, $25.00). Both cream cheese and chocolate melts effortlessly in the microwave. Wrap the cake well and refrigerate; it will stay moist for days.

PICNIC CHICKEN

Makes 6 servings
Preparation time: 15 minutes plus time to marinate
Cooking time: 1 hour

2 chickens, in leg quarters or pieces, about 2 1/2 pounds each, with skin removed
4 teaspoons minced garlic in oil
2 tablespoons herbs de Provence
Salt and black pepper to taste
2 tablespoons balsamic vinegar
1/4 cup olive oil
1/4 cup dried tomatoes, sliced
1/4 cup green olives stuffed with garlic or pimento
1/4 cup capers, with juice
1/4 cup basil leaves
1/4 cup brown sugar
1/2 cup dry white wine
2 tablespoons basil

In a large bowl, combine chicken pieces, minced garlic, herbs de Provence, salt, pepper, vinegar, olive oil, dried tomatoes, olives, capers and juice, and basil. Cover the bowl and marinate, refrigerated, several hours or overnight.

Preheat oven to 350 degrees. Put the chicken pieces in a large, shallow baking pan in a single layer. Spoon the marinade liberally over the chicken. Sprinkle the chicken with brown sugar and pour wine around.

Bake for at least 1 hour, basting frequently with pan juices. The chicken will be done when thigh pieces, pricked with a fork, yield clear yellow (rather than pink) juices.

Transfer chicken, tomatoes and capers to a serving platter. Spoon pan juices over and garnish with basil. Serve hot or at room temperature.

Per serving: 267 calories, 15 grams fat, 19 milligrams cholesterol, 177 milligrams sodium.

CHOCOLATE PUDDING CAKE

Makes 10 servings
Preparation time: 15 minutes
Cooking time: 40 minutes

TOPPING:
8 ounces whipped cream cheese, room temperature
3 ounces unsweetened chocolate, melted
1 egg
1 1-pound box confectioners' sugar, sifted

CAKE:
1 1/2 cups self-rising flour
1 cup sugar
1/4 cup cocoa powder
1 stick unsalted butter, melted
2 eggs
1/2 cup plain non-fat yogurt
1 1/2 teaspoons pure vanilla extract

Preheat the oven to 350 degrees. Grease a 9-by-13-inch cake pan with pan spray or shortening.

To make the topping, put the softened cream cheese, melted chocolate and egg in the workbowl of a food processor or mixing bowl and blend for 1 or 2 minutes (the shorter time in the food processor, longer for a mixer), until smooth. By hand, stir in the sifted confectioners' sugar. Set aside for the assembly.

In another mixing bowl, stir together the flour, sugar and cocoa. In another bowl, whisk together butter, eggs, yogurt and vanilla. Stir the butter mixture into the flour mixture, then beat with a mixer for 3 or 4 minutes. Pour the batter into the prepared cake pan. Spread the cream cheese topping over the cake in an even layer. Bake 40 minutes.

Cool the cake completely (about 4 hours) before cutting to firm the chocolate (otherwise it will just be a pool of chocolate).

Per serving: 540 calories, 22 grams fat, 127 milligrams cholesterol, 174 milligrams sodium.

MONDAY

POTATOES AND WHEELS WITH
FRESH HERB BUTTER
GREEN SALAD *
CHOCOLATE PUDDING CAKE *

Use leftover potatoes and lots of fresh herbs for tonight's pasta dish. It is made with both butter and olive oil for a more complex flavor, but just one of the two fats would be delicious by itself. A flavorful addition to the dish are juniper berries, often available at specialty food stores or farmers

Price: Prices vary with size and are often used as an advertised store special. Specials range from $3.99 to $.99 a pound, and shrimp are often sold individually, such as $.07 or $.09 a piece. Prices go up as the size gets larger and fresh never-frozen shrimp averages at least a $1.00 more per pound than previously frozen shrimp. Look for large sweet Georgia shrimp for $6.99, and previously frozen jumbos for $5.99. As the season progresses, shrimp will grow in size, so sale prices will be offered on increasingly larger sizes later in the summer. Specials are based on availability.

Nutrition: Shrimp is a very low-fat fish. For a 3 1/2-ounce serving (mixed species): 106 calories, 1.7 grams fat, 152 milligrams cholesterol and 480 milligrams Omega-3 fatty acids.

Selection: Most shrimp available has been previously frozen, ask if you don't see a sign indicating this. Choose shrimp that are firm and moist and smell fresh. A stale shrimp may be dry with soft flesh and have an offensive odor. Look for translucent shells that are hard to the touch, not soft or rubbery. Shrimp come in several sizes which include the number of shrimp in a pound. Be sure to look for the count number and not just the size designation, since nomenclature is not consistent for counts per pound in stores. In general, counts are: Medium: 60–70, Large: 36–45, Extra Large 31–35, Jumbo:

26–35, Super Jumbo 16–20, Colossal: 15 or less.

Storage: Fresh or previously frozen shrimp can be stored in a covered container in a very cold refrigerator for 3 to 4 days, cooked shrimp should be refrigerated and eaten within 5 days. Fresh never frozen shrimp can be frozen 2 or 3 months, and previously frozen shrimp, if handled correctly, can also be refrozen for the same amount of

time.

Uses: Shrimp are delicious steamed, boiled, baked and broiled. Use the larger sizes for grilling on kebabs, and put smaller ones in salads, soups, dips and casseroles. If shrimp are to go in a casserole, slightly undercook them first. If you are adding shrimp to a slow-cooking sauce, add the raw shrimp at the end of the cooking time and heat just until done.

markets. Add a green salad, with sliced green Vidalia onions added, and leftover chocolate cake. Save any leftover pasta to serve later in the week.

POTATOES AND WHEELS WITH FRESH HERB BUTTER

Makes 4 servings
Preparation time: 10 minutes
Cooking time: 10 minutes

Salt
8 ounce wheel (or other shaped) pasta
1 pound cooked red potatoes, roughly chopped, warmed up
10 fresh sage leaves or 2 teaspoons dried
2 tablespoons oregano leaves, stemmed
1/4 cup fresh packed parsley, stemmed
4 medium garlic cloves, peeled
1/2 teaspoons salt
2 teaspoons coarsely ground black pepper
2 tablespoons olive oil
1/3 cup unsalted butter

Cook the pasta in a pot of salted water until al dente, 8 to 10 minutes. Drain and toss with the potatoes in a large serving bowl.

Meanwhile, make the herb butter. Put the sage, oregano, parsley, garlic, salt and pepper in the workbowl of a food processor. Process until the herbs are minced. Add olive oil and butter and process again until it makes a smooth paste. Spoon the herb butter over the pasta and potatoes and stir to mix thoroughly.

Per serving: 486 calories, 23 grams fat, 41 milligrams cholesterol, 12 milligrams sodium.

PICNIC CHICKEN *
STEAMED RICE *
STEAMED VIDALIA ONIONS
WITH YELLOW AND
GREEN SQUASH

Serve diced leftover chicken tonight and steamed rice to accompany it. Cook 2 cups of dry rice to make plenty to serve for Saturday night's dinner. If Vidalia onions are gone from the markets, look for the equally sugary Texas Sweet onions, which most grocery stores carry. Save any leftover vegetables to serve in pita breads later in the week.

STEAMED VIDALIA ONIONS WITH YELLOW AND GREEN SQUASH

Makes 6 servings
Preparation time: 10 minutes
Cooking time: 10 minutes

2 large Vidalia or other sweet onions
3 small yellow crookneck squash
3 small zucchini squash
2 tablespoons butter
2 tablespoons water
2 tablespoons fresh herbs, such as parsley, marjoram or basil, chopped if necessary

Cut the onion and squash into thin slices and set aside. Melt the butter in a skillet, add the vegetables and saute about 1 minute. Add the water, cover and steam until the vegetables are tender-crisp, 5 to 8 minutes. Remove from the heat and toss with fresh herbs and serve.

Per serving: 75 calories, 4 grams fat, 10 milligrams cholesterol, 41 milligrams sodium.

STUFFED PITA BREADS
FRESH PINEAPPLE SLICES *

Warmed pita breads can be stuffed with leftovers from the week. Pull out any remaining chicken, broccoli, steamed onions and squash; even the potato and pasta dish can be added. Add fresh pineapple; look for it peeled and cored in the produce section of the grocery store.

STUFFED PITA BREADS

Makes 4 servings
Preparation time: 10 minutes
Cooking time: 10 minutes

1/2 to 1 cup cooked chicken, roughly diced, along with any leftover capers and olives from Picnic Chicken
1/2 to 1 cup cooked broccoli
1 cup steamed vegetables, onions and squash
1 cup cooked potatoes and wheels
4 pita breads, white or whole-wheat, cut in half

Bring the leftover foods to room temperature for 20 or 30 minutes, if possible. Stuff the pita breads and heat in the oven 10 minutes or until the ingredients are heated through. Cover with aluminum foil if necessary to keep the pita breads soft.

Per serving (using 1 cup each of chicken and broccoli): 274 calories, 6 grams fat, 68 milligrams cholesterol, 559 milligrams sodium.

BAKED SWEET POTATOES *

GRILLED HAM SLICES *
MANGO SUBLIME

Make tonight's dinner easy on yourself with sweet potatoes baked in the oven or microwave and grilled ham slices. Add the following drink to go with dinner or as dessert. For another delicious (and lower-fat) drink, substitute citrus sherbet or lemon frozen yogurt for the vanilla ice cream. Key lime juice packs more flavor, but Persian lime juice will do. If you buy bottled Key lime juice, read the label carefully, some are made with Persian limes and only use the word Key in the name.

MANGO SUBLIME

Makes 4 servings
Preparation time: 5 minutes

1 cup milk
1 large scoop vanilla ice cream
2 cups mango, chopped coarsely
1 tablespoon Key lime juice
2 or 3 tablespoons other fruit juice,
    such as pineapple, passion fruit
    or a tropical blend

Place ingredients in a blender or food processor and blend until smooth.
Per serving: 132 calories, 4 grams fat, 16 milligrams cholesterol, 54 milligrams sodium.

FRIDAY

VEGETABLE PLATE SPECIAL *
PECAN CORN MUFFINS *

Look to your favorite family restaurant that features the classic "3 and bread" plate, which means 3 vegetables and your choice of bread. Look for such vegetable offerings as mashed potatoes, butter beans, green beans, collard greens, squash souffle and macaroni and cheese. The works can be picked up on your way home from work or delivered to several parts of town.

SATURDAY

RUM SHRIMP ON THE GRILL
MANGO RICE SALAD
SHORTBREAD COOKIES *

The flavors in tonight's dinner smack of surfing and steel bands, says cookbook authors Chris Schlesinger and John Willoughby (*Thrill of the Grill*, Morrow, $24.95). The dishes are also low in fat and easy on the cook. If you're using wooden skewers, soak them in water for 15 minutes before using, and be careful not to leave any gaps between the shrimp, or the skewers will burn. Purchase good-quality shortbread cookies for dessert.

GRILLED RUM SHRIMP

Makes 4 servings
Preparation time: 10 minutes
Marinating time: 2 to 4 hours
Cooking time: 8 minutes

1/3 cup Key lime juice
1 1/2 cups tropical fruit juice (use a
    combination of passion fruit,
    orange, tangerine, guava,
    pineapple)
1/2 cup dark rum
4 tablespoons chopped cilantro
A few red pepper flakes
1 tablespoon minced garlic in oil
Salt and lots of coarsely ground
    black pepper, to taste
1 1/2 pounds large or jumbo size
    shrimp, raw in shell

In a large nonreactive steel bowl, combine the fruit juices, rum, cilantro, red pepper flakes garlic, salt and pepper. Add the shrimp. Cover and refrigerate to marinate for 2 or 3 hours — no longer — or they will start to cook in the lime juice. Remove the shrimp from the marinade and discard it.
    Thirty minutes before cooking, start the grill or broiler.
    Thread the shrimp on the skewers and grill 3 to 4 minutes on each side, until the shells turn bright red.
Per serving: 158 calories, 1 gram fat, 199 milligrams cholesterol, 229 milligrams sodium.

MANGO RICE SALAD

Makes 4 servings
Preparation time: 20 minutes

2 ripe mangoes
1 small green bell pepper, seeded
    and diced
1 green Vidalia onion, white part
    only, diced
3/4 cup tropical fruit blend or
    pineapple juice
1/3 cup lime juice (2 to 3 large
    limes)
1 teaspoon minced garlic in oil
A handful of cilantro leaves,
    stemmed
Salt and black pepper to taste
1 to 2 cups cooked rice

Peel the mangoes, then cut thick slices of fruit along the long slender pit. Dice the mango, green pepper and onion.
    Combine the mango mixture with the fruit juices, garlic,

cilantro, salt and pepper. This mixture can be refrigerated 2 or 3 days, covered. At serving time, stir in the rice.

Per serving: 170 calories, 2 grams fat, no cholesterol, 5 milligrams sodium.

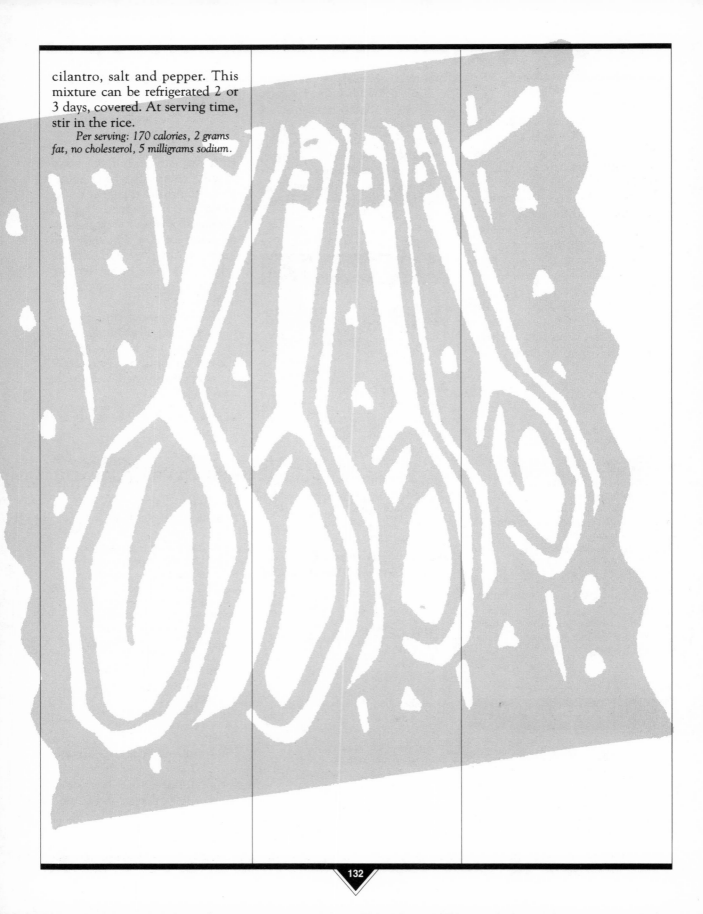

WEEK

25

SHOPPING LIST

Meat, poultry, seafood

- ❑ 1 2 ¹/₂-pound beef roast or large steak (chuck, eye or shoulder underblade), 1 ¹/₂ inches thick
- ❑ 4 6- to 8-ounce turkey cutlets
- ❑ 1 slice thick bacon
- ❑ 1 to 1 ¹/₂ pounds large shrimp, shelled

Produce

- ❑ 2 heads green cabbage
- ❑ 1 medium carrot
- ❑ 1 rib celery
- ❑ 3 pounds new potatoes
- ❑ 1 head garlic
- ❑ 3 bunches green onions
- ❑ 1 medium yellow onion
- ❑ 1 bunch (1 pound) asparagus
- ❑ 1 pint cherry tomatoes
- ❑ 2 tomatoes

- ❑ 1 bell pepper, any color
- ❑ 1 small avocado
- ❑ 1 cup cremini mushrooms
- ❑ 2 heads butter lettuce
- ❑ 1 bunch fresh rosemary
- ❑ 1 bunch parsley
- ❑ 1 bunch mint
- ❑ 1 bunch basil
- ❑ 1 lime
- ❑ 2 large lemons
- ❑ 4 large slices watermelon
- ❑ 4 to 8 peaches
- ❑ 1 navel orange
- ❑ 4 cups fresh blueberries

Dairy

- ❑ 1 pint raspberry frozen yogurt
- ❑ ³/₄ cup plain non-fat yogurt
- ❑ 2 tablespoons butter
- ❑ 3 ounces cream cheese
- ❑ 1 egg

- ❑ 1 cup heavy cream

Deli

- ❑ 3 ounces feta or blue cheese
- ❑ 4 whole-wheat pita breads
- ❑ 1 loaf sourdough bread
- ❑ 4 blueberry muffins

Miscellaneous

- ❑ 3 cups raw rice
- ❑ ¹/₂ cup slivered or chopped almonds
- ❑ ¹/₂ cup dried cherries
- ❑ 1 5-ounce can evaporated milk
- ❑ 4 to 8 chocolate cookies
- ❑ ³/₄ cup low-sodium chicken broth
- ❑ 1 19-ounce can black beans
- ❑ 1 single-crust unbaked

pie shell

Staples

- ❑ Apple cider vinegar
- ❑ Black pepper
- ❑ Cayenne pepper
- ❑ Celery seed
- ❑ Dijon mustard
- ❑ Dried oregano
- ❑ Granulated sugar
- ❑ Ground cumin
- ❑ Horseradish
- ❑ Hot pepper in vinegar
- ❑ Mayonnaise
- ❑ Olive oil
- ❑ Salt
- ❑ White wine (optional)
- ❑ Vanilla bean

* Suggested accompaniments

SPICY GRILLED BEEF ROAST
RICE WITH ALMONDS AND
DRIED CHERRIES *
PETE'S CREAMY COLESLAW

A quick and economical roast beef makes Sunday night's dinner special, and leftovers a certainty. The U.S.D.A. recommends that meat be cooked to an internal temperature of 160 which is medium-cooked meat. Add rice, cooked with almonds and dried cherries. American Spoon Foods, a Michigan company, produces the tartest and most flavorful cherries, ones that don't just taste like big raisins. They're available in specialty stores. Cook plenty of rice to serve later in the week.

There are some ingredients that coleslaw must have to be right: apple cider vinegar and celery seed, to begin with. The slaw should be creamy, but not cloyingly heavy with mayonnaise. The following recipe, adapted from Vince Staten's *Jack Daniel's Old Time Barbecue Cookbook* (Sulgrave Press, $21.95), fits the description perfectly. Another item most coleslaw recipes call for is overnight chilling, to go along with barbecue that's been cooked all night; but this recipe is faster.

Stick a vanilla bean in a small bag of granulated sugar; by the end of the week the sugar will be flavored. Store the sugar this way indefinitely for use in Saturday's dessert and in many others.

SPICY GRILLED BEEF ROAST

Makes 10 servings
Preparation time: 10 minutes
Cooking time: 20-30 minutes

1 tablespoon herbs de Provence
$1/4$ teaspoon cayenne pepper
$1/2$ to 1 teaspoon salt
1 2 $1/2$-pound beef roast or large steak (chuck, eye or shoulder underblade), 1 $1/2$ inches thick

Light the grill or preheat the oven to 500 degrees.

Mix together the herbs de Provence, cayenne pepper and salt in a small bowl. Rub the seasoning mixture all over the top of the roast.

Place the roast on the hot grill, 8 to 10 inches from the heat. Cover with a tent of aluminum foil and cook for 10 to 15 minutes. Turn the meat and cook another 10 to 15 minutes. Test with an instant read thermometer for 150 degrees for medium meat. (If you are cooking in the oven, you may want to turn on the broiler for the last few minutes to get a crisper crust.)

Transfer the meat to a platter and cover with a layer of aluminum foil for 10 to 15 minutes. During this time the internal temperature should rise to 160. To serve, cut on the bias into very thin slices.

Per serving: 277 calories, 22 grams fat, 75 milligrams cholesterol, 166 milligrams sodium.

PETE'S CREAMY COLESLAW

Makes 8 servings
Preparation time: 10 minutes
Chilling time: A few hours or overnight

1 5-ounce can evaporated milk
$1/3$ cup apple cider vinegar
2 tablespoons granulated sugar
1 teaspoon salt
1 teaspoon celery seed
$1/2$ teaspoon black pepper
$1/2$ cup mayonnaise
2 to 3 tablespoons yogurt (optional)
4 cups shredded cabbage
1 medium carrot, shredded
1 rib celery, diced

Stir together the milk, vinegar, sugar, salt, celery seed, pepper, mayonnaise and (optional) yogurt.

Shred the cabbage and carrot by hand or with a food processor. Pour the milk mixture over the cabbage, carrot and celery and mix. Chill and serve.

Per serving: 160 calories, 13 grams fat, 13 milligrams cholesterol, 415 milligrams sodium.

ARMENIAN PITA SANDWICHES
WITH LEMON DRESSING
RASPBERRY FROZEN YOGURT
WITH BLUEBERRIES AND
CRUMBLED CHOCOLATE
COOKIES *

This cheese and vegetable sandwich makes great no-nonsense eating. The lemony dressing recipe makes enough to serve later in the week, so be sure to set some aside. Warm the pita breads if you wish. Pick up raspberry frozen yogurt whenever you can find it and keep it for nights when you want a quick dessert. Pair it with chocolate cookies.

Price: Will range from $1.49 to $1.99 a pint.

Nutrition: One-half cup of blueberries has 42 calories, no fat, and is an excellent source of vitamin C.

Selection: Look for plump, deep-blue berries with no bruises. The grayish, powdery cast is a sign of freshness.

Storage: Refrigerate blueberries in the container they came in, or place them between layers of paper towel and wrap them in plastic up to 1 week. To freeze berries, lay them in a single layer on a cookie sheet and place them in the freezer. When they are firm, put them in bags. It isn't necessary to thaw them before cooking.

Uses: Simply wash blueberries and serve them raw in fruit salads, on breakfast cereal or with ice cream, yogurt or a liqueur. Puree them for yogurt smoothies or add them to pancakes, muffins, marinades, soups or cobblers.

Canadians produce and consume more blueberries than any other nation in the world, but Georgia is right up there with the big leaguers when it comes to production. Georgia is the fifth largest producer of blueberries in the U.S. and production is expected to increase dramatically in the next few years.

As many as 30 farms offer you-pick operations, located all over the state, with individual listings available through the Georgia Department of Agriculture or the Farmers and Consumers Market Bulletin. Organically-grown blueberries are available at Bill Callaway's U-Pick in Cumming, just north of Atlanta.

ARMENIAN PITA SANDWICHES

Makes 4 servings
Preparation time: 20 minutes

1 bunch green onions, chopped
1 1/2 cups cherry tomatoes, stemmed and halved
1 small avocado, peeled, seeded and diced
1 cup cremini mushrooms, thinly sliced
1 cup shredded cabbage
1/4 cup Lemon Vinaigrette (recipe follows)
3 ounces feta or blue cheese, rumbled
4 whole-wheat pita breads, with tops cut off
1/2 cup plain non-fat yogurt

In a large bowl combine the onions, tomatoes, avocado, mushrooms and cabbage. Toss with Lemon Dressing to coat. Sprinkle in the cheese and toss. Fill the pita breads with the mixture and add a dollop of yogurt.

Per serving: 304 calories, 17 grams fat, 19 milligrams cholesterol, 403 milligrams sodium.

LEMON VINAIGRETTE

Makes 1/2 cup
Preparation time: 5 minutes

1/2 cup plus 2 tablespoons chopped fresh mint or cilantro
1/3 cup lemon juice (juice of 2 large lemons)
4 to 6 tablespoons olive oil
Salt and freshly ground black pepper to taste

Put the herbs in the workbowl of a food processor. Pulse to mince, then add the lemon juice, olive oil, salt and black pepper. Process until the mixture is blended, 15 to 20 seconds. Will keep, covered, in the refrigerator for several days. From *The New Harvest* by Lou Seibert Pappas and Jane Horn (101 Productions, $8.95).

Per 1-tablespoon serving: 52 calories, 5 grams fat, no cholesterol, 1 milligram sodium.

TUESDAY

SAUTEED TURKEY CUTLETS *
STEAMED POTATOES
TOSSED IN BUTTER*
SMOTHERED CABBAGE

Slow-cooked cabbage fills the kitchen with a homey aroma, and the price can't be beat right now. Add quick-sauteed turkey cutlets and potatoes tossed in butter. Slice the potatoes thin, and steam or cook in the microwave; cook enough to have three cups left over for later in the week.

SMOTHERED CABBAGE

Makes 4 servings
Preparation time: 10 minutes
Cooking time: 10-15 minutes

1 slice thick bacon
1 garlic clove
1 tablespoon fresh rosemary leaves
1 tablespoon olive oil
2 pounds green cabbage, shredded
1/2 cup low-sodium chicken broth or white wine

Chop the bacon with the garlic and rosemary until well minced. This gets the bacon in small pieces and crushes the rosemary enough to release its fragrance. You can do this with a knife or in the food processor.

Heat the oil in a medium saucepan over medium heat. Add bacon mixture. Cook, stirring constantly, until the mixture begins to sizzle. Stir in the cabbage, tossing to coat well. Cook, covered, over low heat for 10 to 15 minutes, adding stock or wine a little at a time.

Per serving: 127 calories, 7 grams fat, 4 milligrams cholesterol, 114 milligrams sodium.

WEDNESDAY

COLD ROAST BEEF
SANDWICHES *
ASPARAGUS AND MINT
WITH POTATOES
WATERMELON WEDGES *

This meal of great leftovers can go wherever you go — the patio, pool or park. Serve cold beef on thick chunks of sourdough bread with horseradish, mayonnaise and fresh tomatoes. The following salad makes use of leftover potatoes. Don't be scared off by all the onion; it makes a delicious addition.

ASPARAGUS AND MINT WITH POTATOES

Makes 8 servings
Preparation time: 10 minutes
Cooking time: 10 minutes

2 tablespoons olive oil
1 medium yellow onion, thinly sliced
1 pound (or 1 bunch) asparagus, cut into 1-inch pieces
3 cups cooked and sliced potatoes (3 medium potatoes)
3 tablespoons coarsely chopped fresh mint
1 bunch green onions, sliced
1/4 cup chicken or beef broth
Salt and freshly ground black pepper to taste

Put the oil in a medium skillet

and heat over medium heat. Add the yellow onion and saute 4 or 5 minutes, until it begins to brown. Add the asparagus pieces; cook 3 or 4 minutes, stirring. Add the potatoes, mint, green onions and broth. Cover and simmer 5 minutes, tossing carefully to prevent the potato slices from breaking up. Season to taste with salt and pepper.

Per serving: 102 calories, 4 grams fat, no cholesterol, 138 milligrams sodium.

THURSDAY

BEEF AND ASPARAGUS WITH POTATOES*
PETE'S CREAMY COLESLAW *
FRESH PEACHES AND BLUEBERRIES *

Stir bits of leftover beef into the asparagus and potatoes, and serve the salad cold with coleslaw. Peaches purchased at the beginning of the week should be ripe now if you left them at room temperature. Chill the ripe peaches before serving.

FRIDAY

RICE SALAD WITH DRIED CHERRIES AND ORANGES
BUTTER LETTUCE GREENS *
BLUEBERRY MUFFINS WITH CREAM CHEESE *

Leftover rice produces this fragrant and fabulous rice salad. Serve it on tender greens, such as butter lettuce. Try blueberry muffins and softened cream cheese for dessert.

RICE SALAD WITH DRIED CHERRIES AND ORANGES

Makes 4 servings
Preparation time: 10 minutes

3 cups cooked, cooled rice with almonds and dried cherries
1/4 cup Lemon Vinaigrette (see Monday's menu)
1 to 2 teaspoons granulated sugar (optional)
1 navel orange, peeled and cut into 1/2-inch segments
1 to 2 tablespoons fresh mint, roughly chopped

In a large bowl, mix together the rice, lemon dressing and sugar, if desired; blend well. Gently stir in orange segments and mint. Serve cold or at room temperature.

Per serving: 227 calories, 9 grams fat, no cholesterol, 3 milligrams sodium.

SATURDAY

BLACK BEAN AND HOT PEPPER SALAD WITH CUMIN SHRIMP
LETTUCE GREENS *
BLUEBERRY CREAM PIE WITH VANILLA SUGAR

Don't let the list of ingredients scare you; these are simple recipes that take just a few minutes to prepare. If you are using bamboo skewers for the shrimp, soak them in water for 30 minutes to prevent their burning. Mesquite, wood chips, even last year's woody sage stems will add more flavor to the grilling shrimp. The wood (not the herbs) should be soaked in water 30 minutes before adding to the hot coals. Use the vanilla sugar you have been storing

since Sunday in the following pie recipe.

BLACK BEAN AND HOT PEPPER SALAD WITH CUMIN SHRIMP

Makes 6 servings
Preparation time: 25 minutes
Marinating time: 4 hours
Cooking time: 5 minutes

Black Beans
1/4 cup olive oil
1/4 cup vinegar from hot peppers, plus two peppers, minced
1 tablespoon Dijon mustard
Salt to taste
1 19-ounce can black beans, drained and rinsed
1 bell pepper, yellow, red or green, cut in small dice
3 green onions, trimmed and sliced
1/2 cup roughly chopped cilantro
Freshly ground black pepper

SHRIMP:
1/4 cup olive oil
3 tablespoons lime juice
1 tablespoon ground cumin
2 garlic cloves
1/2 teaspoon salt
1 to 1 1/2 pounds large shrimp, shelled

For the bean salad: In a large bowl, whisk together the olive oil, vinegar, minced peppers, mustard and salt. Stir in the beans, bell peppers, onions and cilantro. Add black pepper to taste.

In a blender or food processor combine the olive oil, lime juice, cumin, garlic and salt and process until smooth, 15 seconds. In a large bowl, combine the puree with the shrimp and marinate at least 4 hours. (Or cover and refrigerate overnight. Bring to room temperature before grilling.)

To grill, thread the shrimp on skewers, fitting them closely together. Smear any remaining marinade over the shrimp. Cover the grill and cook, turning the shrimp once, until they are just done, 4 to 5 minutes.

To serve: Spoon the bean salad onto lettuce on serving plates. Slide the shrimp off the skewers onto the salad. Garnish with additional fresh cilantro.

Per serving: 291 calories, 11 grams fat, 115 milligrams cholesterol, 328 milligrams sodium.

BLUEBERRY CREAM PIE WITH VANILLA SUGAR

Makes one 11-inch tart, 8 servings
Preparation time: 15 minutes
Cooking time: 1 hour, 10 minutes

Pastry for a single crust
3 cups fresh blueberries
1 cup heavy cream
1 beaten egg
1 cup vanilla sugar or plain
    granulated sugar

Preheat the oven to 350 degrees. Roll out the pie dough and fit it into a large pie pan. Turn the outer crust underneath to form an edge and crimp the crust. Sprinkle the blueberries thickly over the crust.

Stir together the cream, egg and sugar and pour over the berries. Bake 1 hour and 10 minutes, until the custard has formed. Serve warm.

Per serving: 475 calories, 31 grams fat, 75 milligrams cholesterol, 230 milligrams sodium.

WEEK

26

SHOPPING LIST

Meat, poultry, seafood

- ❑ 4- to 6-pound chum salmon, whole fish
- ❑ 4 slices bacon
- ❑ 1 pound lean ground beef or turkey

Produce

- ❑ 1 bunch sage
- ❑ 1 bunch Italian parsley
- ❑ 1 bunch cilantro
- ❑ 1 bunch fresh basil
- ❑ 2 heads lettuce, any type
- ❑ 4 cups watercress or arugula
- ❑ ¹/₂ pound snow peas
- ❑ 8 medium zucchini
- ❑ 1 10-ounce package shredded spinach leaves
- ❑ 1 bunch green onions
- ❑ 1 pint red cherry tomatoes
- ❑ 2 medium tomatoes

- ❑ 7 small heads fresh garlic
- ❑ 2 ripe avocados
- ❑ 4 lemons
- ❑ 2 pints blueberries
- ❑ 8 nectarines
- ❑ 1 knob fresh ginger
- ❑ 1 cantaloupe
- ❑ 1 pineapple
- ❑ 8 strawberries

Dairy

- ❑ 2 ¹/₂ sticks butter
- ❑ 1 egg
- ❑ 1 cup plain low-fat yogurt
- ❑ 1 cup heavy cream, chilled
- ❑ 2 pints good-quality vanilla ice cream
- ❑ 1 pint raspberry frozen yogurt
- ❑ Assorted cheeses (8 to 12 ounces total)

Deli

- ❑ 2 loaves crusty bread

Miscellaneous

- ❑ 4 ounces finely chopped nuts (pecans, walnuts or almonds
- ❑ ¹/₄ cup chopped peanuts
- ❑ ³/₄ cup fudge sauce
- ❑ 1 cup tomato salsa or picante sauce
- ❑ 20 brine-cured, imported black olives, such as Calamata
- ❑ ²/₃ cup chicken stock or broth
- ❑ 1 pound fresh fettuccine noodles
- ❑ 8 ounces angel-hair pasta
- ❑ 2 cups uncooked fragrant rice

Staples

- ❑ All-purpose flour
- ❑ Baking soda
- ❑ Black pepper
- ❑ Ground allspice
- ❑ Cayenne pepper
- ❑ Granulated sugar
- ❑ Herb vinegar or wine vinegar
- ❑ Olive oil
- ❑ Salt
- ❑ Sherry wine vinegar
- ❑ Soy sauce

* Suggested accompaniments

GRILLED CHUM SALMON *
GRILLED ZUCCHINI WITH
BASIL BUTTER
CRUSTY BREAD *
BLUEBERRY COFFEE CAKE
WITH YOGURT CREAM

Alaskan chum salmon makes a perfect grilled meal. Choose a 4- to 6-pound whole fish, and save leftovers for two more meals. Grill the fish 10 minutes per inch of thickness or until an instant-read thermometer registers 115 degrees in the middle. Brush the outside with olive oil to keep the skin from burning. While the grill is hot, toss on long spears of zucchini and grill for a couple of minutes. Store nectarines for Monday night's dinner at room temperature until they ripen, and reserve leftover yogurt cream for later desserts.

GRILLED ZUCCHINI WITH BASIL BUTTER

Makes 6 servings
Preparation time: 20 minutes (including chilling time)

BASIL BUTTER:
2 green onions, white part only, finely chopped
2 tablespoons finely chopped fresh basil leaves
1/4 teaspoon black pepper
1 teaspoon lemon juice
1 stick butter, room temperature, cut in chunks
8 medium zucchini
Olive oil

Put the green onions, basil, black pepper, lemon juice and butter in the workbowl of a food processor and pulse until combined, scraping with a spatula if necessary.

Turn the butter out onto a large piece of waxed paper or aluminum foil and roll into a 1-inch thick log. Chill or freeze until the butter is firm enough to slice and flavors have blended. The butter can freeze for a few months, or stay refrigerated for several weeks.

Slice zucchini lengthwise into long 1/2-inch slices and brush them with olive oil. Grill or broil them a couple of minutes, until softened and crisp. Serve them topped with a slice of basil butter with grilled salmon.

Per serving: 162 calories, 16 grams fat, 41 milligrams cholesterol, 161 milligrams sodium.

BLUEBERRY COFFEE CAKE WITH YOGURT CREAM

Makes 8 servings
Preparation time: 20 to 25 minutes
Cooking time: 1 hour

1 pint (2 cups) blueberries, washed and dried
2 teaspoons grated lemon peel
1/2 teaspoon ground allspice
2 1/4 cups all-purpose flour
1 cup granulated sugar
1 1/2 sticks unsalted butter, cut in small pieces
1 teaspoon baking soda
1 egg
1/2 cup plain low-fat yogurt

YOGURT CREAM:
1 cup whipping cream, chilled
2 tablespoons granulated sugar
1/3 cup plain yogurt

Preheat the oven to 400 degrees. Grease a round 10-inch baking dish or 10-inch springform pan with pan spray or shortening, then flour, and set aside.

In a medium bowl, toss the blueberries with the lemon peel and allspice; set aside. In a food processor, combine 2 cups of the flour with the sugar. Add the butter and process until the mixture resembles coarse meal. Set 1 1/2 cups of the mixture aside for the crumb topping. To the mixture left in the food processor, add the remaining flour and baking soda and pulse to incorporate. Pour the contents into a large bowl.

In a small bowl, lightly beat the egg. Stir in the yogurt and add to the dry ingredients. Stir briefly just until blended, then fold in 1 cup blueberries, reserving the second cup.

Spread the batter in the prepared baking dish and scatter the reserved 1 cup blueberries over. Sprinkle the reserved crumb mixture over the blueberries. Set the dish in the middle of the oven on a cookie sheet to catch any drips, and bake about 1 hour, or until the topping is golden brown and the sides of the cake are crispy. Remove from the oven and cool 10 minutes in the pan before removing.

Meanwhile, make the sauce. In a mixing bowl combine the cream, sugar and yogurt. Using an electric mixer, beat until it becomes stiff enough to spoon. To firm the cream, refrigerate 20 to 30 minutes.Serve warm or at room temperature with dollops of yogurt cream.

Per serving: 418 calories, 19 grams fat, 83 milligrams cholesterol, 133 milligrams sodium.

MIXED GREEN SALAD *
ROASTED GARLIC
SALAD DRESSING
CHEESE PLATTER WITH CANTALOUPE AND NECTARINES *

Make tonight's dinner light with a large green salad and an unforgettable salad dressing, adapted from Renee Shepherd and Fran Raboff's wonderful book, *Recipes From a Kitchen Garden, Volume 2* (Shepherd's Garden Publishing, $8.95). Roasted garlic tastes mild and sweet and smells wonderful too. Add a hearty cheese-and-fruit platter for dessert.

ROASTED GARLIC SALAD DRESSING

Makes ½ cup
Cooking time: 15 minutes
Preparation time: 10 minutes

3 or 4 large garlic cloves whole
    and unpeeled
2 tablespoons olive oil
1 dried tomato, minced, or 2
    Roma-type fresh tomatoes,
    squeezed of juice and finely
    chopped
1 tablespoon lemon juice
1 green onion, diced
1 tablespoon any herb vinegar or
    wine vinegar
2 tablespoons minced fresh basil or
    oregano

Heat the oven to 350 degrees.

Brush the garlic cloves with a little of the oil, reserving the remaining oil for the dressing. Put the garlic cloves in a shallow or flat baking dish and roast about 15 minutes or until golden and soft. Watch them carefully so they do not get too brown. Remove them from the oven and let cool.

Peel the garlic and put the pulp in the workbowl of a food processor. Add the remaining olive oil, tomatoes, lemon juice, green onion, vinegar and basil. Process 20 to 30 seconds, until smooth.

JULY

With good summer weather, most of the vegetable news is quiet right now, with prices steady and most items available. Eggplant, cucumbers, beans and squash are coming from the Carolinas now, and supplies will continue to move up the coast. Georgia sweet corn is about finished, and more northerly supplies will lag a week, so expect price increases on that vegetable. Mangoes are very low.

In beans, purple hull, black-eyed and pink-eyed peas, half runners, the longer and fuller pole, and the more tender snap beans are plentiful. Even okra, usually coming from Florida now, is plentiful in South Georgia. The price will be coming down. The smaller size is perfect for pickling, while the larger size is fine for slicing and cooking. A full line-up of cantaloupes are available, from the Maguam 45's — the standard grocery store good shipper — to the local Georgia favorite, Edisto — a large delicious melon that doesn't ship well and stays pretty close to home. Peaches are everywhere, and Vidalia onions are taking their last breath of the season. If you plan to buy them, do it now.

Fruit, in general, is cheaper this season due to a huge harvest for most items. Peaches, nectarines and plums are quite cheap, and the smaller sizes of plums are especially rock bottom in price. Florida avocados are back in season after being gone for three months. Look for nice California white peaches, lychees and some early figs. Lemons are reasonable, and limes are even cheaper. Do expect to see high prices on blueberries, as the southern berries are about finished. Sugar cane batons or sticks are starting to come into season and make a great snack. Florida will be out of celery for several weeks as growing areas change; supplies will come from California and likely be higher in price.

Per 2 tablespoons: 71 calories, 7 grams fat, no cholesterol, 5 milligrams sodium.

TUESDAY

GRILLED SALMON AND
ARUGULA SALAD WITH BLACK
OLIVE VINAIGRETTE
STEAMED FRAGRANT RICE *
BLUEBERRY COFFEE CAKE *

Leftover salmon makes a wonderful summer main-course dinner

salad. Here it is paired with the deep flavor of imported olives and spicy watercress. Choose watercress that is not too stemmy, or remove some of the larger stems, if necessary, to make the salad easier to eat. Choose a fragrant rice, such as Texmati or jasmine, available at several local grocery stores and the Dekalb Farmers Market; any leftover rice can go in Thursday's burritos. The most time-consuming part of the meal is the time it takes to pit the olives; substitute canned pitted black olives if you wish, but they won't have as much flavor.

GRILLED SALMON ON WATERCRESS WITH BLACK OLIVE VINAIGRETTE

Makes 4 servings
Preparation time: 15 minutes

20 brine-cured, imported black
    olives, pitted and chopped
1 1/4 cups olive oil
1/4 cup wine vinegar
1/4 teaspoon salt
Freshly ground black pepper
4 cups watercress or arugula leaves,
    washed and dried
3 or 4 cups other lettuce, washed and
    dried
1 pint cherry tomatoes, cut in half
12 to 16 ounces grilled salmon, cut
    into chunks, room temperature
Freshly ground black pepper

In the workbowl of a food processor or in a small bowl, combine the olives, olive oil, vinegar, salt and a generous grind of fresh pepper. Pulse or whisk together.

Toss the vinaigrette with watercress, other greens and tomatoes, reserving a tablespoon or two. Put the salad on 4 serving plates and top with salmon chunks and drizzle with extra vinaigrette. Grind a generous amount of black pepper over and serve.

Per serving: 439 calories, 37 grams fat, 42 milligrams cholesterol, 287 milligrams sodium.

WEDNESDAY

THAI HOT SUPPER SALAD
ANGEL-HAIR PASTA *
RASPBERRY FROZEN YOGURT
WITH BLUEBERRIES AND
NECTARINES *

This beef dish makes extra portions to serve later in the week. You can vary the heat of the dish by using a milder or hotter picante sauce. Offer frozen yogurt and fruit for dessert.

THAI HOT SUPPER SALAD

Makes 6 servings
Preparation time: 10 minutes
Cooking time: 20 minutes

1 pound lean ground beef or turkey
1 to 2 cloves garlic
3/4 cup picante sauce
2 teaspoons soy sauce
1 tablespoon lime or lemon juice
1 tablespoon finely shredded fresh
    ginger
4 cups shredded spinach leaves
1 tomato, cut into thin wedges
1/4 cup chopped peanuts
2 to 4 tablespoons chopped cilantro
2 green onions with tops, sliced

Put the meat and garlic in a large skillet and brown over medium-high heat; then drain the fat and discard. Stir in the picante sauce, soy sauce, lime juice and ginger; cook and stir 4 to 5 minutes or until the sauce has thickened slightly.

Meanwhile, put the spinach and tomatoes on a serving platter; spoon the hot meat mixture over. Sprinkle with peanuts, cilantro and green onions and serve.

Per serving, using turkey: 189 calories, 8 grams fat, 58 milligrams cholesterol, 312 milligrams sodium.

THURSDAY

SUSAN'S GUACAMOLE
BURRITOS FILLED WITH
GRILLED ZUCCHINI
AND SALMON *

FRESH PINEAPPLE SLICES AND
YOGURT CREAM *

Grilled zucchini flavored with basil butter and any leftover salmon pair well in a fat dinner burrito. Add any rice, lettuce, olives and tomatoes you have on hand and pack everything into warmed burrito-size tortillas. Serve homemade chunky guacamole, my newspaper editor Susan Pucket's favorite, alongside or tucked into the burritos. If you have yogurt cream left over, drizzle it over the pineapple and sprinkle with cinnamon.

SUSAN'S GUACAMOLE

Makes 1 cup
Preparation time: 5 minutes

2 ripe avocados
1 tablespoon lemon juice
1/4 cup roughly-chopped tomato
    salsa or picante sauce

Cut the avocados in half and remove the seeds. Scoop out the pulp with a spoon and place in a bowl. Add the lemon juice and mash the avocado with a fork until it is fairly smooth with some creamy chunks of avocado laced throughout. Top with the salsa and serve.

Per 1/4-cup serving: 159 calories, 15 grams fat, no cholesterol, 66 milligrams sodium.

FRIDAY

SAUSAGE CALZONES *
MARINATED ARTICHOKES *
ICE CREAM *

Choose pizza-crust turnovers filled with cheeses and sausage, available at most Italian restau-

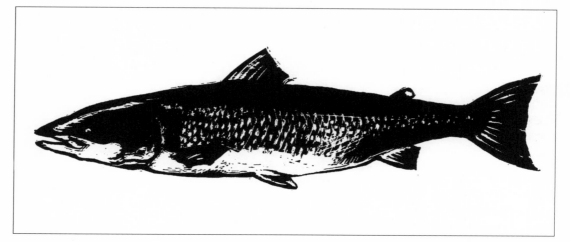

Price: The price ranges from $2.99 to $4.99, but many seafood departments will be featuring special prices on Chum for under $2.00. Look for continuing low prices throughout the summer.

Nutrition: A 3 ¹/₂-ounce serving has 120 calories, 3.8 grams fat, 49 milligrams cholesterol and 1,005 milligrams Omega-3 fatty acids. (As comparison, King salmon has 10 grams fat.)

Selection: Steaks will run about 8 ounces each, whole fish 4 to 9 pounds, which would serve 8 to 16 people. Chum comes whole (headed and gutted) or as steaks. Choose meat that glistens, with no bruises and a uniform silver skin color, free of dark reddish streaks. Don't buy fish that smell, or that are sitting in a puddle of fish juice. Buy fish as you leave the store, and refrigerate it as soon as possible to deter spoilage.

Storage: Store salmon in the coldest part of the refrigera-

tor. Leave it wrapped in the paper and plastic wrapping from the grocery store until use, in 2 or 3 days. After cooking, store tightly covered up to 5 days. No need to freeze the fish, as it will be plentiful all summer.

Uses: Grilling, smoking, baking, broiling or sauteing. Serve it hot or chill after cooking and use cold in a salad.

Alaskan Chum salmon, also called silverbrite, has hit town and plans to stay the summer. The Chum season started last week and will continue through most of October. Then the fish start swimming toward the rivers to spawn and the meat gets soft and loses its elasticity, says Mike Hulsey, retail coordinator at Inland Seafood in Atlanta.

Chum is a wild salmon, as are all Alaskan salmon, and has a more developed flavor than the milder farm-raised salmon from Scotland, Norway or Chile. Many stores will stop carrying imported Atlantic salmon during the summer and concen-

trate on the Chum. It is a good tasting fish — perhaps not as luxurious in taste or texture as King salmon, but the very best value for its reasonable price. It is a fine choice for barbecues and has long been a favorite fish for smoking. A middle-range fish is perfect for the grill, since grilling tends to overpower the flavor of a more subtle fish, says Chris Schlesinger, co-author of *Thrill of the Grill* (William Morrow, $24.95).

Chum are pinkish-orange and paler in color than the brilliant red Alaskan King salmon, due to a lower fat content. And the color varies: last week's Chum from Maine Bay in Prince William Sound was pink; this week's will come from the Yukon River in western Alaska and will be a more pronounced orange. Next week's Chum will come from Bristol Bay in central Alaska and will again be pinkish in color.

rants in Atlanta. Add marinated artichokes and ice cream for dessert.

SATURDAY

FETTUCCINE WITH BROKEN
GARLIC AND SNOW PEAS
CRUSTY BREAD *
ICE CREAM BALLS

The fresh crop of garlic arrives from the fields near Gilroy, California this weekend. The chefs at Berkley's Chez Panisse restaurant celebrate with an evening of garlic dishes, such as the following one adapted from their book *Chez Panisse Pasta Pizza and Calzone* by Alice Waters, Patricia Curtain & Martine Labro (Random House, $17.95). You could choose other vegetables that could stand up to the hearty garlic flavor, such as zucchini, eggplant or green beans. Add this easy ice cream dessert.

FETTUCCINE WITH BROKEN GARLIC AND SNOW PEAS

Makes 4 servings
Preparation time: 10 minutes
Cooking time: 20 minutes

6 small heads garlic, cloves separated
4 slices bacon, diced
16 to 20 fresh sage leaves, roughly
    chopped
1 bunch Italian parsley, left whole
1 pound fresh fettuccine noodles
1/2 to 2/3 cup chicken stock
1/2 pound snow peas
Salt and pepper to taste

With the side of a chef's knife or a cleaver, flatten each of the garlic cloves and slip off the skins.

Cook the pasta in boiling water until al dente.

Meanwhile, put the bacon in a large skillet and begin to fry. Add the garlic cloves, parsley and sage and gently cook without letting the garlic cloves burn; it will take about 10 minutes for the garlic to become golden. Add the peas and enough chicken stock to make a creamy mass without it being too watery.

When the pasta is cooked, drain and toss it, along with the bacon and garlic mixture. Season with salt and black pepper.

Per serving: 484 calories, 12 grams fat, 5 milligrams cholesterol, 282 milligrams sodium.

ICE CREAM BALLS

Makes 4 servings
Preparation time: 15 minutes
Cooking time: 30 seconds

2 pints good-quality vanilla ice cream
4 ounces finely chopped nuts, pecans,
    walnuts or almonds
3/4 cup fudge sauce
Sliced strawberries (for garnish)

Dip ice cream into scoops, a few at a time and roll in nuts. Freeze on a cookie sheet until ready to serve. Divide chocolate sauce among four microwave-safe dessert dishes and heat on medium (50 percent power) for 30 seconds or until the sauce is melted. Place the ice cream balls on top of melted chocolate and garnish with strawberries.

Per serving: 646 calories, 41 grams fat, 59 milligrams cholesterol, 156 milligrams sodium.

WEEK

27

SHOPPING LIST

Meat, poultry, seafood

- ❏ 3 pounds boneless pork butt, cut in 1-inch pieces
- ❏ 1 4- to 5-pound smoked turkey breast

Produce

- ❏ 3 ripe tomatoes
- ❏ 7 medium zucchini
- ❏ 10 garlic cloves
- ❏ 2 bunches green onions
- ❏ 2 shallots
- ❏ 1 large red onion
- ❏ ³/₄ pound Italian chicory and/or Belgian endive
- ❏ 1 3-ounce package sunflower seed sprouts
- ❏ 2 red bell peppers
- ❏ 2 celery stalks
- ❏ ¹/₄ watermelon
- ❏ 2 green mangoes
- ❏ 3 ripe mangoes
- ❏ 1 lime

- ❏ 4 plums
- ❏ 2 peaches
- ❏ 2 cups berries, your choice
- ❏ 1 bunch Italian parsley
- ❏ 2 or 3 bunches basil (to make 2 cups)
- ❏ 1 bunch oregano (optional)
- ❏ 1 bunch cilantro
- ❏ 1 bunch chives
- ❏ A handful of mint or lemon balm (optional)

Dairy

- ❏ 1 8-ounce carton lemon yogurt

Deli

- ❏ 1 loaf crusty bread
- ❏ 4 blueberry muffins
- ❏ 8 slices whole grain bread

- ❏ ²/₃ cup freshly grated Parmesan cheese

Miscellaneous

- ❏ 1 cup pineapple juice
- ❏ 9 tablespoons sesame seeds
- ❏ 3 cups uncooked rice
- ❏ 2 14 ¹/₂-ounce cans artichoke hearts
- ❏ ¹/₄ cup plus 2 tablespoons white vermouth
- ❏ 20 ounces spaghetti
- ❏ ¹/₂ cup smooth peanut butter
- ❏ ¹/₃ cup toasted sesame oil
- ❏ ¹/₄ to ¹/₂ cup roasted peanuts (optional)
- ❏ ¹/₄ cup chopped walnuts
- ❏ 2 cups sparkling water
- ❏ 1 teaspoon freshly grated orange rind
- ❏ 2 cups orange juice
- ❏ ¹/₂ cup blanched almonds

Staples

- ❏ Allspice
- ❏ Cinnamon
- ❏ Cracked black pepper
- ❏ Crushed red pepper flakes
- ❏ Curry powder
- ❏ Grainy mustard
- ❏ Ground cardamom
- ❏ Ground cumin
- ❏ Lemon juice
- ❏ Low-fat mayonnaise
- ❏ Low-sodium soy sauce
- ❏ Olive oil
- ❏ Salt
- ❏ Sugar
- ❏ Turmeric
- ❏ Walnut oil
- ❏ Wine vinegar

* Suggested accompaniments

GRILLED PORK SKEWERS WITH
GREEN MANGO
STEAMED RICE WITH GREEN
ONIONS AND SESAME SEEDS
SLICED TOMATOES *
SLICED WATERMELON *

Both of the following recipes produce copious amounts of delicious leftovers. The pork dish, adapted from *The Thrill of the Grill* by Chris Schlesinger and John Willoughby (Morrow, $24.95), utilizes a less-tender cut of meat that is also inexpensive. Green mango tenderizes meat while offering its characteristic flavor. Both dishes are full of flavor and fragrance. If you are using bamboo skewers, be sure to soak them in water for 30 minutes before cooking to prevent them from burning. This would be a great dish to make in the spring, using the golf-ball bulbs of green Vidalia onions.

GRILLED PORK SKEWERS WITH GREEN MANGO

Makes 8 servings
Preparation time: 30 minutes
Marinating time: 4-5 hours
Cooking time: 15 minutes

2 large green mangoes
1 tablespoon red pepper flakes
1 cup tropical fruit juice blend or
    pineapple juice
2 or 3 tablespoons apple cider vinegar
1/2 teaspoon ground cumin
1/2 teaspoon curry powder
2 large garlic cloves, minced
3 pounds boneless pork butt, cut into
    1-inch cubes
2 red bell peppers, seeded
1 large red onion
Salt and freshly cracked black pepper,
    to taste

To make the marinade: Peel one green mango and slice the fruit away from the pit (See In Season, Page 147). Put the fruit into a blender or food processor and pulse a few times to puree. Add the pepper flakes, fruit juice, vinegar, cumin, curry powder and garlic, and pulse to blend.

Place the pork cubes in a large shallow pan and pour the marinade over. Cover, refrigerate and marinate for several hours. When ready to cook, light the grill or preheat the oven to 350 degrees. Peel the second mango and cut the fruit away from the pit, making 1-inch chunks. Cut the red bell pepper into about 20 chunks, and cut the onion into 1-inch cubes.

Remove the meat from the marinade, and discard any marinade not clinging to the meat. Thread the pork cubes and pieces of mango, red pepper and onion on skewers. Season with salt and pepper. Grill the skewers over medium heat until the pork is cooked, 5 to 7 minutes per side or until the meat is cooked and tender.

Per serving: 474 calories, 33 grams fat, 112 milligrams cholesterol, 1 milligram sodium.

STEAMED RICE SPRINKLED WITH CHIVES AND SESAME SEEDS

Makes 8 servings
Preparation time: 10 minutes
Cooking time: 30 minutes

1 large bunch (about 1/2 cup),
    snipped in small pieces (or 2
    green onions, cut in thin slivers)
4 tablespoons sesame seeds
3 cups uncooked long-grain rice
6 cups water

Place chives in a bowl of cold water and soak for 5 or 10 minutes. To roast the sesame seeds, heat a cast-iron skillet over medium heat. Add the sesame seeds and stir 2 or 3 minutes, until they are lightly brown and fragrant. Take care that the seeds don't fly out; cover the pan if necessary.

Put the rice and water in a large saucepan. Bring to a boil and cover. On low heat, cook for 25 minutes.

Drain the onions and press the moisture out in a cloth or paper towel. Reserve all but 2 cups of the rice for later in the week. Serve the rice, garnished with the onions and sesame seeds.

Per serving: 284 calories, 3 grams fat, no cholesterol, 4 milligrams sodium.

ARTICHOKE HEARTS AND
CHICORY WITH WARM
WALNUT DRESSING
FRUIT TOSSED WITH LEMON
YOGURT AND CINNAMON *
CRUSTY BREAD *

Choose a vegetable main dish tonight to balance the heavier meat dish from yesterday. The elegant original of this recipe from Sally Schneider's *The Art of Low-Calorie Cooking* (Stewart, Tabori & Chang, $35), called for fresh artichoke bottoms; here canned artichoke hearts have been substituted to fit into a weeknight time schedule (but don't hesitate to use the fresh artichoke if you have time). Add summery fruit — plums, peaches and mixed berries — to yogurt and toss for a nice side dish. Add

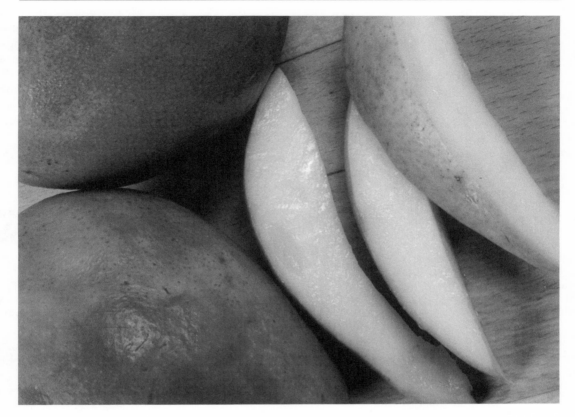

Price: Will range from $.59 to $.95 each.

Nutrition: A 200-gram fruit has 132 calories and is an excellent source of vitamins A and C and a good source of potassium.

Selection: Mangoes ripen from the seed out toward the skin and may be ripe without feeling soft to the touch, so choose mangos by their fragrance rather than by feel. They should be fully colored, and free of blemishes and have a full fruity aroma.

Storage: Mangoes are shipped green (unripe), and most need to be ripened before using. Some recipes (see Menu Planner, page 146) call for green mangoes. Don't refrigerate mangoes until they are completely ripe: while they will soften, refrigerator temperatures stop any sugar development. Instead, allow them to ripen at room temperature, which will take 3 or 4 days. Fully-ripe mangoes will be almost as tender as a ripe avocado. Mangoes require no special handling to prevent browning.

Uses: One medium mango, peeled and pitted yields about 2 cups of fruit. Fresh mango can be cut and added to fruit and meat salads, grilled with seafood or added to milkshakes and ice cream. Green mangoes are used to make delicious chutneys.

The fragrant, melting flesh of the mango, sandwiched between a leathery peel and stubborn pit, is in season now through late August and shouldn't be missed. From now through the end of the season, at least five varieties will pass through stores. Most of the mangoes available locally come from the southernmost part of Florida, Texas, Mexico, Haiti, and Central and South America.

crusty bread for dipping.

ARTICHOKE BOTTOMS AND CHICORY WITH WARM WALNUT DRESSING

Makes 4 servings
Preparation time: 5 minutes
Cooking time: 8 minutes

2 14 ¹/₂-ounce cans artichoke hearts
³/₄ pound total, Italian chicory and
    Belgian endive, leaves
    separated
¹/₄ cup plus 2 tablespoons white
    vermouth
2 shallots, minced
2 teaspoons wine or champagne
    vinegar
1 tablespoon plus 2 teaspoons
    walnut oil
¹/₄ cup walnuts, coarsely chopped
1 tablespoon minced Italian parsley
Freshly ground pepper

Drain the artichokes. Place the chicory and endive in a medium bowl and set aside.

In a small saucepan, combine the vermouth and shallots. Bring to a boil over moderately high heat. Using a long kitchen match, ignite the vermouth and cook until the flames die down, 1 to 2 minutes. Add the vinegar and walnut oil and boil vigorously until the oil and vermouth are combined, about 1 minute.

Put the chicory, endive and artichoke hearts in a large mixing bowl and toss with the warm dressing. Divide among 4 serving plates. Spoon any remaining dressing over. Top the salads with walnuts, parsley and pepper to taste.

Per serving: 244 calories, 12 grams fat, no cholesterol, 97 milligrams sodium.

TUESDAY

COLD PORK SANDWICHES*
ZUCCHINI AND BASIL RICE SALAD

This quick meal makes great picnic or pool fare. Slice the cooked pork into thin slivers and use for sandwiches; it will be so flavorful you won't need additional seasonings. Serve the sandwiches with a grainy mustard, sunflower sprouts and whole grain bread.

The zucchini salad is quintessentially summer. Serve it hot or cold, and leftovers taste better the next day. Because the zucchini is grated and blends in anonymously, it's a good salad for folks who balk at eating this nutritious vegetable. It is also delicious made with orzo, a rice-shaped pasta. Look for large, inexpensive bunches of basil at local farmers markets.

ZUCCHINI AND BASIL RICE SALAD

Makes 8 servings
Preparation time: 15 minutes
Standing time: 20 minutes

4 medium zucchini, coarsely grated
1 teaspoon salt
2 cups packed fresh basil leaves
3 garlic cloves, peeled
1 tablespoon fresh oregano or
    1 teaspoon dried
¹/₂ cup olive oil
3 cups cooked rice, room temperature
¹/₄ cup lemon juice
¹/₄ cup grated Parmesan cheese
3 tablespoons chopped parsley

Sprinkle zucchini with salt in a colander and toss. Let stand 20 minutes, stirring once or twice. Squeeze zucchini dry with your hands or the back of a wooded spoon. Put the zucchini in a large bowl.

Meanwhile, put basil, garlic and oregano together in a food processor or blender and process until the ingredients are well chopped. Add oil and pulse a couple of times. Stir in drained zucchini, rice, lemon juice, cheese and parsley and stir to blend well.

Per serving: 240 calories, 15 grams fat, 2 milligrams cholesterol, 348 milligrams sodium.

WEDNESDAY

SPICY NOODLES WITH PEANUT SAUCE AND VEGETABLES
SMOKED TURKEY BREAST*

Peanutty sesame noodles are always a hit in my household, particularly chilled. Some commercial peanut sauces are available that are as good as homemade, but this version takes only minutes to prepare, and for just pennies.

Toasted sesame oil adds the distinctive flavor that makes this dish so special. Look for Oriental brands or an American brand — Loriva is particularly good. The sauce goes together easier if the peanut butter is slightly warmed and creamy; heat it in the microwave for a few seconds, or over steaming water.

SPICY NOODLES WITH PEANUT SAUCE AND VEGETABLES

Makes 8 servings
Preparation time: 10 minutes
Cooking time: 10 minutes

1 pound dry spaghetti
1/2 cup peanut butter, room
    temperature or slightly warmed
1/3 cup sugar
1/2 cup low-sodium soy sauce
2 to 3 teaspoons red pepper flakes
6 to 8 tablespoons toasted sesame oil
3 large garlic cloves, minced

GARNISHES (optional):
3 green onions, chopped
1/2 cup sunflower seed sprouts
1 tablespoon toasted sesame seeds
1/4 cup roasted peanuts
1/4 to 1/2 cup fresh cilantro, stems
    removed and roughly chopped

Cook pasta in a large pot of boiling salted water until done, about 10 minutes, then drain well.

Meanwhile, put garlic in the workbowl of a food processor and pulse until minced. Add peanut butter, sugar, soy sauce, pepper flakes and sesame oil and process until thoroughly blended.

Toss the sauce with the drained noodles. Serve hot or let stand at room temperature for a few hours if possible to develop flavors, or refrigerate and serve within 2 days. Toss the noodles before serving to redistribute sauce. To serve, place the noodles in a large shallow dish, such as a pasta dish. Top with any of the suggested garnishes.

Per serving: 512 calories, 21 grams fat, no cholesterol, 489 milligrams sodium.

THURSDAY

ZUCCHINI AND BASIL RICE SALAD *
BLUEBERRY MUFFINS *

You'll be glad to find leftover Basil Rice Salad in the refrigerator. Add purchased or prepared blueberry muffins.

FRIDAY

SPICY NOODLES WITH PEANUT SAUCE AND VEGETABLES *
MANGOADE

Leftover cold sesame noodles make a good Friday night dinner. The fabulous and refreshing mango drink perfectly complements the Asian flavor of the noodle dish. Garnish the mangoade with a few (unsprayed) rose petals for a beautiful and fragrant drink. Cut out the slightly bitter white "heels" of the rose petals before you use them.

MANGOADE

Makes 6 servings
Preparation time: 5 minutes
Cooking time: 5 minutes
Chilling time: 10 minutes

1 large mango (enough to make 2
    cups pulp)
1/4 cup sugar, or to taste
2 cups sparkling mineral water
2 cups orange juice
1 teaspoon grated orange rind
Ice cubes
Slices of lime
mint sprigs for garnish (optional)

Peel the mangos and slice the fruit away from the pit. Put all the little and big pieces of mangoes in a blender or workbowl of a food processor and puree.

Combine the sugar, water and orange rind in a saucepan and heat, stirring, until the sugar dissolves. Let the mixture chill, or put in the freezer for 10 minutes to speed up chilling. Stir in the mango puree. Add orange juice and rind. Serve on ice, in tall glasses, decorated with a slice of lime and (optional) mint or lemon balm sprigs.

Per serving: 106 calories, trace of fat, no cholesterol, 2 milligrams sodium.

SATURDAY

MANGO AND SMOKED TURKEY SALAD
ZUCCHINI WITH ALMONDS
CORN ON THE COB *

When it's too hot to cook, you'll be glad to have leftover smoked turkey for a delicious salad, adapted from one of my favorite books, *Uncommon Fruits and Vegetables* by Elizabeth Schneider (Harper & Row, $16.95). Fresh mango, fully ripened during the week, adds a sweet counterpoint to the fragrant spices. Any leftover sunflower seed sprouts would make a good garnish in place of chives.

MANGO AND SMOKED TURKEY SALAD

Makes 4 servings
Preparation time: 20 minutes
Chilling time: 2 or more hours

1/3 to 1/2 cup low-fat mayonnaise
1/2 teaspoon curry powder
Pinch ground cardamom
3/4 to 1 pound sliced smoked turkey
    breast, cut in julienne
2 celery stalks, cut into 1/4-inch dice
1 green onion, sliced in paper-thin
    rings
Pepper, to taste
Ground allspice, to taste
2 large mangoes, ripe but
still firm, peeled and halved
2 tablespoons snipped chives
1/4 cup chopped walnuts (optional)

Place mayonnaise in a small bowl and stir in the curry powder and cardamom. Set aside.

Put turkey in a large mixing bowl with the celery, onion and prepared mayonnaise. Season with pepper and allspice to taste. Cover and chill for a few hours or overnight.

Before serving, peel and cut the mangoes into 1/2-inch slices. Arrange decoratively on four serving plates. Add turkey salad. Sprinkle with chives (optional) and serve.

Per serving: 375 calories, 13 grams fat, 112 milligrams cholesterol, 440 milligrams sodium.

ZUCCHINI WITH ALMONDS

Makes 4 servings
Preparation time: 10 minutes
Cooking time: 3 minutes

1/4 cup olive oil
1/2 cup sliced blanched almonds
3 medium zucchini, cut in large dice
2 or 3 garlic cloves, minced
Salt, to taste
6 tablespoons freshly grated
    Parmesan cheese

Heat the oil in a large skillet. Add the almonds and cook over high heat for a few seconds, stirring constantly, just until golden brown. Remove the almonds with a slotted spoon and drain on paper towels.

Pour off all but 1 or 2 tablespoons of the oil and add the zucchini, garlic and salt. Stir and toss the pieces for about 2 minutes or until they are tender-crisp. Put zucchini in a serving bowl and top with cheese and almonds.

Per serving: 211 calories, 18 grams fat, 5 milligrams cholesterol, 134 milligrams sodium.

WEEK

28

SHOPPING LIST

Meat, poultry, seafood

- ❑ 2 3-pound whole chicken fryers
- ❑ 1 pound shrimp

Produce

- ❑ 4 cloves garlic
- ❑ 3 medium to large onions
- ❑ 2 small red onions or 1 large
- ❑ 1 package celery
- ❑ 4 or 5 carrots
- ❑ 2 to 3 pounds all-purpose potatoes
- ❑ 12 ounces medium mushrooms
- ❑ 5 zucchini or yellow crookneck squash
- ❑ 3 green or red bell peppers
- ❑ 1 head radicchio or other red leaf lettuce
- ❑ 1 head Boston or Bibb lettuce
- ❑ 4 or 5 ripe tomatoes
- ❑ 1 pound okra
- ❑ 5 to 8 large lemons
- ❑ 10 to 12 peaches
- ❑ $^1/_2$ pound nectarines
- ❑ $^1/_2$ pound red plums
- ❑ $^1/_2$ pound blueberries or blackberries
- ❑ 4 bananas
- ❑ 2 cups basil
- ❑ 1 bunch fresh mint

Dairy

- ❑ $^1/_2$ cup low-fat cottage cheese
- ❑ $^2/_3$ cup plain low-fat yogurt
- ❑ 2 tablespoons grated Parmesan cheese
- ❑ 3 cups low-fat milk
- ❑ 1 pint red raspberry frozen yogurt
- ❑ 4 tablespoons unsalted butter
- ❑ 1 cup heavy cream

Deli

- ❑ 4 to 8 bakery rolls
- ❑ 4 popovers
- ❑ 4 blueberry muffins
- ❑ $^1/_2$ pound hard cheese, such as Cheddar or Gouda
- ❑ $^1/_4$ pound salami, thinly sliced

Miscellaneous

- ❑ 1 14 $^1/_2$-ounce can chicken broth, plus $^1/_2$ cup
- ❑ $^1/_2$ cup raspberry or plum jam
- ❑ 1 package active dry yeast
- ❑ 2 cups converted or long-grain rice
- ❑ 20 amaretti or lemon cookies
- ❑ 2 4-ounce packages ramen noodles
- ❑ 1 cinnamon stick

Staples

- ❑ All-purpose flour
- ❑ Bay leaf
- ❑ Black pepper
- ❑ Corn oil
- ❑ Dried oregano
- ❑ Dried red pepper flakes
- ❑ Granulated sugar
- ❑ Hoisin sauce
- ❑ Kosher salt (optional)
- ❑ Lemon juice
- ❑ Light brown sugar
- ❑ Olive oil
- ❑ Salt
- ❑ Thyme
- ❑ Vegetable oil

* Suggested accompaniments

WHOLE ROAST LEMON CHICKEN WITH VEGETABLES
BAKERY ROLLS *
SUMMER FRUIT SIMMERED WITH STAR ANISE

The best-yet chicken dish was inspired by cookbook author, Marlene Sorosky, from her must-have book *Easy Entertaining With Marlene Sorosky* (Harper & Row, $22.50). If you really need to serve a crowd, this dish is equally good, but use the larger roasters instead of fryers, and cook another 20 minutes. Reserve a couple of breasts and thighs for later in the week, and the celery tops for tomorrow night's dinner. If you have vanilla sugar prepared in the pantry, it makes a fine addition to the summer compote; otherwise, use plain sugar. Prepare the batter today for Monday's vegetable fry.

WHOLE ROAST LEMON CHICKEN WITH VEGETABLES

Makes 8 servings
Preparation time: 20 minutes
Cooking time: 1 hour, 10 minutes

2 whole chicken fryers, washed and
    dried inside and out
2 teaspoons salt, or to taste
1 teaspoon black pepper
3 or 4 tablespoons fresh Italian
    parsley, minced
4 cloves garlic, minced
$^1/_3$ to $^1/_2$ cup olive oil, divided
2 large lemons, pierced all over
    with fork
2 medium to large onions, sliced
    $^1/_2$ inch thick
4 or 5 stalks celery, peeled and sliced,
    including leaves
4 or 5 carrots, scrubbed and sliced

2 to 3 pounds all-purpose potatoes,
    cubed
$^2/_3$ cup lemon juice (3 or 4 lemons)
$^1/_3$ cup low-sodium chicken broth

Preheat the oven to 500 degrees.

In a bowl, stir together the salt, black pepper, parsley, garlic and oil. Rub the mixture over the chickens. Put a pierced lemon inside each chicken, then put the vegetables in the bottom of a large shallow roasting pan and put chickens on top, breast side up. Stir together the lemon juice and chicken broth and pour over the chicken and vegetables. Bake, uncovered, for 20 minutes. Turn chickens over and roast, back side up for 20 more minutes, basting the vegetables occasionally.

Lower oven heat to 450 degrees and turn chickens breast side up. Cook 20 minutes, basting vegetables and chickens occasionally. The chicken is done when the drumsticks move easily.

Remove the chickens from the roasting pan and let them rest for 10 minutes; then remove lemons from cavities and reserve. Cut chickens into serving pieces and place on a serving platter with vegetables. Cut the reserved lemons in half and squeeze lemon juice over all. Skim the fat from the pan juices and serve on the side.

Per serving: 762 calories, 35 grams fat, 206 milligrams cholesterol, 418 milligrams sodium.

SUMMER FRUIT SIMMERED WITH STAR ANISE

Makes 6 servings
Preparation time: 15 minutes
Cooking time: 30 minutes

1 $^1/_2$ cups water

$^1/_2$ cup raspberry or plum jam
4 to 6 sprigs fresh mint
1 cinnamon stick
1 star anise
1 tablespoon vanilla or granulated
    sugar
$^1/_2$ lemon, cut in half
2 medium peaches, peeled and sliced
2 nectarines, sliced
2 red plums, sliced
$^1/_2$ cup blueberries or blackberries
Fresh mint, basil or cinnamon basil,
    for garnish

In a large saucepan, combine water, jam, mint, cinnamon stick, star anise, sugar and lemon. Bring to a boil, lower the heat and simmer for 15 minutes. Discard the mint, lemon and cinnamon stick.

Add the peaches and simmer for 5 minutes, the nectarines and simmer for 5 minutes, the plums and simmer 5 minutes. Finally, add the berries and take off the heat and chill. To serve, place in a beautiful bowl and garnish with fresh herbs.

Per serving: 135 calories, less than 1 gram fat, no cholesterol, 2 milligrams sodium.

CHELSEA STREET MIXED VEGETABLE FRY
PLATTER OF CHEESE AND SALAMI *
FRESH PEACHES *

Fresh vegetables — quickly fried and served with lemons and salt — make a great first course, followed by a hearty cheese and salami platter. Cut the vegetables in a uniform size so they cook evenly. If you can find lovage, an anise-flavored vegetable in the celery family, its stems and leaves would make a wonderful substi-

Price: Normal price is $7.99 a pound, on special this week may be as low as $4.99 a pound.

Nutrition: A 3-ounce serving has 90 calories, 95 milligrams cholesterol, a trace of fat and is a good source of zinc.

Selection: Look for 1- to 1 1/2-pound lobsters with both claws the same size (if a claw has broken off and regenerated, the lobster is considered a "cull" and is not as valuable). Look for lobsters that move around and reach back and turn tails under when picked up. If the lobster is limp it may be dead. Look for hard shells and lobsters that seem heavy for their size.

Storage: Refrigerate as soon as possible for 1 to 2 days, but best to eat as soon as possible. Store in a sealed plastic bag in the coldest part of the refrigerator.

Uses: About a third of the weight of a lobster is edible meat. Lobsters may be steamed, baked, boiled or grilled. Use the meat for salads and casseroles. Many grocery stores now steam lobsters while you wait.

The American lobsters (better known as Maine lobsters), that are in Atlanta stores now come from the cold waters around Nova Scotia and northern Maine where they are now in greatest concentration. Many stores will have live lobsters on sale for a couple of weeks, and they are a good summer bargain.

Lobster fishermen have to work harder to get their catch in the winter, as the shallow inlets freeze and lobsters migrate to deeper waters, but winter lobsters are especially meaty and of excellent quality. During the summer lobsters swim back to shallow waters, but their shells have less meat and more water.

Large lobsters are not necessarily tougher than smaller ones, but they are often overcooked.

tute for celery. Pull from the refrigerator the batter you prepared yesterday; the extra day of resting time will develop its flavor. If you didn't make it in advance, allow 30 minutes for it to stand before frying the vegetables.

CHELSEA STREET MIXED VEGETABLE FRY

Makes 4 servings
Preparation time: 20 minutes
Cooking time: 15 minutes

BATTER:
1 1/2 cups warm water
1 package (or 2 teaspoons) active dry
    yeast
1 tablespoon olive oil
1 cup all-purpose or unbleached
    (but not bread) flour
1 teaspoon salt

VEGETABLES:
4 ounces medium mushrooms,
    cleaned, stemmed, quartered
3 zucchini and/or yellow squash, cut
    in 1-inch chunks
2 small red onions, cut in 1-inch
    chunks
1 bunch fresh sage leaves
Vegetable oil for frying
2 lemons, cut into wedges
Salt

In a large bowl, stir together the water, yeast, oil, flour and salt. Cover the bowl with plastic wrap and refrigerate overnight, or at least let it rest 30 minutes before using.

Heat the oven to 250 degrees.

Pour 1 to 2 inches of oil into a deep skillet or heavy kettle. Heat over medium-high heat to 375 degrees or until a drop of batter sizzles instantly.

Dip the vegetables in the batter, then slip a few into the oil one at a time. Fry until golden and puffed, about 3 minutes. Between batches, make sure the oil gets back to 375 degrees, to prevent soggy vegetables. Fry the remaining vegetables. Keep the finished vegetables warm in a 250 degree oven on a baking sheet lined with paper towels.

Serve the vegetables with lemon wedges and salt.

Per serving: 219 calories, 13 grams fat, no cholesterol, 272 milligrams sodium.

TUESDAY

VERY LEMON CHICKEN SALAD POPOVERS *

A food processor and leftover chicken make this delicious dinner a snap. Save any remaining lemon-basil dressing for salads or cold pasta dishes.

VERY LEMON CHICKEN SALAD

Makes 4 to 6 servings and 1 3/4
*   cup dressing*
Preparation time: 15 minutes

1 medium head radicchio, leaves
    separated, rinsed and dried
1 head Boston or Bibb lettuce, leaves
    separated, rinsed and dried
3 cups cooked lemon chicken,
    cut in julienne

LEMON-BASIL DRESSING:
1 cup packed fresh basil leaves
4 tablespoons lemon juice
3/4 cup light mayonnaise
Salt and pepper to taste
Sprigs of fresh basil as garnish

Toss the lettuces in a salad bowl and add the chicken. Set aside.

Put the basil in the work-

bowl of a food processor and process until minced. Add the lemon juice and mayonnaise and pulse to combine. Season to taste with salt and pepper. Process 1 minute or until smooth. Toss with the salad and serve.

Per serving: 367 calories, 28 grams fat, 110 milligrams cholesterol, 344 milligrams sodium.

WEDNESDAY

CREAMY VEGETABLE RISOTTO BLUEBERRY MUFFINS *

This easy version of Italian risotto is quick enough to cook on a weeknight. The cottage cheese adds a creamy texture without the calories. Add purchased or homemade muffins to complete the meal.

CREAMY VEGETABLE RISOTTO

Makes 4 servings
Preparation time: 5 minutes
Cooking time: 20 minutes

1/2 cup low-fat cottage cheese
1/4 cup plain low-fat yogurt
2 tablespoons grated Parmesan
    cheese
1 1/4 teaspoons salt
1/8 teaspoon black pepper
3 cups low-fat milk
1 cup converted or long-grain rice
1/2 large red or green bell pepper,
    seeded and chopped
1 large zucchini or yellow crookneck
    squash, sliced
1 cup mushrooms, sliced

In a food processor, combine cottage cheese, yogurt, Parmesan cheese, salt and black pepper; process until smooth, about 10 seconds. Set aside.

In a medium saucepan, bring

milk just to a boil; stir in rice and reduce heat. Simmer, covered, for 5 minutes. Stir in bell pepper; simmer, covered, for 5 minutes. Stir in squash and mushrooms; simmer, covered, until rice is tender, 5 to 8 minutes longer (not all of the liquid will be absorbed). Remove from heat, stir in cottage cheese mixture and serve immediately.

Per serving: 325 calories, 5 grams fat, 19 milligrams cholesterol, 947 milligrams sodium.

THURSDAY

RAMEN NOODLES WITH VEGETABLES
RED RASPBERRY FROZEN YOGURT *

Dry ramen noodles, available in the soup section of the grocery store, cook in minutes to make an easy dinner of leftovers. Pull any vegetables and chicken pieces from the refrigerator and add to the ramen as it finishes cooking. Look for sweet and sour sauce in the Oriental section of the grocery store, or at specialty stores and farmers markets.

RAMEN NOODLES WITH VEGETABLES

Makes 4 servings
Preparation time: 5 minutes
Cooking time: 10 minutes

1 14-ounce can chicken broth
1/4 to 1/2 cup chopped red (or other) onions, optional
1/2 cup water (optional)
2 4-ounce packages ramen noodles
1 1/2 to 2 cups chopped cooked vegetables — celery, peppers, zucchini, yellow squash, mushrooms, potatoes

2 teaspoons hoisin sauce

Place the chicken broth and any onions in a large saucepan and bring to a boil. Add the noodles, discarding the flavor packets. Stir the noodles occasionally as they cook, about 5 minutes, until they are soft. Add optional water if you prefer a soupy dish; leave it out for a drier dish. Add any cooked vegetables and chicken and cook and toss just until heated through. Toss with sweet and sour sauce and serve.

Per serving: 177 calories, 5 grams fat, less than 1 milligram cholesterol, 807 milligrams sodium.

FRIDAY

CUBAN SANDWICHES *
DILL PICKLE WEDGES *
FRESH SLICED TOMATOES *

Pick up Cuban sandwiches at a deli on the way home from work. The version from Happy Herman's has roasted pork, baked ham, Swiss cheese and their secret mojo sauce, served on Cuban bread.

SATURDAY

SHRIMP GUMBO
STEAMED RICE *
BANANA PEACH CRUMBLE WITH YOGURT CREAM

Make this zesty summer meal in minutes. The fruit crumble can be served warm or at room temperature, so bake it early in the day while the kitchen is still cool.

SHRIMP GUMBO

Makes 4 servings
Preparation time: 10 minutes
Cooking time: 30 minutes

1 medium onion, sliced
1/2 green bell pepper, sliced
2 tablespoons olive oil
2 cups peeled and chopped ripe tomatoes
4 or 5 sprigs thyme
Salt and ground black pepper, to taste
1 pound fresh okra, cut in 1/2-inch rounds
1 pound medium shrimp, peeled and cleaned
1 teaspoon dried red pepper flakes

Saute the onion and green pepper in olive oil. Add the tomatoes, thyme, salt and pepper; simmer, uncovered, for 15 minutes. Add okra to the tomato sauce and cook for about 5 minutes.

Add shrimp and red pepper to the pan; simmer for 5 minutes. Serve over rice.

Per serving: 200 calories, 8 grams fat, 166 milligrams cholesterol, 201 milligrams sodium.

BANANA PEACH CRUMBLE WITH YOGURT CREAM

Make 6 servings
Preparation time: 10 minutes
Cooking time: 20 minutes

CAKE:
4 bananas, cut into 1-inch chunks
4 peaches, peeled, cored and cut into 1-inch chunks
3 tablespoons light brown sugar
1 tablespoon fresh lemon juice
4 tablespoons unsalted butter
20 amaretti or lemon cookies
1 cup yogurt cream (see page 140)

Preheat oven to 350 degrees. Generously butter an 8-inch-square baking dish.

In a bowl, combine bananas, peaches, sugar and lemon juice. Toss to coat; then put in a baking dish. Melt the butter in the microwave oven or a small saucepan.

In the workbowl of a food processor, process the cookies until they resemble coarse crumbs. Stir in the melted butter and sprinkle the crumbs evenly over the fruit. Bake 20 minutes, or until bubbly and the crumbs are golden. Serve hot or at room temperature with yogurt cream.

Per serving: 380 calories, 20 grams fat, 55 milligrams cholesterol, 135 milligrams sodium.

WEEK

29

SHOPPING LIST

Meat, poultry, seafood

- ❑ 1 ¹/₄ pound catfish fillets
- ❑ ¹/₂ pound lean ground beef or sausage
- ❑ 4 8- to 10-ounce T-bone steaks

Produce

- ❑ 4 Italian eggplants or 1 large eggplant
- ❑ 2 peppers, red and/or green
- ❑ 7 large tomatoes
- ❑ 9 garlic cloves
- ❑ 1 green onion
- ❑ 1 bunch fresh spinach
- ❑ 1 head lettuce, any type
- ❑ 3 large red potatoes
- ❑ 1 3-ounce package alfalfa sprouts
- ❑ 1 bunch Italian parsley
- ❑ 1 bunch fresh rosemary
- ❑ 2 bunches basil (enough to make ¹/₂ cup roughly chopped)
- ❑ 1 cantaloupe or other melon
- ❑ 1 pint blueberries

Dairy

- ❑ 1 cup half-and-half
- ❑ 1 pint lemon frozen yogurt

Deli

- ❑ 8 whole wheat pita breads
- ❑ 1 pint coleslaw
- ❑ 1 loaf crusty bread
- ❑ 8 ounces Brie cheese
- ❑ ¹/₂ cup (2 ounces) grated mozzarella cheese
- ❑ 2 ounces freshly grated Parmesan cheese
- ❑ 4 to 8 lemon cookies
- ❑ 1 medium Boboli or other pizza crust
- ❑ 1 cup pitted black olives

Miscellaneous

- ❑ 2 19-ounce cans garbanzo beans (chickpeas)
- ❑ ³/₄ cup sesame paste (tahini)
- ❑ 1 ¹/₂ cups dry fragrant rice
- ❑ ¹/₃ cup dry-roasted peanuts
- ❑ 1 pound linguine
- ❑ 3 cups strong coffee, preferably dark-roast

Staples

- ❑ Black pepper
- ❑ Curry powder
- ❑ Granulated sugar
- ❑ Ground ginger
- ❑ Lemon juice
- ❑ Lemon pepper
- ❑ Light soy sauce
- ❑ Olive oil
- ❑ Salt
- ❑ Sugar
- ❑ Vegetable oil

* Suggested accompaniments

SUNDAY

CASA BLANCA ROASTED
VEGETABLE SALAD
HUMMUS WITH ALFALFA
SPROUTS
HOT PITA BREADS *
MELON WEDGES *

These chilled Mediterranean salads offer intense flavors for summer nights. Hummus, made from pureed garbanzo beans and tahini — a nutty-flavored puree of sesame seeds (available in many grocery stores and health food stores) — adds protein and a smooth counterpoint to the smokey-flavored roasted vegetable salad. Both salads offer leftovers. The hummus freezes beautifully.

Vegetable pieces are easy to grill when you use a pan designed for the purpose; the grated box sits on top of the regular grill rack and makes it impossible to lose slices into the fire. Choose one standard large eggplant or several Japanese eggplants (see In Season, Page 159). The long, skinny Japanese variety or egg-shaped white eggplant has the best flavor, fewer seeds and roasts more quickly than larger, standard varieties.

CASA BLANCA ROASTED VEGETABLE SALAD

Makes 8 to 9 servings
Preparation time: 15 minutes
Cooking time: 20 minutes

4 Italian eggplants or 1 large eggplant
2 peppers, red or green
4 to 6 garlic cloves, left whole
2 large ripe but firm tomatoes, left whole
4 to 6 green onions, chopped
3 tablespoons olive oil
3 tablespoons lemon juice
2 tablespoons chopped fresh Italian parsley
1 to 1 1/2 teaspoons chopped fresh rosemary
Salt and black pepper to taste
4 pita breads

Preheat the grill or oven to 400 degrees.

Prick the eggplants four or five times with the tines of a fork. On the grill or on an unoiled cookie sheet, roast the peppers, eggplant and garlic cloves for 10 minutes, turning the vegetables for even browning. (If using larger eggplants, cook 30 minutes.) Add the tomatoes and green onions and roast another 10 minutes. The eggplants and peppers are done when they are tender and sunken-looking.

While still hot, place the peppers in a paper bag and put in the freezer for 10 minutes for later peeling. Allow the other vegetables to cool.

Scoop the eggplant pulp from the skin and chop it. Peel the pepper skins off and discard, then chop the peppers into 1/2-inch pieces. Remove the garlic skins and mince the garlic. Cut the tomatoes in half; remove seeds and extract juice. Chop the tomato into 1/2-inch pieces.

Mix the roasted vegetables together with the oil, lemon juice, garlic, onion, parsley, rosemary, salt and pepper and serve stuffed in warm pita bread halves.
Per serving: 55 calories, 4 grams fat, no cholesterol, 6 milligrams sodium.

HUMMUS

Makes 8 servings
Preparation time: 10 minutes

2 19-ounce cans garbanzo beans, slightly drained
4 garlic cloves, minced
1/3 to 1/2 cup lemon juice
3/4 to 1 cup sesame tahini (pureed sesame seeds)
Freshly ground black pepper
1 tablespoon olive oil (optional)
1 3-ounce package alfalfa sprouts
4 pita breads

Place the beans, garlic, lemon juice, tahini and a generous amount of black pepper in a food processor and process until smooth and creamy. If the mixture seems too stiff, add a tablespoon more of lemon juice or olive oil. Refrigerate until serving time.

Just before serving time, heat the pita breads in a warm oven (300 degrees) for 5 minutes. Let guests stuff pita bread halves with hummus, roasted vegetables and alfalfa sprouts.
Per serving: 296 calories, 13 grams fat, no cholesterol, 420 milligrams sodium.

MONDAY

CURRIED CATFISH,
THAI STYLE
STEAMED FRAGRANT RICE *
COLESLAW *

For this light dinner, catfish fillets bake in only eight minutes. Serve fragrant rice, such as jasmine Thai rice, steamed with almonds. Cook enough to have leftover rice.

CURRIED CATFISH, THAI STYLE

Makes 4 servings
Preparation time: 5 minutes
Cooking time: 8 minutes

2 tablespoons light soy sauce
1 tablespoon vegetable oil
2 teaspoons curry powder
1/2 teaspoon ground ginger

Price: Prices will be as low as $.49 a pound for large eggplant to $1.49 a pound for some of the specialty varieties.

Nutrition: A one-cup cooked portion has about 38 calories and is not especially rich in any one vitamin or mineral.

Selection: Eggplant are available all year, but peak from July through October. Look for firm eggplant that is heavy for its size, with taut, glossy, deeply colored skin. An oval mark at the blossom end indicates fewer seeds and firmer flesh; a round mark indicates the opposite. The stem should be bright green. Dull skin and rust-colored spots indicate old age.

Storage: Refrigerate, unwashed, in a plastic bag for up to 5 days.

Uses: Allow about $1/2$ pound per serving. One large eggplant weighs about $1 1/2$ pounds and should serve 4 people. A one-pound eggplant will yield 4 cups of diced flesh. Eggplant may be stuffed, fried, sauted, stir-fried, roasted whole, baked, layered or added to a spaghetti sauce in a traditional Sicilian recipe.

Lemon pepper, to taste
$1 1/4$ pound catfish fillets
$1/3$ cup dry-roasted peanuts

Preheat the oven to 475 degrees. Grease a baking sheet with vegetable spray.

Combine the soy sauce, oil, curry powder, ginger and lemon pepper in a plastic bag. Add the catfish fillets and toss to coat. Arrange the fillets in a single layer on the baking sheet and bake 8 minutes. Top with peanuts and serve.

Per serving: 274 calories, 16 grams fat, 82 milligrams cholesterol, 332 milligrams sodium.

TUESDAY

LINGUINE WITH TOMATOES AND BASIL
CRUSTY BREAD *
BLUEBERRIES WITH LEMON FROZEN YOGURT *

Tonight, let the warm kitchen do the cooking for you. This uncooked tomato pasta sauce mellows and melts with room-temperature cheese. Along with fresh basil leaves, it has a lively, fresh flavor that cooked sauces can't match. Save leftovers for Thursday night.

LINGUINE WITH TOMATOES AND BASIL

Makes 8 servings
Preparation time: 15 minutes
Cooking time: 10 minutes

4 large, very soft and ripe tomatoes, cut into $1/2$-inch chunks
8 to 10 ounces Italian Fontina or Brie, rind removed (to make about 6 or 8 ounces), and torn into small pieces
$1/2$ cup packed basil leaves, roughly chopped
2 to 3 garlic cloves, minced
$1/2$ cup olive oil
1 teaspoon salt
$1/4$ teaspoon freshly ground black pepper
1 pound linguine
Freshly grated Parmesan cheese (optional)

In a large shallow bowl, combine the tomatoes, cheese, basil, garlic, olive oil, salt and pepper. Put this together a few hours before your meal and set aside at a warm room temperature.

Bring a large pot of salted water to a boil and cook the pasta 8 to 10 minutes, until al dente. Drain the pasta and toss with the pasta sauce. Serve at once. Sprinkle with grated Parmesan cheese if desired.

Per serving: 420 calories, 20 grams fat, 21 milligrams cholesterol, 440 milligrams sodium.

WEDNESDAY

ROASTED EGGPLANT AND MOZZARELLA PIZZA
LEMON COOKIES *

Leftover roasted vegetables from Sunday's dinner will make an excellent pizza topping. Save $1/2$ cup for tomorrow night's dinner, if you have it to spare.

ROASTED EGGPLANT AND MOZZARELLA PIZZA

Makes 4 servings
Preparation time: 5 minutes
Cooking time: 8-15 minutes

1 to 1 1/2 cups leftover roasted
vegetables
1 medium Boboli or other pizza crust
1/2 cup (2 ounces) grated mozzarella
cheese
1 tablespoon chopped fresh parsley

Preheat the oven to 425 degrees.

Spread the vegetable mixture over the pizza crust, sprinkle with grated cheese and parsley. Bake for 8 to 15 minutes, until the cheese is melted and all the ingredients are thoroughly heated.

Per serving: 257 calories, 8 grams fat, 11 milligrams cholesterol, 398 milligrams sodium.

THURSDAY

LINGUINE WITH TOMATOES, BASIL AND HAMBURGER CRUSTY BREAD*

This dish illustrates how easy it is to transform leftovers into a second wonderful meal. The linguine dish with uncooked tomato sauce can be tossed with cooked hamburger or sausage and any remaining roasted vegetables for a delicious dinner. Leftover rice, gazpacho or other tomato-based soup or sauce make good additions.

LINGUINE WITH TOMATOES, BASIL AND HAMBURGER

Makes 6 servings
Cooking time: 10 minutes

1/2 pound lean hamburger
4 cups leftover Linguine With
Tomatoes and Basil
1/2 cup cooked rice (optional)
1/2 cup roasted vegetables
Salt and black pepper to taste

In a large skillet, fry the ham-

burger until the pink is gone. Drain any fat in the skillet. Toss in the leftover linguine, rice and any roasted vegetables. Add salt and black pepper to taste and serve hot.

Per serving: 373 calories, 20 grams fat, 45 milligrams cholesterol, 321 milligrams sodium.

FRIDAY

HUMMUS *
WARM PITA BREADS *
SPINACH AND BLACK OLIVES *

Leftover hummus will taste better after a few days. Again, stuff it into warmed pita breads with spinach leaves and black olives.

SATURDAY

T-BONE STEAKS *
TOSSED SPINACH AND GREEN SALAD WITH TOMATOES *
SUMMER POTATOES BAKED WITH HERBS
SINGLE SHOT ESPRESSO ICE

This summery meal needs no explanation. Steaks, usually on sale this time of year, go well with herb-infused roasted potatoes and a green salad. Be sure to use vine-ripe red tomatoes for the salad. Also look for delicious California Long White potatoes, or other locally-grown potatoes, such as the Kennebec, some of which should be in the markets by now. Put the Espresso Ice together early in the day, to allow time for it to harden sufficiently.

SUMMER POTATOES BAKED WITH HERBS

Makes 4 servings
Preparation time: 5 minutes
Cooking time: 35 minutes

3 large all-purpose potatoes, unpeeled
and sliced 1/4-inch thick
1 tablespoon olive oil
1 tablespoon fresh rosemary
Salt and black pepper to taste

Preheat oven to 425 degrees.

Place the potatoes in an 8-inch baking dish, drizzle with oil and toss. Sprinkle with rosemary, salt and pepper. Bake until the potatoes can be easily pierced with a fork, about 35 minutes.

Per serving: 198 calories, 4 grams fat, no cholesterol, 13 milligrams sodium.

SINGLE SHOT ESPRESSO ICE

Makes 8 servings
Preparation time: 5 minutes
Cooking time: 5 minutes
Freezing time: 3-6 hours

3 cups prepared Italian, French or
other dark-roast coffee
1 cup half-and-half
1 1/4 cup granulated sugar

Combine the coffee, half-and-half and sugar in a medium saucepan over medium heat. Heat, stirring, until the mixture almost comes to a boil and the sugar has dissolved.

Pour the mixture into a shallow pan, such as a cake pan and chill to room temperature, then put in the freezer. It will take 3 to 6 hours to freeze completely, and will be quite dense. Thirty minutes before serving, set the mixture in the refrigerator, then stir just before serving.

Per serving: 139 calories, 4 grams fat, 11 milligrams cholesterol, 14 milligrams sodium.

WEEK

30

SHOPPING LIST

Meat, poultry, seafood

- ❑ 2 frying chickens
- ❑ 10 medium shrimp, peeled
- ❑ 1 ¹/₂ pounds lean ground beef

Produce

- ❑ 2 pints fresh lima beans, shucked
- ❑ 21 Kirby cucumbers
- ❑ ¹/₂ pound tender green beans
- ❑ 6 medium shallots
- ❑ 2 garlic cloves
- ❑ 2 green onions
- ❑ 4 large portabella mushrooms, or 12 cremini
- ❑ 4 ears sweet corn
- ❑ 6 large, plus 2 medium, ripe tomatoes
- ❑ 2 zucchini
- ❑ 1 red onion
- ❑ 1 large orange

- ❑ 1 Sharlyn or other melon
- ❑ 4 peaches
- ❑ 1 lemon (optional)
- ❑ 1 pound blackberries
- ❑ 1 bunch dill
- ❑ 1 bunch oregano (optional)
- ❑ 1 bunch mint
- ❑ 1 bunch parsley
- ❑ 2 sticks lemongrass or 1 large bunch basil

Dairy

- ❑ 1 ¹/₂ cups light sour cream
- ❑ 1 quart buttermilk
- ❑ 1 quart vanilla ice cream
- ❑ 1 stick butter
- ❑ 4-8 ounces Cheddar cheese

Deli

- ❑ 1 large focaccia or other flat bread

- ❑ 4 to 8 slices whole wheat or other bread
- ❑ 4 ounces blue cheese
- ❑ 2 or 3 ounces feta cheese
- ❑ 4 hamburger buns

Miscellaneous

- ❑ 4 cups dry long-grain rice
- ❑ 2 ounces (¹/₂ cup) slivered almonds
- ❑ 2 ounces (¹/₂ cup) small almond cookies, crushed
- ❑ 1 cup low-sodium chicken broth
- ❑ 8 slices whole-grain bread
- ❑ 1 pound linguine
- ❑ 2 tablespoons poppy seeds

Staples

- ❑ Balsamic vinegar
- ❑ Black pepper
- ❑ Cider vinegar

- ❑ Confectioners' sugar
- ❑ Crackers
- ❑ Freshly grated nutmeg
- ❑ Olive oil
- ❑ Salt
- ❑ Spicy mustard
- ❑ Vegetable oil
- ❑ Vinaigrette with garlic
- ❑ Worcestershire sauce

* Suggested accompaniments

PERFUMED RICE WITH VEGETABLES NONYA-STYLE BARBECUED CHICKEN * FRESH LIMA BEANS TOSSED WITH MINT * BLACKBERRY ALMOND CRUMBLE

This Malaysian rice dish is perfumed with fresh herbs and gently cooked like a superior fried rice, adapted from Madhur Jaffrey's public television show and accompanying cookbook, *Madhur Jaffrey's Far Eastern Cookery* (Harper & Row, $17.95). Presoaking decreases the amount of water used in cooking the rice, but more importantly, it produces sticky rice that holds together between chopsticks. Use fresh lemongrass, available at farmers' markets, or substitute fresh basil leaves and grated lemon peel. Kirby cucumbers don't need to be peeled or seeded; if you use a slicing cucumber, do both. Fresh limas will round out the dinner and, along with the other dishes, provide leftovers.

PERFUMED RICE WITH VEGETABLES NONYA-STYLE

Makes 8 servings
Preparation time: 30 minutes
Cooking time: 25 minutes

4 cups long-grain rice
5 1/3 cups water
2 teaspoons salt
2 sticks fresh lemon grass (6 inches long) or 30 basil leaves plus 3 tablespoons grated lemon rind
2 Kirby cucumbers, cut into tiny dice
1/2 pound tender green beans, cut in 1/4-inch pieces

4 tablespoons vegetable oil
6 medium shallots or 1 small onion, cut in paper-thin slices
10 medium shrimp, peeled and cut into 1/4-inch dice
Salt to taste

Place the rice in a bowl and cover with water. Let soak for 30 minutes, then drain. Combine the rice, 5 1/3 cups water and salt in a large, heavy saucepan. Bring the water to a boil, cover and turn the heat to very low. Cook for 20 minutes. If not serving right away, the rice will stay warm, covered, for 45 minutes.

Meanwhile, trim the lemon grass, discarding the hard casings, and cut the pieces into thin rounds. Combine lemon grass (or basil and lemon rind) with the cucumbers and beans in a bowl, and cover.

Place the oil in a frying pan over medium heat. When the oil is hot, add the shallots and stir-fry until they are golden brown and crispy, about 1 minute. Remove with a slotted spoon and drain on paper towels. Add the shrimp to the pan and cook 1 minute. Remove and place in a bowl and lightly salt, then reserve. Save the oil in the pan.

Put the rice into a large serving bowl, breaking up any lumps with the back of a spoon. Top with the cooked shrimp and reserved oil, lemongrass (or basil leaves) and cucumber mixture. Garnish with the crispy shallots and serve warm or at room temperature.

Per serving: 442 calories, 8 grams fat, 22 milligrams cholesterol, 622 milligrams sodium.

BLACKBERRY ALMOND CRUMBLE

Makes 4 servings
Preparation time: 10 minutes

Cooking time: 5 to 10 minutes
Chilling time: 30 minutes

2 ounces (1/2 cup) slivered almonds, chopped and browned
1 pound blackberries
1/4 cup confectioners' sugar, or to taste
2 ounces (1/2 cup) small almond cookies, crushed
1 1/2 cups light sour cream, thinned with a little buttermilk

To brown the almonds: Place them on a baking sheet in a 350-degree oven and bake for 5 to 10 minutes. As soon as they are browned, put them in the workbowl of a food processor along with the cookies and pulse to roughly chop.

Mix the berries with sugar and reserve.

Fold the browned nuts and cookies into the sour cream, fold in the berries and chill before serving.

Per serving: 511 calories, 25 grams fat, 6 milligrams cholesterol, 144 milligrams sodium.

CASE'S PORTABELLA MUSHROOMS WITH BLUE CHEESE SUMMER SQUASH TOSSED WITH CHOPPED TOMATOES * FOCACCIA *

Produce buyers often are great vegetable cooks, and Case Lichtveldt, produce buyer for the famed Harry's Farmers Market in Atlanta is one great cook. For this easy dish, he chooses the large and dramatic-looking portabella mushrooms, really just oversize brown creminis (buy creminis if necessary). These meaty and flavorful mushrooms can be a little tough, so a preliminary blanching tenderizes them before broiling or grilling. For other occasions, Case stuffs the large caps with chopped vegetables, shrimp, sauce or bread crumbs. Add a purchased or prepared focaccia or other flat bread, and save leftovers (to make 3 cups) to serve later in the week.

CASE'S PORTABELLA MUSHROOMS WITH BLUE CHEESE

Makes 4 servings
Preparation time: 5 minutes
Cooking time: 7 minutes

1 cup water
1 teaspoon Worcestershire sauce
4 large portabella mushroom caps, stems cut off
4 ounces blue cheese, crumbled

Preheat the broiler or grill.

Place water and Worcestershire sauce in a large skillet and bring to a boil. Add the mushroom caps, lower the heat to a low boil and cook 5 minutes.

Remove mushrooms to a broiler pan or place on grill. Sprinkle the tops with crumbled cheese and cook until the cheese melts, 1 or 2 minutes (longer on the grill).

Per serving: 108 calories, 8 grams fat, 21 milligrams cholesterol, 409 milligrams sodium.

TUESDAY

COOL CUCUMBER SOUP
SWEET CORN *
CRACKERS *

Even though cucumbers are 96 percent water, the remaining 4 percent holds a tantalizing flavor that keeps us buying and slicing

AUGUST

There's no better time than now to buy vegetables. Georgia, Tennessee and North Carolina produce is abundant and a good value. Look for beans, mountain tomatoes, squash and a variety of butter beans, lima beans and zipper peas. Green peanuts are also available now.

Sweet corn is still well priced. Squash and cabbage prices, however, are higher and supplies are tight for the moment, as growing regions change from the south to the north. Look for prices to lower in another week or two as those growing areas get up to speed. The dry weather has caused a drop in harvest volume, but the quality is excellent. Western heat can hurt the lettuce market and drive up those prices, while new California Long White potatoes and Eastern Shore potatoes are beautiful this month.

This is a good month to buy the sweetest of summer melons: canary melon, cantaloupe, crenshaw, honeydew, orange flesh honeydew, and the super-sweet Sharlyn, which has a Brix level of 14 right now, the sweetest of any melon on the market. Kent mangos are in, along with figs and lots of grape varieties.

Most of the soft summer fruits — peaches, plums and nectarines — are still plentiful, cheap and delicious. Red plum supplies are tight, but the crunchy and sweet Black Friar plums are plentiful for now. Blueberries have a week or two left, and other fruits are dwindling now, so buy them while the quality is still good. The first of the muscadine grapes are in the stores, and early apples and pears are in too. Cool nighttime temperatures in California are holding back the sugar in Thompson and Flame grapes.

them for salads and pureeing them into refreshing summer soups like the one below.

COOL CUCUMBER SOUP

Makes 4 servings
Preparation time: 10 minutes
Chilling time: 4 hours

10 Kirby cucumbers, cut into chunks
1 cup low-sodium chicken broth
3 cups buttermilk
3 or 4 tablespoons fresh mint leaves
1 tablespoon fresh dill
Salt and black pepper to taste

Place the cucumbers, chicken broth, buttermilk, mint, dill, salt and black pepper in a food pro-

cessor or blender and puree. Chill for at least 4 hours, then garnish with extra snipped dill.

Per serving: 158 calories, 3 grams fat, 6 milligrams cholesterol, 226 milligrams sodium.

WEDNESDAY

STUFFED TOMATOES
CHEESE TOAST *
PEACHES AND ICE CREAM *

This is a cold dish, perfect for the muggy weather we've been having lately. Serve it with cheddar cheese broiled on whole-wheat bread.

STUFFED TOMATOES

Makes 4 servings
Preparation time: 20 minutes

4 large tomatoes, very ripe
Salt
1 cup cooked rice
1 cup lima beans, cooked
$^1/_4$ cup olive oil
2 teaspoons balsamic vinegar
1 tablespoon parsley, chopped
Freshly ground black pepper
2 tablespoons mint, chopped

Slice off the stem end of the tomatoes, leaving two-thirds of the tomato. Hollow out the tomatoes, reserving the pulp. Sprinkle salt inside the tomatoes, turn them upside down to drain for 10 minutes. Meanwhile, coarsely chop all pulp and combine in a large bowl with the rice, beans, oil, vinegar, parsley, and pepper.

Spoon the bean mixture into the tomatoes and garnish with mint.

Per serving: 272 calories, 14 grams fat, no cholesterol, 24 milligrams sodium.

THURSDAY

TUSCAN BREAD SALAD
SHARLYN MELON WEDGES *

Raw vegetables and stale bread can make a substantial dinner salad for a hot summer night. This version of an Italian bread salad uses leftover focaccia, which has lots of herby flavor, and feta cheese for protein. It uses the small, sweet Kirby cucumbers, which don't need to be peeled or seeded. Use the standard, larger cucumbers if you wish. The salad makes a great party dish. It is easily doubled just

as it is, or in a pinch, just toss in more bread. Add wedges of the sweetest melon in the markets these days, the Sharlyn, available at farmers markets. Substitute any melon if you wish.

TUSCAN BREAD SALAD

Makes 4 servings
Preparation time: 20 minutes
Standing time: 30 minutes
Cooking time: 5 minutes

2 medium fresh and juicy tomatoes, cut in $^1/_2$-inch cubes
2 or 3 Kirby cucumbers, cut into $^1/_2$-inch cubes
2 tablespoons chopped fresh basil
1 tablespoon chopped fresh parsley
1 tablespoon chopped fresh oregano (optional)
1 or 2 green onions, chopped
4 tablespoons vinaigrette with garlic
Salt and freshly ground black pepper to taste
2 ounces feta cheese, crumbled
2 cups stale foccacia, cut into 1 $^1/_2$-inch cubes

In a large bowl, combine tomatoes, cucumbers, basil, parsley, (optional) oregano, onion, vinaigrette, salt and black pepper. Let the mixture marinate at room temperature for 30 minutes.

At serving time, add the cheese and bread cubes and toss.

Per serving: 184 calories, 11 grams fat, 13 milligrams cholesterol, 268 milligrams sodium.

FRIDAY

CHICKEN SANDWICHES *
GRATED ZUCCHINI SLAW *

Leftover chicken should make substantial sandwiches, accompanied by whole-grain bread, red onions and a spicy mustard.

Zucchini can be grated and tossed with vinaigrette for a side dish.

SATURDAY

HAMBURGERS ON THE GRILL *
ORANGE POPPY SEED NOODLES
KIRBY CUCUMBERS IN BALSAMIC VINAIGRETTE

For a change from the usual hamburger tagalongs of potato salad or slaw, try these marinated cucumbers and orange-flavored noodles, adapted from Sharon Tyler Herbst's *Cooking Smart* (Harper Collins, $25).

ORANGE POPPY SEED NOODLES

Makes 4 servings
Preparation time: 10 minutes
Cooking time: 10 minutes

1 pound dry spaghetti
1 large or 2 medium Valencia juice oranges
1 tablespoon fruity vinegar
1 stick butter, cut into 6 pieces, at room temperature
$^1/_4$ teaspoon grated cloves
2 tablespoons poppy seeds
Salt and black pepper to taste
1 tablespoon additional grated orange peel (optional)

Cook pasta in large pot of boiling salted water 8 to 10 minutes, until al dente. While it is cooking, remove the peel from the orange with vegetable peeler or zester and chop fine. Squeeze the juice from the orange and reserve.

In small saucepan over medium-high heat, cook juice and vinegar until reduced to 3 tablespoons, about 5 minutes. Whisk

Price: Will average $.79 a pound.

Nutrition: Four ounces of raw cucumber has 17 calories and, unpeeled, is a fair source of vitamin A, C and iron.

Selection: Look for cucumbers that are firm and fresh looking, not flabby or have indentations or sunken spots. Watch for soft ends.

Storage: Unlike slicing cucumbers, Kirbys are not waxed, so will not last quite as long as a waxed cucumber. Cucumbers can give off aromas, so store them in a plastic bag in refrigerator 3 to 4 days. Place them in the crisper, which offers high humidity.

Uses: Allow 2 Kirby cucumbers per serving. One pound of peeled cucumbers will yield about 2 cups. Cucumbers can be served raw, pickled, in vinaigrette, lightly sauteed with other vegetables and fresh herbs, or pureed into a refreshing summer soup.

When one giant cucumber seems to be too big for a small family, or too much to use in salads, look for the small, firm Kirby cucumbers, often sold as pickling cucumbers earlier in the season. And while they are easily made into delicious pickles, they are just as useful as a fresh vegetable. Look for them at local farmers markets and grocery stores throughout the summer.

We all know that cucumbers are refreshing and cool, otherwise, why would some people be called "cool as a cucumber?" Cucumbers have the ability to retain large amounts of water and to remain cool; in fact, the inside of a cucumber can be up to 20 degrees cooler than the outside.

Besides their value for their refreshing coolness and crunch they add to salads, cucumbers are used as an aid to sunburn and as a skin refresher, and some people like to cut slices and place them on their closed eyelids while taking a catnap.

in the butter, a piece at a time until the sauce is creamy. Stir in the cloves.

Drain the pasta and put in a shallow pasta dish. Toss with the butter mixture, poppy seeds; add salt and pepper. Garnish with (optional) orange peel.

Per main-course serving: 669 calories, 26 grams fat, 62 milligrams cholesterol, 238 milligrams sodium.

KIRBY CUCUMBERS IN BALSAMIC VINAIGRETTE

Makes 4 servings
Preparation time: 10 minutes

6 Kirby cucumbers
$^1/_3$ cup olive oil
2 to 3 tablespoons balsamic vinegar
Salt and black pepper to taste
1 tablespoon fresh herb (mint, basil or other)

Slice cucumbers on bias in $^1/_4$-inch slices and place in large, shallow bowl. Cover with oil, vinegar, salt, pepper and herbs. Serve chilled or at room temperature.

Per serving: 166 calories, 14 grams fat, no cholesterol, 7 milligrams sodium.

WEEK 31

SHOPPING LIST

Meat, poultry, seafood

- [ ] 1 6-pound leg of lamb, cut into steaks
- [ ] 8 soft-shell crabs, fresh or frozen

Produce

- [ ] 1 lemon
- [ ] 1 head lettuce, any type
- [ ] 1 head romaine lettuce
- [ ] 2 tomatoes
- [ ] 12 garlic cloves
- [ ] 1 pound small mushrooms
- [ ] 1 medium red onion
- [ ] 1 medium onion
- [ ] 1 carrot
- [ ] $^1/_2$ pound greens: Swiss chard, spinach, beet greens or kale
- [ ] 1 yellow squash
- [ ] 3 banana peppers
- [ ] 1 $^1/_4$ pounds tiny okra
- [ ] 1 small knob ginger
- [ ] 1 orange (optional)
- [ ] 3 bunches Red Flame grapes
- [ ] 1 melon
- [ ] 3 peaches
- [ ] 1 cup blueberries
- [ ] 1 pint strawberries
- [ ] 1 bunch rosemary
- [ ] 1 bunch oregano
- [ ] 2 bunches herbs, combination of parsley, oregano, tarragon, basil or mint

Dairy

- [ ] 2 tablespoons butter (optional)
- [ ] 10 eggs
- [ ] 16 ounces plain non-fat yogurt
- [ ] $^1/_2$ cup whipping cream

Deli

- [ ] 4 pita breads

- [ ] 1 loaf crusty bread
- [ ] 4 to 8 corn muffins
- [ ] 1 lemon meringue pie
- [ ] 1 focaccia or flat bread
- [ ] 2 to 3 ounces feta cheese
- [ ] 2 or 3 tablespoons grated Parmesan cheese
- [ ] 1 pint potato salad

Miscellaneous

- [ ] 2 cups dry rice
- [ ] $^1/_2$ cup dry red wine
- [ ] $^1/_2$ cup dry white wine
- [ ] 1 14 $^1/_2$-ounce can low-sodium chicken broth or 4 teaspoons chicken bouillon granules
- [ ] 1 19-ounce can garbanzo beans
- [ ] $^1/_2$ sheet toasted nori (optional)
- [ ] $^1/_2$ cup almond-flavored liqueur (amaretto)
- [ ] 4 tablespoons slivered almonds

Staples

- [ ] Freshly ground black pepper
- [ ] Granulated sugar
- [ ] Non-fat mayonnaise
- [ ] Olive oil
- [ ] Red wine vinegar
- [ ] Salt
- [ ] Sesame oil
- [ ] Sesame seeds
- [ ] Soy sauce
- [ ] Vegetable oil
- [ ] Vinaigrette

* Suggested accompaniments

LAMB GRILLED WITH HERBS
DE PROVENCE
STEAMED LEMON RICE *
GRILLED MUSHROOM KEBABS
WARM PITA BREADS *
LEMON MERINGUE PIE *

Grilled mushrooms and a lettuce salad get tucked in pita breads for a different vegetable dish. Purchase a semi-boneless leg of lamb rather than the more expensive lamb chops and have the butcher cut it into eight steaks for you. (These will be about 1 inch thick; if you need to serve more people, have them cut thinner.) This will also yield about ½ pound of leg bone with meat, perfect for lamb stew. Save leftover lamb and mushrooms to serve in Tuesday's meal.

LAMB GRILLED WITH HERBS DE PROVENCE

Makes 8 servings
Preparation time: 5 minutes
Marinating time: 2 hours
Cooking time: 20 minutes

3 garlic cloves, minced
2 tablespoons herbs de Provence
1 6-pound semi-boneless leg of lamb,
    cut into 8 steaks
½ cup dry red wine
¾ to 1 cup olive oil
Salt and black pepper to taste

Put the garlic in the workbowl of a food processor and pulse to mince; add the herbs de Provence and pulse again to combine. Rub the seasonings onto one side of the steaks. Put the steaks into a shallow dish, pour the wine and olive oil over and marinate, covered, for about 2 hours, or covered and refriger-

ated for several hours.

Preheat the grill or oven to 400 degrees.

Remove the steaks, season with salt and pepper and grill over a hot fire, 8 minutes per side for medium.

Per serving: 540 calories, 43 grams fat, 139 milligrams cholesterol, 84 milligrams sodium.

GRILLED MUSHROOM KEBABS

Makes 4 servings (with leftover
    mushrooms)
Preparation time: 15 minutes
Marinating time: 1 hour
Cooking time: 15 minutes

½ cup red wine
3 tablespoons chopped fresh herbs,
    such as parsley, basil, tarragon or
    mint
5 or 6 tablespoons olive oil
2 or 3 garlic cloves, crushed and
    peeled
1 pound small mushrooms, cleaned,
    stemmed and patted dry
4 pita breads
4 tablespoons non-fat mayonnaise
2 cups shredded crisp lettuce
¼ cup vinaigrette

To make the marinade: Mix wine, herbs, olive oil and garlic in a large bowl. Add the mushrooms for 1 or more hours. Meanwhile, soak the skewers if you are using bamboo.

Heat the grill or oven to 350 degrees.

Thread the mushrooms onto skewers and barbecue on the grill for about 15 minutes, turning occasionally and brushing with marinade, until cooked through. Just before serving, wrap the pita breads in foil and heat them on the grill for about 10 minutes.

Off the grill, split the pitas open and spread the insides with mayonnaise. Toss the lettuce with vinaigrette and divide the

lettuce among the pitas. Remove the mushrooms from the skewers and fill over the lettuce.

Per serving: 282 calories, 19 grams fat, 8 milligrams cholesterol, 161 milligrams sodium.

SPINACH, FETA AND RED
ONION SALAD WITH FRESH
HERB VINAIGRETTE
FOCACCIA*
RED FLAME GRAPES AND
MELON WEDGES*

The dressing makes enough for two meals, so save half and store it in the refrigerator. Carefully wrap or freeze half the focaccia to keep it fresh to serve later. Crunchy California Red Flame grapes are at their finest this month, so serve them out-of-hand or simmer them quickly in red wine and let them steep till cool, for a fabulous dessert.

SPINACH, FETA AND RED ONION SALAD WITH FRESH HERB VINAIGRETTE

Makes 4 servings
Preparation time: 15 minutes

3 tablespoons fresh oregano leaves
2 tablespoons red wine vinegar
1 large garlic clove
½ teaspoon salt
¼ teaspoon freshly ground black
    pepper
½ cup olive oil
1 large bunch spinach, cleaned and
    patted dry
½ medium red onion, peeled and
    sliced into thin rings
2 to 3 ounces feta cheese, rinsed and
    crumbled
Freshly ground black pepper

Price: Will range from $.89 to $1.39 a pound.

Nutrition: Per cup, 102 calories, and are low in sodium. They are a good source of fiber.

Selection: Look for well-colored, plump grapes that are firmly attached to the stem. Bunches should be held together on green, pliable stems. Avoid bunches that are straggly, with shriveled, crushed or wet grapes.

Storage: Store grapes unwashed in the refrigerator for 2 to 5 days. Grapes don't continue to ripen after harvesting, so don't expect them to develop more flavor.

Uses: Table grapes are mostly eaten out-of-hand, in fruit or vegetable salads or in pies or cakes. One pound equals about 3 cups.

A flavorful seedless grape is in season now, and it isn't white. The white Thompson Seedless is better now, and cheaper, but the Red Flame Grape is sweeter. It is gaining in popularity as people discover the crunch and flavor that, as one retailer described, "explodes in your mouth." The Red Flame from California, also called Flame or Red Seedless, is in season June through August, with Chilean supplies coming in the late winter months.

Grapes develop more sugar as their season progresses, and thus taste sweeter. But they don't continue to ripen or develop sugar after harvesting; they must be fully edible when cut.

While grapes grow in every state of the U.S., most of America's table grapes come from California's hot interior valley, with smaller amounts coming from Arizona. Current Red Flame harvests are coming from the Coachella Valley and Delano area in Southern California and will work their way up as far north as Modesto, California.

Table grapes with adherent skins are derived from European stock, and they need long, warm-to-hot, dry summers and cool winters. Native American grape species (often called slip-skinned), such as the Concord, Scuppernong and Muscadine, grow better in Washington state and east of the Rockies.

Combine the oregano, vinegar, garlic, salt and pepper in the workbowl of a food processor and process 30 seconds. With the machine running, add the olive oil in a thin stream.

Put the spinach in a large salad bowl. Drizzle the fresh oregano dressing over the spinach, scatter the feta and onion over the dressing, and season with pepper.

Per serving: 299 calories, 31 grams fat, 13 milligrams cholesterol, 460 milligrams sodium.

TUESDAY

OMELET WITH LAMB, MUSHROOMS AND RED ONION
CRUSTY BREAD *

Omelets make a great, quick dinner. Leftover lamb can be sliced and tucked in with leftover grilled mushrooms and fresh red onion.

OMELET WITH LAMB, MUSHROOMS AND RED ONION

Makes 4 servings
Preparation time: 15 minutes
Cooking time: 10 minutes

2 tablespoons butter or oil
1 garlic clove, minced
1/4 to 1/2 red onion, minced
1 cup mushrooms, sliced
1/2 to 1 cup cooked lamb, sliced thin, room temperature
2 tablespoons fresh herbs, such as oregano, tarragon or parsley
6 eggs
2 tablespoons water
2 to 3 tablespoons grated Parmesan cheese

Heat a large skillet over moderate heat. Add 1 tablespoon of butter.

When it is melted and hot, add the garlic and onion and cook, stirring, 1 to 2 minutes. Add the mushrooms, lamb and herbs and continue to cook, stirring, until the lamb is heated through and starting to brown. Remove the contents of the pan to a bowl.

Place the eggs in a mixing bowl and mix slightly with the water. Add the remaining butter to the pan; when it is hot, add the eggs and cook until slightly set. Spoon in the cooked ingredients and cheese and continue to cook, with pan partially covered, until eggs are set.

Per serving: 290 calories, 23 grams fat, 440 milligrams cholesterol, 165 milligrams sodium.

WEDNESDAY

GARLICKY CHICKPEA SOUP WITH GREENS
CORN MUFFINS *
STRAWBERRY YOGURT SMOOTHIE *

This soup has a light broth and substantial ingredients, so it's filling without being heavy on a hot night. Nori, commonly used to wrap sushi rolls, is a toasted sea vegetable available in health food stores. It not only adds delicious flavor but is loaded with protein, vitamins and minerals, especially calcium and iron. Greens, especially Swiss chard or beet greens, are also rich in calcium. Process strawberries and yogurt together to make a great-tasting yogurt shake.

GARLICKY CHICKPEA SOUP WITH GREENS

Makes 4 servings
Preparation time: 10 minutes

Cooking time: 20 minutes

1 tablespoon olive oil
1/2 medium onion, chopped
2 garlic cloves, minced
6 cups chicken broth or water
1 14 1/2-ounce can low-sodium chicken broth or 4 teaspoons chicken bouillon granules
1 carrot, grated
1/2 sheet toasted nori, or salt to taste
1 19-ounce can garbanzo beans (chickpeas), drained and rinsed
1/2 pound greens: Swiss chard, spinach, beet greens or kale, roughly chopped
2 to 3 teaspoons finely minced orange peel (colored part only; optional)

In a large saucepan, heat the oil. Saute the onion 3 minutes, add the garlic and saute 2 more minutes. Add the chicken broth or water and chicken bouillon granules and grated carrot. Simmer, uncovered, for 5 minutes.

Meanwhile, if using nori, shred the sheet with scissors or your hands and add to the soup, otherwise season with salt at this point. Add the chickpeas and simmer until heated through, about 2 minutes. Add the greens and turn off the heat. The greens will heat through and wilt in a minute or two. Garnish the soup with orange peel, if desired.

Per serving: 309 calories, 6 grams fat, no cholesterol, 514 milligrams sodium.

THURSDAY

STIR-FRY WITH OKRA, YELLOW SQUASH AND BANANA PEPPERS
STEAMED RICE *

Leftover rice and almost any extra vegetables you may find

make this a tasty dish. Okra stir-fries beautifully if you add it at the end and cook it quickly, before it starts to get mushy. Other peppers, celery, broccoli and any greens, such as spinach or Swiss chard, also would make good additions. Toast the sesame seeds for 5 minutes in a 350-degree oven if you have the time; it will give them a nuttier, fuller flavor.

STIR-FRY WITH OKRA, YELLOW SQUASH AND BANANA PEPPERS

Makes 4 servings
Preparation time: 10 minutes
Cooking time: 5 minutes

1 teaspoon vegetable oil
1 garlic clove, minced
2 teaspoons grated fresh ginger
1 yellow squash, sliced
2 banana peppers, cored, seeded and sliced
1/4 pound fresh tiny okra, stems removed
1 tablespoon soy sauce
1 tablespoon sesame seeds
1 teaspoon sesame oil

Heat a large skillet or wok; add oil over moderately high heat. When hot, add garlic and ginger and stir for 30 seconds. Add squash and peppers and stir-fry for 1 to 2 minutes, until the vegetables are tender-crisp. Add the okra and stir-fry for 1 to 2 minutes. Place the lid over the pan if okra doesn't seem to be cooking quickly enough.

Toss with soy sauce and sprinkle with sesame seeds and sesame oil just before serving.
Per serving: 67 calories, 4 grams fat, no cholesterol, 265 milligrams sodium.

FOCACCIA SANDWICHES *
GREEN SALAD WITH FRESH TOMATOES*
FRESH OREGANO DRESSING *

Split leftover focaccia and layer with slices of ripe tomato and sprinkle with feta cheese and basil leaves. This is an effortless meal you can carry to the pool or enjoy on the run. Use leftover oregano dressing for a green salad.

FRIED SOFT-SHELL CRABS *
POTATO SALAD *
SUMMER SAUTE OF FANCY OKRA AND BANANA PEPPERS
PEACHES WITH AMARETTO ZABAGLIONE

From the crabs to the peaches, this meal is summer itself. Quickly sauteed tiny okra, called fancy, retains its bright color and crisp texture, so follow cooking times carefully. Zabaglione is a rich custard usually made with a sweet wine; here it is flavored with the almond liqueur called amaretto. Serve it with fresh fruit and almonds.

SUMMER SAUTE OF FANCY OKRA AND BANANA PEPPERS

Makes 4 servings
Preparation time: 10 minutes
Cooking time: 10 minutes

1 pound fresh okra, fancy size (very small, 1 to 1 1/2 inches long)
3 to 5 tablespoons olive oil

3 large garlic cloves, minced
2 or 3 banana peppers, seeded and thinly sliced
4 or more tablespoons fresh basil, chopped
Salt and black pepper to taste

Wash the okra and pat dry. Trim off the stems.

Heat 1 tablespoon oil in a large skillet over medium heat. Add half the okra and saute 3 to 5 minutes or until tender-crisp. With a slotted spoon, remove okra to a warm serving platter or bowl. Cover to keep warm. Repeat with second batch of okra, using another tablespoon olive oil as needed, and remove to warm platter.

Add a third tablespoon of oil to the skillet over very medium heat. Add the banana pepper slices and saute 2 minutes or until softened, fragrant and starting to get crispy. Remove to warm platter. In leftover oil in the pan, add the garlic and basil and cook 30 seconds or just until garlic releases its fragrance. (Do not overcook or use high heat or garlic may burn.) Pour the garlic-basil oil over the okra and add salt and pepper to taste.
Per serving: 89 calories, 5 grams fat, no cholesterol, 7 milligrams sodium.

PEACHES WITH AMARETTO ZABAGLIONE

Makes 4 servings
Cooking time: 15 minutes
Chilling time: 1 hour

4 egg yolks, room temperature
1 tablespoon granulated sugar
1/2 cup amaretto
1/2 cup whipped cream
3 tablespoons slivered almonds
3 peaches, sliced
1 cup blueberries or raspberries, washed and drained

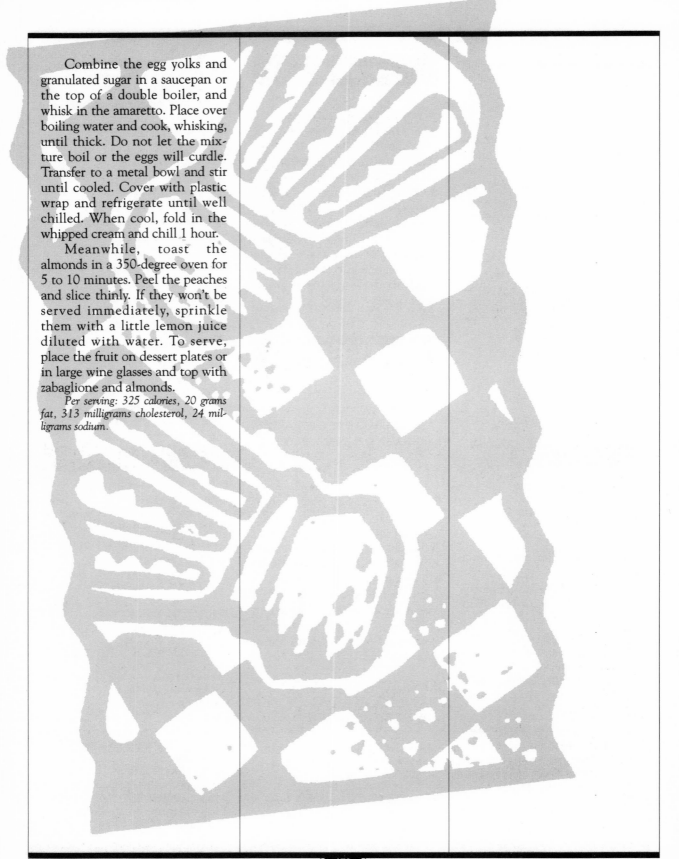

Combine the egg yolks and granulated sugar in a saucepan or the top of a double boiler, and whisk in the amaretto. Place over boiling water and cook, whisking, until thick. Do not let the mixture boil or the eggs will curdle. Transfer to a metal bowl and stir until cooled. Cover with plastic wrap and refrigerate until well chilled. When cool, fold in the whipped cream and chill 1 hour.

Meanwhile, toast the almonds in a 350-degree oven for 5 to 10 minutes. Peel the peaches and slice thinly. If they won't be served immediately, sprinkle them with a little lemon juice diluted with water. To serve, place the fruit on dessert plates or in large wine glasses and top with zabaglione and almonds.

Per serving: 325 calories, 20 grams fat, 313 milligrams cholesterol, 24 milligrams sodium.

WEEK

32

SHOPPING LIST

Meat, poultry, seafood

- ❑ 4 whole red snappers, 10 ounces each
- ❑ ³/₄ pound ground turkey
- ❑ ³/₄ pound ground beef
- ❑ 4 veal chops, 8-10 ounces each

Produce

- ❑ 3 Hass (black) avocados
- ❑ 7 or 8 plum tomatoes
- ❑ 9 green onions
- ❑ 1 yellow onion
- ❑ 3 sweet onions (or use yellow)
- ❑ 3 shallots
- ❑ 1 garlic clove
- ❑ 6 ears corn
- ❑ 1 pound carrots
- ❑ 1 pound broccoli
- ❑ 1 head lettuce, any type
- ❑ 1 turnip
- ❑ 4 ounces mushrooms
- ❑ 1 peeled and cored pineapple

- ❑ 2 kiwi fruit
- ❑ 1 orange
- ❑ 1 cup strawberries
- ❑ 4 limes
- ❑ 4 to 6 nectarines
- ❑ ¹/₄ watermelon
- ❑ 3 large bunches cilantro (2 make 2 cups)

Dairy

- ❑ ¹/₂ cup milk
- ❑ ¹/₂ cup plain non-fat yogurt
- ❑ 2 eggs
- ❑ 1 pint vanilla frozen yogurt
- ❑ 1 pint coffee ice cream

Deli

- ❑ 1 large bag tortilla chips
- ❑ 1 ¹/₂ cups (4 ounces) Pepper Jack cheese
- ❑ 4 to 8 flour or corn tortillas

Miscellaneous

- ❑ 4 cups chicken broth
- ❑ 1 15-ounce can refried beans
- ❑ ¹/₂ cup salsa
- ❑ 2 cups uncooked white rice
- ❑ 2 6-ounce jars marinated artichoke hearts
- ❑ 8 to 12 pitted black olives
- ❑ ³/₄ cup pasta sauce
- ❑ ¹/₄ cup pecans
- ❑ ¹/₂ cup bread and butter pickles (optional)
- ❑ 1 teaspoon anchovy paste or mashed fillets
- ❑ 2 tablespoons toasted almond slices

Staples

- ❑ Almond extract
- ❑ Black pepper
- ❑ Bread crumbs
- ❑ Dried sage

- ❑ Ground nutmeg
- ❑ Honey
- ❑ Hot sauce
- ❑ Lemon juice
- ❑ Minced garlic in oil
- ❑ Olive oil
- ❑ Powdered espresso
- ❑ Red chili flakes
- ❑ Rum (optional)
- ❑ Rum extract (optional)
- ❑ Salt
- ❑ Seasoned salt (optional)
- ❑ Vegetable oil
- ❑ Walnut oil (optional)

* Suggested accompaniments

SUNDAY

GUACAMOLE
TORTILLA CHIPS *
GRILLED WHOLE
RED SNAPPER *
CORN SOUP WITH PESTO

Make this light-hearted meal for a casual Sunday dinner. Red snapper is a good value this time of year. Stuff whole fish with fresh basil leaves and lemon slices, or wonderful lemon verbena leaves if you have them. Brush the outsides with lemon juice and butter and grill or broil 10 minutes per inch of thickness. Save about 12 ounces of cooked fish and 1 cup of guacamole for meals later in the week. Don't omit the corn cobs from the simmering soup, adapted from *Jane Brody's Good Food Gourmet* (Norton, $25.00); they add plenty of flavor. This is a good time of year to make cilantro puree, and store it in the freezer for a quick flavor-infusion of vegetables, chicken breasts or soups all year long.

GUACAMOLE

Makes 2 cups
Preparation time: 15 minutes

2 ripe Hass avocados
6 plum tomatoes, chopped with seeds and juice removed
Juice of 2 limes
2 teaspoons hot sauce
4 tablespoons minced green onions

Cut the avocados in half and remove the pits. Using a spoon, scoop the flesh out of the skin and put it in a medium-size bowl. Roughly mash the avocado with the back of a fork until it is smooth with a few creamy pieces of avocado. Add the tomatoes, lime juice, hot sauce and onions to the avocado and mix well. Place the guacamole in a covered container and refrigerate until serving time.

Per 1/4-cup serving: 86 calories, 7 grams fat, no cholesterol, 17 milligrams sodium.

CORN SOUP WITH CILANTRO PESTO

Makes 6 servings
Preparation time: 15 minutes
Cooking time: 30 minutes

2 sweet (such as Vidalia) or yellow onions, peeled and chopped
1 shallot, peeled and minced
1 tablespoon olive oil (or unsalted butter)
2 teaspoons olive oil
6 ears of corn, kernels cut from the cobs and the cobs reserved
1 sweet banana pepper, seeded and chopped
4 cups low-sodium chicken broth, divided
3 cups water
1/2 cup milk
Salt and pepper to taste
1 cup packed cilantro leaves, rinsed and patted dry
2 to 3 tablespoons freshly grated Parmesan cheese (optional)

Put the oil or butter in a large saucepan and add the onions. Saute over medium-low heat for 5 to 7 minutes, until they are soft and fragrant. Add the shallot and cook another minute without letting it brown.

Add the corncobs, all but 1/4 cup of the broth and the water to the saucepan. Bring the mixture to a boil, reduce the heat and simmer for 10 minutes. Add the corn kernels, and simmer the soup for another 10 minutes. Remove and discard the cobs from the soup.

Stir in the milk, salt and pepper and simmer another 5 minutes. Process the soup to a chunky puree, in batches, in the workbowl of a food processor or blender. Transfer the soup to a bowl and chill for 2 or 3 hours.

Meanwhile, puree the cilantro, adding the remaining olive oil and broth. At serving time, ladle the soup into bowls and swirl a spoonful of the cilantro puree into each serving, then sprinkle with (optional) cheese.

Per serving (no salt added): 174 calories, 6 grams fat, 2 milligrams cholesterol, 546 milligrams sodium.

MONDAY

TACO SALAD DIP
TORTILLA CHIPS *
NECTARINE SLICES WITH
VANILLA FROZEN YOGURT *

Everyone seems to like layered taco salad for parties or family dinners, and the dish goes together in minutes. Health food stores sell a wonderful line of refried black beans that are quite spicy and delicious. Mexican cream is available in the dairy department of many grocery stores; it would add more calories but is also a suave and delicious substitute for non-fat yogurt. (Or thin sour cream with a little yogurt or buttermilk.) Save the leftovers to serve later in the week.

TACO SALAD DIP

Makes 8 servings
Preparation time: 15 minutes

1 15-ounce can spicy refried pinto
    or black beans
1 1/2 cups grated Pepper Jack cheese
1 cup (leftover) guacamole
1/2 cup salsa
1/2 to 3/4 cup plain non-fat yogurt
    or Mexican cream
4 or 5 plum tomatoes, seeded and
    chopped
6 green onions, chopped, with part
    of the green tops
1/2 cup cilantro leaves, roughly
    chopped

In a 10-inch deep-dish ceramic
pie pan, spread the beans evenly
over the bottom. Sprinkle the
cheese over the beans. Place in a
microwave oven for 30 seconds
on high power until the cheese
melts.

Spread the guacamole over
the cheese, then a thin layer of
the salsa. Gently spread the
yogurt over the salsa.

Arrange the tomatoes decoratively in a ring around the
outer edge of the dish. Inside the
tomatoes, sprinkle the green
onions. Top the dish with
chopped cilantro and serve with
a basket of tortilla chips.

*Per serving: 212 calories, 12 grams
fat, 23 milligrams cholesterol, 641 milligrams sodium.*

TUESDAY

RED SNAPPER SALAD WITH
HONEY LIME DRESSING
STEAMED CARROTS *
STEAMED WHITE RICE *

The honey lime dressing complements the red snapper, but
you may want to use the dressing
on other salads as well. Add
steamed carrots and rice, and
cook extras for later in the week.

RED SNAPPER SALAD
WITH HONEY LIME
DRESSING

Makes 4 servings
Preparation time: 20 minutes

1/2 head leaf lettuce, any kind
12 ounces cooked red snapper
    fillets, separated into slivers or
    chunks
2 6-ounce jars marinated artichoke
    hearts, drained
1 avocado, peeled and sliced
8 to 12 pitted black olives, sliced

HONEY LIME DRESSING:
1/4 cup walnut or vegetable oil
Zest of 2 limes (the green part
    of the peel)
2 tablespoons lime juice
1 tablespoon honey
1 tablespoon chopped shallots
Salt and black pepper to taste

Wash, pat dry and tear the lettuce leaves into large pieces and
place on 4 dinner plates. Place
the fish, artichoke hearts, avocado slices and olives over the lettuce leaves and set aside.

Mix together the vinaigrette
ingredients and pour over the
salad and serve.

*Per serving (assuming 2/3 of the
dressing is eaten): 367 calories, 19
grams fat, 40 milligrams cholesterol, 217
milligrams sodium.*

WEDNESDAY

LUCY'S VEGETABLE
MEATLOAF
GREEN SALAD *
BISCUITS *

Lucy Keeble's meatloaf is delicious served hot or cold in sandwiches with pickles, and the following recipe makes plenty for
both purposes. If you are using
any leftover potatoes in the
meatloaf mixture, use bread
crumbs instead of rice. If you
don't use the leftovers later in the
week, put them in the freezer.

LUCY'S VEGETABLE
MEATLOAF

Makes 8 servings
Preparation time: 10 minutes
Cooking time: 1 hour

3/4 pound ground turkey
3/4 pound lean ground beef
1 turnip, grated
1 onion, chopped fine
1 cup grated cooked vegetables —
    carrots, potatoes or cabbage or
    combination
1/2 cup bread crumbs or cooked rice
2 eggs
1/4 cup pasta sauce
1 teaspoon minced garlic in oil
Salt, seasoned or plain, and black
    pepper to taste
1 teaspoon dried sage
1/2 cup pasta sauce

Preheat the oven to 350 degrees.
Mix together the turkey, beef,
turnip, onion, other vegetables,
bread crumbs, eggs, salt and pepper and form the mixture into a
loaf. If the mixture seems soft,
add more vegetables or bread
crumbs to hold the mixture
together more firmly.

Bake the loaf for 45 min-
utes, then drizzle pasta sauce
over the top and bake 15 more
minutes.

*Per serving: 247 calories, 12 grams
fat, 128 milligrams cholesterol, 90 milligrams sodium.*

Price: Look for five or six ears for $1.00 for the next few weeks.

Nutrition: 1 ear of cooked corn has about 70 calories and is a good source of vitamin A.

Selection: Choose fresh-looking ears with green husks, moist stems and silk ends that are free of decay and worm injury. When pierced with a thumbnail the kernels should give a spurt of milky juice. Tough skin indicates overmaturity.

Storage: Store in the refrigerator in the husks and in damp paper towels and plastic bag and use within a few days. Or store in the shrink-wrap plastic the corn comes in from the grocery store.

Uses: Allow one or two ears per serving. Corn can be microwaved, boiled, or grilled and served hot or cold in salads or other prepared foods.

"Most people grossly overcook sweet corn," said Emil Wolf, professor emeritus of horticulture with the University of Florida. "All you really need to do with this new super sweet corn is eat it. If you want it hot, cook it just long enough to heat it."

Sweet corn is the best "fast food" around, perfect for an afterschool snack or quick supper food. Two or three minutes in the microwave is plenty for piping-hot corn. It doesn't take much longer in boiling water — about five minutes.

I harbor an affection for sweet corn that goes beyond just appreciating its wonderful fla-

vor: I grew up between midwestern corn fields, thousands of acres of them. Corn was my daily bread and the backbone of our economy. And I think I know quite a bit about how corn should taste, how to grow it and how quickly it should get to the pot of boiling water.

But I had never been offered a raw ear of corn. Or one so delicious. The new sugar enhanced and super-sweet hybrids have taken sweet corn

to new levels.

The new hybrid corn being grown in Florida these days is three time sweeter than traditional sweet corn, Dr. Wolf said. It owes part of its sweetness to a gene taken from the sugar beet plant. Like any other corn, it diminishes in sweetness after picking, but because it starts out with so much more sugar, it also ends up with more sugar.

THURSDAY

TORTILLAS WITH
TACO SALAD DIP *
FRESH PINEAPPLE ROYALE

Make tonight's dinner effortless with leftover taco salad stuffed in tortillas and reheated. Serve the refreshing pineapple salad for dessert. For convenience, purchase a pineapple already peeled and cored.

FRESH PINEAPPLE ROYALE

Makes 4 servings
Preparation time 20 minutes
Freezing time: 1 hour

THE SAUCE:
1/2 cup frozen vanilla yogurt, softened slightly
1/4 teaspoon almond extract
1/4 teaspoon rum or rum extract
1/8 teaspoon ground nutmeg

THE FRUIT:
1 fresh pineapple, peeled and cored
2 kiwi fruit, peeled and sliced
1 orange, peeled and sectioned
1 cup strawberries, halved
2 tablespoons toasted almond slices

Combine the sauce ingredients and place in the freezer for 15 minutes to 1 hour. If frozen hard, let the sauce stand 10 minutes to soften before serving.

Meanwhile, cut the pineapple into slices. Arrange the fruits on a serving plate and refrigerate until serving time. Serve the fruit with the sauce; garnish with almond slices.

Per serving: 177 calories, 3 grams fat, 2 milligrams cholesterol, 24 milligrams sodium.

FRIDAY

COLD MEATLOAF
SANDWICHES *
BREAD AND BUTTER PICKLES*
WATERMELON SLICES *

Serve leftover meatloaf in sandwiches with thick-sliced white bread, sweet onion slices and mayonnaise. Bread and butter or other sweet pickles would make a good addition, along with watermelon slices served outside.

SATURDAY

GRILLED VEAL CHOPS *
RICE PILAF *
ITALIAN BROCCOLI
GELATO SPAZZACAMINO

Prepare tender veal chops on the grill and serve simply sprinkled with salt and pepper. Reheat leftover rice with mushrooms and pecans. Add the intensely flavored broccoli dish; a tube of anchovy paste is a good addition to your pantry, as a teaspoon of it can brighten plenty of simple dishes. Finish with a grown-up ice cream dessert that will dazzle anyone that needs to be dazzled, from the chefs at Atlanta's restaurant, Veni Vedi Vici.

ITALIAN BROCCOLI

Makes 4 servings
Preparation time: 10 minutes
Cooking time: 15 minutes

1/4 cup olive oil

1/2 teaspoon dried red chili flakes
1 teaspoon anchovy paste or mashed fillets
1 garlic clove, flattened and peeled
1 pound broccoli
Salt and black pepper to taste
Juice of 1/2 lemon

Place oil, pepper flakes, anchovy paste and garlic in a small saucepan. Heat over low heat, 30 seconds to 1 minute, or until the garlic turns golden. Let sit until it cools to room temperature and reserve.

Cut the florets from the broccoli stem, and cut them to similar sizes. Peel the stems, then cut them into julienne. Microwave the broccoli in a little water, in a microwave-safe dish on High power for 4 minutes. Drain immediately and run cold water over to stop the cooking.

Place the broccoli in a serving bowl and pour the reserved oil mixture through a sieve over them. Add salt and pepper to taste, and drizzle with lemon juice. Serve hot or at room temperature.

Per serving (no added salt): 154 calories, 14 grams fat, no cholesterol, 68 milligrams sodium.

GELATO SPAZZACAMINO

Makes 4 servings
Preparation time: 5 minutes

8 teaspoons ground dry espresso beans, powdered in a blender
8 scoops custard gelato or vanilla ice cream
4 tablespoons Scotch whisky

Grind regular espresso beans in the blender at high speed to a fine powder (or use the coffee grinder at the grocery store when you buy the beans).

Spoon the gelato or ice cream into individual shallow bowls, sprinkle 2 teaspoons espresso powder over each serving and pour whisky over all. From Veni Vidi Vici Restaurant in Atlanta.

Per serving (using one 6-ounce scoop vanilla ice cream each): 451 calories, 21 grams fat, 88 milligrams cholesterol, 190 milligrams sodium.

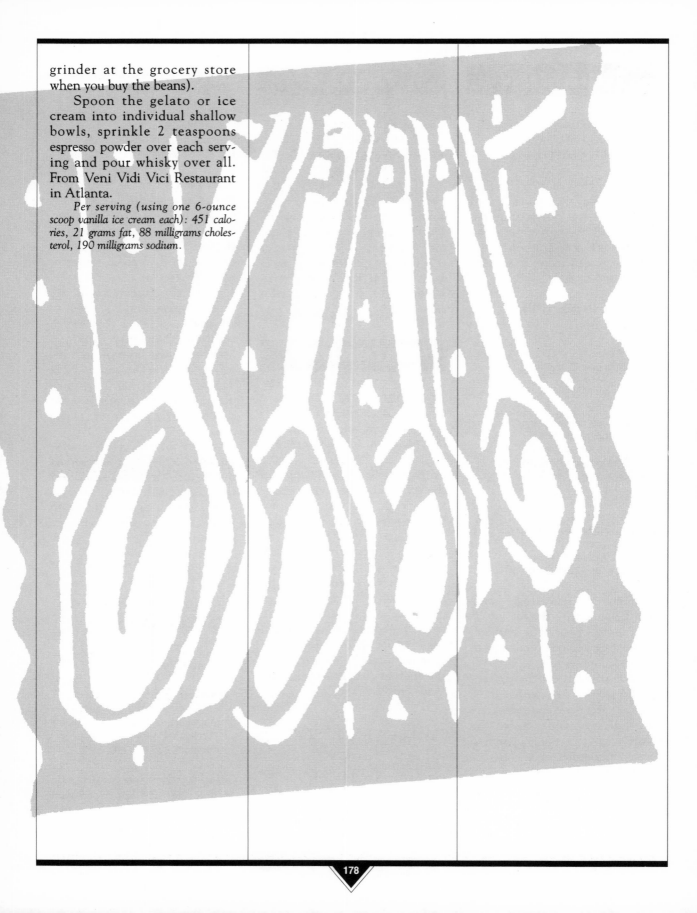

WEEK

33

SHOPPING LIST

Meat, Poultry, Seafood

- ❏ 7 to 8 chicken breasts
- ❏ 1 1/2 pounds kielbasa, fully cooked (optional)
- ❏ 4 6-ounce orange roughy fillets
- ❏ 3/4 pound beef tenderloin

Produce

- ❏ 1 bunch green onions
- ❏ 1 small onion
- ❏ 8 sweet banana peppers
- ❏ 6 or 7 plum tomatoes
- ❏ 2 tomatoes
- ❏ 2 large carrots
- ❏ 2 pounds snow peas
- ❏ 12 ounces mushrooms
- ❏ 1 head lettuce, any type
- ❏ 2 stalks celery
- ❏ 6 cloves garlic
- ❏ 2 shallots
- ❏ 1 to 1 1/2 cups blackberries
- ❏ 1 pineapple

- ❏ 2 lemons
- ❏ 2 limes
- ❏ 1 pint strawberries
- ❏ 2 or 3 bunches (1 1/2 cups) basil leaves
- ❏ 1 bunch mint—apple or regular
- ❏ 1 bunch dill

Dairy

- ❏ 5 large eggs
- ❏ 1 cup heavy cream
- ❏ 3 tablespoons non-fat yogurt
- ❏ 1 pint vanilla ice cream
- ❏ 3 or 4 tablespoons unsalted butter

Deli

- ❏ 1 loaf crusty bread, plus 4 slices
- ❏ 3/4 pound Havarti or Muenster cheese

Miscellaneous

- ❏ 1 8- to 12-ounce jar sweet and sour sauce
- ❏ 3/4 cup slivered or sliced almonds
- ❏ 2 14-ounce cans artichoke hearts
- ❏ 6 ounces pitted black olives
- ❏ 1 16-ounce can garbanzo beans
- ❏ 1 15-ounce can kidney beans (or use part of a larger can)
- ❏ 1 15 1/2-ounce can mandarin oranges
- ❏ 1 1/2 cups orzo
- ❏ 1/4 cup tropical fruit juice blend
- ❏ 3/4 cup beef broth
- ❏ 1/4 cup dry red wine
- ❏ 1 piece crystallized ginger
- ❏ 2 dried tomatoes
- ❏ 2 tablespoons capers

Staples

- ❏ Black pepper
- ❏ Granulated sugar
- ❏ Lemon juice
- ❏ Light mayonnaise
- ❏ Minced garlic in oil
- ❏ Olive oil (good quality)
- ❏ Powdered sugar
- ❏ Pure vanilla extract
- ❏ Red wine vinegar
- ❏ Salt
- ❏ Soy sauce
- ❏ Vegetable oil
- ❏ Vinaigrette
- ❏ White wine
- ❏ Worcestershire sauce

* Suggested accompaniments

SWEET AND SOUR CHICKEN BREASTS*
SNOW PEAS AND BANANA PEPPERS LACED WITH GARLIC
ALMOND AND RASPBERRY MERINGUE CAKE

Use a commercial sweet and sour sauce to marinate chicken breasts for an easy Sunday dinner, and cook extra chicken to serve later in the week. The snowpea recipe also makes plenty to serve later in the week. Jicama, a crunchy and refreshing Mexican vegetable, tastes much like water chestnuts for a fraction of the price. The raspberry meringue cake is light and delicious for a summer evening and easy to prepare.

SNOW PEAS AND BANANA PEPPERS LACED WITH GARLIC

Makes 8 to 10 servings
Preparation time: 10 minutes
Cooking time: 5 minutes

4 tablespoons vegetable oil
4 or 5 cloves garlic, finely chopped
3 sweet yellow banana peppers, seeded and diced
2 pounds snowpeas, trimmed
1 tablespoon hot pepper vinegar

In a wok or deep skillet, heat the oil. Add the banana peppers and saute until softened and fragrant, about 2 minutes. Add the garlic and snowpeas and saute until cooked but still tender-crisp, 2 to 3 minutes. Sprinkle with hot pepper vinegar and toss. Serve hot or room temperature.

Per serving: 89 calories, 6 grams fat, no cholesterol, 313 milligrams sodium.

ALMOND AND BLACKBERRY MERINGUE CAKE

Makes 8 servings
Preparation time: 20 minutes
Cooking time: 1 hour

3/4 cup slivered or sliced almonds
5 large egg whites at room temperature
1 1/4 cups granulated sugar
1/2 teaspoon vanilla
1 cup heavy cream
1 to 1 1/2 cups blackberries
1 piece crystallized ginger, minced
Confectioners' sugar

Preheat oven to 350 degrees. Prepare 2 9-inch round cake pans with grease and parchment paper. Set aside.

Put the nuts in a shallow baking pan and roast for 10 minutes, then cool. Put them in the workbowl of a food processor and pulse a few times to finely chop.

In a mixing bowl, beat the egg whites until stiff, then add the granulated sugar bit by bit, and continue to beat; the mixture will be stiff and glossy. Fold in the vanilla and chopped nuts. Divide the mixture between the cake pans. Bake 35 to 40 minutes, then cool to room temperature. Remove the cakes from the pans and place one on a serving platter.

Whip the cream in a chilled metal bowl until it holds peaks. Fold in the powdered sugar and blackberries. Spread the blackberry cream over the meringue on the serving platter, top with the second meringue and sprinkle crystallized ginger and sift confectioners' sugar over the top. Cut into wedges to serve.

Per serving: 185 calories, 17 grams fat, 41 milligrams cholesterol, 44 milligrams sodium.

ANTIPASTO SALAD BOWL
CRUSTY BREAD AND BUTTER *

This easy dinner salad makes enough to serve two nights running. Omit the kielbasa if you want a meatless dinner, but if you use it, be sure the kielbasa is cooked, or cook it yourself and chill before using. Cremini mushrooms will offer a deeper mushroom flavor and are available at most local grocery stores.

ANTIPASTO SALAD BOWL

Makes 12 servings
Preparation time: 20 minutes
Chilling time: 30 minutes

1 1/2 pounds sliced kielbasa, fully cooked (optional)
2 14-ounce cans artichoke hearts, quartered, drained
8 ounces fresh mushrooms, sliced
1 6-ounce can pitted black olives
4 or 5 sweet banana peppers, peeled and diced
1 16-ounce can garbanzo beans, drained
3/4 pound Havarti or Muenster cheese, cubed
1/2 cup fresh basil leaves, roughly chopped
2 cloves garlic, minced
3/4 cup vinaigrette (homemade or storebought)
Salt and black pepper to taste

In a large bowl, combine the kielbasa, artichoke hearts, mushrooms, olives, peppers, garbanzo beans, cheese and basil leaves.

Mix together the garlic, vinaigrette and salt and pepper and pour over the antipasta ingredients. Mix gently, cover and refrigerate 30 minutes to several hours. Serve cold or at room temperature.

IN SEASON • BANANA PEPPERS

Price: Prices range from $1.69 to $2.99 a pound, with an average of $1.99.

Nutrition: Peppers are rich in fiber and vitamins A, C and E and have about 20 calories each.

Selection: Choose bright, crisp and glossy peppers that are well shaped; avoid those with soft spots or that are wrinkled.

Storage: Refrigerate, unwashed, in a plastic bag for up to 5 days.

Uses: Allow 1 or 2 peppers per person. Banana peppers can be served as you would bell peppers; raw as a salad ingredient or eaten out of hand, grilled, sauteed, added to stir-fries, stuffed or pickled with hot vinegar and served over cooked greens.

Sweet banana peppers and their slightly hotter cousins are favorite Southern vegetables that are in peak season during the hot summer months. Because they are sweet or only mildly warm, they are versatile in myriad recipes. Look for a good variety of locally-grown peppers and good prices now until frost.

Per serving, including kielbasa and no added salt: 451 calories, 37 grams fat, 67 milligrams cholesterol, 932 milligrams sodium.

TUESDAY

MANDARIN CHICKEN SALAD
GARLICKY SNOWPEAS SAUTE *
FRESH PINEAPPLE SLICES *

Make this wonderful chicken salad with leftover chicken breasts, and accompany it with leftover snowpeas and fresh pineapple slices.

MANDARIN CHICKEN SALAD

Makes 4 servings
Preparation time: 10 minutes

4 large lettuce leaves
3 cooked chicken breast halves
2 stalks celery
1 15-ounce can mandarin oranges, drained
1 tablespoon fresh tarragon, chopped
1 teaspoon white wine Worcestershire sauce
1/3 cup light mayonnaise
3 tablespoons plain non-fat yogurt

Clean and pat dry the lettuce leaves. Put on serving plates and set aside.

Cut the meat into slivers and place in a medium-size bowl. Dice the celery and add, along with the remaining ingredients. Combine thoroughly and serve on a plate of lettuce leaves.

Per serving: 211 calories, 8 grams fat, 62 milligrams cholesterol, 86 milligrams sodium.

WEDNESDAY

LEMON AND ORANGE
ROUGHY
STEAMED ORZO WITH
DILL FLECKS *
TOSSED GREEN SALAD *

The new fresh fruit blends available now really add flavor to the meek flavor of orange roughy. Look for tangerine juice, passion fruit, mango or guava to enhance the fish. Cook plenty of orzo, a rice-shaped pasta, and refrigerate the extras to serve later in the week.

LEMON AND ORANGE ROUGHY

Makes 4 servings
Preparation time: 10 minutes
Cooking time: 20 to 25 minutes

1/4 cup tropical fruit juice blend
4 6- to 8-ounce orange roughy fillets
2 tablespoons vegetable oil
1/4 cup tablespoons apple or other mint leaves
1 tablespoon coarsely ground black pepper
Grated peel (green part only) of 2 limes
Grated peel of 2 lemons

Preheat the oven to 350 degrees.

Put the fish fillets in a large shallow baking dish. Brush with oil and pour the juice over.

Sprinkle the fillets heavily with the mint, black pepper and lemon and lime peels. Bake until the fish flakes easily when opened with a form, about 20 minutes.

Per serving: 395 calories, 24 grams fat, 108 milligrams cholesterol, 130 milligrams sodium.

THURSDAY

ANTIPASTO SALAD BOWL *
BASIC BRUSCHETTA

You can't beat the heady flavors of basil, garlic and red-ripe tomatoes for perfect summer food. Serve this Italian garlic bread with leftover antipasto salad.

BASIC BRUSCHETTA

Makes 4 servings
Preparation time: 15 minutes
Cooking time: 5 minutes

6 or 7 fresh ripe plum tomatoes, diced
2 dried tomatoes in olive oil, minced
1/2 cup packed basil leaves
2 tablespoons capers with some juice
Salt and black pepper to taste
1/3 cup good quality olive oil
4 large garlic cloves, peeled and minced
1 extra-large or 2 medium shallots
4 thick slices crusty bread, such as sourdough, Italian or French

Preheat the oven to 450 degrees.

Combine the fresh and dried tomatoes in a large bowl. Add the basil, capers, salt and pepper and half the olive oil. Set aside.

Heat the remaining olive oil in a small skillet and saute the slivered garlic and shallots until fragrant and soft, 1 or 2 minutes.

Meanwhile, toast the bread. Brush the slices with the garlic oil and spoon the tomato mixture over and serve.

Per serving: 258 calories, 16 grams fat, no cholesterol, 166 milligrams sodium.

FRIDAY

BUFFALO WINGS *
CARROT AND CELERY STICKS *
BLUE CHEESE DRESSING *

Make this a finger-food night by picking up tabasco-doused buffalo chicken wings either at your supermarket deli or a restaurant that offers wings-to-go. Add carrot and celery sticks (from the salad bar if they are offered there). Serve the wings and the veggies with your favorite blue cheese dressing.

SATURDAY

PEPPERED PARTY BEEF
KAREN'S CARROT
AND ORZO SALAD
STRAWBERRIES AND OREO
COOKIE ICE CREAM *

Enjoy the richness of this marinated beef tenderloin for tonight's dinner. Put leftover orzo flecked with dill to good use in the following pasta salad, and finish with the easiest summer dessert of all, strawberries and ice cream.

PEPPERED PARTY BEEF

Makes 4 servings
Preparation time: 10 minutes
Cooking time: 20 minutes

1 pound beef tenderloin
3 or 4 tablespoons fresh oregano
1 tablespoon coarsely ground black pepper
1 tablespoon unsalted butter
1 cup sliced fresh mushrooms, stemmed
1 small onion, thinly sliced
3/4 cup beef broth
1/4 cup dry red wine

Heat the oven to 250 degrees.

Trim any fat from the beef and cut into 4 slices. Liberally sprinkle the black pepper on the beef slices and rub in. Heat a large heavy skillet with the butter and add the beef slices. Cook 4 or 5 minutes on each side, until medium done. Put beef slices on a heat-proof platter and keep warm in the oven while cooking the sauce.

In the same skillet cook the mushrooms and onion over medium heat for 2 or 3 minutes. Stir in beef broth and wine and reduce to several tablespoons. Serve over the beef slices.

Per serving: 257 calories, 12 grams fat, 76 milligrams cholesterol, 245 milligrams sodium.

KAREN'S CARROT AND ORZO SALAD

Makes 6 to 8 servings
Preparation time: 20 minutes
Chilling time: 30 minutes

DRESSING:
2 tablespoons lemon juice
2 tablespoons red wine vinegar
Salt and black pepper to taste
1 garlic clove, minced
1/4 cup olive oil

SALAD:
1/4 cup green onions, finely chopped
1 15-ounce can kidney beans, drained
3 cups cooked orzo
2 large carrots, shredded
2 tomatoes, halved and cut into thin slices

To make the dressing, put the lemon juice, red wine vinegar, garlic clove and salt and pepper in the workbowl of a food processor and pulse to combine. With the motor running, add the olive oil in a thin stream to make a creamy vinaigrette.

In a large bowl, combine the green onions, beans, orzo and carrots. Spoon the salad on a serving platter, then arrange the tomato slices across the middle. Drizzle the dressing over the salad. Serve immediately or let the salad sit for a few minutes to let the flavors mingle.

Per serving: 230 calories, 9 grams fat, no cholesterol, 275 milligrams sodium.

WEEK

34

SHOPPING LIST

Meat, poultry, seafood

- ❑ 6 thick-cut pork chops, smoked if possible
- ❑ 4 6- to 8-ounce tilapia fillets
- ❑ 2 chicken fryers, quartered

Produce

- ❑ 1 large eggplant
- ❑ 2 or 3 sweet banana peppers
- ❑ 3 bell peppers
- ❑ 3 onions
- ❑ 1 bunch green onions
- ❑ 1 small bunch ($^1/_3$ cup minimum) bean sprouts
- ❑ 2 garlic cloves
- ❑ 7 tomatoes
- ❑ 1 head salad chicory
- ❑ 2 zucchini
- ❑ 2 pounds shelled butter beans
- ❑ 1 cucumber
- ❑ 1 knob ginger root

- ❑ 4 lemons
- ❑ 4 limes
- ❑ 8 small plums
- ❑ $^1/_2$ cup blueberries
- ❑ 1 small bunch basil
- ❑ 1 bunch dill
- ❑ 12 cherry tomatoes
- ❑ 1 3-ounce package Sunnies sunflower sprouts

Dairy

- ❑ 3 sticks unsalted butter
- ❑ $^1/_4$ cup half-and-half
- ❑ 1 8-ounce carton lemon yogurt
- ❑ 1 3-ounce package low-fat cream cheese
- ❑ 1 pint lemon sherbet
- ❑ 1 egg
- ❑ $^3/_4$ cup milk

Deli

- ❑ 4 blueberry muffins
- ❑ 1 strawberry pie

Miscellaneous

- ❑ $^1/_4$ cup almonds
- ❑ $^1/_4$ cup peanuts (optional)
- ❑ 2 cups dry rice
- ❑ $^1/_4$ cup sherry or vermouth
- ❑ 1 cup chicken broth
- ❑ 2 cups tomato or V-8 juice

Staples

- ❑ Black pepper
- ❑ Brown sugar
- ❑ Cinnamon
- ❑ Confectioners' sugar
- ❑ Granulated sugar
- ❑ Ground cumin
- ❑ Ground nutmeg
- ❑ Key lime juice
- ❑ Lemon juice
- ❑ Lime juice
- ❑ Olive oil
- ❑ Paprika
- ❑ Peanut oil

- ❑ Peanut sauce (optional)
- ❑ Rice wine vinegar
- ❑ Salt
- ❑ Self-rising flour
- ❑ Sesame oil
- ❑ Soy sauce
- ❑ Vanilla extract
- ❑ Vegetable oil

* Suggested accompaniments

SUNDAY

GRILLED SMOKED
PORK CHOPS *
GRILLED VEGETABLES
WILD PLUM UPSIDE -
DOWN CAKE

Fire up the grill for more great summer food: grilled smoky pork chops and effortless vegetables that also get tossed onto the grill. Cook plenty and save leftovers to puree into a summer soup later in the week. Don't miss the plum cake, similar to the familiar pineapple upside-down cake, when you find beautiful plums in the markets. The small sugar plums are often in farmers markets, and they are the ones I seek out for this dish. And plenty of times, I haven't bothered to pit the plums, but warned my dinner guests instead.

GRILLED VEGETABLES

Makes 8 servings
Preparation time: 20 minutes
Cooking time: 10-20 minutes

1 large eggplant, peeled and thickly
    sliced
1 red pepper, sliced
1 yellow pepper, sliced
2 onions, peeled and thickly sliced
5 tomatoes, halved
2 zucchini, halved lengthwise
1/4 cup olive oil

Preheat the grill.

Brush prepared vegetables with olive oil and grill over a low fire (if you can't grill, cook the vegetables in a cast-iron pan over medium heat). Cook until browned and tender. (Some will cook faster than others.) Adapted from *Metropolitan Home*, July 1992.

Per serving: 103 calories, 7 grams fat, no cholesterol, 9 milligrams sodium.

WILD PLUM UPSIDE-DOWN CAKE

Makes 1 large cake (10 servings)
Preparation time: 20 minutes
Cooking time: 30 minutes

8 small plums
1/2 cup blueberries
1/2 cup butter, divided, room
    temperature
1/2 cup packed brown sugar
1/2 teaspoon grated nutmeg
1/4 cup water
3/4 cup granulated sugar
1 egg
3/4 cup milk, approximately
1 1/2 cups self-rising flour
Confectioners' sugar, sifted, for
    garnish (optional)

Wash the fruit and pit the plums, but do not peel them. Preheat oven to 350 degrees.

Melt 2 tablespoons butter in a 9-inch cake pan over medium heat. Add brown sugar, nutmeg and water to the pan and bring to a boil, stirring. Remove from heat and place the plum halves around the pan, skin-side down. Scatter the blueberries in between the plums.

With a mixer or in the workbowl of a food processor, cream the remaining butter. Add the sugar and continue to beat, then add the egg and milk. With a spoon, stir in the flour, alternating with the liquid. Pour the batter over the fruit.

Bake about 30 minutes until the top is brown and well set. Cool on a rack for a few minutes, then turn out onto a plate. Pour any sauce left within the bottom of the pan over the cake. Sprinkle (optional) powdered sugar over.

Per serving: 284 calories, 10 grams fat, 53 milligrams cholesterol, 315 milligrams sodium.

MONDAY

SPECKLED BUTTER BEANS
STEAMED RICE *
SLICED TOMATOES *
FRESH FRUIT TOSSED WITH
LEMON YOGURT AND
CINNAMON *

Southern butter beans are fresh in the markets now (see In Season, page 185) and make for a memorable meal that is high in fiber, complex carbohydrates and vitamins. Look for shelled beans at farmers markets and roadside stands; otherwise, you will have to shell them yourself. (Or look for frozen beans and shorten the cooking time.) This simmered dish, inspired by Louisvillian Ronni Lundy in her book *Shuck Beans, Stack Cakes and Honest Fried Chicken* (Atlantic Monthly Press, $24.95), brings out their simplest and best flavor; save leftovers for later in the week. Cook enough rice to reheat later in the week. You can gild the lily with fresh herbs, but why?

SPECKLED BUTTER BEANS WITH SALT AND PEPPER

Makes 12 servings
Preparation time: 5 minutes
Cooking time: 30 minutes

4 cups water
2 pounds shelled butter beans

Price: Look for prices to average from $.99 a pound for unshelled and $1.69 or more for shelled. Farmers markets charge less for shelled than the roadside vegetable trucks.

Nutrition: Fresh shelled beans are high in vitamin C, B complex, sodium, niacin and have about 190 calories per cooked cup. They are also rich in fiber and complex carbohydrates, and lower blood cholesterol and help control blood sugar in diabetics.

Selection: Choose beans in pods that are broad and filled out and tightly closed. Shelled beans should be plump and fresh looking, not watery, slimy or dried up.

Storage: Refrigerate unwashed pods or shelled beans in a plastic bag for up to 4 days. Rinse the shelled beans before cooking.

Uses: Allow about $1/4$ pound shelled or $3/4$ pound unshelled per serving. One pound unshelled beans yields about 1 cup shelled beans. Beans must be cooked before serving and can then be served hot or cold. Add fresh-shelled beans to soups or combine several kinds of cooked shelled and edible-pod beans, such as green beans, in cold salads.

Southerners know a good vegetable when they see one, and butter beans are one of the best, and a harbinger of a deep South summer. These first cousins to lima beans have a creamy texture and buttery flavor that sets them apart from other fresh legumes. They are also very nutritious and a good meat substitute.

Local butter beans are grown in the Cordell and Thomasville areas of Georgia and are now in season. Supplies are excellent and prices lower than last summer, as farmers grew a bumper crop.

They should be available in farmers markets and local produce stands now until autumn. Because butter beans are so popular and are a seasonal item, they sell out quickly each day. That means shop early in the day or you may miss them. Shelled beans will cost slightly more, but may be worth the inconvenience.

4 tablespoons butter
1/4 cup half-and-half
Salt, to taste

In a large saucepan, bring the water to a boil. Add the butter beans, cover and bring the water back to a boil. Reduce the heat and simmer for 15 minutes, or until tender. Stir the beans occasionally to keep them from sticking and add small amounts of water if necessary. (You want most of the water to cook out of the beans during cooking.)

Add butter to the beans and when it has melted, stir in the half-and-half. Cover and simmer on low heat another 5 minutes or until the butter forms a sauce. Add salt to taste and serve hot.

Per serving: 126 calories, 5 grams fat, 12 milligrams cholesterol, 47 milligrams sodium.

TUESDAY

FLORIDA TILAPIA WITH KEY LIMES AND GINGER
STIR-FRIED RICE WITH TOASTED ALMONDS *
PLUM UPSIDE-DOWN CAKE *

Quick-cooking tilapia fillets, similar to orange roughy and a good bargain at the grocery store, get baked with tropical juices and fresh ginger root for an effortless meal. Stir-fry leftover rice with toasted almonds, then garnish with fragrant lemon or orange peel.

FLORIDA TILAPIA WITH KEY LIMES AND GINGER

Makes 4 servings

Preparation time: 5 minutes
Cooking time: 10 to 20 minutes

4 6- to 8-ounce tilapia fillets
1/4 cup dry sherry
1/4 cup Key lime juice
2 tablespoons grated ginger root
1/4 teaspoon pepper
2 tablespoons unsalted butter, cut in pieces

Preheat oven to 400 degrees.

Place fillets in a single layer in a glass baking dish. Pour the sherry and lime juice over. Top with ginger root and sprinkle liberally with black pepper. Dot with the pieces of butter. Bake about 15 to 20 minutes or until the fish flakes easily with a fork.

Per serving: 283 calories, 18 grams fat, 34 milligrams cholesterol, 187 milligrams sodium.

WEDNESDAY

ROASTED VEGETABLE SOUP
BLUEBERRY MUFFINS WITH LOW-FAT CREAM CHEESE *

Save those leftover grilled vegetables for this great summery soup — a gazpacho with the added flavor that comes from smoked food. Add prepared or purchased blueberry muffins with a low-fat cream cheese for added protein.

ROASTED VEGETABLE SOUP

Makes 4 servings
Preparation time: 10 minutes
Chilling time: 1 hour

1/2 eggplant, sliced and grilled
1 bell pepper, or halves of different colored ones, sliced and grilled

1/4 to 1/2 large grilled onion
1/2 zucchini, sliced and grilled
1/2 cucumber, diced
2 tablespoons olive oil
2 tablespoons fresh basil leaves
3/4 to 1 cup chicken broth
2 cups tomato or V-8 juice
1 teaspoon ground cumin (optional)
Salt and freshly ground pepper to taste

Place the cold, grilled vegetables in the bowl of a food processor, reserving a few slivers of bell pepper and the cucumber. Pulse until the vegetables are pureed, then add the oil, basil, broth, tomato juice, cumin, salt and pepper, and puree again. Add more tomato juice if it is too thick. Pour into a large bowl or other serving container (a pitcher if you are going to the pool).

Chop the reserved bell pepper and cucumber and add the chunks to the soup. Chill for an hour before serving.

Per serving: 115 calories, 7 grams fat, no cholesterol, 598 milligrams sodium.

THURSDAY

PORK AND BUTTER BEAN STIR-FRY
SLICED TOMATOES *
LEMON SHERBET *

The week's leftovers make a filling meal that will expand to accommodate any number of diners. Leftover zucchini, tomatoes or peppers can be added to the mix, and a sprinkling of chopped peanuts complements the flavors of pork and beans.

PORK AND BUTTER BEAN STIR-FRY

Makes 4 servings
Preparation time: 10 minutes
Cooking time: 10 minutes

2 tablespoons peanut oil
1 small onion, diced
1 garlic clove, minced
1 cup diced cooked pork
3 to 4 cups cooked butter beans
2 to 3 tablespoons chopped fresh
   basil or mint
1/4 cup chopped peanuts (optional)
   as garnish

Heat the oil in a large skillet. Saute the onion until soft, about 5 minutes, then add the garlic and saute 1 more minute. Stir in the pork and butter beans and cook and toss until they are heated through, about 5 minutes. Remove from the heat and stir in basil and sprinkle with peanuts, if desired.

Per serving: 344 calories, 17 grams fat, 33 milligrams cholesterol, 48 milligrams sodium.

Per serving, with peanuts: 398 calories, 21 grams fat, 33 milligrams cholesterol, 49 milligrams sodium.

FRIDAY

COLD PASTA SALAD *
CHEESE BREAD *
GIANT CHOCOLATE
CHIP COOKIES *

Look for summer variations of deli offerings: pasta salad with lots of black olives and gutsy capers, cheese-filled bread and giant chocolate chip cookies for dessert.

SATURDAY

LEMON-LIME CHICKEN
SUNNIES AND GREENS WITH
GINGER VINAIGRETTE
SAUTEED BUTTER BEANS *
STRAWBERRY PIE *

This dinner is delicious and healthful, inspired by Jane Weston Wilson's recipe from her book *Eating Well When You Just Can't Eat the Way You Used To* (Workman, $12.95). Look for crinkled chicory or endive for the pretty salad; Sunnies is a brand name for delicious sunflower sprouts, big enough to be considered a green all their own. Quickly saute fresh butter beans for a filling side dish, and finish with a purchased strawberry pie.

LEMON-LIME CHICKEN

Makes 8 servings
Preparation time: 5 minutes
Marinating time: 4 hours
Cooking time: 50 minutes

2 chicken fryers, quartered, rinsed
   and dried
1/2 cup lemon juice (about 4
   lemons)
1/2 cup lime juice (about 4 limes)
2 teaspoons minced ginger root
1 large garlic clove, minced
Salt and black pepper to taste
3 tablespoons snipped fresh dill
6 tablespoons unsalted butter,
   melted

Place the chicken pieces in a large glass or stainless steel container. Combine the lemon and lime juices, ginger root, garlic, salt and pepper. Pour over the chicken and marinate, covered, 4 hours in the refrigerator.

Preheat the oven to 450 degrees.

Line a large baking pan with parchment paper. Arrange the chicken in a layer, skin side up, and sprinkle with the dill and brush with the melted butter.

Bake the chicken for 20 minutes, turning once. Reduce heat to 350 and cook 30 to 35 minutes or until the juices run clear when the thigh joint is pricked with a fork.

Per serving: 334 calories, 24 grams fat, 109 milligrams cholesterol, 85 milligrams sodium.

SUNNIES AND GREENS WITH GINGER VINAIGRETTE

Makes 6 servings
Preparation time: 10 minutes

1 head salad chicory, shredded
2 green onions, chopped
1 cup sunflower sprouts
2 sweet banana peppers, cored,
   seeded and julienned
Ginger Vinaigrette (recipe follows)
12 cherry tomatoes, halved
1/4 cup chopped fresh herbs

Place the shredded chicory, onions, bean sprouts and sweet pepper in a large bowl. Pour the Ginger Vinaigrette over the salad and mix well. Add tomatoes and toss again. Serve, garnished with chopped herbs.

Per serving: 114 calories, 5 grams fat, no cholesterol, 71 milligrams sodium.

GINGER VINAIGRETTE

Makes 1/2 cup or 8 servings
Preparation time: 5 minutes

1/4 cup vegetable oil
1 tablespoon sesame oil
1 tablespoon rice wine vinegar

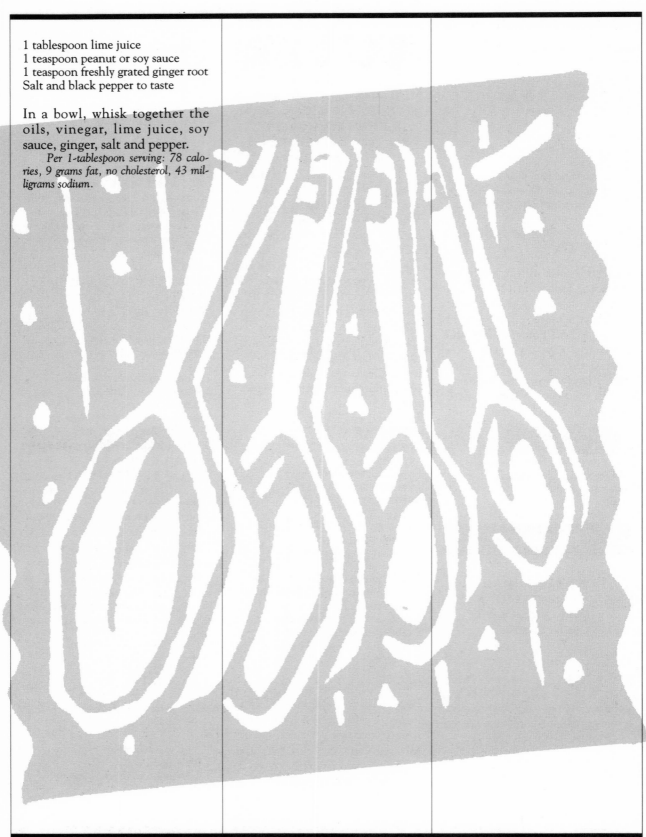

1 tablespoon lime juice
1 teaspoon peanut or soy sauce
1 teaspoon freshly grated ginger root
Salt and black pepper to taste

In a bowl, whisk together the oils, vinegar, lime juice, soy sauce, ginger, salt and pepper.

Per 1-tablespoon serving: 78 calories, 9 grams fat, no cholesterol, 43 milligrams sodium.

WEEK

35

SHOPPING LIST

Meat, poultry, seafood

- [ ] 1 ½ pounds boneless smoked turkey
- [ ] 1 1- to 1 ½-pound ham steak
- [ ] 4 lamb chops

Produce

- [ ] 2 pounds shelled White Acre peas (or other small, fresh peas or beans)
- [ ] 6 medium ripe tomatoes
- [ ] 2 ribs celery
- [ ] 4 green onions
- [ ] 1 yellow onion
- [ ] 1 garlic clove
- [ ] 3 yellow squash or zucchini or combination
- [ ] 2 or 3 yellow banana peppers or 1 bell pepper
- [ ] ¾ pound green beans
- [ ] 1 large head lettuce

- [ ] 13 new russet potatoes
- [ ] 1 bunch Italian parsley
- [ ] 1 bunch chives
- [ ] ½ cup blackberries
- [ ] 1 melon
- [ ] 1 lime
- [ ] 3 pounds Italian prune plums
- [ ] 1 or 2 Sharlyn melons

Dairy

- [ ] 1 tablespoon low-fat sour cream or yogurt
- [ ] ½ cup shredded Cheddar cheese
- [ ] ½ cup grated Italian Fontina cheese
- [ ] 3 sticks butter
- [ ] 2 large eggs
- [ ] ¼ cup whipping cream
- [ ] 1 pint cinnamon ice cream (optional)

Deli

- [ ] 1 dried-cherry focaccia (or other kind of coffee cake)
- [ ] 3 tablespoons pesto
- [ ] 8 corn tortillas
- [ ] 8 slices sandwich bread

Miscellaneous

- [ ] ½ cup commercial poppy seed dressing
- [ ] ½ cup fruit liqueur, such as cassis, kirsch, port or frozen fruit juice concentrate, thawed (apple or orange, for example)
- [ ] 2 cups dry white rice
- [ ] 1 cup dry wild rice
- [ ] 1 cup semisweet chocolate chips
- [ ] 1 5-ounce package corn bread mix
- [ ] 2 14 ½-ounce cans low-sodium chicken broth

- [ ] 1 ¼ cups sliced almonds
- [ ] ½ cup chopped pecans or walnuts

Staples

- [ ] All-purpose flour
- [ ] Almond extract
- [ ] Bread crumbs
- [ ] Brown sugar
- [ ] Coarse bread crumbs
- [ ] Hot sauce
- [ ] Granulated sugar
- [ ] Ground allspice
- [ ] Hot sauce
- [ ] Light corn syrup
- [ ] Olive oil
- [ ] Salt
- [ ] Vegetable oil
- [ ] Vinaigrette

* Suggested accompaniments

WHITE ACRE PEAS WITH FRESH TOMATOES STEAMED WILD AND WHITE RICE *
CORN BREAD *
ITALIAN PLUM CRUMBLE WITH CINNAMON ICE CREAM

Late summer produce is still my favorite: the combination of summer harvests and the first fall offerings mingle in robust dishes. Delicate Southern White Acre peas are still available at most farmers markets, usually already shelled, so use them while the season lasts. If you can't find them, substitute black-eyed peas, crowder peas, butter beans or limas, but expect to cook them 15 to 20 minutes longer. With rice and corn bread, the peas make a delicious and substantial meal. The recipe makes plenty to use throughout the week. To bring out their fullest flavor, don't refrigerate the tomatoes.

Use a combination of wild and white rice packaged together, available from Uncle Ben's, or cook the rices separately. Be sure to make enough to have 4 cups of cooked rice leftover. Prune plums are at the end of their season but still available and wonderfully sweet, or look for locally-grown plums. This dessert will be a hit, but try to save leftovers for tomorrow's holiday dinner.

WHITE ACRE PEAS WITH FRESH TOMATOES

Makes 8 servings
Preparation time: 5 minutes
Cooking time: 20 minutes

2 pounds shelled White Acre peas or other peas or beans
8 cups combination water and low-sodium chicken broth or ham broth
1/2 to 1 teaspoon salt (optional)
Freshly ground black pepper, to taste
4 ripe and juicy tomatoes, cut into chunks

Place the peas, broth and (optional) salt in a large saucepan and bring to a boil over high heat. Lower the heat and simmer, covered for 15 minutes. If you like a thick pot liquor, allow the peas to cook for another 10 or 15 minutes or until they begin to burst. Serve the peas in a bowl, topped with black pepper and chopped tomatoes.
Per serving: 389 calories, 1 gram fat, no cholesterol, 319 milligrams sodium.

ITALIAN PLUM CRUMBLE

Makes 12 servings
Preparation time: 20 minutes
Cooking time: 40-45 minutes

3 pounds Italian prune plums, pitted and cut in large pieces
A few handfuls blue or blackberries (optional)
1 1/4 cup brown sugar, packed
1/2 cup fruit-based liqueur, such as cassis, kirsch, port or frozen fruit juice concentrate, thawed (apple or orange, for example)
1 cup all-purpose flour
3/4 cup dried bread crumbs, coarsely ground
1/2 cup chopped pecans or walnuts
2 teaspoons ground allspice
1/4 teaspoon salt
3/4 cup (1 1/2 sticks) unsalted butter, cold, cut into small pieces
1 large egg, lightly beaten
1 pint cinnamon ice cream

Preheat the oven to 375 degrees.
Combine the plums and any berries if you wish, 1/2 cup of the brown sugar and the liqueur together in a rectangular 12-by-8-inch or equal size shallow baking dish. In the workbowl of a food processor, combine the flour, oats, pecans, remaining brown sugar, cinnamon and salt. Add the butter and pulse several times until mixture resembles coarse meal. Add egg and process a few seconds until moist and crumbly. Sprinkle the topping evenly over the plums in the baking dish.

Bake until the plums are bubbling and the top is golden brown, 40 to 45 minutes. Serve warm or at room temperature, with ice cream.
Per serving: 361 calories, 16 grams fat, 53 milligrams cholesterol, 36 milligrams sodium.

WILD RICE AND SMOKED TURKEY SALAD WITH BLACKBERRY DRESSING
ITALIAN PLUM CRUMBLE *

This picnic dish will celebrate Labor Day in great late-summer, early-fall fashion. Leftover rice gets transformed into a delicious dish that can be expanded to feed plenty of people, or save the leftovers to serve later in the week. Save the remaining turkey for sandwiches.

WILD RICE AND SMOKED TURKEY SALAD WITH BLACKBERRY DRESSING

Makes 8 servings
Preparation time: 15 minutes

2 cups cubed smoked turkey

1/2 cup chopped celery
2 green onions, chopped
3 cups cooked long-grain and wild
    rice, room temperature
1/2 cup blackberries
1/2 cup commercial poppy seed
    dressing
Lettuce leaves

In a large bowl, toss together the turkey, celery, onions and rice and set aside.

Puree the blackberries in a food processor. If you want to remove the seeds, rub the puree through a sieve or food mill. In a small bowl, whisk together the blackberry puree and poppy seed dressing. Toss the dressing with the salad mixture.

To serve, arrange lettuce leaves on a serving platter and place salad mixture on top.

Per serving: 223 calories, 9 grams fat, 24 milligrams cholesterol, 708 milligrams sodium.

TUESDAY

HAM STEAKS *
BAKED POTATOES *
MIXED GREEN SALAD *
CREAMY PARSLEY SALAD
DRESSING

This looks like an ordinary dinner, except for the exceptional flavor of the newly dug potatoes. Their extra-sweet flavor and moisture make them a late-summer treat. Bake in the oven to produce a crisp skin and fluffy interior. For faster results, microwave 4 potatoes for about 15 minutes. The result is a more moist potato with a soft skin, much like a boiled or steamed potato. Cook 2 or 3 extra potatoes to tuck into tacos later in the week.

SEPTEMBER

Vegetables prices are a little higher now, with supplies coming from the midwest. As supplies start to move South again, prices should drop. Sweet corn is coming from Colorado and is excellent now. Look for supplies of greens — collards, turnips and mustards — to start up again with cooler temperatures. The Norkota new russet potato is in from Idaho, with Burbanks coming in a few weeks. New potatoes are always a little more expensive than storage potatoes, but also more delicious. Green peanuts have been in for a few weeks, sweet potatoes will start soon. Stores are getting fresh cider in — right now it is made from red and yellow delicious apples; later in the season we will get cider made from the spicier Macintosh apple.

Fall squashes, apples and pears are the news now. Cabbage is still low in price, and lettuce, especially red and green lettuce, is expensive. Rutabagas are in, as well as Florida radishes, sweeter than the earlier Michigan radishes. Vidalia onions are in stores, higher in price than in the spring, but welcome just the same. Shallots are a good value.

California tree fruit — peaches, plums and nectarines — is winding down. The colorful O'Henry peaches and Red Jim nectarines are gone, and late varieties will be just as flavorful — they just won't have the color of earlier peaches.

The new crop of Washington state Golden Delicious apples is in, and Royal Galas have been in stores for a week or so. Georgia and Virginia apple harvests are in full swing and are available in many stores, farmers markets and at apple houses in north Georgia.

Late summer is the best time for California grapes because they are at their sweetest now. Shoppers often mistakenly shy away from grapes with a yellow cast, thinking they are past their prime, but the color indicates extra sweetness. Variety melons, such as the Sharlyn Casaba, and Honeydew, are also at their sweetest now, so look for good prices for a few weeks, until temperatures start to drop.

Add a green salad with a delicious salad dressing made with low-fat sour cream. Flat Italian parsley and freshly ground black pepper will make a better dressing, and the optional addition of blue cheese will really pep up the flavor. The salad dressing is a great potato topper, too.

CREAMY SALAD DRESSING WITH PARSLEY AND BLUE CHEESE

Makes 1/2 cup
Preparation time: 10 minutes

1/4 cup vegetable oil

3 tablespoons fresh parsley leaves, minced
2 green onions, finely chopped
$1/4$ teaspoon salt
$1/4$ teaspoon black pepper
1 tablespoon low-fat yogurt or low fat sour cream
1 tablespoon blue cheese, crumbled (optional)

Combine the oil, parsley, onions, salt and pepper in a food processor and process until blended. With the machine running, add the yogurt or sour cream and blue cheese, blending thoroughly, although lumps of blue cheese will be fine. Refrigerate in an airtight container until ready to use.

Per 1-tablespoon serving without blue cheese: 69 calories, 7 grams fat, less than 1 milligram cholesterol, 76 milligrams sodium.

WEDNESDAY

VEGGIE AND RICE TOSS WITH PESTO DRIED-CHERRY FOCACCIA *

Leftover rice works its way into another great dinner dish, and this one is a personal favorite to use my garden bounty of peppers, yellow squash and basil. Purchase pesto or prepare your own. When I find basil in abundance in the markets, I prepare pesto in ice cube trays and store in the freezer year round for a quick flavor infusion, such as in the recipe below.

A dried-cherry foccaccia, available at local bakeries and farmers markets, is a sweet version of an Italian flat bread. Laced with the haunting flavor of dried cherries and sprinkled with

powdered sugar, it begs to be pulled apart and enjoyed with a cup of coffee.

VEGGIE AND RICE TOSS WITH PESTO

Makes 4 servings
Preparation time: 10 minutes
Cooking time: 15 minutes

1 tablespoon olive oil
$1/2$ yellow onion, chopped
2 or 3 yellow banana peppers or 1 bell pepper, seeded and chopped
1 garlic clove, peeled and minced
3 summer squash, zucchini or yellow or combination, roughly chopped
1 cup cooked rice, room temperature
3 tablespoons pesto
$1/4$ cup grated Parmesan cheese
Salt and black pepper to taste

In a large, deep skillet, heat the oil. Saute the onion for a couple of minutes, until softened, then add the peppers and cook a couple minutes more. Add the garlic and cook about 1 minute.

Add the squash and continue to cook, stirring for about 5 minutes or until the squash is softened and the entire dish is fragrant. Add the rice; cook and toss a couple of minutes until heated through. Add the pesto and cheese and toss and cook a minute. Add salt and black pepper if necessary.

Per serving: 193 calories, 12 grams fat, 4 milligrams cholesterol, 90 milligrams sodium.

THURSDAY

WHITE ACRE PEAS AND POTATO TACOS MELON WEDGES WITH LIME JUICE *

Leftover peas and potatoes make their way into tonight's meal. White Acre peas may not be traditional in tacos, but their great flavor and nutrition are welcomed anyway. Add slices of late-summer melon, sprinkled with lime juice for dessert.

WHITE ACRE PEAS AND POTATO TACOS

Makes 4 servings
Preparation time: 5 minutes
Cooking time: 10-15 minutes

1 tablespoon olive oil or lard
$1/2$ onion, chopped
2 or 3 cooked potatoes, roughly chopped, room temperature
$1/2$ to $3/4$ cup cooked White Acre peas, room temperature
8 corn tortillas
$1/2$ cup shredded Cheddar cheese
2 cups lettuce, shredded
Hot sauce

In a large skillet, heat the oil. Saute the onion until soft and fragrant, about 3 minutes. Add the potatoes and cook over medium-high heat, tossing until they turn brown and crispy. Pull them to one side of the skillet and add the peas. Lower the heat slightly and mash the peas lightly with a potato masher or fork and let them cook until warmed. Set aside.

Meanwhile, heat the tortillas on a dry griddle or skillet with no oil, just until warm and softened, 1 or 2 minutes.

To serve, spread some of the mashed peas on the warm tortillas, top with potatoes, cheese, lettuce and hot sauce and serve.

Per serving: 391 calories, 16 grams fat, 33 milligrams cholesterol, 309 milligrams sodium.

Price: Tomatillos range from $.69 to $2.00 a pound.

Nutrition: Tomatillos have about 35 calories each and are a good source of vitamin C. They also provide vitamin A, thiamin and niacin.

Selection: Tomatillos are light green but may be soft yellow. Choose fruits that are firm and dry with clean, close-fitting husks that show no blackness or mold. They should be hard; they do not give like tomatoes.

Storage: Tomatillos can be stored in the refrigerator for two or three weeks; place them in a paper-lined dish or basket and simply let them be.

To freeze: Husk, wash and cook them just until softened. Cool and freeze them in the cooking liquid. Then use them along with the liquid for sauce-making.

Uses: Generally, tomatillos are cooked before using to bring out their sweetness and more mellow flavor and soften their tough skins. Use in soups, sauces and salad dressings or add raw to gazpacho or guacamole.

An integral ingredient in Mexican sauces is the small green tomato called tomatillo, actually related to gooseberries and not at all related to tomatoes. Tomatillos are generally available year around now, but will be more plentiful and a bargain in late summer. Look for them with specialty products and chili peppers in the produce section of most grocery stores.

These green golf-balls are wrapped in delicate paper husks which must be removed before cooking.

Raw tomatillos can be sliced into soups and sauces, but they retain their acidic character. If cooked in water or roasted for just a few minutes, they soften and yield a lemony flavor and fragrance, and the acid diminishes. Their slightly gelatinous texture also lends body to sauces.

FRIDAY

**SMOKED TURKEY
SANDWICHES ***
**WHITE ACRE PEAS WITH
FRESH TOMATOES TOSSED IN
VINAIGRETTE ***

Leftovers continue to offer easy fixings for tonight's meal. Smoked turkey makes terrific sandwiches, while leftover peas are great tossed in a basil vinaigrette. Use a tablespoon of pesto left over from Wednesday's meal for the basil flavoring.

SATURDAY

LAMB CHOPS *
**ACCORDIAN ROASTED
POTATOES**
**SAUTEED GREEN AND
YELLOW WAX BEANS ***
HARVEST MOON COOKIES

This pretty little dinner will treat guests to the best. The lamb chops may get ignored for the potatoes, especially if you get freshly dug and moist russets, adapted from Renee Shepherd's book, *Recipes From a Kitchen Garden* (Shepherd's Garden Publishing, $7.95). The delicate almond cookies, inspired by Debbi Fields's book, *Mrs. Field's Cookie Book* (Time-Life Books, $12.95), offer an elegant ending; they are delicious unadorned, or you can drizzle them with melted chocolate.

ACCORDIAN ROASTED POTATOES

Makes 6 servings

Preparation time: 10 minutes
Cooking time: 1 ¹/₂ hours

6 large russet baking potatoes, peeled
Cold water
4 to 6 tablespoons butter, melted
Salt, to taste
6 tablespoons chopped fresh chives
¹/₂ cup Italian Fontina or other cheese, grated
4 tablespoons bread crumbs

Preheat the oven to 350 degrees.

Put peeled potatoes in a bowl of cold water until ready to use. Dry thoroughly and cut a thin slice off the long side of each potato so it can sit flat. Cut slits from the top almost to the bottom of each potato, being careful not to cut all the way to the bottom.

Dip the cut potatoes in melted butter and sprinkle with salt. Bake in a baking pan for 1 hour and 15 minutes, basting with the butter left from dipping. When the potatoes are cooked, the cut slits will open in accordion fashion as they bake.

In the last 15 minutes of baking, combine the chives, cheese and bread crumbs. Stuff the mixture into the slits in the potatoes.

Per serving: 339 calories, 15 grams fat, 43 milligrams cholesterol, 440 milligrams sodium.

HARVEST MOON COOKIES

Makes 1 ¹/₂ dozen
Preparation time: 20 minutes
Cooking time: 15 minutes

¹/₄ cup almonds
¹/₂ cup unsalted butter, softened
³/₄ cup granulated sugar
1 large egg
1 teaspoon almond extract
1 cup all-purpose low-protein flour (such as White Lily)
1 to 1 ¹/₂ cups (4 ounces) slivered

almonds
1 cup hard chocolate sauce (optional)

Preheat oven to 350 degrees.

Put the almonds in the food processor and process until they are ground fine, then set aside.

Put the butter and sugar in the workbowl of a food processor and process until the mixture turns to a paste, scraping the sides of the bowl once or twice. With the machine running, add the egg and almond extract and process for about 30 seconds.

Add the ground almonds and flour and process another 10 to 15 seconds, scraping the sides of the bowl as necessary. With a teaspoon, form the dough into 1-inch balls. Flatten the balls slightly by pressing them into the ground almonds, coating each ball thoroughly.

Bake the cookies on an ungreased cookie sheet, 2 inches apart for 15 minutes or until the cookies start to color on the edges.

Let cookies cool slightly, then drizzle chocolate sauce over them. Serve when chocolate hardens.

Per cookie with chocolate drizzled over: 225 calories, 15 grams fat, 34 milligrams cholesterol, 59 milligrams sodium.

WEEK

36

SHOPPING LIST

Meat, poultry, seafood

- ❏ 2 pounds boneless pork shoulder or sirloin cubes
- ❏ 1 ¹/₄ pounds smoked turkey, sliced
- ❏ 1 pound sea scallops

Produce

- ❏ 4 onions
- ❏ 1 green bell pepper
- ❏ 6 cloves garlic
- ❏ 3 all-purpose potatoes
- ❏ 2 pounds green beans
- ❏ 1 quart shelled lady peas
- ❏ 1 large butternut squash
- ❏ 1 leek
- ❏ 1 pint cherry tomatoes
- ❏ 2 tomatoes
- ❏ 1 bunch spinach
- ❏ 1 extra-large portabella, 4 or 5 ounces shiitake or cremini mushrooms
- ❏ 1 bunch sage
- ❏ 1 bunch cilantro
- ❏ 1 bunch mint leaves

- ❏ 1 bunch fresh dates
- ❏ 4 Paula Red apples
- ❏ 3 Sharlyn melons

Dairy

- ❏ 1 cup milk
- ❏ 1 cup ricotta cheese
- ❏ 8 ounces Italian Fontina or Cheddar cheese
- ❏ 4 ounces blue cheese
- ❏ ¹/₂ cup grated Parmesan cheese
- ❏ 2 sticks butter
- ❏ 4 toffee ice cream bars

Deli

- ❏ 1 loaf country-style white bread
- ❏ 1 pint coleslaw
- ❏ 4 corn muffins
- ❏ Corn bread

Miscellaneous

- ❏ 4 14 ¹/₂-ounce cans low-

sodium chicken broth
- ❏ 2 cups fresh or frozen corn
- ❏ 1 16-ounce can pinto or garbanzo beans
- ❏ 1 cup chopped pecans
- ❏ ¹/₂ cup jam
- ❏ ¹/₂ cup hot pepper jelly
- ❏ 1 9-ounce package lemon angel-hair pasta
- ❏ 1 6-ounce package pesto sauce
- ❏ 1 3-ounce package ramen noodles
- ❏ 1 cup Italian arborio rice
- ❏ Baking parchment
- ❏ ¹/₂ cup ruby port or cassis

Staples

- ❏ Black pepper
- ❏ Chili powder
- ❏ Crushed red pepper flakes
- ❏ Dried oregano
- ❏ Granulated sugar

- ❏ Kosher salt
- ❏ Olive oil
- ❏ Salt
- ❏ Soy sauce
- ❏ Sugar
- ❏ Vegetable oil

* Suggested accompaniments

CHILE SUNDAY
CORN BREAD *
SHARLYN MELON IN PORT

Prepare this wonderful chili on Sunday when you have time on your hands for the slow cooking it requires. Save the extras to serve later in the week. The famous dessert melon of Provence is the Cavaillon; but here in the States, few can compare with the late summer Sharlyn, with a Brix of 14. Perfectly ripe, perfumed melon is essential for the following dessert.

CHILE SUNDAY

Makes 8 servings
Preparation time: 20 minutes
Cooking time: 1 hour

1 tablespoon vegetable oil
2 pounds boneless pork shoulder or sirloin cubes, cut into 1 1/2-inch cubes
1 large onion, chopped
4 to 6 sweet banana peppers or 2 green bell peppers, chopped
4 garlic cloves, minced
1 handful cilantro stems, leaves reserved for garnish
3 to 4 tablespoons chili powder, depending on its heat
1 to 1 1/2 teaspoons salt
1 teaspoon crushed red pepper
4 to 6 cups water
3 cups cubed potatoes, cut into 1-inch pieces
2 cups fresh or frozen corn
1 15-ounce can pinto or garbanzo beans, drained

Heat the oil in a Dutch oven or other large casserole. Brown pork over medium-high heat, 8 to 10 minutes. Stir in the onions, green pepper, garlic, cilantro stems, chili powder, salt, red pepper and water. Cover; cook over medium-low heat for 45 to 55 minutes or until the meat is tender. Add potatoes, corn and beans. Cover;

cook 15 to 20 minutes longer. Garnish with cilantro leaves and serve.

Per serving: 528 calories, 22 grams fat, 102 milligrams cholesterol, 971 milligrams sodium.

SHARLYN MELON IN PORT

Makes 4 servings
Preparation time: 20 minutes
Chilling time: 15 minutes

1 perfectly ripe Sharlyn melon or cantaloupe
2 to 4 tablespoons sugar
1/4 to 1/2 cup ruby port or cassis

Cut the melon in half and remove the seeds. Remove the pulp in chunks or with a melon baller and put the balls in a serving bowl. Chill.

Ten or 15 minutes before serving, remove the fruit from the refrigerator and sprinkle lightly with sugar and moisten with muscatel or port and serve.

Per serving: 81 calories, less than 1 gram fat, no cholesterol, 13 milligrams sodium.

LADY PEAS WITH FRESH MINT
STEAMED GREEN BEANS *
THICK-SLICED BREAD WITH
RICOTTA CHEESE AND JAM *

The tiny white lady peas, also called white acre peas, have a delicate flavor and cook faster than other peas. Look for them shelled at farmers markets, or buy frozen lady peas. Cook plenty of green beans to use later in the week, and add bread and a soft cheese, such as ricotta, to round out the meal.

LADY PEAS WITH FRESH MINT

Makes 6 to 8 servings

Preparation time: 5 minutes
Cooking time: 15 minutes

2 quarts water
1 quart shelled lady peas
1 small onion, quartered
Salt and black pepper to taste
2 to 3 tablespoons fresh mint leaves

Bring the water to a boil in a large saucepan. Add the peas and onion and lower the heat to medium-low. Cook the peas for 10 to 15 minutes, add salt and pepper to taste. To serve, ladle the peas out of the broth, toss with mint leaves and serve.

Per serving without added salt (8 servings): 96 calories, less than 1 gram fat, no cholesterol, 4 milligrams sodium.

SMOKED TURKEY AND
CHEDDAR SANDWICHES
HOT PEPPER JELLY *
STEAMED BUTTERNUT
SQUASH *
MELON BALLS WITH MINT *

A sweet and hot pepper jelly is just right for these crusty sandwiches, but a thick and spicy chutney or cranberry sauce would be equally delicious. Purchase a large butternut squash and cook half for tonight's dinner and save the rest to cook later in the week.

SMOKED TURKEY AND CHEDDAR SANDWICHES

Makes 4 servings
Preparation time: 5 minutes
Cooking time: 10 minutes

4 thick slices of a large country-style or sourdough bread, slices large to flip over
1/2 cup hot pepper jelly
8 ounces Italian Fontina or Cheddar cheese, sliced thin
3/4 pound smoked turkey breast, sliced, skin and fat removed
1/2 to 1 stick unsalted butter, melted

Price: Melons will average $2.49 for small melons and $3.49 for larger ones.

Nutrition: Melons are a good source of vitamin C. Half a 5-inch cantaloupe has 80 calories, a 7-by-2-inch honeydew wedge has 50 calories.

Selection: Specialty melons peak in late August and September, as harvests move up the western coast. Melons often taste sweeter later in the season than earlier, as sugar content builds up in the fruit. The blossom end of a melon is generally sweeter than the stem end, the top side sweeter than the part that rests on the ground, and the center flesh sweeter than that closer to the rind.

Storage: Melons should last 4 days refrigerated, unless they are very ripe when you buy them. To soften a hard melon, place the whole melon in a loosely-closed paper bag. Once picked, melons won't get any riper or sweeter, only softer. Refrigerate cut melon tightly sealed in plastic, as the ethylene gas melons give off can hasten spoilage of other produce in the refrigerator.

Uses: Two-thirds to 1 pound of melon yields about 1 cup

cubed melon. Eat melon fresh, simply cut and served by itself or in a mixed fruit salad, with a squeeze of lemon or lime juice, salt, fresh mint, crystallized ginger or liqueur. Serve with proscuitto or dry salami, pureed into a chilled soup or yogurt smoothie.

Spread 1 side of each of the bread slices with pepper jelly. Add sliced cheese over the jelly, then turkey slices. Invert the remaining cheese-covered bread on top of the turkey.

Heat a griddle or large cast-iron skillet over medium heat until warm. Add half the butter to the skillet, and brush the remainder on the top sides of the sandwiches.

Cook, covered, until the bread is crisp and golden brown on the bottom and the cheese is beginning to melt, 3 or 4 minutes. Flip and cook the other side, 2 or 3 minutes. Cut in wedges and serve.

Per serving: 545 calories, 32 grams fat, 96 milligrams cholesterol, 574 milligrams sodium.

WEDNESDAY

LEMON PASTA WITH PESTO
LADY PEAS, GREEN BEANS AND
CHERRY TOMATOES IN PESTO*

This flavorful meal goes together in minutes and takes advantage of the last of summer vegetables. Pesto sauce is widely available, or make your own. Lemon angel-hair pasta is available in most deli sections of the grocery store; the Trio brand makes a good version.

LEMON PASTA WITH PESTO

Makes 4 servings
Preparation time: 5 minutes
Cooking time: 10 minutes

1 teaspoon olive oil
1 cup cooked lady peas
1 cup cooked green beans
1 cup cherry tomatoes, halved
1 6-ounce package pesto sauce
1 9-ounce package fresh lemon
    angel-hair pasta
¼ cup Parmesan cheese (optional)

In a skillet heat the olive oil; add the lady peas, green beans and tomatoes and toss until heated through and the tomatoes are softened. Stir in a couple tablespoons of the pesto sauce and set aside.

Meanwhile, cook the pasta in boiling water about 2 minutes. Drain, toss with the remaining pesto sauce. Place in a large, shallow serving dish and top with the vegetables and serve. Pass Parmesan cheese.

Per serving, including Parmesan: 511 calories, 32 grams fat, 5 milligrams

cholesterol, 131 milligrams sodium.

THURSDAY

RAMEN NOODLES WITH LADY PEAS AND SMOKED TURKEY
FRESH SLICED TOMATOES *
FRESH DATES *

Look for ramen noodles in the soup section of the grocery store, or for fuller-flavored and whole-grain versions, try West-brae Natural ramen from a health-food store. Cubes of firm tofu could be substituted for turkey. If you don't have fresh mint leaves, add a few drops of hot chili or sesame oil to the top of the soup just before serving.

RAMEN NOODLES WITH LADY PEAS AND SMOKED TURKEY

Makes 4 servings
Preparation time: 10 minutes
Cooking time: 10 minutes

3 to 4 cups water, vegetable or
    chicken broth
1 3-ounce package ramen noodles
2 cups cooked lady peas with juice

¼ to ½ cup sliced or chopped
    smoked turkey
Salt or soy sauce, to taste
1 bunch spinach, cleaned and
    stemmed
Fresh mint leaves

Bring the water or broth to a boil in a large saucepan, then add the flavor packet from the noodles and let it dissolve. Add the ramen noodles and cook 5 minutes; add the lady peas with any juices that naturally collect in a ladle, turkey and salt or soy sauce. Cook 5 minutes; turn off heat and add spinach leaves. Garnish with mint and serve the soup immediately, the spinach leaves will just wilt slightly.

Per serving without added salt or soy sauce: 166 calories, 3 grams fat, 12 milligrams cholesterol, 240 milligrams sodium.

FRIDAY

CHILE SUNDAY *
COLESLAW *, CORN BREAD *
TOFFEE ICE CREAM BARS *

Serve the leftovers from Sun-day's dinner tonight; the time in the refrigerator will have developed the flavors even more. Throw in a handful of freshly chopped cilantro to brighten the flavor. Add coleslaw, corn muffins and toffee ice cream bars.

SATURDAY

RISOTTO WITH WILD
MUSHROOMS
SEARED SCALLOPS WITH
MINT BUTTER *
WINTER SQUASH AND LEEKS
BAKED IN PARCHMENT
FRESH DATES, APPLES AND
BLUE CHEESE *

Autumn flavors abound in this meal — from wild mushrooms to winter squash flavored with sage.

For a simple first course, do as the Italians do and serve risotto, a creamy, comforting rice dish. Use the Italian arborio rice, a short-grain white rice that melts into a creamy mass when cooked; it's available in most grocery stores and at farmers markets.

The dish is traditionally a difficult dish to master, but it's easy in the microwave. For an autumn flavor, we cook it with portabella mushrooms, those overgrown creminis with an earthy flavor. Use creminis or other mushrooms if necessary.

Some dishes are simply impossible to improve on, such as Deborah Madison's Winter Squash and Leeks Baked in Parchment, from her book *The Greens Cookbook* (Bantam Books, $22.95).

RISOTTO WITH WILD MUSHROOMS

Makes 6 first-course servings
Preparation time: 5 minutes
Cooking time: 35 minutes

4 tablespoons unsalted butter
4 tablespoons olive oil
1 large yellow onion, minced
1 heaping cup Italian arborio rice
6 cups chicken broth
1 extra large portabella mushroom or
    4 or 5 ounces shiitake mush-
    rooms, cleaned and sliced
Salt and black pepper to taste
1/4 cup grated Parmesan cheese

Heat the butter, oil and onions in a large microwave-safe dish, about 11 by 14 inches. Add the rice and cook on high (100 percent power) for 4 minutes. Add the broth and the mushrooms and cook, uncovered, for 12 minutes. Stir and cook for 12 minutes more. Remove from the oven and let stand, uncovered for 5 min-utes, to let the rice absorb the remaining liquid, stirring several times. Stir in salt, pepper and cheese before serving.

Per serving without added salt: 340 calories, 19 grams fat, 25 milligrams cholesterol, 857 milligrams sodium.

WINTER SQUASH AND LEEKS BAKED IN PARCHMENT

Makes 4 servings
Preparation time: 20 minutes
Cooking time: 25 minutes

2 cups peeled butternut squash, cut
    into ¼-inch cubes
1 large leek, chopped into ½-inch
    pieces
2 or 3 garlic cloves, minced
4 teaspoons olive oil
Salt and black pepper to taste
4 pieces baking parchment, 12 by 15
    inches
1 to 2 tablespoons unsalted butter,
    softened, cut in pieces
8 fresh sage leaves

Preheat the oven to 400 degrees.

Put the squash, leeks, garlic and olive oil in a large bowl and toss, then sprinkle with salt and black pepper; set aside.

Fold the parchment paper in half and make a crease. Open it up and generously butter the bottom half, covering all but an inch from the edge. (It is important to coat the surfaces thoroughly, or the sugars in the squash will stick to the paper and burn.) Heap the vegetables into the center of the buttered area and tuck in 2 sage leaves. Add some butter pieces on top of the vegetables, then fold the upper half of the parchment over. Roll the edges tightly over themselves to make a half-circle. Bake for 25 minutes.

Open the packages carefully so the hot steam doesn't hit your face, and serve.

Per serving: 127 calories, 8 grams fat, 8 milligrams cholesterol, 39 milligrams sodium.

WEEK

37

SHOPPING LIST

Meat, poultry, seafood

- ❏ 6 boneless, skinless chicken breasts
- ❏ 2 or 3 slices bacon
- ❏ 4 6- to 8-ounce turkey cutlets

Produce

- ❏ 4 plum tomatoes
- ❏ 7 green onions
- ❏ 3 large yellow crookneck squash
- ❏ 3 small onions
- ❏ 2 celery stalks
- ❏ 1 or 2 tablespoons garlic or alfalfa sprouts
- ❏ 2 carrots
- ❏ 1 head leaf lettuce
- ❏ 1 bunch spinach
- ❏ 2 pounds snap beans
- ❏ 8 tomatillos
- ❏ 4 banana peppers
- ❏ 1 jalapeno pepper
- ❏ 2 Anaheim or 2 bell peppers

- ❏ 2 garlic cloves
- ❏ 4 all-purpose white potatoes
- ❏ 1 bunch cilantro
- ❏ 1 bunch mint or apple mint (optional)
- ❏ 2 Black Friar plums
- ❏ 2 Paula Red or Gravenstein apples
- ❏ 1 pint blackberries
- ❏ 1 bunch sage leaves
- ❏ 1 bunch chives

Dairy

- ❏ 6 tablespoons butter or margarine
- ❏ 6 tablespoons Parmesan cheese
- ❏ 1/2 pint strawberry yogurt
- ❏ 1/2 cup grated Monterey Jack cheese
- ❏ 1/2 cup diced Gruyere or Swiss cheese
- ❏ 2 eggs
- ❏ 1 cup cold milk

Deli

- ❏ 1 chocolate marble poundcake
- ❏ 4 to 8 flour tortillas

Miscellaneous

- ❏ 1 5-ounce package corn bread mix
- ❏ 1 15-ounce can black beans
- ❏ 1 16-ounce can corn (or use fresh ears)
- ❏ 1 15 1/2-ounce can artichoke hearts
- ❏ 1/2 cup lime or lemon juice
- ❏ 8 ounces soba noodles
- ❏ 1 12-ounce can water-packed tuna
- ❏ 1 14 1/2-ounce can chicken broth
- ❏ 1 cup barley
- ❏ 1 9-inch chocolate crumb pie crust
- ❏ 2 or 3 tablespoons capers

Staples

- ❏ All-purpose flour
- ❏ Balsamic vinegar
- ❏ Black pepper
- ❏ Confectioners' sugar
- ❏ Ground cumin
- ❏ Olive oil
- ❏ Red pepper flakes
- ❏ Red wine vinegar
- ❏ Salt
- ❏ Sugar
- ❏ Vegetable oil

* Suggested accompaniments

PUREE OF YELLOW
SQUASH SOUP
BLACK BEAN AND
CORN SALAD
CORN BREAD *
CHOCOLATE MARBLE
POUNDCAKE *

Take advantage of overgrown yellow squash that most gardens have in late summer to prepare a creamy squash soup. Late summer in Georgia often kills off vegetable plants, but they perk up again with cooler temperatures, so look for good quality corn and squash now. If corn is still expensive, use canned or frozen corn. Purchase or prepare corn bread, and serve a purchased chocolate marble poundcake, available in the deli section of most grocery stores, and save extras to serve later in the week.

PUREE OF YELLOW SQUASH SOUP

Preparation time: 20-30 minutes
Cooking time: 30-40 minutes
Yield: 4 to 6 servings

3 large yellow crook-neck squash, diced or grated
1 large onion, chopped
1 garlic clove, minced
2 tablespoons unsalted butter
4 or 6 fresh sage leaves
1 teaspoon salt
1/2 cup dry white wine
2 cups milk or half-and-half
Freshly ground black pepper
Minced chives or green onion tops

Heat the butter in a large saucepan or a Dutch oven, then saute the onions and garlic for about 5 minutes, or until the onions are soft and fragrant (take longer if you have the time, the onions turn sweeter with longer cooking). Add the squash, sage leaves and salt. Stir, cover and continue to cook about 10 minutes. Continue to cook over medium-low heat for 5 minutes.

Stir in the white wine, cover, and simmer 10 to 15 minutes. Remove from the heat and chill a few minutes before pureeing.

Puree the soup with the milk in a food processor or blender and return it to the pan. Add salt and pepper to taste. Heat gently just before serving. To serve, garnish with long sprigs of chives.

Per serving: 528 calories, 22 grams fat, 102 milligrams cholesterol, 971 milligrams sodium.

BLACK BEAN AND CORN SALAD

Makes 8 servings
Preparation time: 10 minutes
Blending time: 1 hour

1 15-ounce can black beans, drained and rinsed
1 16-ounce can corn, drained, or 3 or 4 ears of corn, briefly cooked and drained
4 plum tomatoes, diced
2 Anaheim or 1 bell pepper, seeded and diced
1 jalapeno pepper, seeded and diced
4 green onions, sliced
1/4 cup minced cilantro
3 tablespoons red wine vinegar
1/2 teaspoon ground cumin
3 tablespoons olive oil
Salt and black pepper to taste
Cilantro leaves for garnish
1 or 2 tablespoons garlic or alfalfa sprouts
Lettuce leaves

Mix the beans, corn, tomatoes, peppers, onions, cilantro, vinegar, cumin and oil together in a large mixing bowl about an hour before serving. Be sure the black beans have been rinsed, so the color doesn't bleed on the other ingredients. Before serving add salt and pepper to taste. Top with cilantro and garlic sprouts and serve on lettuce leaves.

Per serving, using 3 ears of fresh corn: 139 calories, 6 grams fat, no cholesterol, 204 milligrams sodium.

CHILE GRILLED
CHICKEN BREASTS *
TOMATILLO GREEN SAUCE
STEAMED GREEN BEANS *

Quicker to make and healthier than chicken enchiladas is this lovely green sauce simply served with grilled chicken breasts, adapted from Elizabeth Schneider's *Uncommon Fruits and Vegetables* (Harper & Row, $16.95). The lemony-herbal flavor of tomatillos comes out with gentle cooking, and a fistful of cilantro adds more lemony accent. Be sure to taste the banana pepper for hotness before adding it. Cook plenty of chicken, sprinkled with your favorite chile powder, and green beans to offer leftovers for later in the week, and reserve leftover green sauce for a later meal.

TOMATILLO GREEN SAUCE

Makes 6 servings
Cooking time: 10 minutes
Preparation time: 10 minutes

8 or 9 tomatillos, husks removed and washed

Friar plums made their yearly debut last week. These tart black-skinned plums have a sweet, juicy white flesh and are considered to be the best tasting midsummer plum, perhaps the best plum of the summer, according to Jerry Daniels, produce buyer at Super Value Retail Support Center in Atlanta. Don't be fooled by the dark red Simkas or Larodas that are also available now — their flesh is tarter than the Friar, he says. Friars are good eaten out of hand and excellent for cooking.

And until the popular bright-red Cassleman comes into season in mid-August, the Friar is the pick of the crop. July is the peak month of the plum season, even though early varieties start in May and late varieties are still around in October. Some South American imports are available during the winter, but they are expensive and sour from early picking.

The flavor of a good ripe plum has a luscious sweet-tart balance that distinguishes it as one of the finest fruits. Plums can be as small as a cherry or as large as a baseball, either very round, elongated or heart-shaped. Colors range from yellow, green, red, blue, purple to black.

Plums are divided into two types: Japanese and European. Japanese plums, which make up the majority of California plum varieties, are tarter tasting, juicier and larger than European plums. They also come in the widest range of colors. European plums are blue or purple, longer and more oval-shaped, smaller and sweeter than the Japanese. When dried, these plums are called prunes.

Price: About $.98 a pound.

Nutrition: One plum has 33 calories, and is rich in vitamin A, potassium and fiber, and contains a fair amount of iron.

Selection: Choose fruits with good color, that are plump, slightly soft, and free of bruises and shriveled skin. Ripe plums often have a light dusting on their skin called "bloom." It occurs naturally and is perfectly safe to eat. Friar plums are dark purple-to-black in color and very large. Friars may be labeled simply "black plums" in grocery stores.

Storage: If plums are ripe, store them in a plastic bag in the refrigerator and use within several days. If they need to ripen, leave them at room temperature to mature.

Uses: Plums are good eaten out of hand, cooked into tarts and cobblers, cakes, jams, ices and mousses, or stewed. They make good relishes and sauces for game and poultry.

1 small onion, quartered
1 or 2 sweet yellow banana peppers,
    seeded and roughly chopped
1 garlic clove, minced
1 or 2 tablespoons lemon juice
2 to 3 tablespoons minced fresh
    cilantro, mint or apple mint

Put the tomatillos in a small saucepan and add enough water to cover the fruits. Bring to a boil; lower the heat and simmer 3 to 6 minutes, until not quite soft, and before the fruits burst.

Meanwhile, combine onion, peppers and garlic in the work-bowl of a food processor. Drain tomatillos from their cooking water and add to processor. Pulse a few times to make a chunky texture. Scoop the contents into a bowl and add lime juice to taste. Top with the cilantro or apple mint and serve.

Per serving: 16 calories, trace of fat, no cholesterol, 4 milligrams sodium.

TUESDAY

TUNA AND CAPERS ON SOBA NOODLES
STEAMED GREEN BEANS *
BLACK FRIAR PLUMS AND
PAULA RED APPLES *

Any dry or fresh pasta will work well here, but buckwheat pasta, called soba, available in health food stores, complements the tuna and caper flavors. Lemon pasta, such as one made by Trio and available in the deli section of many grocery stores, is equally delicious. Toss the steamed green beans with the pasta dish, or serve them alongside. Offer crunchy Black Friar plums and sweet-tart Paula Red or Gravenstein apples for dessert.

TUNA AND CAPERS ON SOBA NOODLES

Makes 4 servings
Preparation time: 10 minutes
Cooking time: 8 minutes

8 ounces soba noodles
2 tablespoons balsamic vinegar
2 or 3 tablespoons olive oil
1 large garlic clove, peeled and
    minced
2 to 4 tablespoons grated Parmesan
    cheese
Salt to taste
1 12-ounce can water-packed tuna,
    drained
2 or 3 green onions, chopped
2 sweet banana peppers or 1 red bell
    pepper, seeded and diced
2 or 3 tablespoons capers, for
    garnish (optional)

Cook the pasta in a pot of salted, boiling water until al dente, about 8 minutes, but don't overcook. Drain and place in a large, shallow serving bowl.

Meanwhile, in the work-bowl of a food processor, combine the vinegar, oil, garlic, cheese and salt, to taste. Pulse a few times just to combine. Toss the dressing, tuna, onions and peppers with the hot pasta and serve with capers.

Per serving: 322 calories, 11 grams fat, 37 milligrams cholesterol, 393 milligrams sodium.

WEDNESDAY

BARLEY AND CHICKEN CASSEROLE
CHOCOLATE MARBLE POUNDCAKE WITH
FROZEN YOGURT *

This satisfying dinner costs pennies and cooks effortlessly while you take care of after-work chores. Add chunks of leftover chicken and another can of artichoke hearts, even roasted potatoes, as much as you want, if you need to stretch the servings. Barley is available in all grocery stores, or you could easily substitute kashi, a delicious blend of barley, buckwheat, oats, rice and sesame seeds, available at health food stores.

BARLEY AND CHICKEN CASSEROLE

Makes 6 servings
Preparation time: 10 minutes
Cooking time: 25 minutes

1 tablespoon vegetable oil
1 onion, chopped
2 celery stalks, diced
2 carrots, sliced
1 15 ^{1}/2-ounce can chicken broth
    (and enough water to make 2
    ^{1}/2 cups)
1 teaspoon salt (optional)
1 cup quick-cooking barley
1 15-ounce can artichoke hearts,
    halved
1 cup cooked, shredded chicken
    with chile powder
Salt and black pepper to taste
2 tablespoons grated Parmesan
    cheese

Heat the oil in a large skillet or Dutch oven. Saute the onion, celery and carrots until softened, about 5 to 8 minutes. Stir in the chicken broth, (optional) salt and barley. Cover, reduce heat to simmer and cook about 20 minutes, or until the barley has absorbed the liquid. Stir in the artichoke hearts and chicken and cook until heated through, about 5 minutes. Add salt and pepper to taste. Garnish with cheese and serve.

Per serving, without added salt: 278 calories, 11 grams fat, 26 milligrams cholesterol, 586 milligrams sodium.

FLOUR TORTILLAS
WITH GREEN SAUCE
BLACK BEAN AND
FRESH CORN SALAD *
BLACKBERRIES WITH
STRAWBERRY YOGURT *

Tortillas with green sauce is an everyday Mexican dish, but it becomes a special dish when you use homemade green sauce, freshly made with tomatillos, lime juice and cilantro. Use leftover sauce and bean salad you made earlier in the week.

FLOUR TORTILLAS WITH GREEN SAUCE

Makes 4 servings
Preparation time: 10 minutes
Cooking time: 5 minutes

2 or 3 slices bacon
4 flour tortillas
$1/2$ cup salsa verde
$1/3$ to $1/2$ cup grated Monterey
    Jack cheese

Cook the bacon, then crumble it and set aside.

Heat the flour tortillas in a skillet, griddle or in a warm oven. When they are softened and pliable, spread the green sauce, cheese and bacon over the four tortillas and heat in the oven just until the cheese is melted, about 5 minutes.

Per serving: 166 calories, 7 grams fat, 14 milligrams cholesterol, 133 milligrams sodium.

PUREE OF YELLOW
SQUASH SOUP *
BARLEY SKILLET DINNER *
CORN BREAD *

Tonight's the time to clean out the refrigerator, and chances are the leftovers will taste better tonight, with a few days to allow flavors to develop. Sprinkle some grated cheese over the soup before serving.

SAUTEED TURKEY CUTLETS *
KAREN'S CHIVES AND
CHEESE HASH BROWNS
SPINACH SALAD *
LIGHTER THAN AIR
LEMON ICEBOX PIE

Cut the potatoes in small dice and you will have one of the best potato dishes ever, made in minutes. Meanwhile saute lean turkey cutlets in a small amount of oil or butter and toss an easy spinach salad. Prepare the chiffon pie earlier in the day and serve at room temperature or chilled.

KAREN'S CHIVES AND CHEESE HASH BROWNS

Makes 6 servings
Preparation time: 10 minutes
Cooking time: 20 minutes

4 medium potatoes (1 $1/2$ pounds)
    cut in small dice
1/4 cup unsalted butter
1 small onion, chopped
4 to 6 tablespoons cilantro leaves,
    roughly chopped
$1/2$ cup grated Gruyere or Swiss
    cheese
$1/2$ teaspoon salt
$1/4$ teaspoon pepper
2 tablespoons water

Cut the potatoes into $1/4$-inch strips.

Melt the butter in a 10-inch skillet. Add potatoes and onions and salt and pepper to taste. Cook partially covered over medium heat, turning frequently, until potatoes start to brown, about 10 minutes. Add the cilantro and cheese and continue to cook until brown and crusty.

Per serving: 162 calories, 7 grams fat, 21 milligrams cholesterol, 252 milligrams sodium.

LIGHTER THAN AIR LEMON ICEBOX PIE

Makes 6 servings
Preparation time: 15 minutes
Cooking time: 35 minutes

3 tablespoons unsalted butter,
    softened
$2/3$ cup sugar
2 large eggs, separated
$1/4$ cup lemon juice
Zest of 1 lemon
1 tablespoon low-protein all-purpose
    flour, such as White Lily
1 cup cold milk
1 9-inch chocolate crumb pie crust
Confectioners' sugar

Preheat the oven to 350 degrees.

Put the butter and sugar in the workbowl of a food processor and process until light and fluffy. Add the eggs, juice, zest and flour. Stir in the milk. In a separate bowl, beat the egg whites until stiff. Gently fold the lemon mixture into the egg whites and spoon into the pie shell.

Bake 30 to 35 minutes, or until the filling is set and golden brown. Sprinkle the pie with confectioners' sugar, pressed through a sieve and serve.

Per serving: 289 calories, 14 grams fat, 105 milligrams cholesterol, 261 milligrams sodium.

WEEK

38

SHOPPING LIST

Meat, poultry, seafood

- ❏ 1 ¹/₂ pounds Italian sausage, mild or hot
- ❏ 6 to 8 skinless, boneless chicken breasts
- ❏ 10 slices pancetta, sliced ¹/₁₆-inch thick, or bacon

Produce

- ❏ 2 heads leaf lettuce
- ❏ 1 pint Sunnies sunflower sprouts or alfalfa sprouts
- ❏ 1 medium head cauliflower
- ❏ 1 jicama
- ❏ 3 pounds new potatoes
- ❏ 3 red bell peppers
- ❏ 1 yellow bell pepper
- ❏ 1 green bell pepper
- ❏ 1 or 2 stalks celery
- ❏ 2 zucchini
- ❏ 6 Italian frying peppers or banana peppers
- ❏ 6 garlic cloves
- ❏ 2 medium onions (1

sweet)
- ❏ 4 large shallots
- ❏ 8 ounces snow peas
- ❏ 8 to 10 black mission figs
- ❏ 1 medium apple
- ❏ 20 3-inch stems rosemary (see note on recipe)

Dairy

- ❏ 4 tablespoons butter or margarine
- ❏ 1 stick plus 1 tablespoon butter
- ❏ ¹/₂ cup plain non-fat yogurt
- ❏ ¹/₄ cup light mayonnaise

Deli

- ❏ 4 French rolls
- ❏ 8 slices sturdy rye bread
- ❏ 1 loaf crusty bread
- ❏ 6 to 8 ounces sharp Cheddar or blue cheese
- ❏ 1 loaf bread and chocolate

- ❏ 6 to 8 ounces grated Parmesan cheese
- ❏ 1 cheesecake

Miscellaneous

- ❏ 2 26- to 32-ounce jars tomato pasta sauce
- ❏ 1 16-ounce package lemon cookies
- ❏ ¹/₂ cup non-fat dry milk
- ❏ 2 tablespoons espresso instant coffee powder
- ❏ 2 cups Italian arborio rice
- ❏ 1 cup bulgur
- ❏ ¹/₂ cup roasted, unsalted peanuts
- ❏ 12 ounces dry spaghetti
- ❏ ¹/₂ cup dry white wine
- ❏ 3 14 ¹/₂-ounce cans unsalted chicken stock
- ❏ 2 tablespoons sweet pickle (optional)

Staples

- ❏ Black pepper
- ❏ Cider vinegar
- ❏ Cinnamon
- ❏ Granulated sugar
- ❏ Hot chili paste or hot sauce
- ❏ Minced garlic in oil
- ❏ Olive oil
- ❏ Salt
- ❏ Soy sauce
- ❏ Toothpicks (optional)
- ❏ Vegetable oil

* Suggested accompaniments

ITALIAN PEPPER AND SAUSAGE GRINDERS MIXED GREEN SALAD * CAPPUCCINO GRANITA

For today's dinner, take advantage of the array of sweet and hot peppers still available through early fall. The 6- to 8-inch long Italian frying peppers and sweet and hot yellow banana peppers have just enough of a bite to let you remember them, without the pain of a jalapeno. Grinders, or hoagie sandwiches, are good in small amounts for the family and expand to serve dozens of people.

Saute the peppers with Italian sausage and tomato sauce and serve the meaty sauce on French rolls with a green salad. Save leftover sauce to serve over spaghetti later in the week.

The refreshing coffee ice goes together in seconds and makes a cool ending to this Italian meal.

ITALIAN PEPPER AND SAUSAGE GRINDERS

Makes 4 servings with leftovers
Preparation time: 5 minutes
Cooking time: 30 minutes

1 ¹/₂ pounds Italian sausage
   (mild or hot)
1 cup water
6 Italian frying peppers or banana
   peppers, split, ribbed and seeded
4 garlic cloves, chopped
1 jar (26 to 32 ounces) tomato pasta
   sauce
4 French rolls

Prick the sausages and cut them into 4-inch lengths. Put them and the water in an uncovered skillet and cook on moderate heat, about 10 minutes. The water will evaporate and the sausages will start to cook in their own fat. Cook another 10 minutes, or until the sausages are done.

Remove them from the pan and set aside. Drain part of the fat and add the peppers and garlic to the oil in the pan. Cook 5 minutes, or until the peppers are soft. Drain the remaining fat and add the jar of tomato sauce. Cook 5 to 10 minutes more to blend the flavors and thicken the sauce. To serve, split grinder rolls and hollow out a bit of the bread to accommodate the sausage and filling.

Per sandwich: 613 calories, 31 grams fat, 77 milligrams cholesterol, 1,323 milligrams sodium.

CAPPUCCINO GRANITA

Makes 4 servings
Preparation time: 5 minutes

2 tablespoons espresso powder
¹/₂ cup non-fat dry milk
1 cup ice cubes
2 tablespoons granulated sugar
Ground cinnamon

Combine the coffee powder, dry milk, ice cubes and sugar in the work bowl of a food processor. Process 10 seconds, or until ground to a chunky slush. Spoon into a freezer container and freeze for 10 to 20 minutes, stirring the slush a couple of times. At serving time, spoon into 4 dessert dishes and sprinkle lightly with cinnamon.

Per serving: 45 calories, trace of fat, 2 milligrams cholesterol, 52 milligrams sodium.

SUNFLOWER SPROUT AND GRILLED CHEESE SANDWICHES LEMON COOKIES *

Look to the deli department of the grocery store for good-quality rye bread, which makes these sandwiches especially delicious. Sunnies sprouts — organic, sweet and delicious — are available at most groceries and natural food stores. If you can't find them, substitute alfalfa sprouts or another green. Purchase lemon cookies to serve for dessert.

SUNFLOWER SPROUT AND GRILLED CHEESE SANDWICHES

Preparation time: 10 minutes
Cooking time: 5 to 10 minutes

4 tablespoons softened butter or
   margarine
8 slices sturdy rye bread
1 pint Sunnies sunflower seed sprouts
6 to 8 ounces sharp Cheddar or blue
   cheese, sliced

Melt 2 tablespoons of the butter in a large, heavy skillet, and spread the remaining 2 tablespoons on one side of 4 slices of bread. Layer sunflower sprouts, sliced cheese and remaining bread slices. Cook the sandwiches in the melted butter, with unbuttered sides down. When golden brown, turn and cook other side.

Per sandwich: 409 calories, 28 grams fat, 76 milligrams cholesterol, 732 milligrams sodium.

Price: Will average $2.49 a pound.

Nutrition: One medium fig has about 40 calories, is an excellent source of fiber and a good source of potassium, calcium and iron.

Selection: For the greatest sugar content and best eating quality, figs must be tree-ripened, but because they are so perishable, most figs are picked and shipped firm-ripe. Ripe figs give readily to pressure; avoid hard, dry figs and those with flattened sides, splits or signs of mold. They should smell sweet, not sour.

Storage: Use ripe fruit as soon as possible. Store ripe fruit in a single layer on a paper-towel-lined tray, cover with plastic wrap and refrigerate for 3 days.

Uses: Use figs fresh, by themselves or with other fruits and nuts, or wrapped in prosciutto. They can be threaded on skewers and quickly grilled or sauteed in butter, made into jams and steamed puddings and cakes.

From figgy pudding to Fig Newtons, the luxurious flesh of this fruit is in season through the late summer months. In warm countries where the fig grows easily, it is a cheap and staple food. In other climates, fresh figs are a luxury and are more commonly sold in their dried form. Figs have two seasons, a smaller season in June with larger fruit, and a second season of smaller fruit in late August and September. They will be available another month in local stores and farmers markets.

When the Spanish padres built the first missions along the California coast, some of the first trees they planted were figs — and came to be known as mission figs.

Today, Black Mission figs — thin-skinned with deep pink, sweet flesh — are still one of America's favorite and flavorful figs, both fresh and dried. Also available at local farmers markets and some grocery stores are the thicker-skinned Kadota, grown both in Florida and California and large-sized Calimyrna , usually only available dried. Some stores and farmers markets will carry the red-fleshed local Brown Turkey figs.

The flesh of figs is so delicate they are at their best either eaten out-of-hand or just barely sauteed or grilled. Fig preserve is a favorite local condiment.

TUESDAY

SAUTEED CHICKEN BREASTS *
STEAMED NEW POTATOES *
QUICK SAUTEED
CAULIFLOWER AND
RED PEPPERS

This homey meal goes together fast and will provide leftovers for later in the week. Cook extra chicken and 1 ½ extra pounds of potatoes to use later (don't bother to peel them); those 3-pound bags of new potatoes would be the perfect size to buy.

QUICK SAUTEED CAULIFLOWER AND RED PEPPERS

Makes 6 large servings
Preparation time: 10 minutes
Cooking time: 10 minutes

2 tablespoons minced garlic in oil
1 cauliflower, cut in small florets
½ jicama, peeled and cut in julienne
1 colored bell pepper, seeded and cut in strips
Salt to taste
2 to 3 tablespoons fruity vinegar

Heat the garlic and oil in a deep skillet or wok. Add the cauliflower and jicama and saute over medium-high heat for 5 minutes, stirring frequently. Add pepper strips, salt and vinegar and cook another 2 or 3 minutes, until tender-crisp.
Per serving: 79 calories, 5 grams fat, no cholesterol, 21 milligrams sodium.

WEDNESDAY

BULGUR AND VEGETABLES

BREAD AND CHOCOLATE *

This hearty vegetable and grain dish has lots of flavor and staying power; it may become a staple dish in your kitchen. Bulgur is simply parched, cracked wheat with a nutty flavor, and it cooks quickly. For dessert, serve bread and chocolate, a delicious bread full of chunks of chocolate, available at Harry's Farmers Market. Heat it in the oven to melt the chocolate. This bread is also a wonderful after-school snack for children. If necessary, substitute a good-quality chocolate bar and a loaf of fresh bread: Simply grate the chocolate over the sliced bread and set in a warm oven just long enough to barely melt the chocolate.

BULGUR AND VEGETABLES

Makes 4 servings
Preparation time: 5 minutes
Cooking time: 15 minutes

1 cup bulgur
1 medium onion, chopped
2 tablespoons minced garlic in oil
1 bell pepper, any color, cut in thin strips
8 ounces snow peas, cut in halves
½ jicama, peeled and cut in thin slices
1 to 2 tablespoons soy sauce
1 teaspoon hot chili paste or several drops hot sauce

Put 3 cups water and bulger in a large, deep skillet and bring to a boil. Reduce heat, add onion and cook 5 minutes, until the onion is softened and the bulgur doubled in size. Add the bell pepper strips, snow peas and jicama and continue cooking until the water is absorbed. Add soy sauce to taste, and stir a tiny amount of hot chili paste into the mixture, going slowly, as it is very hot.
Per serving: 323 calories, 18 grams fat, no cholesterol, 274 milligrams sodium.

THURSDAY

SWEET ONION, POTATO AND
CHICKEN SALAD
LEMON COOKIES *

This healthful potato salad can be served with or without chunks of leftover chicken; either way it is fabulous and takes advantage of leftover cooked potatoes. Use a sweet onion if you can find one; some Vidalias are coming out of storage now, or choose a red onion. Add lemon cookies for dessert.

SWEET ONION, POTATO AND CHICKEN SALAD

Preparation time: 15 minutes

1 ½ pounds cooked new potatoes, halved or quartered
1 medium sweet white onion, quartered and thinly sliced
1 or 2 stalks celery, thinly sliced
1 medium apple, cored and diced or 2 tablespoons sweet pickle, chopped (optional)
1 to 2 cups cooked chicken, cut in chunks
½ cup low-fat yogurt
¼ cup light mayonnaise

Mix together the potatoes, onion, celery, apple, pickles and chicken.

In a small bowl, combine yogurt and mayonnaise. Add salt and pepper to taste. Mix gently. Fold into the potato mixture. Cover and chill 30 minutes or longer to blend the flavors.

Per serving: 313 calories, 6 grams fat, 43 milligrams cholesterol, 69 milligrams sodium.

FRIDAY

SPAGHETTI
QUICK SAUTEED
CAULIFLOWER AND
RED PEPPERS *
CRUSTY BREAD *

This quick meal is as easy to put together as waiting for takeout at the deli department. The grinder sauce left from Sunday should provide a full flavor when added to a jar of commercial pasta sauce. Add leftover sauteed vegetables from earlier in the week and thick slices of Italian bread. Wonderful Italian breads are available from several stores in Atlanta. Special Delivery, a takeout caterer on Peachtree Avenue, sells breads from the Bread Garden. If you give 24-hour notice, you'll get the bread of your choice, but the potluck choices are equally delicious.

SPAGHETTI

Makes 4 servings
Preparation time: none
Cooking time: 10 minutes

12 ounces dry spaghetti
1 tablespoon olive oil
Leftover grinder sauce
1 26- to 32-ounce jar tomato pasta sauce
4 to 8 tablespoons grated Parmesan cheese

Bring water to a boil in a large pot and cook the spaghetti until al dente. Drain and toss with 1 tablespoon olive oil to keep it

from sticking.

Mix together the leftover grinder sauce and as much of the jar of pasta sauce as necessary to make about 4 cups of sauce. Heat the sauce while the pasta is cooking. Serve the pasta and sauce separately, and pass the Parmesan cheese.

Per serving: 471 calories, 18 grams fat, 43 milligrams cholesterol, 632 milligrams sodium.

SATURDAY

SAUTEED FIGS WITH
PANCETTA AND ROSEMARY
COUNTRY-STYLE RISOTTO
SALAD GREENS *
CHEESECAKE *

Scott Peacock, past executive chef at the Georgia Governor's Mansion, makes this fabulous fig dish for late summer and autumn dinners. Wrapped in pancetta, a cured bacon-type Italian meat, these make a hearty and unforgettable fall dish. Fresh rosemary is crucial; if you can't find enough fresh to use as toothpicks, use regular toothpicks and sprinkle fresh rosemary over the cooking figs (reserve 1 tablespoon leaves for the second recipe). Pancetta is available at specialty markets; if you must, use regular bacon and blanch it for 5 minutes in boiling water to remove the smoky flavor.

Constant stirring turns short-grain rice into a creamy mass, without a drop of cream. Look for unsalted chicken stock (Pritikin makes a good one) otherwise, the Parmesan cheese will make the finished risotto too salty. Doused with cheese and vegetables, risotto makes a hearty main course;

but roasted chicken could be served alongside. Chunks of goat cheese could be substituted for the Parmesan for a different taste. Pick up a cheesecake for dessert.

SAUTEED FIGS WITH PANCETTA AND ROSEMARY

Makes 4 servings
Preparation time: 20 minutes
Cooking time: 5 minutes

8 to 10 black mission figs
10 slices pancetta, sliced $1/16$-inch thick, or 10 slices bacon
20 toothpicks or 3-inch tips of rosemary
4 tablespoons unsalted butter

Cut the figs in half lengthwise. Cut pancetta or bacon in half. Wrap a piece of pancetta around each fig half and stick a rosemary sprig or toothpick through to secure the meat. Repeat with the remaining figs.

Heat the butter, preferably in two skillets, so all the figs finish cooking at the same time. When the butter is bubbling, add the figs and saute briefly, turning to finish on the other side. Serve immediately.

Per serving: 195 calories, 12 grams fat, 38 milligrams cholesterol, 239 milligrams sodium.

COUNTRY-STYLE RISOTTO

Makes 4 main-course servings or 8 side-dish servings
Preparation time: 5 minutes
Cooking time: 25 minutes

5 tablespoons unsalted butter
4 large shallots, minced
1 tablespoon rosemary leaves, crushed
$1/2$ cup dry white wine
2 cups Italian arborio rice or other short-grain rice

5 to 6 cups unsalted chicken stock,
    simmering
4 to 6 ounces grated Parmesan cheese
    or Fontina or goat cheese, in
    chunks
2 small zucchini, cut in thin rounds
Salt and black pepper to taste

Melt the butter in a heavy skillet over medium-low heat. Add the shallots and rosemary and cook 1 minute. Pour in the wine. Raise the heat slightly and cook, stirring constantly, until almost all the liquid has evaporated, about 4 minutes.

Stir the rice into the mixture until coated. Add 2 cups of the simmering chicken broth and cook, stirring constantly, on medium heat, until almost all liquid has been absorbed, about 10 minutes.

Add 2 more cups of broth and continue to cook, stirring frequently, until almost all liquid has been absorbed. Check to see if the rice is tender; if not add another cup of broth to the rice and continue to cook, stirring frequently, until the rice is tender, 5 to 10 minutes longer. Add the zucchini, then the cheese, stirring. Add salt and pepper to taste.

Per serving: 676 calories, 25 grams fat, 62 milligrams cholesterol, 543 milligrams sodium.

WEEK
39

Meat, poultry, seafood

- ❏ 1 2- or 3-pound beef tenderloin
- ❏ 4 Cornish hens

Produce

- ❏ 1 pound green beans
- ❏ 10 cloves garlic
- ❏ 2 2- to 3-pound butternut squash
- ❏ 4 medium zucchini
- ❏ 1 onion
- ❏ 1 head chicory or curly endive
- ❏ 1 bunch arugula
- ❏ 12 firm, ripe pears
- ❏ 1 lemon
- ❏ 1 small bunch cilantro

Dairy

- ❏ 2 sticks unsalted butter
- ❏ 1 8-ounce carton lemon yogurt (optional)
- ❏ 1 pint frozen lemon yogurt
- ❏ 1/2 pint (1 cup) heavy cream (optional)

Deli

- ❏ 1 loaf crusty bread
- ❏ 4 corn muffins
- ❏ 3 tablespoons Parmesan cheese

Miscellaneous

- ❏ 2 tablespoons white wine
- ❏ 2 or 3 tablespoons Cognac, brandy or lemon juice
- ❏ 2 tablespoons Jack Daniel's (optional)
- ❏ 1/2 cup raisins or currants
- ❏ 1 28-ounce can tomato sauce
- ❏ 1 14 1/2-ounce can corn
- ❏ 1 15-ounce can great Northern or pinto beans
- ❏ 2 cups (16 ounces) chicken broth

- ❏ 1 16-ounce can chickpeas
- ❏ 2 tablespoons pesto sauce
- ❏ 2 10-ounce boxes couscous
- ❏ 1/2 cup slivered or chopped almonds
- ❏ 2 1/2 cups walnuts
- ❏ 1 8-ounce package egg noodles
- ❏ 4 pita bread rounds
- ❏ 1 package (10 ounces) frozen corn kernels
- ❏ 1 jar (4 ounces) pickled sweet cherry peppers
- ❏ 1 jar (3 ounces) cocktail onions
- ❏ 2 pickled jalapeno peppers
- ❏ 1 teaspoon sauce from chipolete peppers (optional)

Staples

- ❏ Black pepper
- ❏ Brown sugar
- ❏ Confectioners' sugar
- ❏ Dried oregano
- ❏ Ground cinnamon
- ❏ Olive oil
- ❏ Red pepper flakes
- ❏ Salt
- ❏ Unbleached flour

* Suggested accompaniments

BEEF TENDERLOIN*
BRAISED GARLICKY
WINTER SQUASH
STEAMED GREEN BEANS*
SAUTEED PEARS WITH RAISINS
AND COGNAC

This squash is braised Italian-style, and it's more than delicious. Choose a winter squash with a smooth rather than pebbly or ribbed skin for this dish; otherwise, it will be too hard to peel. Smaller dice will cook faster than larger chunks. Serve a beef tenderloin or other beef roast that offers leftovers. Peel and dice an extra squash and steam or microwave for 10 minutes separately to use in later dishes.

BRAISED GARLICKY WINTER SQUASH

Makes 6 servings
Preparation time: 15 minutes
Cooking time: 40 minutes

3 tablespoons unsalted butter
3 tablespoons white wine
8 cloves garlic, flattened and peeled
2 2- to 3-pound butternut squash, peeled, seeded, diced (reserve one for microwaving separately for other dishes)
Salt and black pepper to taste (optional)

Melt 1 tablespoon butter in a large heavy skillet over low heat. Add the wine and garlic. Cook, covered, stirring occasionally 10 to 20 minutes. The garlic will brown slightly but should not burn.

Mash up the garlic with a fork. Stir the remaining butter and squash in the pan and toss.

Cook, covered, stirring occasionally, until the squash is tender, about 20 minutes. Add salt and pepper to taste and serve.

Per serving: 120 calories, 6 grams fat, 15 milligrams cholesterol, 10 milligrams sodium.

SAUTEED PEARS WITH RAISINS AND COGNAC

Makes 6 servings
Preparation time: 10 minutes
Cooking time: 5 minutes

4 to 6 large firm-ripe pears, cored, peeled and sliced
1 or 2 tablespoons butter
2 tablespoons brown sugar
1/2 cup raisins or currants
2 or 3 tablespoons cognac, brandy or orange juice

Melt 2 tablespoons butter in a large skillet over medium heat. Add the pears and sprinkle with brown sugar. Cover and saute, stirring occasionally until the pears soften, 4 or 5 minutes.

Uncover, add the raisins and saute for another couple of minutes, stirring. Remove the skillet from the heat, stir in the cognac and toss with the pears until it is absorbed.

Per serving: 147 calories, 2 grams fat, 5 milligrams cholesterol, 23 milligrams sodium.

EASY TOMATO
VEGETABLE SOUP
CRUSTY BREAD *

Put this satisfying soup together in minutes with ingredients from your pantry. Add a loaf of crusty bread, either from the grocery store or from a takeout deli, such as Special Delivery, 1841 Peachtree Road, or Partner's Pantry, 1397 N. Highland Ave. N.E. Pesto sauce is now available in the deli sections of most grocery stores, and Sanremo makes a good bottled version.

EASY TOMATO VEGETABLE SOUP

Makes 6 servings
Preparation time: 5 minutes
Cooking time: 20 minutes

1 tablespoon olive oil
1 onion, chopped
1 28-ounce can tomato sauce
1 cup water
1 14 1/2-ounce can corn, undrained
1 15-ounce can great Northern or pinto beans, drained
1 to 2 tablespoons pesto sauce
1 to 2 teaspoons dried oregano

In a large saucepan, heat the vegetable oil and saute the onion until soft. Add the remaining ingredients. Bring to a boil, then lower the heat to a simmer and cook for 10 minutes. Add more water if the soup seems too thick.

Per serving: 202 calories, 5 grams fat, no cholesterol, 197 milligrams sodium.

COUSCOUS WITH SQUASH
AND CHICKPEAS
SAUTEED PEARS *

Weeknights don't offer enough time to prepare traditional couscous, a spicy North African dish made with steamed, crushed semolina grain and chicken or lamb. This quick version is quite good and provides leftovers to serve later in the week. Use some cooked butternut squash (or sweet potatoes), along with fresh zucchini and canned chickpeas. Couscous is available in boxes with other grains in most grocery stores.

COUSCOUS WITH SQUASH AND CHICKPEAS

Makes 8 servings
Preparation time: 5 minutes
Cooking time: 15 minutes

6 tablespoons butter, divided
2 tablespoons olive oil
4 medium zucchini, scrubbed and
    sliced
1 cup cooked, diced butternut squash,
    room temperature
$^1/_2$ teaspoon red pepper flakes
2 cups (10 ounces) quick-cooking
    couscous
2 cups canned chicken broth
1 16-ounce can chickpeas, drained
    and rinsed

In a large skillet over high heat, melt 2 tablespoons of butter with the olive oil. Add the zucchini and cook, stirring occasionally, until softened, about 5 minutes. Halfway through the cooking, stir in the cooked butternut squash. Remove from the skillet with a slotted spoon. Reserve the skillet.

In a medium saucepan, over moderate heat, melt the remaining butter. Add the pepper flakes and cook 1 minute. Stir in the couscous, coating the grains with butter, and then the chicken broth. Lower the heat, cover, and cook until the liquid is absorbed, about 5 minutes. Turn off the heat and let the couscous sit for 5 minutes, then fluff it with a fork.

Meanwhile, put the squash,

OCTOBER

Asparagus is high now, coming from Peru and Guatemala, while cabbage and other locally-grown vegetables are showing reasonable or lower prices. Look for large-sized carrots and fluctuating prices on lettuce as harvest areas move. Fresh water chestnuts are back in season.

Most lettuces, broccoli, cauliflower, yellow squash and zucchini are all widely available and have nice quality. Collard greens seem to be hard to get, but mustard and turnip greens are plentiful. California spinach is looking good. Southern peas are at their end — butter beans, lady peas, black eye peas are all but finished. Look for supplies of Hubbard and other specialty winter squashes, acorn and butternut. Asian pears are very nice right now and will be in season through the winter. The price of watercress has dropped, while other specialty greens, including arugula, are steady. Supplies are moving down the coast from North Carolina, with a few harvests starting from Georgia fields.

Apples are everywhere, and Georgia apples are especially sweet and inexpensive when you can get them. Look for supplies of Jonathon, Empire and the early Gala, which are coming out of storage. In specialty apples, the Mutzu, Empire and Georgia Romes are all finished, but Jonagold, Braeburn and Fugi are still available.

Hamlin juice oranges from Florida are in most of the stores, still early and without fully developed flavor. Florida navels are improving in flavor and prices are slowly dropping. Look for Dancy tangerines and extra sweet Spanish clementines, which will be available through December. Clementines and tangerines look very similar, so watch the produce signs carefully.

Asian pears are in the stores, as well as European pears. Prices are a little high. The first of the fall cranberry shipments have arrived, with prices the same as last year.

The pomegranates season has started with early arrivals of the Wonderful variety. Be careful with pomegranates; sometimes the outsides look beautiful but the insides have both red and under-ripe white seeds. Look for harvests to get increasingly sweeter as the season continues. Oriental persimmons have also started, some of which are sweet and ready to eat even when firm to the touch.

Carambola (star fruit) is of excellent quality now and is a wonderful addition to fruit salads and poultry dishes; just be sure to wait until it is completely yellow to eat. Barlett and Bosc pears are especially nice right now. Mexican melons are available and sweet, just expensive.

zucchini and chickpeas in the skillet over medium heat. Season to taste with salt, cover, and cook until just warmed through, stirring once or twice, about 5 minutes. Serve over hot couscous.

Per serving: 77 calories, 2 grams fat, 2 milligrams cholesterol, 140 milligrams sodium.

WEDNESDAY

SQUASH CASSEROLE WITH PARMESAN CHEESE
CORN MUFFINS *

This dish makes good use of bits of leftovers you may find in your refrigerator. If Monday's tomato soup has thickened into a sauce, so much the better.

SQUASH CASSEROLE WITH PARMESAN CHEESE

Makes 4 servings
Preparation time: 5 minutes
Cooking time: 15 minutes

2 cups cooked butternut squash
1 cup leftover tomato soup
2 to 3 tablespoons grated Parmesan cheese

Preheat oven to 350 degrees.
    Place the chunks of cooked butternut squash in an 8-inch baking dish. Spoon over the tomato soup, including corn and beans. Sprinkle with Parmesan cheese and bake until hot throughout and bubbly, about 15 minutes.

Per serving: 77 calories, 2 grams fat, 2 milligrams cholesterol, 140 milligrams sodium.

THURSDAY

ROAST BEEF SANDWICHES *
CORN AND
TWO-PEPPER RELISH

All Southerners know about corn and pepper relish, and this two-pepper recipe should become a favorite. Chipotle peppers, available in many specialty and Mexican stores, are smoked and add an intense flavor, so use them and their accompanying sauce sparingly. Slice leftover roast beef thinly and serve on bread spread with mayonnaise.

CORN AND PEPPER RELISH

Makes 2 cups
Preparation time: 5 minutes

1 package (10 ounces) frozen corn kernels, thawed
5 pickled cherry peppers
1 3-ounce jar cocktail onions, drained
2 pickled jalapeno peppers
2 to 3 tablespoons cilantro leaves, roughly chopped
Salt, to taste
1 teaspoon sauce from canned chipotle peppers (optional)

Place the corn in a mixing bowl. Put the pickled peppers, onions and cilantro in the workbowl of a food processor and pulse a few times to roughly chop. Stir into the corn; season to taste with salt. Cover and refrigerate until serving time.

Per 1/2-cup serving: 70 calories, trace of fat, no cholesterol, 390 milligrams sodium.

FRIDAY

COUSCOUS WITH SQUASH
AND CHICKPEAS *
WARM PITA BREADS *
FROZEN LEMON YOGURT *

Reheat couscous reserved from Tuesday's meal for tonight's dinner. Add warmed, sliced pita breads and frozen lemon yogurt for dessert.

SATURDAY

GARLICKY CORNISH HENS
WINTER GREEN SALAD
WITH WALNUTS*
BUTTERED NOODLES *
PEAR PIE WITH
WALNUT CRUST

This elegant meal takes advantage of full-flavored autumn foods, such as bitter greens, ripe pears and walnuts. And nothing says autumn better than Mollie Katzen's recipe for pear pie, adapted from her book *Still Life With Menu* (Ten Speed, $24.95).

GARLICKY CORNISH HENS

Makes 4 servings
Preparation time: 10 minutes
Cooking time: 50 minutes

1/4 cup olive oil
2 garlic cloves, peeled and minced
4 Cornish hens
4 garlic cloves, peeled and cut in slivers

Preheat the oven to 425 degrees.

Price: Comice pears will average $.99 a pound, Barletts and other varieties may be a little less. Different sizes are available in different grocery stores, and prices may reflect the size.

Nutrition: A medium pear has about 100 calories and is high in the fiber pectin, potassium and levulose sugar — a valuable aid to diabetics who digest this type of sugar more easily than glucose.

Selection: The season for pears runs from August to December, with pears coming out of storage through May. The Comice is available September through March. It is a short, fat pear, with a short stem and upon ripening has a greenish yellow skin with a crimson blush. Minor blemishes on the skin do not matter, and most ripe pears will have some russeting (brown webbing) on the skin.

Storage: Most pears are sold green and need to ripen for perfect eating. Allow them to ripen at room temperature in a loosely closed bag until they give to gentle pressure — 3 to 7 days. Some varieties don't change color as they ripen. Refrigerate ripe pears unwashed for up to 3 days.

Uses: One pound pears (about 3 medium fruit) yields about 2 cups sliced fruit. Many dishes can be cooked with pears — such as chutneys, cakes, tarts, and breads, or they can be poached in wine, but they are best shown off when perfectly ripe and served simply, with a properly aged cheese. To prevent the white flesh from darkening, brush it with lemon juice or Fruit Fresh. The skins of pears are exceptionally flavorful.

The "butter fruit" as European pears are called, are back in season and make great pairings with fall dinners. With flavors that range from spicy to sweet, and a texture that literally melts, pears are worthy of their high status.

Don't be disappointed with the texture and flavor of pears; usually it's just a matter of allowing them to ripen to the optimum point of juiciness and tenderness, then enjoying them immediately.

The Comice is an exceptional variety that should not be missed: the name "Comice" translates as "best of show," and one bite proves it. This delicate pear doesn't ship well, so the skin may look a bit tattered, but don't let that stop you — it is the finest pear for eating fresh — buttery and very juicy.

Put the olive oil and garlic in a small skillet. On low heat, saute for 5 minutes; then set aside to cool.

To split the hens in half, place each one breast-side down on a work surface with the legs facing you. Use poultry shears or heavy scissors to cut down center to the tail, then continue cutting through backbone. With the back of your hand, firmly press down on the breastbone to flatten. Rinse the hens and your hands.

Rub each hen with the garlic oil and tuck extra slivers of garlic under the skin. Salt the hens lightly. Roast the hens 45 minutes, or until the leg joints move freely and the skin is crispy and golden brown.

Per serving: 457 calories, 23 grams fat, 172 milligrams cholesterol, 98 milligrams sodium.

PEAR PIE IN A WALNUT CRUST

Makes 8 servings
Preparation time: 35 minutes
Baking time: 35 minutes

CRUST:
Pan spray or 1 tablespoon butter, softened
2 cups walnuts
$^1/_2$ cup unbleached white flour
3 tablespoons (packed) brown sugar
$^1/_4$ teaspoon cinnamon
3 or 4 tablespoons water

FILLING:
5 to 6 average-size firm, ripe pears
2 tablespoons unbleached white flour
$^3/_4$ teaspoon ground cinnamon
2 tablespoons (packed) brown sugar
Grated rind of 1 lemon
1 tablespoon lemon juice
$^1/_2$ pint heavy cream (optional)
Confectioners' sugar, to taste (optional)
2 tablespoons Jack Daniel's (optional)

Generously grease a 9-inch pie pan with pan spray or 1 tablespoon soft butter and set aside. Preheat the oven to 375 degrees.

Put the walnuts in the workbowl of a food processor and process almost to a paste. Add the flour, sugar and cinnamon and pulse to combine. With the motor running, add the water 1 tablespoon at a time until the dough sticks to itself, but not to the workbowl. Pat the dough evenly into the bottom and sides of the pie pan and set aside.

Peel and slice the pears and place them in a bowl. Sprinkle the pears with the flour, cinnamon, sugar, lemon rind and juice and toss. Turn the pear mixture into the crust and bake 35 minutes.

Meanwhile, whip the cream with sugar and Jack Daniel's and refrigerate until serving time. Serve the pie warm.

Per serving: 355 calories, 30 grams fat, 45 milligrams cholesterol, 94 milligrams sodium.

WEEK

40

SHOPPING LIST

Meat, poultry, seafood

- ❑ 1 5-to 7-pound roasting chicken
- ❑ 1 1/2 pounds lean ground beef
- ❑ 6 thin slices bacon
- ❑ 12 large sea scallops

Produce

- ❑ 1 pound carrots
- ❑ 4 pounds Yukon Gold or russet potatoes
- ❑ 1 turnip
- ❑ 2 pounds green beans
- ❑ 13 cloves garlic
- ❑ 4 large yellow onions
- ❑ 2-3 zucchini
- ❑ 10 apples
- ❑ 3/4 cup fresh apple cider

Dairy

- ❑ 3 sticks unsalted butter
- ❑ 7 eggs
- ❑ 1/2 cup heavy cream
- ❑ 1 1/4 cup milk
- ❑ 1 pint vanilla ice cream (optional)

Deli

- ❑ 1 focaccia bread
- ❑ 4 ounces freshly grated Parmesan cheese
- ❑ 4 ounces Cheddar or other hard cheese

Miscellaneous

- ❑ 1 9-inch pie shell
- ❑ 1 28-ounce can whole tomatoes, crushed

- ❑ 4 to 8 premade crepes
- ❑ 1 14 1/2-ounce can corn
- ❑ 1 cup dry red wine
- ❑ 3 tablespoons dry sherry or white wine
- ❑ 1 cup dry rice
- ❑ 1 10-ounce box frozen chopped spinach
- ❑ 1 5-ounce package biscuit dough
- ❑ 1 cup wild rice

Staples

- ❑ All-purpose flour
- ❑ Bay leaves
- ❑ Black pepper
- ❑ Brown sugar
- ❑ Cornstarch
- ❑ Freshly grated nutmeg
- ❑ Granulated sugar
- ❑ Ground cinnamon

- ❑ Hungarian paprika
- ❑ Lemon juice
- ❑ Olive oil
- ❑ Salt

* Suggested accompaniments

ROAST CHICKEN*
GREAT MASHED POTATOES
WITH GARLIC AND ONIONS
STEAMED CARROTS*
CINNAMON-CRUMB
TOPPED APPLE PIE

Potatoes cooked and mashed with garlic and onion are better tasting than plain potatoes, and healthier than those lathered with butter, cream or cheese. If you use Yukon Gold potatoes, their golden color will look as if they have been laced with butter. Don't throw away those potato peels. Put them in a plastic bag and freeze, then fry along with french fries. Cook a 5- to 7-pound roasting chicken and reserve 2 cups of cooked meat for a later meal. Tape the recipe for this apple pie, adapted from *American Country Cooking* by Mary Emmerling (Clarkson Potter, $35), to your kitchen wall and don't ever lose it.

GREAT MASHED POTATOES WITH GARLIC AND ONIONS

Makes 8 servings
Preparation time: 20 minutes
Cooking time: 20 minutes

4 pounds yellow (Yukon or Finnish) potatoes or russet baking potatoes, peeled and cut into 1-inch pieces
8 large garlic cloves, peeled and quartered
2 large yellow onions, coarsely chopped
Unsalted butter to taste (about 4 tablespoons) (optional)
Salt and pepper to taste

Put the potatoes in a large saucepan of salted water and bring to a boil. Add the onion and garlic and cook for 20 to 25 minutes, until the potatoes are quite tender.

Puree the potatoes with a potato masher. Stir in the butter, a piece at a time, if desired. Stir in $^1/_2$ cup or so of the reserved potato cooking liquid, or just enough to achieve a nice smooth consistency. Season with salt and pepper and serve.

Per serving without butter or added salt: 216 calories, trace of fat, no cholesterol, 12 milligrams sodium.

CINNAMON-CRUMB TOPPED APPLE PIE

Makes 8 servings
Preparation time: 20 minutes
Cooking time: 1 hour

PIE:
6 cups sliced, peeled baking apples, such as Golden Delicious or Jonagold
1 9-inch unbaked deep-dish pie shell in pie pan
1 $^1/_4$ cups sugar
3 tablespoons cornstarch
4 tablespoons unsalted butter, melted and cooled
3 large egg yolks, beaten
$^1/_2$ cup heavy cream
$^1/_4$ cup milk
2 tablespoons lemon juice

CRUMB TOPPING:
11 tablespoons (1 stick plus 3 tablespoons) unsalted butter, softened
$^1/_2$ cup packed brown sugar
1 $^2/_3$ cup all-purpose flour
1 $^1/_2$ teaspoons ground cinnamon

Preheat oven to 350 degrees.

To make the pie: Place the apples in the pie shell. In a large bowl or food processor, combine the sugar, cornstarch, butter and egg yolks. Process until the sugar has dissolved. Add the cream, milk and lemon juice and process several seconds, until smooth. Set the filling aside.

To make the crumb topping, put the butter and brown sugar in the workbowl of the food processor and process until well blended. Add the flour and cinnamon and process until the mixture forms medium-size crumbs.

Pour the filling over the apples in the pie shell, then sprinkle the topping evenly over the apples. Place the pie pan on a baking sheet and bake for 1 hour to 1 hour and 10 minutes, until the crumbs are golden brown.

Cool on a wire rack to room temperature to allow the custard to set. The pie may still be soupy, but no one will notice.

Per serving: 675 calories, 35 grams fat, 181 milligrams cholesterol, 183 milligrams sodium.

MELISSA'S VEGETABLE STEW
FOCACCIA *

This hearty vegetable soup can go together quite fast, but if you have time to spare, an additional 20 minutes of cooking on a simmer will deepen the flavors. Leftover carrots, dried, cooked beans or grains would be welcome in this soup, and if you need to stretch the servings, add another can of tomatoes. Save leftovers to serve later in the week.

Look for a fococcia topped with onions, rosemary and thyme — sold at bakeries and farmers markets in most cities. One focaccia is quite large and should last a couple of meals. To keep it fresh-tasting, freeze the leftover bread.

MELISSA'S VEGETABLE STEW

Makes 8 servings
Preparation time: 10 minutes
Cooking time: 30 minutes

1 large onion, chopped
4 garlic cloves, peeled and
    smashed
3 tablespoons olive oil
2 medium potatoes, cut into
    chunks
2 large carrots, cut into $^1\!/_2$-inch
    rounds
1 turnip, peeled and diced
2 tablespoons sweet Hungarian
    paprika
1 to 2 cups water or stock
1 28-ounce can crushed tomatoes
    with Italian seasoning
2 bay leaves
1 cup dry red wine
1 or 2 zucchini squash, sliced
3 cups mushrooms, sliced
Salt and black pepper to taste

Put the oil, onion and garlic in a large soup pot and saute until soft, 8 or 10 minutes. Stir in the potatoes, carrots, turnip and paprika and saute for 3 minutes, being careful not to let the paprika burn. Pour in the water or stock, tomatoes, bay leaves and wine. Cover and bring to a boil, then simmer about 10 minutes.

Add the zucchini, mushrooms, salt and pepper and continue to cook, covered, 5 to 10 minutes.

Per serving: 208 calories, 6 grams fat, no cholesterol, 309 milligrams sodium.

TUESDAY

CHICKEN CREPES

STEAMED RICE *
APPLE PIE *

Make use of Sunday's leftover chicken for a quick but nice meal. Make your own crepes or buy premade crepes in the produce section of most grocery stores. Cook plenty of rice for later in the week, and serve leftover apple pie for dessert.

CHICKEN CREPES

Makes 4 servings
Preparation time: 5 minutes
Cooking time: 15 minutes

1 tablespoon butter or margarine
1 cup mushrooms, sliced
1 tablespoon flour
$^1\!/_2$ to 1 cup milk or half-and-half
Salt to taste
2 cups cooked chicken, sliced or
    shredded
2 tablespoons dry sherry or white
    wine
4 to 8 crepes, warmed

In a skillet or wide sauce-pan, melt the butter, then quickly saute the mushrooms. Remove mushrooms; set aside. Stir in flour and gradually whisk in milk to make a white sauce. Gently salt. Add chicken, reserved mushrooms and sherry and cook over medium-low heat until warmed through. Spoon a portion into each crepe to serve.

Per serving, using milk: 158 calories, 6 grams fat, 56 milligrams cholesterol, 156 milligrams sodium.

WEDNESDAY

WEDNESDAY'S CASSEROLE
GREAT MASHED POTATOES
WITH GARLIC AND ONIONS *

This no-nonsense weeknight dinner goes together fast. Shape leftover mashed potatoes into patties and saute or simply reheat before serving. Save leftovers from the casserole for later in the week.

WEDNESDAY'S CASSEROLE

Makes 8 servings
Preparation time: 5 minutes
Cooking time: 15 minutes

1 medium onion, chopped
1 clove garlic, minced
3 tablespoons olive oil
1 10-ounce package frozen chopped
    spinach, thawed and liquid
    squeezed out
1 zucchini, grated
Salt and black pepper to taste
Freshly grated nutmeg
1 $^1\!/_2$ pounds lean ground beef
4 eggs, beaten
Grated Parmesan cheese

Put the oil, onion and garlic in a saucepan and saute until the onion is transparent. Add zucchini and cook a few minutes, just until it is slightly crisp. Remove from the heat. Add spinach to the onion mixture, add salt, pepper and nutmeg to taste.

In a large frying pan, cook the beef over medium heat until it browns. Drain on paper towels and return to the frying pan. Over medium heat, stir in the onion mixture. Push the meat mixture to one side and add the eggs. Cook them until lightly set, then stir into the meat and continue to cook until they are thoroughly cooked. Sprinkle with Parmesan.

Per serving, with 1 tablespoon Parmesan: 324 calories, 22 grams fat, 209 milligrams cholesterol, 137 milligrams sodium.

Price: Will range from $.49 a pound for common varieties to over $1.50 a pound for some unusual ones. Organic apples run about $1.79 for regular varieties to over $2.00 a pound for exotic varieties. Sold by the pound at most stores and farmers markets and by the peck or bushel at apple houses.

Nutrition: One medium-sized apple has 81 calories, no cholesterol, almost no fat or sodium, and is high in vitamin A, fiber, potassium, boron and complex carbohydrates.

Selection: Late September through November is the season for late varieties. The surface should be firm, unbroken and free of bruises. Look for the appropriate color, either orange, red, green or yellow, or a color blend depending on the cultivar. Immature fruit has a dark grass-green undercast, ripe apples have a soft, light green undercast, and overripe fruit has a dull, yellowish green background and soft, often bruised skin. Many eastern apples have low sugar this year, due to cool spring weather and heavy rains.

Storage: Apples ripen best at room temperature; you may put them in a bag with a banana (the ethylene gas produced by the banana will speed up ripening). After ripening, refrigerate them in a loose or perforated plastic bag to keep them crisp. To store apples for a few months, keep refrigerated or in a cool basement.

Uses: One pound of

apples (4 small, 3 medium or 2 large) yields 3 cups diced fruit or 2 ½ cups peeled, sliced fruit. Eat out of hand, cut up in fruit or vegetable salads or cook into pies, cakes, sauces or chutneys; press for juice or cider. Apples are great paired in savory combinations with cabbage, sausage, game, pork, and pair off quite naturally with other fall foods, such as beans, sweet potatoes and winter squashes.

The late, assertive fruit is upon us. From all across the country, Winesaps, Romes, old Georgia varieties such as Yates, Arkansas Black, and the newest darling of the orchard, the Fuji , are in full harvest.

We know that early apples are usually soft and fragrant, with mid-season apples coming in sweet, even bland. Later apples, harvested from mid-October through November, again turn spicy, tart and hard, in readiness for winter storage.

THURSDAY

VEGETABLE POT PIE
CHEESE AND APPLES *

Leftover vegetable soup can be turned into a warming dinner in minutes. Add chunks of Cheddar cheese, flavorful apples and pears, and dinner is complete. Make your own biscuit dough or purchase refrigerated dough.

VEGETABLE POT PIE

Makes 4 servings
Preparation time: 10 minutes
Cooking time: 20 minutes

4 cups of solids of vegetable soup,
    with liquid strained and
    reserved
Biscuit dough to make 6 to 10
    biscuits

Preheat oven to 375 degrees.

Strain the tomato liquid from the vegetable soup, leaving only the solids. Refrigerate or freeze the liquid for another use.

Place the soup solids (the potatoes, tomatoes, corn and beans) in a saucepan and heat until warmed through. Place them in an 8-inch square baking dish or 1-quart casserole. Pat out the biscuit dough and place on top, pressing the dough to the edges of the pan.

Bake in the oven for 10 to 15 minutes, until the biscuit dough is puffed and golden brown. Serve immediately.

Per serving: 217 calories, 5 grams fat, no cholesterol, 636 milligrams sodium.

FRIDAY

WEDNESDAY'S CASSEROLE *
PITA BREADS *
PUMPKIN SEEDS *

Make an easy dinner by reheating leftovers of Wednesday's casserole and stuffing it into warmed, halved pita breads. And what to do with those leftover pumpkin seeds from Halloween? Roast them for a healthful snack easy enough for a child to make.

SATURDAY

BAKED SCALLOPS WITH
BACON, APPLES AND
CIDER SAUCE
STEAMED WILD RICE *
GREEN BEANS PARMESAN

The meaty texture of scallops goes well with bacon and a svelte cider sauce. Add steamed wild rice and a simple vegetable dish that everyone in the family will appreciate.

BAKED SCALLOPS WITH BACON, APPLES AND CIDER SAUCE

Makes 4 servings
Preparation time: 5 minutes
Cooking time: 25 minutes

6 thin slices bacon, halved crosswise
2 large Golden Delicious apples,
    cored and cut into 8 wedges
12 large sea scallops, about 1 pound
2 tablespoons unsalted butter
Pinch sugar
3/4 cup apple cider

Preheat oven to 425 degrees.

Saute bacon in a large skillet just until it renders its fat; do not brown, about 4 minutes. Transfer the bacon to paper toweling to drain. Discard the bacon fat and wipe out the skillet. Cut up the apples while the bacon cooks.

Lightly butter a baking dish and arrange the scallops in a single layer without touching. Place a bacon slice on top of each scallop. Bake just until the bacon browns and the scallops are cooked, 8 to 12 minutes.

Meanwhile, heat the butter in the skillet until melted. Add the apple slices and sprinkle with a pinch of sugar; saute over medium heat, stirring and turning until the apples turn golden, about 5 minutes. Remove the apple slices and set aside. Add the cider to the skillet. Cook, stirring, until the sauce bubbles and thickens slightly. Serve the scallops topped with the cider sauce and garnished with apple slices.

Per serving: 267 calories, 12 grams fat, 61 milligrams cholesterol, 337 milligrams sodium.

GREEN BEANS PARMESAN

Makes 6 servings
Preparation time: 5 minutes
Cooking time: 5 minutes

2 pounds green beans, ends trimmed
1/4 to 1/3 cup unsalted butter
1 tablespoon dry sherry (optional)
1/4 to 1/3 cup freshly grated
    Parmesan cheese

Bring a large pot of salted water to a boil. Add the beans, bring the water back to a boil and cook 4 to 5 minutes, or until they're crisp-tender and bright green. Drain the beans and put in a serving bowl.

Meanwhile, in a small saucepan, melt butter over low heat. Add the (optional) sherry and let it heat for less than a minute, then stir in the cheese and toss the sauce with the beans.

Per serving: 168 calories, 13 grams fat, 34 milligrams cholesterol, 83 milligrams sodium.

WEEK

41

SHOPPING LIST

Meat, poultry, seafood

- ❑ 3 pounds flank steak
- ❑ ³/₄ to 1 pound bacon
- ❑ 4 Cornish game hens

Produce

- ❑ 6 ounces cremini or shi- itake mushrooms
- ❑ 8 to 10 garlic cloves
- ❑ 1 ¹/₂ pound large shallots
- ❑ 1 to 1 ¹/₂ pounds green beans
- ❑ 1 pound carrots
- ❑ 1 bunch spinach
- ❑ 4 pounds red or white waxy (round, all pur- pose) potatoes
- ❑ 2 medium onions
- ❑ 6 large sweet onions (about 2 pounds)
- ❑ 2 navel oranges
- ❑ 1 pomegranate
- ❑ 7 to 8 firm-ripe pears
- ❑ 6 apples
- ❑ 4 or 5 kiwi fruit

- ❑ 2 large bunches parsley
- ❑ 1 bunch rosemary
- ❑ 1 head red leaf lettuce
- ❑ 1 head Bibb lettuce

Dairy

- ❑ 14 to 16 tablespoons unsalted butter

Deli

- ❑ 4 whole-wheat pita breads
- ❑ 4 to 8 flour tortillas
- ❑ 4 blond brownies
- ❑ ¹/₃ cup grated Parmesan cheese

Miscellaneous

- ❑ 1 cup bourbon
- ❑ 1 8-ounce can spicy tomato juice
- ❑ 1 pound dry soba noodles
- ❑ 1 cup oil-cured black olives

- ❑ 3 cups small dried fava beans or black-eyed peas
- ❑ ¹/₂ cup low-sodium chicken broth
- ❑ 2 cups mixed wild and white rice
- ❑ ¹/₂ cup pecans
- ❑ ¹/₂ cup raisins or currants
- ❑ 2 or 3 tablespoons cognac or brandy
- ❑ ¹/₂ teaspoon orange- flower water
- ❑ 2 tablespoons poppy seeds
- ❑ 2 cups wood chips

Staples

- ❑ Apple cider vinegar
- ❑ Brown sugar
- ❑ Coarsely ground black pepper
- ❑ Dark corn syrup or molasses
- ❑ Dark, unrefined peanut oil
- ❑ Granulated sugar

- ❑ Ground allspice
- ❑ Ground cinnamon
- ❑ Lemon juice
- ❑ Olive oil
- ❑ Paprika
- ❑ Poppy seeds
- ❑ Salt
- ❑ Star anise
- ❑ Vegetable oil

* Suggested accompaniments

SUNDAY

GRILLED BOURBON-GLAZED
FLANK STEAK
CRISPY SHALLOTS AND
MUSHROOMS ON SOBA
NOODLES
STEAMED CARROTS *
PLATTER OF FALL FRUIT *

Robust autumn flavors abound in this Sunday dinner. The dishes are simple, yet deeply flavored and satisfying, such as the steak, adapted from *Cooking Smart* by Sharon Tyler Herbst (Harper Collins, $25.00). Look for a good peanut oil in health food stores, or the brand Loriva: this peanut oil actually tastes like peanuts. Leeks or sweet Vidalia onions could be easily substituted for shallots. Look for the largest shallots for easier peeling. Soba, or buckwheat noodles, offer a good fall flavor, but lemon or egg noodles would taste fine. Cook extra carrots and hold on to leftovers of everything for later meals. Add a platter of fall fruits, including kiwi.

GRILLED BOURBON-GLAZED FLANK STEAK

Makes 8 servings
Preparation time: 5 minutes
Marinating time: 8 hours to overnight
Cooking time: 10 minutes

1 cup bourbon
1 cup spicy tomato juice
$1/2$ cup dark corn syrup
$1/4$ cup dark, unrefined peanut oil
3 garlic cloves, flattened and peeled
2 teaspoons coarsely ground pepper
1 teaspoon salt
2 star anise
3 pounds flank steak, about $1/2$ inch thick
2 cups wood chips (optional)

In a shallow glass or ceramic pan large enough to hold the steak, combine the bourbon, tomato juice, corn syrup, peanut oil, garlic, pepper, salt and star anise; stir well.

Trim visible fat from the steak. If it is thicker than $1/2$-inch, pound it with the edge of a plate or meat mallet. With a sharp knife, score it in a diamond pattern on each side, cutting about $1/8$-inch deep. Dip the meat in the marinade and turn, and leave it in marinade. Cover the dish with plastic wrap and refrigerate at least 8 hours or overnight. Turn occasionally.

If desired, one hour before grilling, soak 2 cups wood chips in water to cover. Light the grill or heat the broiler.

Drain marinade into a small saucepan. Bring to a boil and cook 5-7 minutes. Cover and keep warm over low heat.

Sprinkle the soaked wood chips over coals. Grill steak over high heat or broil in oven for 3 to 5 minutes per side. Carve immediately, cutting diagonally across the grain. Drizzle marinade over steak slices and pass remaining sauce on the side.

Per serving: 334 calories, 20 grams fat, 86 milligrams cholesterol, 395 milligrams sodium.

CRISPY SHALLOTS AND MUSHROOMS ON BUTTERED SOBA NOODLES

Makes 8 servings
Preparation time: 15 minutes
Cooking time: 20 minutes

Vegetable oil for frying, about 4 tablespoons
1 to 1 $1/4$ pound large shallots, peeled and thinly sliced crosswise
6 ounces cremini or shiitake mushrooms, stemmed and sliced
1 pound dry soba noodles
3 or 4 tablespoons unsalted butter
Salt and freshly ground black pepper, to taste

Heat the oil in a large skillet over moderately high heat. Add the shallots and mushrooms and fry, stirring occasionally, 4 to 6 minutes, or until they are golden. Transfer them with a slotted spoon to paper towels to drain.

Bring a pot of salted water to boil, add the noodles and cook 8 to 10 minutes or until al dente. Drain the noodles and return them to the pan. Over low heat toss the noodles with the butter, salt and pepper to taste. Place the noodles in a shallow pasta dish and top with shallots and mushrooms.

Per serving: 444 calories, 14 grams fat, 86 milligrams cholesterol, 14 milligrams sodium.

MONDAY

BLACK-EYED PEAS WITH
LEMON AND GARLIC
OIL-CURED BLACK OLIVES *
WARM WHOLE-WHEAT
PITA BREAD *

Called ful medames in Egypt, this earthy dish has sustained Egyptians for thousands of years. Here it is adapted from one of the best books of the decade, *Recipes From an Ecological Kitchen* by Lorna J. Sass (Morrow, $25). Ms. Sass uses the pressure cooker for equally fast results, which you might want to investigate. Save leftovers to serve later in the week.

Price: 6 to a pound, 3 or 4 for $1.00 at retail stores, or about 6 for $1.00 (1 pound) at U-pick farms.

Nutrition: An average kiwi fruit contains about 55 calories, is low in sodium, is an excellent source of vitamin C and a good source of potassium.

Selection: Choose firm, rather than soft fruit, as softer fruit can be mealy and lacking in flavor. Fruit that are small or unevenly shaped are as delicious as perfect-looking fruit. Vine-ripened fruit will be sweeter.

Storage: If refrigerated, kiwi fruit can be kept for weeks, even months. Because the fruit comes protected in a furry coat, it does not bruise easily. If the fruit is hard and unripe, ripen it by setting it, unpeeled, in a bowl at room temperature or enclose in a paper bag with a banana for a day or two. Once ripened, refrigerate the fruit and serve within a week.

Uses: Kiwi fruit can simply be cut in half and eaten with a spoon, or peeled and sliced to use raw in fruit, vegetable or meat salads. The slices make a good garnish that won't discolor. The puree can be used in fruit sauces or to make ices and sorbets, but prolonged pureeing crushes the seeds and amplifies their slightly bitter flavor.

Aptly called the "enfant terrible" of nouvelle cuisine, kiwi fruit has finally settled into a comfortable marriage with mainstream American cooking. After 20 years of being touted as an exotic, this delightful lemon-

flavored tropical fruit can now be found as readily in children's lunch boxes as at serious dinner parties. Hardly anyone remembers when it was called the Chinese gooseberry.

While kiwi fruit are available in most grocery stores year-round, domestic supplies, grown in California, are available from now through May. During the remaining months of the year, kiwi fruit are imported from New Zealand or Chile. With the passage of the 1990 Farm Bill, imported fruits must now contain the same sugar content (called the Brix level) at harvest as domestic fruit. All kiwi fruit supplies should now have comparable flavor and sweetness.

Still, nothing quite approximates the flavor of vine-ripened fruit. The good news for Southerners is that kiwi fruit is now being grown and harvested in a 100-mile swath through South Carolina, Georgia and Alabama that approximates the fall (or gnat) line.

BLACK-EYED PEAS WITH LEMON AND GARLIC

Makes 8 servings
Preparation time: 5 minutes
Cooking time: 30 minutes

1 16-ounce bag frozen black-eyed peas
4 cups water
4 garlic cloves, peeled and thinly sliced
4 to 6 tablespoons olive oil
1 cup tightly packed minced fresh parsley
4 to 6 tablespoons lemon juice
2 teaspoons salt, or to taste
1 lemon, cut in sections

Put the beans, water, garlic and half the oil in an a heavy 3-quart saucepan. Bring to a boil, reduce heat to a simmer, cover and cook until the beans are tender, about 10 minutes.

While the beans are hot, stir in the parsley, the remaining olive oil, lemon juice and salt. Pass lemon slices at the table.

Per serving: 277 calories, 8 grams fat, less than 1 milligram cholesterol, 606 milligrams sodium.

TUESDAY

CRISPY SHALLOTS AND MUSHROOMS ON SOBA BUTTERED NOODLES STEAMED GREEN BEANS AND CARROTS*

A classic use of leftover pasta is to pan- or oven-bake it until it develops a crisp golden crust. The process is simple and fast, and good for a weeknight when comfort food is a requirement. During frying, the poppy seeds get toasted and sweeter.

FRIED BUTTER NOODLES WITH CRISP BROWNED SHALLOTS

Makes 4 servings
Cooking time: 8-10 minutes

1 to 2 tablespoons butter
4 servings leftover noodles, shallots and mushrooms, room temperature
2 tablespoons minced fresh parsley

Place a heavy medium skillet on low heat. Add the butter just to cover the bottom of the pan. When it foams, add the leftover shallots, pasta and parsley. Press the pasta down into the butter to form a dense pancake. Lower heat to medium and cook uncovered, about 10 minutes. Check occasionally so the shallots don't burn. The pasta is done when it forms a golden bottom crust. Cut into pie-shaped pieces and serve immediately.

Per serving: 470 calories, 17 grams fat, 94 milligrams cholesterol, 44 milligrams sodium.

WEDNESDAY

GERMAN POTATO SALAD STEAMED GREEN BEANS * APPLE SLICES SPRINKLED WITH CINNAMON AND SUGAR *

Unless you are able to maintain great self-control, you will be hard-pressed to get eight servings of this potato salad classic to the table, or out of the pan for that matter. Serve this delicious salad warm on fresh spinach for a well-rounded meal, and save leftovers for later. Also, it is delicious hot, but if it sits for an hour, the flavors will be even more intense. Serve leftover steamed green beans from earlier in the week, tossed with a vinaigrette or added to the potato salad.

GERMAN POTATO SALAD

Makes 8 servings
Preparation time: 10 minutes
Cooking time: 20 minutes

4 pounds red or white round (waxy) potatoes, thinly sliced
3/4 to 1 pound bacon, cut in 1-inch pieces
2 medium onions, peeled and chopped
3 shallots (or garlic cloves)
1/2 cup low-sodium chicken broth
1/2 cup apple cider vinegar
1/4 cup minced fresh parsley
Salt to taste

Place potatoes in a large saucepan and add salted water to cover. Bring to a boil, lower heat to medium and cook until potatoes are cooked through, about 20 minutes.

Meanwhile, in a large skillet, cook the bacon. When it is half done, add the onions, and in a few minutes, the shallots. Cook until the onions are softened and starting to turn golden, 8 to 10 minutes. Add the chicken broth and vinegar, turn up the heat and cook until most of the liquid has evaporated.

When the potatoes are cooked, drain and turn them into the skillet. Toss with the hot bacon mixture and the parsley and salt to taste.

Per serving: 330 calories, 11 grams fat, 18 milligrams cholesterol, 357 milligrams sodium.

THURSDAY

**FLOUR TORTILLAS WITH
REFRIED BLACK-EYED PEAS
AND FLANK STEAK SLICES***
**KIWI, ORANGE AND
GRENADINE SALAD**

Leftover black-eyed peas make good fodder for tortillas. Mash them lightly and heat in a hot skillet with a bit of oil. Add bits and slices of leftover meat, hot sauce and any leftover vegetables, such as carrots. Top with lettuce and sliced green onions to serve.

Kiwis, oranges and pomegranates are all in season and this beautiful tropical salad is a good complement to tortillas. If you are lucky enough to live near a kiwi orchard, what fun it is to pluck them from the vines, and be able to see what odd shapes them come in — only one oval shape makes it to the grocery stores! Follow the quick directions for opening a pomegranate to remove the seeds without piercing them.

KIWI, ORANGE AND GRENADINE SALAD

Makes 4 servings
Preparation time: 15 minutes

2 navel oranges, all rind and pith
    removed
1 to 2 tablespoons granulated sugar
2 or 3 tablespoons grenadine
    (pomegranate-flavored syrup)
3 large kiwis, peeled and sliced
1 pomegranate, opened and seeds
    removed

Halve the oranges and slice into half-moons as thin as you can slice them. To get the pomegranate, cut the fruit partially open, then pull it the rest of the way open with your hands. Pull the seeds out with your fingers or the top of a paring knife.

Layer the kiwi slices and orange slices in a bowl, preferably glass, sprinkling them with sugar, pomegranate seeds and grenadine.

Per serving: 105 calories, less than 1 gram fat, no cholesterol, 5 milligrams sodium.

FRIDAY

GERMAN POTATO SALAD *
MIXED GREEN SALAD *
BLOND BROWNIES *

Leftovers are surely welcome on Friday night; all you have to do here is reheat the potato salad and add a salad, either of your own making or from the salad bar of the grocery store. Add purchased brownies for dessert.

SATURDAY

**ROAST CORNISH HENS
STUFFED WITH WILD RICE
AND PECANS ***
**BAKED SWEET ONIONS
SCENTED WITH ROSEMARY**
**SPICED RED FLAME AND
CHAMPAGNE GRAPES**
CHEESE PLATTER *

This is a dressy meal for favorite friends. Cook wild and white or brown rice with pecans and parsley before stuffing and roasting the hens along with the onions. Tiny Champagne grapes are the sweetest in the world; try them marinated in balsamic vinegar and red wine.

BAKED SWEET ONIONS SCENTED WITH ROSEMARY

Makes 6 servings
Preparation time: 5 minutes
Cooking time: 1 hour

6 large sweet onions, peeled and cut
    in thick slices
6 tablespoons unsalted butter
3 teaspoons fresh rosemary leaves
Salt and freshly ground black pepper,
    to taste
$1/3$ cup freshly grated Parmesan
1 $1/4$ teaspoons paprika, divided

Preheat oven to 400 degrees.

Put the onion slices in a large buttered baking dish. Dot with butter and tuck rosemary leaves and sprigs in among the layers. Sprinkle with salt and pepper and Parmesan cheese. Add $1/2$ cup water to the pan and cover with aluminum foil. Bake for 30 minutes, or until the onions are meltingly tender. Remove the foil and sprinkle with the remaining cheese and paprika. Bake another 10 minutes, or until the onions are golden brown.

Per serving: 172 calories, 13 grams fat, 34 milligrams cholesterol, 74 milligrams sodium.

SPICED RED FLAME AND CHAMPAGNE GRAPES

Makes 4 to 6 servings
Preparation time: 5 minutes
Marinating time: 2 days
Cooking time: 5 minutes

1 pound seedless red grapes, stemmed
2 bunches champagne grapes,
    stemmed
1 cup red wine vinegar and 1 cup
    white wine vinegar

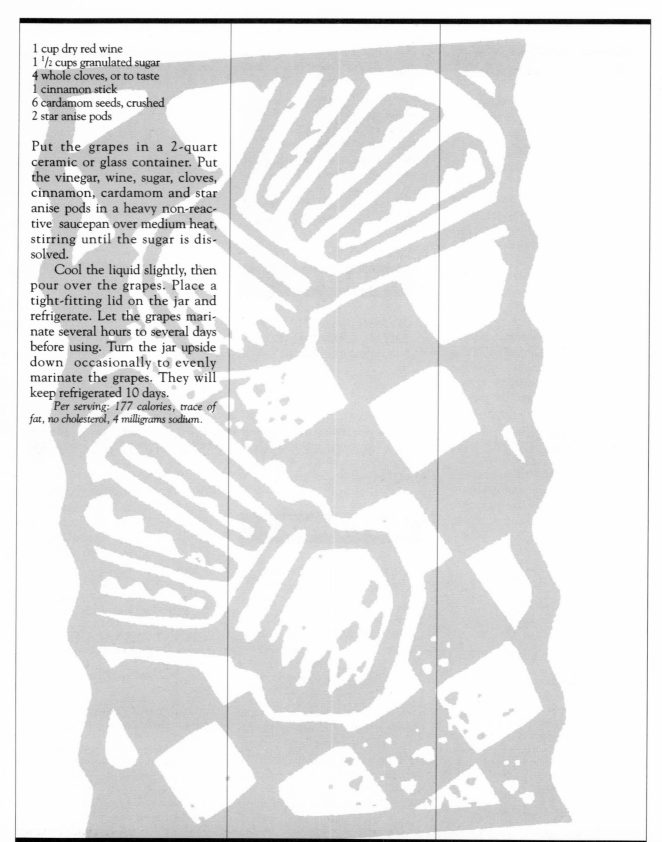

1 cup dry red wine
1 ¹/₂ cups granulated sugar
4 whole cloves, or to taste
1 cinnamon stick
6 cardamom seeds, crushed
2 star anise pods

Put the grapes in a 2-quart ceramic or glass container. Put the vinegar, wine, sugar, cloves, cinnamon, cardamom and star anise pods in a heavy non-reactive saucepan over medium heat, stirring until the sugar is dissolved.

Cool the liquid slightly, then pour over the grapes. Place a tight-fitting lid on the jar and refrigerate. Let the grapes marinate several hours to several days before using. Turn the jar upside down occasionally to evenly marinate the grapes. They will keep refrigerated 10 days.

Per serving: 177 calories, trace of fat, no cholesterol, 4 milligrams sodium.

WEEK 42

SHOPPING LIST

Meat, poultry, seafood

- ❑ 1 ¹/₂ to 2-pounds smoked turkey breast, boned
- ❑ ¹/₄ to ¹/₂ pound bacon
- ❑ 1 ¹/₂ pounds sole fillets
- ❑ 4 pork loin chops, ³/₄ inch thick

Produce

- ❑ 2 ripe tomatoes
- ❑ 2 bunches Swiss chard (or turnip greens)
- ❑ 8 garlic cloves
- ❑ 1 large red onion
- ❑ 1 large yellow onion
- ❑ 4 medium red potatoes
- ❑ 1 bunch broccoli
- ❑ 2 ¹/₂ pounds winter squash, such as butternut or kabocha
- ❑ 3 pounds new potatoes
- ❑ 1 head fennel (or anise or Florence fennel)
- ❑ 2 large or 4 small heads lettuce, any type
- ❑ 1 bunch fresh sage leaves
- ❑ 3 large bunches flat-leaf parsley (to make 1 ¹/₄ cups packed)
- ❑ ¹/₂ cup apple cider
- ❑ 10 medium to large apples (4 may be apples not good for cooking, such as Red Delicious, or McIntosh)
- ❑ 1 fresh pineapple, cored and peeled

Dairy

- ❑ 3 large egg whites
- ❑ 1 large egg
- ❑ 3 tablespoons butter
- ❑ 1 ¹/₂ cups buttermilk or sweet milk
- ❑ 1 cup heavy cream

Deli

- ❑ 8 to 16 rye crackers
- ❑ 8 ounces (2 cups) grated sharp Cheddar cheese
- ❑ 1 ¹/₂ ounces low-fat cream cheese

Miscellaneous

- ❑ 4 ounces unsweetened chocolate
- ❑ ¹/₂ cup pureed prunes
- ❑ ³/₄ cup chopped walnuts
- ❑ 6 14 ¹/₂-ounce cans beef or chicken stock or 12 bouillon cubes
- ❑ 2 15-ounce cans cannellini (white kidney beans)
- ❑ 1 pint spicy tomato pasta sauce
- ❑ 1 10-ounce package frozen fried okra
- ❑ 1 ¹/₂ cups popcorn cornmeal or other cornmeal
- ❑ 2 or 3 tablespoons grits (optional)
- ❑ 2 cups frozen corn
- ❑ 3 cups frozen lima or butter beans
- ❑ ¹/₄ cup dry white wine (optional, may use cider)
- ❑ 4 flour tortillas

Staples

- ❑ All-purpose unbleached (if possible) flour
- ❑ Baking soda
- ❑ Black pepper
- ❑ Caraway seeds
- ❑ Dry mustard
- ❑ Granulated sugar
- ❑ Lemon juice
- ❑ Low-fat mayonnaise
- ❑ Miso (optional)
- ❑ Olive oil
- ❑ Paprika
- ❑ Pure vanilla extract
- ❑ Salt
- ❑ Self-rising flour
- ❑ Vegetable oil
- ❑ Walnut oil
- ❑ Wine vinegar
- ❑ Worcestershire sauce

* Suggested accompaniments

SUNDAY

SMOKED TURKEY BREAST *
CHARD CHOWDER WITH
BEANS AND COUNTRY HAM
SLICED TOMATOES *
LOW-FAT FUDGE BROWNIES

Make this warming and healing soup for your family and a few close friends on a chilly Sunday night. Use intensely-flavored country ham, available in 12-ounce packages in many grocery stores. Omit the meat entirely if you wish, or chill the soup for a few hours after cooking, then skim off the fat from the surface. It gets better after a day or two in the refrigerator, so be sure to hold some soup for leftovers. Miso adds a wonderful flavor addition instead of beef stock, and is sold in health food stores and oriental markets. Smoked turkey is effortless and, like the soup and dessert, offers leftovers.

You won't believe these brownies have no butter or added fat; they taste too good. The secret ingredient is the new darling of the no-fat wars: pureed canned prunes, developed by the California Prune Board.

CHARD CHOWDER WITH BEANS AND COUNTRY HAM

Makes 10 servings
Preparation time: 15 minutes
Cooking time: 25 minutes

2 or 3 ounces country ham or $^1/_4$ pound bacon, diced
2 bunches Swiss chard, stems cut, leaves coarsely chopped
4 garlic cloves, minced
1 large onion, peeled and chopped
2 tablespoons fresh sage leaves
4 medium red potatoes, cut in small dice
6 14 $^1/_2$-ounce cans beef stock or red

miso (with enough water added to make 12 cups)
2 15-ounce cans cannellini (white kidney beans), drained
Salt and pepper to taste
$^1/_2$ cup chopped flat-leaf parsley

Put the country ham in a large pot and cook over medium-high heat until it is heated through, 3 or 5 minutes. (The ham won't render much fat, but if you use bacon, remove all but a tablespoon or two of the fat after cooking.)

Put the chard stems, garlic, onion and sage in the pot and cook until the vegetables are soft, about 5 minutes. Stir in the chard leaves, potatoes, stock, water and beans and bring to a boil.

Partially cover and reduce the heat to a simmer. Cook for 15 minutes, then season with salt and pepper and stir in parsley.

Per serving: 244 calories, 5 grams fat, 5 milligrams cholesterol, 443 milligrams sodium.

LOW-FAT FUDGE BROWNIES

Makes 2 dozen brownies
Preparation time: 10 minutes
Cooking time: 30 minutes

4 ounces unsweetened chocolate
$^1/_2$ cup pureed prunes
3 large egg whites
1 cup granulated sugar
1 teaspoon salt
1 teaspoon vanilla
$^1/_2$ cup all-purpose flour
$^1/_4$ cup chopped walnuts

Preheat the oven to 350 degrees. Coat an 8-inch-square baking pan with vegetable spray and set aside.

Cut chocolate into 1-inch pieces and place in a microwave-proof bowl. Melt in the microwave for 2 or 3 minutes on medium (50 percent power); set aside.

In a mixing bowl, combine the prune puree, egg whites,

sugar, salt and vanilla and beat until blended thoroughly. Mix in the flour. Spread batter in the prepared pan and sprinkle with walnuts. Bake about 30 minutes until springy to the touch. Cool completely on a rack before cutting into 1 $^1/_2$-inch squares.

Per brownie: 79 calories, 3 grams fat, no cholesterol, 105 milligrams sodium.

MONDAY

MONDAY NIGHT FISH FRY
APPLE-PINEAPPLE TOSS *
MIXED GREEN LETTUCES *

This low-fat fried fish puts the fat in the sauce, where it really matters, without wasting it in the pan. Use sole, orange roughy or tilapia, whatever you find on sale. Mix apple and pineapple slices and toss in a small amount of low-fat mayonnaise; serve over fresh lettuce.

MONDAY NIGHT FISH FRY

Makes 4 servings
Preparation time: 5 minutes
Cooking time: 8-10 minutes

Olive oil
1 $^1/_2$ pounds sole fillets, cut in 3- or 4-inch pieces
$^1/_4$ to $^1/_2$ cup all-purpose flour
$^1/_2$ cup fresh parsley leaves
1 teaspoon paprika
$^1/_2$ teaspoon minced, dried orange peel
$^1/_2$ cup water
$^1/_4$ cup lemon juice
2 tablespoons unsalted butter, cut in pieces
Salt and freshly ground black pepper, to taste

Blend the flour, parsley, paprika and orange in a shallow bowl; then dip the fish in the flour mixture and shake off any excess.

Spray a large non-stick skil-

Price: Most ciders cost about $3.00 a gallon. Most roadside stands will be open through mid-November, and a few until Christmas. A telephone call will determine which ones are open and have fresh cider.

Selection: Look for freshly-pressed cider that is caramel colored, opaque and unfiltered. Be sure it has been refrigerated since pressing, and that it is less than 2 weeks old.

Storage: Always keep fresh cider refrigerated, as it has not been pasteurized and will turn sour and spoil. Be sure to loosen the cap to allow the fermenting gases to escape, rather than explode. Most ciders will be good for about 2 weeks. Cider may also be frozen for up to one year with no loss of flavor, in fact it will likely taste sweeter after freezing. Be sure to pour out 1 cup of juice from the container, to allow for expansion of the cider during freezing. To serve, thaw and shake the cider well before using.

Uses: Fresh cider can be drunk cold or heated with spices; added to donut and muffin batters, apple pie, chutney, mincemeat, and applesauce, used to marinate chicken or pork or added to the liquid as those meats stew, or to finish a meat sauce.

---

let with pan spray. Heat the skillet over medium heat until very hot. Add the fish and saute, until the pieces start to color golden, about 2 minutes. Turn and cook the fish on the other side until firm, about 2 minutes. Put the fish on serving plates.

Add the water and lemon juice to the skillet and increase the heat to medium-high. Scrape up any browned bits on the bottom of the pan and boil, stirring, until syrupy, about 2 minutes. Turn off the heat and add the butter a piece at a time. Season with salt and pepper and pour the sauce over the fish.

Per serving: 218 calories, 8 grams fat, 120 milligrams cholesterol, 194 milligrams sodium.

TUESDAY

FRIED OKRA WITH SPICY TOMATO SAUCE *
POPCORN CORN BREAD

Johnny Burt of Burt's Pumpkin Farm near Dawsonville in North Georgia says his popcorn, ground into meal by water at a vintage mill nearby, makes the best corn bread in the South. And I think he's right: This is the crispiest, crunchiest and most delicious corn bread I've tried yet.

If you don't have buttermilk, stir 1 tablespoon vinegar into 1 ½ cups sweet milk and let it sit 5 or 10 minutes to sour it slightly. If you can't find popcorn cornmeal, add a tablespoon or two of dry grits to the batter to give it a crunchy texture. To order popcorn cornmeal, call Burt's Pumpkin Farm, 706-265-3701.

Use any standard tomato sauce or your favorite pasta sauce over fried okra, which is low in price right now.

POPCORN CORN BREAD

Makes 12 pie-shaped slices
Preparation time: 5 minutes
Cooking time: 25 minutes

1 ½ cups popcorn cornmeal (or other cornmeal)
½ teaspoon baking soda
½ cup self-rising flour
1 tablespoon granulated sugar
¼ cup vegetable oil
1 ½ cups buttermilk (or soured milk)
1 egg, well beaten

Preheat oven to 475 degrees. Place a well-seasoned and greased cast-iron skillet or other heavy 10-inch square baking pan in the oven while the oven is heating.

In a large bowl, stir together the cornmeal, baking soda, flour and sugar. In a separate bowl, combine the oil, egg and milk. Stir the milk mixture into dry ingredients.

Pour the batter into the hot skillet and bake until the sides turn crispy and the top is golden brown.

Per serving: 137 calories, 6 grams fat, 24 milligrams cholesterol, 143 milligrams sodium.

WEDNESDAY

SAUTEED SMOKED TURKEY SLICES *
SUCCOTASH WITH SAGE
POPCORN CORN BREAD *

This dish uses America's favorite native foods: corn, beans and squash. It cooks quickly on the stovetop, and is great spooned over halved and toasted slices of corn bread. Save leftovers for another meal. The meat in the menu isn't necessary for a meal with complete protein, but it adds a nice flavor counterpoint to the vegetable dish.

SUCCOTASH WITH SAGE

Makes 8 servings
Preparation time: 20 minutes
Cooking time: 12-15 minutes

1 1/2 cups water
1 large onion, peeled and coarsely chopped
4 or 5 fresh sage leaves
2 1/2 pounds winter squash (butternut and kabocha or other), peeled, seeded and cut into 1-inch chunks
3 cups frozen and defrosted lima beans or butter beans
2 cups frozen (defrosted) corn kernels
1/4 cup tightly packed, finely chopped fresh parsley
1/2 teaspoon salt, or to taste

Put the water, onion, sage, squash and salt in a large saucepan and bring to a boil. Reduce the heat, cover and simmer until the squash is tender, about 10 minutes. Add the limas and cook another 5 to 7 minutes. Add the corn and cook until the corn is thoroughly heated through. The water should be evaporated. Remove the vegetables and toss with the parsley and salt to taste.

Per serving: 166 calories, less than 1 gram fat, no cholesterol, 187 milligrams sodium.

THURSDAY

APPLE CIDER CHEESE
RYE CRACKERS *, APPLE SLICES*
RAW BROCCOLI *

This different-tasting spread from the Georgia Apple Com-mission is delicious on cold slices of apples or crackers. Spread the dip on raw broccoli as well for a quick meal.

APPLE CIDER CHEESE

Makes 1 1/2 cups
Preparation time: 5 minutes

2 cups sharp Cheddar cheese, grated
1 1/2 ounces cream cheese
1/4 cup apple cider
1/2 teaspoon Worcestershire sauce
1/2 teaspoon dry mustard
1/8 teaspoon paprika
1 teaspoon caraway seeds

Combine cheese, cream cheese, cider, Worcestershire sauce, paprika and caraway seeds in the bowl of a food processor. Serve at room temperature.

Per 1-tablespoon serving: 93 calories, 8 grams fat, 24 milligrams cholesterol, 136 milligrams sodium.

FRIDAY

WARM FLOUR TORTILLAS
SUCCOTASH WITH SAGE *
CHARD CHOWDER WITH
BEANS AND COUNTRY HAM *
LOW-FAT FUDGE BROWNIES *

Almost anything can be tucked into a warm flour tortilla and called dinner. Here, it's leftover succotash from Wednesday. Add leftover soup and brownies for dessert.

SATURDAY

PORK CHOPS WITH APPLES
AND CIDER SAUCE
ROASTED NEW POTATOES
WITH GARLIC AND FENNEL *
GREEN SALAD WITH WALNUTS
AND WALNUT VINAIGRETTE *

The flavors of pork and apples and cider go together perfectly. Here, quick-cooking pork chops are paired with a wonderful cider sauce. Add an easy salad and potatoes roasted with slivers of garlic and fennel, sometimes called Florence fennel or anise.

PORK CHOPS WITH APPLES AND CIDER SAUCE

Makes 4 servings
Preparation time: 10 minutes
Cooking time: 30 minutes

4 to 6 apples, quartered, cored and thinly sliced
4 pork loin chops, about 3235/4 inch thick
Salt to taste
1 tablespoon unsalted butter or vegetable oil
1/4 cup fresh apple cider or dry white wine
1 cup heavy cream
Pepper to taste

Preheat the oven to 400 de-grees. Butter or grease a gratin dish or other baking pan large enough to hold the chops side by side.

Spread the apples in the prepared dish and bake for 15 minutes. Meanwhile, put the oil in a large skillet and cook the pork chops over medium heat until nicely colored on each side — 7 or 8 minutes per side. Place the chops on top of the apples and set aside.

To deglaze the skillet, add the cider to the pan drippings and stir on medium heat, scraping up any bits of food. Cook until the cider is reduced by half, then stir in the cream and salt and pepper to taste.

Pour the sauce over the pork chops and shake the dish gently so the cream penetrates the bed of apples. Bake 15 minutes longer.

Per serving: 593 calories, 38 grams fat, 178 milligrams cholesterol, 132 milligrams sodium.

WEEK

43

Meat, poultry, seafood

- ❏ 1 ¹/₂ pounds country-style pork ribs, cut apart
- ❏ 22 ¹/₂-pound chickens cut-up, or pieces of same weight
- ❏ 1 to ¹/₄ pounds catfish fillets
- ❏ 2 boneless New York strip steaks (10 to 12 ounces each)

Produce

- ❏ 1 medium onion
- ❏ 1 small red onion
- ❏ 1 Vidalia onion
- ❏ 2 cloves garlic
- ❏ 2 to 2 ¹/₂ pounds Brussels sprouts
- ❏ ³/₄ pound collard greens
- ❏ 1 head lettuce
- ❏ 1 small head white cabbage
- ❏ 2 large tomatoes
- ❏ 1 bunch broccoli

- ❏ 1 3-ounce package spicy or onion sprouts
- ❏ 8 Seckle pears
- ❏ 1 tart cooking apple (Cortland, Granny Smith or Jonathon)
- ❏ 2 lemons
- ❏ 2 cups cider (optional)

Dairy

- ❏ 4 tablespoon butter or margarine
- ❏ 1 cup skimmed milk
- ❏ ¹/₂ pint whipping cream

Deli

- ❏ 4 ounces blue cheese
- ❏ 10 to 12 ounces Fontina or cheddar cheese

Miscellaneous

- ❏ 1 pound dry white navy beans
- ❏ 8 slices firm white or

whole wheat bread
- ❏ 1 7-ounce can chipotles peppers
- ❏ 2 cups white or brown rice
- ❏ 1 8-ounce package mixed dried fruit
- ❏ ¹/₂ cup nuts (almonds, pecans or walnuts)
- ❏ ¹/₄ cup pecans
- ❏ 1 tablespoon cocoa or carob powder
- ❏ ¹/₂ cup wheat germ
- ❏ 1 12-ounce package cornmeal mix
- ❏ ¹/₃ cup sesame seeds
- ❏ ¹/₄ cup orange marmalade
- ❏ 2 tablespoons cassis

Staples

- ❏ Balsamic vinegar
- ❏ Black pepper
- ❏ Brown sugar
- ❏ Cayenne pepper
- ❏ Cider vinegar

- ❏ Cornmeal
- ❏ English dry mustard
- ❏ Flour
- ❏ Ground ginger
- ❏ Olive oil
- ❏ Oregano
- ❏ Peanut oil
- ❏ Salt
- ❏ Star anise pods
- ❏ Vegetable oil

VERMONT
APPLE-BAKED BEANS
BAKED COUNTRY RIBS
BRUSSELS SPROUTS IN BUTTER
PEARS WITH BLUE CHEESE*

There's nothing better than home-baked beans when the weather turns cool, and this recipe cooked with country ribs and a spicy apple is one of the best. The beans take longer to bake than to cook in a soup, but the baking gives them a dense texture and fuller flavor. The following recipe makes plenty for lunches and dinner later in the week. As the ribs bake on top of the beans, their drippings help to flavor this wonderful dish; offer a small amount of meat with each serving of beans.

Serve simply cooked Brussels sprouts (cook extras for later in the week) and finish with a platter of flavorful pears (see In Season, page 215) and a wedge of ripe blue cheese: an Italian gorgonzola, the domestic Maytag Blue or a fine English Stilton.

VERMONT APPLE-BAKED BEANS

Makes 10 servings
Preparation time: 5 minutes
Cooking time: 3 1/2 hours

1 pound dry navy beans
2 tablespoons vegetable oil (optional)
1 to 1 1/2 pounds country-style pork ribs, cut apart
1 large onion, chopped
1 teaspoon English dry mustard
1/2 cup brown sugar (packed)
1/2 teaspoon freshly ground black pepper
2 cups cider or water
1 tart apple (about 1/2 pound), peeled, cored, diced
Salt to taste

Put the beans in a large pot and cover with water. Bring to a boil, turn off the heat and let the beans soak for 1 hour, then drain. (Alternatively, soak the beans overnight, then drain.)

Preheat the oven to 300 degrees.

Put the oil and ribs in a large heavy Dutch oven on high heat and saute until the ribs are well browned on all sides. Set them aside.

Reduce the heat under the Dutch oven to medium, add the onion and cook 5 minutes, until the onions are softened but not brown. Stir in the mustard, brown sugar, maple syrup, pepper and water. Add the drained beans and apple. Place the pork ribs on top of the beans.

Cover and bake for 2 hours. Reduce heat to 275 degrees and continue to bake until the beans are tender, about 1 1/2 hours. If the beans are still quite wet, remove the ribs and keep warm, then bake the beans uncovered in the oven for about 20 minutes. Add salt to taste.

Per serving: 407 calories, 17 grams fat, 49 milligrams cholesterol, 66 milligrams sodium.

GRILLED CHEESE WITH
SMOKED CHILES AND
SPICY SPROUTS
MIXED GREEN SALAD*

Another variation on the comfy cheese sandwich, this one is packaged for stout tastebuds. Chipotle puree is made from chipotle peppers, actually smoked jalapeno peppers. Look for the canned chipotles at specialty stores that carry Mexican products. Puree the chilies (with a bit of the sauce) with just enough vegetable oil to make a smooth paste. Store the puree in the refrigerator and use to season dishes such as this one. Nutty-flavored Fontina cheese melts beautifully for a great sandwich; spicy sprouts are actually radish sprouts and the size of tiny alfalfa sprouts, but the resemblance stops with their size. Their nippy bite, similar to watercress, adds a good punch to the sandwiches. Substitute onion or garlic sprouts, basil or cilantro.

GRILLED CHEESE WITH SMOKED CHILES AND RADISH SPROUTS

Makes 4 servings
Preparation time: 5 minutes
Cooking time: 5 minutes

Soft butter or margarine
8 slices white or whole wheat bread
2 teaspoons or more chipotle puree
10 to 12 ounces Fontina (or white cheddar), thinly sliced
2 large tomatoes, sliced
1 small red onion, thinly sliced into round
2 tablespoons radish sprouts

Butter the outsides of the bread for grilling. Spread the insides with the chipotle puree, putting a scant 1/4 teaspoon on each slice. Layer the cheese, tomato and onion and top with another bread slice.

Heat a griddle or heavy skillet and grill the sandwiches on

Price: About $1.29 to $1.39 a pound.

Nutrition: One-half cup cooked Brussels sprouts have about 24 calories. Sprouts are high in vitamin C and are a good source of vitamin A, potassium and phosphorus. Like other members of the cabbage family, Brussels sprouts are considered helpful in the prevention of certain types of cancer, according to the American Cancer Society.

Selection: Available year-round, but peaking September through February. Look for firm sprouts that are compact and fresh looking with a bright green color. They should feel heavy for their size. Purchase sprouts that are uniform in size for uniform cooking. Smaller sprouts are younger and more tender.

Storage: Pull off any yellowed or limp leaves, then refrigerate, unwashed, for up to 3 days.

Uses: One pound has about 3 cups of sprouts. Allow ¼ cup pound per person. Cut a shallow x in the bottom of each sprout to speed up cooking. Boil in a large amount of water or steam sprouts about 5 to 10 minutes or microwave on High 6 to 7 minutes, but overcooking turns them mushy and bitter-tasting. Top cooked sprouts with butter and fresh herbs or a vinaigrette, or add to a hearty salad.

Brussels sprouts are the tiniest and sweetest member of the cabbage family. In Belgium they have been grown since the 1200s and are considered the official vegetable. There they are often paired with smoky sausages or ham. They are equally good simply steamed and sauced in butter and fresh herbs. Autumn recipes could include walnuts or other fall nuts.

Autumn is the official season for Brussels sprouts, and some fans claim that like collard greens or persimmons, they turn sweeter after the first frost or snow fall. "It makes sense. Whenever you chill starches, they turn to sugar," said Shirley Corriher, Atlanta food scientist and cooking teacher.

While tiny, young sprouts are sweet, the large, older ones are tough and coarse and have a strong, cabbagy flavor. In Belgium, the best sprouts are served when only the size of a child's fingernail. While you may not find them quite that small, tiny ones are available in local stores and are worth the search.

one side until the cheese melts, 3 to 4 minutes; turn and grill the other sides. Add sprouts to the insides and serve.

Per serving: 433 calories, 24 grams fat, 84 milligrams cholesterol, 241 milligrams sodium.

TUESDAY

LEMON CHICKEN
STEAMED RICE*
BRUSSELS SPROUTS IN
BROWNED BUTTER*

There's nothing difficult about tonight's dinner, and if you have put the chicken in the marinade before you leave for work, it will be ready to cook right away. Use whichever chicken pieces you find on sale. Cook double portions of chicken and rice to use later in the week. Steam Brussels sprouts until tender, then quickly finish in a tablespoon of butter that you have let brown slightly.

LEMON CHICKEN

Makes 8 servings
Preparation time: 5 minutes
Marinating time: 20 minutes
Cooking time: 10 to 15 minutes

2 2 $^1/_2$ to 3-pound chickens, cut up, or pieces (such as thighs or legs)
Juice of 2 lemons
4 to 6 teaspoons olive oil
2 garlic cloves, minced
1 teaspoon allspice
A few sprinkles cayenne pepper

Cut visible fat from chicken and remove as much skin as possible. Put the chicken in one layer in a shallow baking dish.

In a small dish, combine the lemon juice, oil, garlic, allspice and cayenne and mix well. Pour over chicken and turn to coat all sides. Let the chicken marinate at room temperature for 20 minutes or cover and refrigerate overnight.

Preheat the broiler or grill and cook chicken 10 to 15 minutes, turning once, until the juices are clear.

Per serving: 286 calories, 16 grams fat, 98 milligrams cholesterol, 56 milligrams sodium.

WEDNESDAY

BAKED BEANS*
STEAMED BROCCOLI*
LOVE-IN-BLOOM FRUIT AND
NUT SQUARES

This is an easy dinner, with beans warmed (and now even tastier) from earlier in the week. Add steamed broccoli and homemade cookies that the kids will want to help make. The cookies, adapted from *Smart Cookies* by Jane Kinderlehrer (Newmarket Press) will be good in the lunch box too. Look for nuts in bulk in the produce section of the grocery store or at some farmers markets.

LOVE-IN-BLOOM FRUIT AND NUT SQUARES

Makes 1 dozen
Preparation time: 15 minutes

18-ounce package (1 cup) mixed dried fruits
$^1/_4$ cup nuts (pecans, almonds or walnuts)
1 tablespoon cocoa or carob powder
1 tablespoon honey
$^1/_4$ cup wheat germ
2 tablespoons slivered almonds or

other nuts.

Put the dried fruits in the workbowl of a food processor and pulse to mince. Remove and add the nuts; pulse until they are chopped. Put the fruit and nuts in a bowl; stir in the cocoa and honey. Press dough into walnut-sized balls. Put the wheat germ on a sheet of wax paper and roll the balls in the wheat germ. Press each down slightly, into a square. Top each piece with an almond or walnut, and they are ready to eat.

Per serving: 78 calories, 2 grams fat, no cholesterol, 2 milligrams sodium.

THURSDAY

ALIX'S CATFISH
VIDALIA ONIONS AND
WILTED COLLARD GREENS
CORN MUFFINS*

Even when catfish fillets aren't on sale they are a good bargain, but this week several stores will feature them at a special price, so don't miss them. The following dish, from Alix Kenagy-Carson, co-owner of Indigo Coastal Grill in Atlanta, makes good use of their bland flavor and firm texture.

Vidalia onions are out of California storage and in most grocery stores until Thanksgiving, so take advantage of their sweet flavor in the collard dish while they last. Some stores sell collard greens loose, so you can choose your own leaves: look for young, tender greens, the smallest leaves you can find. Time the cooking of the dishes so that the greens go into the pan after the catfish are finished cooking; otherwise they will overcook.

ALIX'S CATFISH

Makes 4 servings
Preparation time: 5 minutes
Cooking time: 5 minutes

4 tablespoons peanut oil
1 pound catfish fillets
1 cup skim milk
$^1/_3$ cup all purpose flour
$^1/_3$ cup cornmeal
$^1/_3$ cup sesame seeds

Heat the peanut oil in a wide skillet. Wash and pat dry the fillets. Place the milk in a shallow bowl or pie plate, and the flour, cornmeal and sesame seeds in another shallow bowl. Dip the fillets first in the milk, then in the flour mixture.

Place the fillets in the hot fat so that they aren't crowded. Saute them until they are cooked, about 4 to 5 minutes, turning once. Serve over wilted collard greens and sprinkle with toasted pecans.

Per serving: 451 calories, 31 grams fat, 93 milligrams cholesterol, 335 milligrams sodium.

WILTED COLLARD GREENS

Makes 4 servings
Preparation time: 10 minutes
Cooking time: 15 minutes

$^1/_4$ cup toasted pecans
2 tablespoons peanut oil
1 small Vidalia onion, chopped
$^3/_4$ pound collard greens, washed, stemmed and leaves cut in long strips
1 tablespoon balsamic vinegar

Heat the oven to 300 degrees.

To toast the pecans, place them on a baking sheet. Put them in the oven, stirring every few minutes, until they start to color and release their fragrance,

8 to 10 minutes. Set aside.

Heat the peanut oil in a large skillet, saute the Vidalia onion until it has softened, 5 minutes. Add the collard greens, turn off the heat, and toss until the greens have wilted, about 30 seconds. Sprinkle and toss with balsamic vinegar. Place the wilted greens on a plate and top with a cooked catfish fillet. Sprinkle the top with toasted pecans.

Per serving: 124 calories, 12 grams fat, no cholesterol, 14 milligrams sodium.

FRIDAY

LEMON CHICKEN*
BROCCOLI, BRUSSELS SPROUTS, CHOPPED ONIONS AND SPICY SPROUTS*
FRUIT AND NUT SQUARES*

Pull some cold barbecued chicken from the refrigerator for tonight's dinner, and pair it with cooked vegetables for a nutritious no-work meal.

SATURDAY

ORANGE-GLAZED STEAKS
RAISIN-WALNUT RICE*
MIXED CABBAGE AND LETTUCE SALAD*
PEARS IN ZINFANDEL WITH CASSIS CREAM

Orange marmalade and cider vinegar add a piquant touch to New York strip steaks. Add a couple tablespoons orange juice, golden raisins and chopped walnuts to the rice for a delicious

pilaf. Add a green salad and pears poached in a spicy red zinfandel — Seckle are a good choice for their smooth, dense texture and because they cook quickly. Adapted from *Chez Panisse Menu Cookbook* by Alice Waters (Random House, $16.95). Also, four halves on a plate make a beautiful presentation. Cook the pears earlier in the day, refrigerate until before serving time, then serve them at room temperature. Choose pears that are partially ripened but not so soft they will fall apart during cooking.

ORANGE-GLAZED STEAKS

Makes 4 servings
Preparation time: 5 minutes
Cooking time: 10 to 12 minutes

2 boneless New York strip (top loin) steaks, 10 to 12 ounces, cut 1-inch thick
$^1/_2$ teaspoon coarse grind black pepper, divided
$^1/_4$ cup orange marmalade
2 teaspoons cider vinegar
$^1/_4$ teaspoon ground ginger
$^1/_8$ teaspoon salt (optional)

Press pepper evenly over both sides of steaks. Place the steaks on rack in broiler pan so surface of meat is 3 to 4 inches from the heat. Combine marmalade, cider vinegar and ginger; brush the tops of the steaks with half the marmalade mixture, reserve the remainder. Broil steaks 10 to 12 minutes for medium-done. During cooking, turn steaks once and brush with reserved marmalade mixture. Season with (optional) salt. Carve and serve.

Per serving: 226 calories, 24 grams protein, 8 grams fat, 61 milligrams sodium, 65 milligrams cholesterol.

POACHED PEARS IN ZINFANDEL WITH CASSIS CREAM

Makes 4 servings
Preparation time: 10 minutes
Cooking time: 15 minutes
Standing time: 20 minutes

8 ripe Seckle pears (or 4 Bosc or
    D'Anjou)
4 to 6 cups Zinfandel
1 cup sugar
1 cup water
1 or 2 star anise pods
1 cup whipping cream, very cold
1 or 2 tablespoons cassis

Peel the pears, leaving the stems on. Cut them in half and cut out the seeds. To poach them, bring the wine, sugar, water and star anise to a boil. Stir to dissolve the sugar, add the pears and reduce the heat. Poach the pears at a simmer until their outer coating is translucent and they give slightly to the touch but are still firm, 10 to 15 minutes. Remove the pears from the heat and let them cool in the poaching liquor for 20 or more minutes. They should be soft to the core but not mushy, and should retain their shape.

To make the cassis cream, beat the whipping cream until it barely forms soft peaks. Fold in cassis. Refrigerate until serving time.

To serve, place four pear halves in spoke fashion on a dessert plate, spoon over them some of the poaching liquor. Add some cassic cream in the center of the dish.

Per serving: 263 calories, 9 grams fat, 33 milligrams cholesterol, 12 milligrams sodium.

WEEK

44

SHOPPING LIST

Meat, poultry, seafood

- ❏ 6 8-ounce pork chops
- ❏ 1 8-pound turkey
- ❏ ¼ pound lean bacon

Produce

- ❏ 2 heads romaine lettuce
- ❏ 1 bunch watercress
- ❏ 1 bunch spinach
- ❏ 5 medium onions
- ❏ 1 garlic clove
- ❏ 1 leek
- ❏ 8 ounces mushrooms, such as cremini
- ❏ 3 pounds new red potatoes
- ❏ 2 pounds green beans
- ❏ 1 fennel bulb (anise)
- ❏ 1 pound peeled lima beans
- ❏ 1 ½ cups cranberries, fresh or frozen
- ❏ ½ bunch parsley
- ❏ 1 bunch rosemary
- ❏ 1 bunch sage leaves
- ❏ 2 ripe persimmons (Japanese)

Dairy

- ❏ 4 sticks plus 2 tablespoons unsalted butter
- ❏ 8 eggs
- ❏ 2 cups buttermilk
- ❏ 3 cups milk
- ❏ 1 pint ice cream

Deli

- ❏ 2 ounces Parmesan cheese
- ❏ 2 baguettes French bread
- ❏ 12 1-ounce slices Gruyere or Swiss cheese
- ❏ 8 ounces Cheddar cheese

Miscellaneous

- ❏ 2 cups dry white wine
- ❏ 2 to 3 tablespoons red (dark) miso
- ❏ 1 ½ cups walnuts
- ❏ ¼ cup cognac
- ❏ 2 4-ounce packages ramen noodles
- ❏ 1 16-ounce can cranberry sauce
- ❏ 1 cup wild rice
- ❏ 1 5-ounce package self-rising corn bread mix
- ❏ 1 16-ounce package lemon cookies
- ❏ 1 pound fresh vegetable or cheese ravioli
- ❏ 1 cup low-sodium chicken broth
- ❏ 1 cup crushed tomatoes with Italian seasoning

Staples

- ❏ All-purpose flour
- ❏ Black pepper
- ❏ Cornmeal
- ❏ Dried sage
- ❏ Granulated sugar
- ❏ Fruity vinegar
- ❏ Hot chili oil
- ❏ Orange extract
- ❏ Peanut oil
- ❏ Salt
- ❏ Sherry vinegar
- ❏ Vegetable oil
- ❏ Walnut oil

*Suggested accompaniments

ROASTED TURKEY BREAST
WITH FENNEL AND
WILD RICE DRESSING
SAUTEED LIMA BEANS *
BREAD PUDDING WITH
CRANBERRIES
ICE CREAM *

Don't save turkey and the works just for the end of the month: the flavors of wild rice, crunchy and anise-flavored fennel, cranberries and turkey start tasting good as soon as the weather turns cold. Cook the rice and cornbread ahead of time, and save some for later meals. This meal should provide lots of leftovers. Purchase a 5- to 7-pound turkey breast. Rub it outside of the turkey with butter and maple syrup or cider and either stuff it or bake the dressing in a casserole dish. Don't miss the wonderful bread pudding adapted from *Jasper White's Cooking From New England* (Harper & Row, $27.95).

WILD RICE DRESSING

Makes 8 to 10 servings
Preparation time: 25 minutes
Cooking time: 45 minutes

¼ pound lean bacon, cubed
1 medium onion, chopped
½ fennel bulb, diced
4 ounces mushrooms, sliced
¼ teaspoon black pepper
4 or 5 fresh sage leaves
2 cups cooked wild rice
2 to 3 cups corn bread crumbs
4 tablespoons unsalted butter,
    melted
½ cup low-sodium chicken broth

Preheat oven to 325 degrees.

Brown the bacon in a large skillet, then drain the fat. In the same skillet, saute onions and fennel in the drippings until softened and golden brown, about 8 minutes. Add the mushrooms, pepper and sage; saute, stirring occasionally, for 5 to 8 minutes. Stir in cooked wild rice, corn bread crumbs, butter and chicken broth and toss until it forms a damp mass. (Put this in a large mixing bowl or roasting pan if the skillet isn't big enough.) Put in a baking dish and bake 45 minutes, or stuff the cavity of the turkey and roast according to the size of the turkey.
Per 1-cup serving: 423 calories, 20 grams fat, 37 milligrams cholesterol, 477 milligrams sodium.

BREAD PUDDING WITH CRANBERRIES

Makes 10 servings
Preparation time: 20 minutes
Resting time: 10 minutes
Cooking time: 30 minutes

6 tablespoons unsalted butter, melted
6 to 8 slices stale sour dough or
    French bread, cut ½ to ¾-
    inch thick, crusts removed
1 cup fresh or frozen cranberries
½ cup chopped walnuts
3 cups milk
6 whole eggs
¾ cup sugar
1 teaspoon orange extract

Grease a loaf pan with butter, shortening or pan spray and set aside. Scatter half the cranberries and half the walnuts over bottom of baking dish. Brush both sides of bread pieces with melted butter and layer the bread so pieces overlap slightly.
Preheat the oven to 350 degrees.
Mix the milk, eggs, sugar and orange extract in a bowl until smooth. Pour the custard over the bread and cranberries; let it sit for 10 minutes, occasionally pushing down on the bread so it absorbs as much custard as possible.
Sprinkle the remaining cranberries and walnuts over the bread and bake for 30 minutes or until edges are golden brown and the center set. Let the pudding sit for 10 or 15 minutes before serving. Cut into squares to serve.
Per serving: 339 calories, 15 grams fat, 188 milligrams cholesterol, 252 milligrams sodium.

FRENCH ONION SOUP
GREEN SALAD*
COFFEECAKE *

If you can, use the full cooking times called for in the soup recipe to bring out the sweet onion flavor and to develop more body in the soup. Miso adds a wonderful salty flavor and makes a great meatless substitute for beef broth. Extra soup can be refrigerated and served later — just replace the toasted bread and cheese topping. Add a big green salad and a moist coffeecake.

FRENCH ONION SOUP

Makes 6 servings
Preparation time: 10 minutes
Cooking time: 1 hour

4 tablespoons unsalted butter
3 medium onions, thinly sliced
2 cups dry white wine
2 cups water
3 to 4 tablespoons red (dark) miso
    (or 1 beef boullion cube)
Salt and pepper to taste
6 slices sourdough or French bread

NOVEMBER

Some nappa cabbage supplies have black spots due to aphid damage, but as the weather gets cooler, the bug problems should disappear. Every variety of winter squash is available at rock bottom prices.

With the Florida rains continuing, some vegetables are scarce and expensive, such as pole beans, celery and summer squashes, and prices may go higher. Cauliflower is very high now and broccoli may jump any day.

Thanksgiving produce is looking good this week, with good quality and prices on cranberries, most nuts, squash and beans. Asparagus is coming from Chili and Argentina, and prices vary according to the country of origin. Yukon Gold, Yellow Finn and extra-sweet organic purple potatoes will add flavor and a new look to the Thanksgiving table.

A fresh harvest of pecans is in; look for paler skins and moist nut meat to be sure you are getting the new harvest. Fresh chestnuts are in from Italy. They are delicious in the shell and easy to roast in the fire, or peeled can be added to sauteed vegetables or turkey stuffing. A little frost has sweetened up the collards and turnip and mustard greens, but head lettuce has some tip-burn problems, which isn't noticeable until you cut open the lettuce.

Hamlin oranges are tasting great, and navel oranges are excellent too. Mineola tangelos, an early variety that will be in stock for a few months, are in, juicy and sweeter than this normally tart fruit. Lemons and limes are cheap. Look for lots of apple varieties of excellent value. The late season varieties are very tangy, crisp and juicy, so enjoy them for a few more months. Fresh Medjool dates are in some stores through the holidays.

Chilean fruit has started. The sizes are small but flavor is excellent. California avocados are well priced and available, but Florida avocados are more scarce. Citrus continues with great quality and prices, and a wide variety of winter apples continue to be available — look for the newest variety, a red Granny Smith, at local farmers markets. Look for the newly-arrived Honey tangerine — the sweetest of them all. Florida juice oranges continue to get sweeter.

Florida citrus is in full swing, with delicious grapefruit at good prices, navel oranges and sweet kumquats. Look for lots of apple varieties right now, especially the Braeburn and Fuji, Jonagold and Mutsu.

The large green Florida avocados have a couple more weeks before they finish. Look for California Haas to continue, and the Chilean Haas to start next week; prices may fluctuate due to the two suppliers.

Prices are still good on California grapes, while Washington State apple prices are higher than Eastern apples. Central American pineapple is quite inexpensive right now.

With so much produce coming in from Georgia and North Florida, prices are stable and quality is excellent. As long as the weather holds up with no frosts, all the vegetables should be of good quality. With a frost, look for potential problems with celery and other leafy vegetables. Sweet potatoes are looking good now, with the Red Jewel and honey-colored Vardeman cooking and baking the same; the only difference is the pigment of the flesh. Idaho and russet potatoes are also being harvested.

6 thin slices Gruyere or Swiss cheese
Freshly grated Parmesan cheese

Melt the butter in a heavy, large pot over medium heat. Add onions and saute until deep golden brown, stirring occasionally, 10 to 20 minutes. Add the wine; cover and cook 10 minutes. Add both stocks and water and bring to a boil. Reduce heat and simmer uncovered 5 minutes, stirring occasionally. Stir in miso, then season to taste with salt and pepper. Meanwhile, toast the bread slices and preheat the broiler.

Ladle soup into broiler-proof soup crocks. Top with toasted bread and cheese slices and broil just until the cheese melts and bubbles. Sprinkle with Parmesan cheese and serve.

Per serving with 1 teaspoon Parmesan, ¹/₂ ounce Swiss and 1 slice bread: 284 calories, 13 grams fat, 36 milligrams cholesterol, 706 milligrams sodium.

TUESDAY

GRILLED ROSEMARY
PORK CHOPS
BAKED NEW POTATOES *
STEAMED GREEN BEANS
WITH SHERRY VINEGAR *

Besides offering a delicious pork dish, this is a night of generating leftovers: cook two extra pork chops and save 2 cups of cooked potatoes and green beans for later in the week.

GRILLED ROSEMARY PORK CHOPS

Makes 6 servings
Preparation time: 5 minutes
Cooking time: 10 minutes

6 8-ounce pork chops

4 to 6 teaspoons peanut oil
2 tablespoons fresh rosemary leaves, chopped and crushed to release their fragrance
Salt and pepper to taste

Preheat the broiler and place the rack 6 to 8 inches from the heat.

Brush the chops with peanut oil, then sprinkle them with the rosemary, salt and pepper. Put the chops on a broiling pan and broil 4 to 6 minutes per side.

Per serving: 475 calories, 30 grams fat, 162 milligrams cholesterol, 126 milligrams sodium.

WEDNESDAY

RAMEN NOODLES WITH
PORK AND FENNEL
FRESH, RIPE PERSIMMONS *

Two packages of ramen noodles, with pork, chopped fennel and onions added, make an instant dinner that's substantial and fragrant.

RAMEN NOODLES WITH PORK AND FENNEL

Makes 4 servings
Preparation time: 10 minutes
Cooking time: 15 minutes

1 tablespoon vegetable oil
¹/₂ cup chopped onion
¹/₂ bulb fennel, sliced thin
2 14 ¹/₂-ounce cans chicken or vegetable broth
2 4-ounce packages ramen noodles
2 cooked pork chops, cut into 1-inch cubes
¹/₂ cup cooked green beans
Dash hot chili oil

In a medium skillet, heat the oil, then saute the onion and celery 5 minutes. Add the chicken broth

and bring to a boil. Add the noodles and cook 5 minutes, until the noodles are soft. Add the pork and green beans and serve in soup bowls. Sprinkle a dash or two of hot chili oil on each serving.

Per serving: 385 calories, 21 grams fat, 82 milligrams cholesterol, 880 milligrams sodium.

THURSDAY

POTATOES, LEEKS
AND CHEESE
CORN BREAD *

Reheat leftover cornbread from Sunday's dinner, sprinkled with water if it is a little dry. Break the bread up in a large, shallow bowl and spoon the potato mixture over.

POTATOES, LEEKS AND CHEESE

Makes 4 servings
Preparation time: 5 minutes
Cooking time: 15 minutes

¹/₄ cup chicken broth or 2 tablespoons butter
1 leek, white part only, sliced thin
2 cups cooked potatoes, sliced, at room temperature
1¹/₂ to ³/₄ cup grated Cheddar cheese

In a heavy skillet, heat the broth and saute the leeks until soft, about 5 minutes. Add the potatoes and continue to cook until heated through, stirring occasionally, about 8 to 10 minutes. Remove from the heat, sprinkle with grated cheese and put the cover on the pot for a minute to melt the cheese.

Per serving, using chicken broth: 127

Price: Wild rice prices vary according to harvesting technique, growing location and grades. The longest grains are from Canada, are often organic and have the least amount of polishing or milling. Hand-harvested lake rice and organic will be more expensive; smaller grains with more polishing (that which is machine-harvested and blends with brown or long-grain white rice) will be considerably cheaper. It comes in packages as small as 4 ounces up to a pound or can be purchased bulk at farmers markets and health food stores. Packaged prices average $1.95 for 4 ounces (average $8.64 a pound) to bulk supplies at about $7.00 a pound.

Nutrition: A half-cup cooked serving has 70 calories, is low in fat and is a good source of protein, B vitamins, minerals and fiber.

Selection: Choose kernels that are dry and whole and not broken or soft.

Storage: Store wild rice in a sealed container in the refrigerator. One hundred percent wild rice will keep 5 years, while blends will keep 1 year.

Uses: The rice multiplies four times during cooking. Cook it and serve alone, as a side dish to game and poultry or add to soups, casseroles and other baked dishes. Cooked and chilled, it is excellent in salads

Wild rice has for too long been a premium product. Today, prices are getting more reasonable, and because this nutty-flavored whole grain is

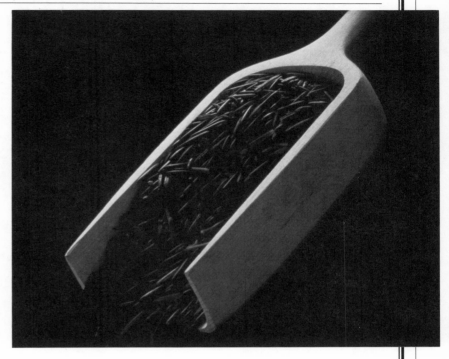

so nutritious and cooks to such great volume, the price has become reachable for more people. While wild rice is available year round, it complements winter foods and hearty flavors of the holiday season. Look for it in packages, in bulk and in blends with other rices in most stores.

For centuries, the Anishinabe (pronounced Ojibwe) Indian tribe in Minnesota has harvested this autumn grain from their canoes, paddling through the northern lakes. Today, they continue to harvest it the same way, and this rice, now labeled "Lake rice," draws premium prices.

A much larger commercial harvest comes from rice paddies in California, Oregon and Idaho, and the larger harvest has helped to bring prices down.

Cooking instructions in recipes often cause confusion. Some call for presoaking, and cooking times can vary from 20 to 60 minutes. The longest, blackest kernels have had less processing and polishing and will take the longest to cook, while smaller kernels that have had more of the bran polished off can cook in as little as 20 minutes. Presoaking can shorten cooking time by 15 minutes on the largest grains.

Take care to not overcook the rice; especially if it is to go into a casserole or soup with further cooking. Overcooked rice will split open to show its' white interior and will be starchy and mushy.

calories, 5 grams fat, 15 milligrams cholesterol, 143 milligrams sodium.

FRIDAY

TURKEY AND STUFFING ROLL-UPS
GREEN SALAD*
BREAD PUDDING WITH CRANBERRIES*

Make this sandwich from the week's leftover turkey, stuffing, even cranberry sauce.

TURKEY AND STUFFING ROLL-UPS

Makes 4 servings
Preparation time: 10 minutes
Cooking time: 15 minutes

8 large slices cooked turkey
2 cups leftover wild rice stuffing
4 to 8 tablespoons cranberry sauce
4 slices ($1/8$-inch thick) Cheddar
    cheese (optional)
1 cup potatoes, leeks and cheese, left
    over (optional)

Preheat the oven to 350 degrees.

Lay a slice of turkey on a plate. Fill it with a few spoonfuls of stuffing, cranberry sauce, cheese and potatoes and top with a second turkey slice. Roll up the sandwiches as if they were crepes, and secure them with a toothpick.

Place the roll-ups in a baking pan and cover the top with aluminum foil. Bake for 15 minutes or until the ingredients are warmed through. Serve hot.

Per serving, using 3 ounces turkey and 1/2 ounce cheese: 509 calories, 25 grams fat, 81 milligrams cholesterol, 560 milligrams sodium.

SATURDAY

RAVIOLI WITH MUSHROOM AND SAGE SAUCE
WATERCRESS AND SPINACH SALAD*
LEMON COOKIES*

Take advantage of pre-made ravioli to make tonight's wintry dinner, adapted from *The New Basics* by Julee Rosso & Sheila Lukins (Workman, $18.95). For the salad, toss watercress and fresh spinach with a vinaigrette made with walnut oil and a fruity vinegar.

RAVIOLI WITH MUSHROOM AND SAGE SAUCE

Makes 4 servings
Preparation time: 40 minutes
Cooking time: 20 minutes

$1/4$ cup cognac
$1/4$ cup chicken broth
4 ounces cremini mushrooms,
    stemmed and sliced
$1/2$ cup fresh sage leaves, coarsely
    chopped
8 tablespoons (1 stick) unsalted
    butter
1 cup crushed tomatoes with Italian
    seasonings
Vegetable oil
1 pound fresh vegetables or cheese
    ravioli
$1/2$ cup toasted walnuts

Put the cognac and chicken broth in a large saucepan and bring to a boil. Add the mushrooms and simmer, uncovered for 5 to 8 minutes. Remove the mushrooms and pat dry.

Melt the butter in a large, shallow saucepan. Add the sage, mushroom cooking liquid and tomatoes and cook over medium heat for 5 to 10 minutes, uncovered, until the mixture evaporates and thickens some. Stir in the cooked mushrooms and cook, uncovered, a few minutes longer to develop the flavors.

Meanwhile, cook ravioli. To serve, drain the ravioli, toss with the sage sauce and garnish with walnuts.

Per serving: 537 calories, 37 grams fat, 72 milligrams cholesterol, 192 milligrams sodium.

WEEK 45

SHOPPING LIST

Meat, poultry, seafood

- ❑ 4 pounds boneless beef chuck
- ❑ 4 to 6 pork chops
- ❑ 4 to 5 pounds stone crab claws

Produce

- ❑ 4 pounds all-purpose potatoes
- ❑ 1 pound green beans
- ❑ 1 bunch Swiss chard
- ❑ 11-pound bag carrots
- ❑ 15-pound bag yellow onions
- ❑ 2 cloves garlic
- ❑ 24 ounces brown cremini mushrooms
- ❑ 1 ounce dried porcini mushrooms
- ❑ 2 red bell peppers
- ❑ 2 small acorn squash
- ❑ 1 head Romaine lettuce
- ❑ 4 ounces firm tofu
- ❑ 1 large (or 2 smaller) bunches mint
- ❑ 1 bunch fresh rosemary
- ❑ 1 bunch Italian parsley
- ❑ 5 bananas
- ❑ 3 large pears, Comice or Bosc
- ❑ 2 lemons
- ❑ 1 large Persian lime or 2 or 3 Key limes
- ❑ 2 persimmons

Dairy

- ❑ 3 sticks plus 1 tablespoon unsalted butter
- ❑ 9 eggs
- ❑ 1 pint whipping cream
- ❑ 1 pint vanilla ice cream or yogurt
- ❑ $^1/_3$ cup sour cream

Deli

- ❑ 2 loaves crusty bread
- ❑ 4 ounces freshly grated Parmesan cheese
- ❑ 4 whole wheat pita breads
- ❑ 1 cup dry bulgur
- ❑ 4 blueberry muffins
- ❑ 8 ounces oyster crackers

Miscellaneous

- ❑ 2 14 $^1/_2$ ounce cans beef broth
- ❑ 4 14 $^1/_2$-ounce cans unsalted chicken broth
- ❑ 8 ounce pasta wheels, spirals or shells
- ❑ $^1/_3$ cup pecans
- ❑ $^1/_2$ cup unsalted peanuts
- ❑ $^1/_4$ cup rum
- ❑ 15-ounce jar black olives
- ❑ 1 14-ounce can artichoke hearts
- ❑ 1 16-ounce can garbanzo beans
- ❑ $^1/_3$ cup apple butter
- ❑ 2 tablespoons Amaretto
- ❑ 1 cup Creole or other stone-ground mustard
- ❑ 1 10-inch pie crust
- ❑ $^1/_4$ cup sesame seeds (optional), unhulled if possible

Staples

- ❑ All-purpose flour
- ❑ Baking soda
- ❑ Black pepper
- ❑ Brown sugar
- ❑ Corn meal
- ❑ Granulated sugar
- ❑ Hungarian paprika
- ❑ Lemon juice
- ❑ Olive oil
- ❑ Peanut oil
- ❑ Pure vanilla extract
- ❑ Salt
- ❑ Self-rising flour
- ❑ Tomato paste
- ❑ Vegetable oil
- ❑ Vinaigrette

RAGOUT OF BEEF WITH MUSHROOMS
MASHED POTATOES*
STEAMED MIXED VEGETABLES*
BANANA CORN MEAL CAKE

Cold weather comes just in time for this fabulous beef stew. After a few minutes preparation of chopping and sauteing, the pot goes in the oven to cook. Use the most flavorful mushrooms you can find — the brown Italian cremini are robust and meaty, and dried porcini will add depth to the flavors of the dish. Beef leftovers won't be used until Friday night, so it would be wise to freeze the remains of tonight's dinner until then.

Add mashed potatoes and a mixture of steamed vegetables — swiss chard, green beans and carrots, fennel or squash. Toss the vegetables with lemon juice and fresh herbs, such as parsley or mint. Cook extra potatoes and vegetables to use later in the week. Corn meal adds sweetness and crunch to the banana cake. It is quite dense and should offer leftovers during the week.

RAGOUT OF BEEF WITH MUSHROOMS

Makes 6 to 8 servings
Preparation time: 10 minutes
Cooking time: 1 1/2 hours

4 pounds boneless beef chuck, cut into 1-inch cubes
5 to 7 tablespoons vegetable oil
Salt and pepper to taste
3 large onions chopped
2 garlic cloves, minced
1 teaspoon imported Hungarian paprika
2 tablespoons tomato paste
2 14 1/2-ounce cans beef broth
1 1/2 pounds cremini mushrooms, stemmed and sliced
2 teaspoons peanut oil
1 ounce dried porcini mushrooms
Italian parsley, minced, for garnish

Preheat oven to 350 degrees.

Heat half the vegetable oil in a heavy Dutch oven over medium-high heat. Add the beef cubes a few at a time and saute until well browned on all sides, seasoning with salt and pepper. Use more oil as needed. Remove the meat and reserve.

Add the onions and garlic to the pot, and cook over low heat until the onions become soft and fragrant, but do not let them burn, 8 to 10 minutes. Stir in the paprika, tomato paste, cooked onion mixture and all but 1 cup of the beef broth, bring to a boil, lower heat and simmer, covered. Reserve the 1 cup broth to cook the dried mushrooms.

Meanwhile, in a medium skillet, heat the peanut oil over medium heat. Add the cremini mushrooms and saute until lightly browned; add to the beef and onion mixture. Put the pot in the oven, covered and braise for 1 hour.

While the beef is braising, rinse the porcini mushrooms to remove sand. Put the porcini in a small saucepan with 1 cup reserved beef broth; and simmer over medium heat for 10 to 15 minutes, or until they are tender. Discard the broth and cut the porcini mushrooms into fine julienne and set aside.

When the beef is tender, remove it from the pot with a slotted spoon to a side dish. If the pan juices are too thin, bring to a boil on top of stove, uncovered, and reduce slightly. Whisk in bits of beurre manie (see recipe below) until the sauce thickens. Add salt and pepper to taste. Sprinkle the stew with the porcini and parsley and serve.

Per serving: 664 calories, 36 grams fat, 222 milligrams cholesterol, 495 milligrams sodium.

BUERRE MANIE

Makes 2 servings
Preparation time: 5 minutes

2 tablespoons unsalted butter, softened
2 tablespoons all-purpose flour

Combine the butter and flour in the workbowl of a food processor and process until smooth. Refrigerate the mixture until it is firm enough to shape with your hands into small balls. Refrigerate the balls or they can be frozen for 2 to 3 months.

Per serving: 129 calories, 11 grams fat, 31 milligrams cholesterol, 2 milligrams sodium.

BANANA CORN MEAL CAKE

Makes 16 to 20 servings
Preparation time: 20 minutes
Cooking time: 45 minutes

STREUSEL:
1/3 cup chopped pecans
1/2 cup all-purpose flour
1/4 cup packed brown sugar
1/4 cup (1/2 stick) butter or margarine, melted

1 1/2 cups sugar
2 eggs
1 1/4 cups mashed ripe banana (about 4 medium)
1/4 cup rum
1 teaspoon vanilla
1 1/2 cups self-rising flour
3/4 cup corn meal
1/2 teaspoon baking soda
Whipped cream
Banana slices

Preheat oven to 350 degrees. Grease a 10-inch tube pan.

Add the pecans to a food

Price: Will average $.85 to $1.00 each for large fruit.

Nutrition: One 3 ¹/₂-ounce serving of persimmon has 77 calories and is an excellent source of vitamin A, a good source of fiber, potassium and phosphorus, has three times as much vitamin C as citrus fruits, and is low in sodium.

Selection: Generally two varieties of California-grown fruit are available September through mid-December; during other months the fruit probably comes from Chili. Two varieties are generally available and both should be deep, rich orange with no trace of yellow color. The flesh of some persimmons may show some black discoloration, but it should not affect quality. The acorn-shaped Hachiya should be completely soft to lose its astringency. The rounder-shaped Fuyu may be crisp-hard. The Hachiya must be completely ripened and soft to be edible, while the Fuyu will be sweet and can be eaten while still crisp.

Storage: To ripen persimmons, place the fruit in a plastic bag stem- side up with a cut-up apple or pour a few drops of rum, bourbon or other liquor on a paper towel and add it to the bag before closing. The fruit or liquor will produce ethylene fumes which will speed ripening in three to six days. Do not try to ripen persimmons by freezing, as they will remain bitter and become very mushy.

Uses: One large, soft persimmon yields 3/4 to 1 cup

puree. One large crisp persimmon yields ³/₄ to 1 cup sliced fruit. Serve the fruit melting-soft by slicing in half and scooping out the soft pulp, broil with brown sugar or use the pureed pulp in puddings, breads and pies, much as you would pureed pumpkin. The fruit also dries beautifully.

Persimmons can be as sweet as liquid nectar or as puckery as a lemon, a characteristic the Japanese have been working to subdue for centuries. Either way, this fruit which is growing in popularity in America, is in season for the next couple of months and available at all local grocery stores and farmers markets.

They are a luxurious fruit, a combination of plum, mango and honey. Perhaps at their best

when least tampered with, they are wonderful to eat simply out of the peel with a spoon. Some Californians simply cut off the top and eat the fruit as they would a grapefruit.

Two Japanese varieties grown in California are the predominant varieties available commercially. These fruits are large and opulent and are considered the quality standard for persimmons. A few Georgia farmers have started growing the Fuyu variety in the south part of the state, and local agriculture researchers think it is an ideal crop for the Southeast, according to Jerry Payne, lead scientist for the fruit unit at the USDA's Southeastern Fruit and Tree Nut Research Laboratory at Byron, Georgia.

processor and process until chopped. Add flour, brown sugar and butter, process just until crumbly. Set aside.

In a mixer, beat together the butter and sugar until fluffy. (You may use the food processor also, but will get less volume.) Add eggs, one at a time, beating well after each addition. Blend in banana, rum and vanilla. Add combined dry ingredients, mixing just until blended. Pour into prepared pan. Sprinkle with streusel mixture.

Bake 45 minutes or until a wooden pick inserted in center comes out clean. Cool completely, then remove from the pan. Garnish with (optional) sweetened whipped cream and banana slices, if desired.

MONDAY

ANTIPASTO PLATTER
OF BLACK OLIVES
AND ARTICHOKE
HEARTS*
BEAN SOUP WITH
PASTA SHELLS
CRUSTY BREAD

If a meal made with one complex carbohydrate is good, why can't two be better? This warming and nurturing pasta soup gets its thickening power from garbanzo beans, cooked with fragrant rosemary and pureed. Add a ladle of last-night's beef ragout to the simmering stew if you like. Save any soup leftovers for later in the week.

Add artichoke hearts, perhaps lightly tossed in the saute pan with some butter, and a crusty, chewy bread perfect for dipping into the soup.

BEAN SOUP WITH PASTA SHELLS

Makes 6 servings
Preparation time: 5 minutes
Cooking time: 15 minutes

1 medium yellow onion, chopped
2 tablespoons fresh rosemary leaves, chopped
3 tablespoons olive oil
1 16-ounce can garbanzo beans, drained
2 to 3 tablespoons Italian parsley leaves, roughly chopped
6 chicken boullion cubes and 6 or 8 cups water, or 2 quarts low-sodium chicken broth
8 ounces pasta wheels, spirals or shells
2 to 3 tablespoons freshly grated Parmesan cheese
1 tablespoon olive oil (optional)

Heat the oil in a large frying pan. Add the onion and saute until golden and fragrant, about 5 minutes. Add the garbanzo beans and parsley; saute for five minutes.

Remove half the onion-bean mixture and puree; set aside. Add the chicken broth to the remaining beans, bring to a boil and add the pasta. When the pasta is cooked, 8 to 10 minutes, stir in the pureed beans. Serve with grated cheese and parsley and a splash of (optional) olive oil.

TUESDAY

BULGUR SALAD WITH
TOFU AND PEANUTS
HOT PITA BREAD*

Tonight, serve this healthy dinner of the wonderful nutty-tasting bulgur (cracked, roasted wheat berries), vegetables and tofu, adapted from *Monday through Friday* by Michele Urvater (Workman Publishing, $14.95). Warm, the salad is good stuffed into pita breads; serve later as a cold salad or stuffed into bell peppers. A finely-ground bulgur will absorb the liquid quicker, but won't have that special crunch we bulgur-lovers crave. Look for the finer-ground in the produce section, where folks might be looking for tabouli ingredients; the coarser-ground, organic supplies are available in health food stores. Substitute cashews or other nuts, if you wish. Soy sauce or miso makes a great flavor substitution for salt in this dish.

BULGUR SALAD WITH TOFU AND PEANUTS

Makes 6 to 8 servings
Preparation time: 15 minutes

4 whole wheat pita breads, cut in half
1 cup bulgur
$1/4$ cup sesame seeds (optional), unhulled, if possible
2 cups boiling, salted water
1 red bell pepper, seeded and diced
$1/4$ cup lemon juice
$1/2$ cup unsalted peanuts
$1/4$ cup packed mint leaves
$1/3$ cup good-quality peanut oil (unrefined or Loriva brand)
Salt and black pepper to taste
4 ounces firm tofu, diced

Turn the oven to 300 degrees and heat the halved pita breads for 5 minutes.

Combine the bulgur with boiling, salted water in a large bowl and let sit until the bulgur has softened and absorbed the water, 10 to 30 minutes. Drain the bulgur and press out any excess water with your hand.

Put the pepper, lemon juice, peanuts, mint and oil in the workbowl of a food processor and process until smooth; season to taste with salt and pepper. Stir in the drained bulgur, sesame seeds and tofu; toss everything well. Serve the salad at room temperature.

Per serving: 267 calories, 15 grams fat, no cholesterol, 113 milligrams sodium.

WEDNESDAY

PAN-FRIED PORK CHOPS*
MASHED POTATO PANCAKES*
STEAMED VEGETABLES
TOSSED WITH VINAIGRETTE*
AMARETTO PEARS

A homey meal here with a splash of an ending; the dessert is nice enough for company, but why not give your family the treat?

Choose the butter-smooth Comice or slightly grainier Bosc pears. After slicing, get them cooking quickly, otherwise you will need to sprinkle them with lemon juice or Fruit Fresh to prevent darkening. The pears are lower-fat when broiled, but you can just as easily saute them in a bit of butter on top of the stove, tossing them with the apple butter as they warm. The almond flavor of Amaretto explodes during cooking; if you have a handful of slivered almonds, throw them in the pot as well.

Make potato pancakes from Sunday's leftover potatoes and toss leftover steamed vegetables as well.

AMARETTO PEARS

Makes 4 servings
Preparation time: 5 minutes
Cooking time: 5 minutes

2 or 3 large, ripe pears, such as Comice or Bosc
2 tablespoons cold butter or margarine (optional)
1/4 to 1/3 cup apple butter
1 to 2 tablespoons Amaretto
1 pint vanilla ice cream or yogurt

Preheat the broiler.

Peel, halve and core the pears. Slice the halves in 1/4-inch thick slices and fan them out on a cookie sheet. Dot the slices with apple butter and sprinkle with Amaretto. Place under the broiler a couple of minutes, just until the apple butter sizzles. Serve the pears warm with ice cream or yogurt.

Per serving: 245 calories, 13 grams fat, 45 milligrams cholesterol, 117 milligrams sodium.

THURSDAY

BULGUR STUFFED IN AN
ACORN SQUASH
BLUEBERRY MUFFINS*

The flavors of winter squash and bulgur go together perfectly and fit into most weeknight schedules. While precooking the squash in the microwave oven will speed up meal time, the slower, dry cooking in the oven will bring out the squash's sweetest flavor. Add purchased blueberry muffins for a nutritious vegetarian dinner.

BULGUR STUFFED IN AN ACORN SQUASH

Makes 4 servings

Preparation time: 10 minutes
Cooking time 30 minutes

2 small acorn squash
2 cups leftover bulgur salad
1/2 to 1 red bell pepper
1/4 cup vinaigrette made with peanut oil

Preheat the oven to 350 degrees.

Cut open the acorn squash and remove the seeds and membrane. Sprinkle the halves with water and place in a microwave oven and cook for 10 minutes on high.

Meanwhile, cut the bell pepper into dice. Stir the bell pepper and vinaigrette into the bulgur salad. When the squash is finished cooking, stuff the halves with the bulgur mixture. Place in a baking dish, add a cup or two of water to the bottom of the pan and bake for about 30 minutes, or until the squash is soft and cooked.

Per serving: 494 calories, 11 grams fat, no cholesterol, 15 milligrams sodium.

FRIDAY

FRIDAY SOUP*
OYSTER CRACKERS*
BANANA CORN MEAL
CAKE*

When it comes to soup, the aged flavors of leftovers can't be duplicated with new ingredients. Stir together Sunday's beef ragout, leftover pasta soup, a handful of steamed vegetables and unattached fresh herbs — rosemary and Italian parsley, and simmer the lot together.

STONE CRAB CLAWS WITH
MUSTARD SAUCE
CRUSTY BREAD*
CAESAR SALAD*
LEMON TART WITH FRESH
PERSIMMON SLICES

Stone crab is too good by itself, so don't hide its wonderful, lobster-like flavor with heavy sauces or complicated cooking instructions. They come from Florida precooked, so a short time in boiling water is all they need. This recipe is adapted from one of Florida's newest popular chefs, Norman Van Aken, in his book *Feast of Sunlight* (Ballantine Books, $22.50). Serve the crab with a grainy mustard mayonnaise, Caesar salad and lemon tart made with the first tart Florida lemons of the season. And don't be shy about putting a lobster napkin at your neck.

STONE CRAB CLAWS WITH MUSTARD SAUCE

Makes 4 servings
Preparation time: 5 minutes
Cooking time: 5 minutes

4 to 5 pounds stone crab claws
1 cup Creole mustard
1/3 cup low-fat sour cream
2 to 4 tablespoon fresh lime juice
The grated peel of 1 Persian or 2
    Key limes

Bring a large pot of water to a boil. When it is boiling, add the crab claws and allow the water to return to a boil. When it does, the crab claws are heated through.

In a bowl, combine the mustard, sour cream, lime juice and peel. To serve, put a thick towel on the counter and crack the crab shells open. A firm rap with a small hammer or the back of a large knife works well. Serve the sections of crab and pass the mustard sauce.

Per serving: 159 calories, 5.5 grams fat, 65 milligrams cholesterol, 1,629 milligrams sodium.

LEMON TART WITH FRESH PERSIMMON SLICES

Makes 8 servings
Preparation time: 20 minutes
Cooking time: 1 hour 15 minutes

1 10-inch pie crust
5 large eggs
1 large egg yolk
1 cup sugar
2/3 cup whipping cream
5 tablespoons fresh lemon juice
3 tablespoons finely chopped lemon
    peel (yellow part only)
2 ripe Japanese persimmons, thinly
    sliced
1 tablespoon brown sugar

Preheat oven to 325 degrees. Grease and lightly flour a 10-inch-diameter tart pan with removable bottom. Roll dough out on lightly floured surface to 12-inch round; transfer the dough to prepared pan; finish edges. Refrigerate crust 15 minutes.

To prebake the crust, line it with parchment or foil, then fill with dried beans or pie weights. Bake until crust is set, about 10 minutes. Remove beans and parchment, bake crust until golden brown, 15 to 20 minutes more. Transfer to rack and cool. Maintain oven temperature.

To make the filling, whisk together the eggs, yolk and sugar in a medium bowl. Gradually mix in cream, lemon and chopped peel.

Pour the filling into crust and bake until filling is set, about 40 minutes. Cool to room temperature on rack.

To serve, slice the tart and serve with slices of persimmon, sprinkled with brown sugar.

Per serving: 351 calories, 19 grams fat, 232 milligrams cholesterol, 189 milligrams sodium.

WEEK

46

SHOPPING LIST

Meat, poultry, seafood

- ❏ 3 ¹/₂ to 4 pounds chicken pieces
- ❏ 1 pound crab meat
- ❏ 4 10-ounce salmon steaks

Produce

- ❏ 2 bunches spinach
- ❏ ¹/₂ pound mustard greens
- ❏ 2 large onions
- ❏ 1 medium green pepper
- ❏ 1 head garlic
- ❏ 3 medium carrots
- ❏ 1 small butternut squash
- ❏ 5 medium-to-large white potatoes
- ❏ 2 medium zucchini
- ❏ 1 medium yellow squash
- ❏ 2 large fennel (anise) bulbs
- ❏ 1 pound mushrooms, shiitake (and large white combined, optional)
- ❏ 4 pears

- ❏ 1 lemon
- ❏ 1 pineapple, cored and peeled
- ❏ 2 juice oranges
- ❏ 6 apples
- ❏ 1 bunch fresh thyme
- ❏ 1 bunch fresh rosemary (optional)
- ❏ 1 bunch chives
- ❏ 1 bunch cilantro
- ❏ 1 2-ounce knob fresh ginger

Dairy

- ❏ 1 stick plus 5 tablespoons unsalted butter
- ❏ 1 egg
- ❏ 1 cup buttermilk
- ❏ 4 ounces Pepper Jack or Monterey Jack cheese (grated or block)

Deli

- ❏ 2 ounces blue cheese
- ❏ 8 corn tortillas

- ❏ 1 loaf crusty bread
- ❏ 4 pita breads, whole-wheat or white flour
- ❏ ¹/₂ pound cake
- ❏ 1 10-ounce jar Creole mustard

Miscellaneous

- ❏ 1 8-ounce jar lemon curd
- ❏ 2 14 ¹/₂-ounce cans stewed tomatoes
- ❏ 1 19-ounce can garbanzo beans
- ❏ ¹/₄ cup raisins
- ❏ 1 cup couscous
- ❏ 29-ounce package Trio's Hot Red Pepper Linguini
- ❏ 4 ounces walnut halves
- ❏ 3 to 3 ¹/₂ cups chicken stock
- ❏ ¹/₂ cup dry white wine (optional)
- ❏ 1 10-ounce package frozen raspberries in lite syrup

Staples

- ❏ Black pepper
- ❏ Brown sugar
- ❏ Cider vinegar
- ❏ Cinnamon
- ❏ Ground cumin
- ❏ Honey
- ❏ Hot sauce (optional)
- ❏ Minced garlic in olive oil
- ❏ Olive oil
- ❏ Parmesan cheese
- ❏ Salt
- ❏ Self-rising flour
- ❏ Turmeric
- ❏ Vegetable oil
- ❏ Walnut oil (optional)

SUNDAY

COUSCOUS WITH CHICKEN
MIXED SPINACH SALAD*
GINGERBREAD WITH
LEMON CURD

The beguiling fragrances that waft through the kitchen while cooking this Moroccan stew are only the beginning — the flavors that follow are even better. Don't let the list of ingredients scare you; many are seasonings, and as the dish cooks away you have time to do other things. And the dish, adapted from *Jane Brody's Good Food Book* (Bantam, $13.95) offers plenty of leftovers. You will cut the fat in half by first skinning the chicken pieces. Couscous pasta — tiny grains of semolina pasta — is available in some grocery, health and specialty stores and farmers markets. The Near East brand is a common one and Casbah makes a whole-wheat version that is delicious. Add a few strands of saffron during cooking if you wish.

The combination of fresh ginger and lemon makes the dessert memorable, and the flavors go well with couscous. On the gingerbread, spread purchased or homemade lemon curd, a cooked mixture of lemon juice and eggs available at some grocery stores and specialty stores. The gingerbread recipe makes enough servings for desserts later in the week.

COUSCOUS WITH CHICKEN

Makes 8 servings
Preparation time: 15 minutes
Cooking time: 45 minutes

1 large onion, sliced
2 large cloves garlic, minced
1 tablespoon olive oil
3 ½ to 4 pounds mixed chicken pieces, skinned
Salt and black pepper to taste
2 14 ½-ounce cans stewed tomatoes, undrained
3 medium carrots, cut into 1-inch lengths
1 butternut squash, halved, seeded and pulp cut into 1-inch chunks
1 teaspoon cinnamon
½ teaspoon ground cumin
¼ teaspoon turmeric
Several dashes hot sauce
2 teaspoons honey
1 zucchini, sliced
¼ cup raisins
1 19-ounce can garbanzo beans, drained
1 cup couscous
1/4 cup minced fresh cilantro or mint

In a Dutch oven, saute the onions and garlic in the oil over medium heat for 3 minutes. Remove the onion and garlic from the pan, leaving the oil behind. Brown the chicken pieces in the oil, adding a little more oil if necessary. Add salt and pepper to taste.

Return the onion mixture to the pan, add tomatoes and liquid, carrots, squash, cinnamon, cumin, turmeric, hot sauce and honey. Stir the ingredients gently to combine, leaving the chicken pieces at the bottom of the pan. Bring the stew to a boil, cover, reduce heat and simmer about 25 minutes. Add the zucchini, raisins and garbanzo beans; cover and simmer another 10 to 15 minutes.

Meanwhile, cook the couscous according to package directions. Serve the stew over the cooked couscous. Sprinkle with cilantro or mint.

Per serving: 413 calories, 8 grams fat, 126 milligrams cholesterol, 498 milligrams sodium.

GINGERBREAD WITH LEMON CURD

Makes 12 to 16 servings
Preparation time: 10 minutes
Cooking time: 35 minutes

½ cup unsalted butter, softened
½ cup packed brown sugar
½ cup honey
1 egg, beaten
1 ½ cups self-rising flour
½ cup buttermilk
1 2-ounce knob fresh ginger, peeled and grated
½ cup prepared lemon curd
The grated peel of 1 lemon

Preheat oven to 350 degrees. With a food processor or mixer, cream together the butter and brown sugar; add the syrup and egg and beat until smooth. Whisk in the flour, buttermilk, then ginger.

Grease an 8-inch square pan with pan spray, pour in the batter and bake 35 to 40 minutes. The cake will have a soft texture. Serve warm or at room temperature spread with lemon curd and garnished with peels of grated lemon.

Per serving: (16 servings) 138 calories, 4 grams fat, 27 milligrams cholesterol, 59 milligrams sodium.

MONDAY

HOT RED PEPPER LINGUINI
WITH CHIVE BUTTER
STEAMED ZUCCHINI AND
YELLOW SQUASH*
FRESH PEARS AND CHEESE*

The chive butter used in the following recipe is a handy item to keep in the freezer; simply pull out a sliver to melt over roasted chicken or a plate of vegetables,

Price: $.49 to $.89 per lb., the higher range for organic supplies.

Nutrition: Boiled, winter squashes have 90 calories per cooked cup, and baked, they have about 130 calories per cooked cup (spaghetti squash has only 45 calories per cooked cup). They are an excellent source of vitamin A, potassium and fiber, a good source of niacin, iron and protein, and are low in sodium.

Selection: Choose hard, thick-shelled squash that feel heavy for their size, with no soft spots. They weigh 2 to 4 pounds.

Storage: Store whole squash, unwrapped, in a cool, dry, dark place with good ventilation for up to 2 months. Wrap cut pieces in plastic wrap and refrigerate for up to 5 days.

Uses: Allow 1/3 to 1/2 pound per person. Butternut squash can be microwaved, steamed, baked or stir-fried. Add cooked squash to casseroles, stews and soups.

With fall comes foods with richer flavors, and one of the best of the bunch is the American native, winter squash. They come in all shapes and sizes, with bumps and warts, and some so huge the American colonists considered their size "too uncivilized to contemplate," according to the late Bert Greene in his book *Greene on Greens*.

The sweet, nutty and creamy textured butternut squash is in season now and will last throughout the late winter. This tan-colored squash, thick-necked and bell-shaped on the end, may have the sweetest and nuttiest flavor of all the squashes.

Don't let looks scare you — the larger size just means they stayed on the plant longer and therefore may be more mature and sweeter tasting.

The deep flavor of squash comes from starches turning to sugars. While some people microwave squash for the convenience, a dense, caramelized flavor and drier texture can only come from long slow baking or cooking on top of the stove. Boiling produces tender flesh with a custard-like texture.

or as below, over hot pasta. The hot red pepper linguini is not overly hot but very flavorful and would be equally delicious served with pesto sauce. Add summer squash with pears and cheese for dessert. Choose a robust cheese, such as a blue, and make sure the pears are very ripe and juicy.

HOT RED PEPPER PASTA WITH CHIVE BUTTER

Makes 8 servings
Preparation time: 5 minutes
Cooking time: 2 minutes

1 bunch chives
8 tablespoons unsalted butter, softened
29-ounce packages Trio's Hot Red Pepper Linguini

In a food processor, process the chives until finely minced, add the butter and pulse a few times to mix thoroughly. Set aside.

Cook the pasta in boiling water for 2 minutes, or until al dente. Drain the pasta in a colander, then place in a large shallow bowl. Top with the chive butter and toss until melted.

Per serving: 264 calories, 12 grams fat, 31 milligrams cholesterol, 117 milligrams sodium.

TUESDAY

SEAFOOD TACOS
PINEAPPLE AND
ORANGE SLICES*

If you're really in a hurry, purchase chopped onions and green peppers from the salad bar sec-

tion of the grocery store. But even if you chop your own, this light dish is ready in minutes and is low in fat. The tortillas can be fried the traditional way, but the method shown below is a healthier version that still shows off the flavor and fragrance of the corn tortilla. Any leftover squash from last night's meal could be tucked in for a healthy addition.

Choose the sweet juice oranges and serve with rings of fresh pineapple. For ease, look for pineapple already cored and peeled in the produce section. Let the fruits' individual juices mingle on the dessert plate.

SEAFOOD TACOS

Serves 4
Preparation time: 10 minutes
Cooking time: 10 minutes

2 tablespoons vegetable oil
1 medium onion, thinly sliced
1 medium green pepper, cored and cut into thin strips
1 pound crab meat, flaked
^{1}/3 cup buttermilk
^{1}/4 cup cilantro, chopped
Salt and black pepper to taste
8 corn tortillas
4 ounces (^{1}/4 cup) Pepper Jack or Monterey Jack cheese, grated

Preheat oven to 300 degrees.

Heat oil in a large saute pan or skillet over medium-high heat. Saute onions until soft and fragrant, about 4 minutes. Add pepper strips and crab; saute about 1 minute more.

Reduce heat to medium, add buttermilk and cilantro, stir, and cook about 2 minutes or until sauce is slightly thickened. Season with salt and pepper to taste.

Meanwhile, place tortillas in hot oven, directly on a shelf,

until softened, 1 to 2 minutes. Remove them from the oven while still soft and pliable. If the tortillas are warmed before the filling is cooked, place them in a large coffee mug; as they cool they will form a rounded shape perfect for holding the filling. Divide filling among the 8 tortillas and top each with a heaping teaspoon of grated cheese.

Per serving: 383 calories, 19 grams fat, 39 milligrams cholesterol, 764 milligrams sodium.

WEDNESDAY

FRAGRANT FENNEL SOUP
CRUSTY BREAD*
FRESH APPLES AND WALNUTS

If you want a soothing and fortifying meal that is also light, try the following fennel (sometimes called anise) soup. The vegetable's anise aroma will fill your house, and by the time the soup is cooked, you will already feel partly restored. If the dish seems a bit too light, add a sprinkling of Parmesan cheese. Serve thick slices of bread that will hold up to dunking in the soup.

For dessert, offer slices of flavorful apples, such as McIntosh or Cortland and walnut halves.

FRAGRANT FENNEL SOUP

Makes 4 generous servings
Preparation time: 10 minutes
Cooking time: 16 minutes

2 large fennel bulbs
1 tablespoon olive oil
^{1}/2 medium or 1 small onion, sliced
1 teaspoon minced garlic in olive oil

1 medium-to-large white potato,
    scrubbed and cubed
1 medium or 2 small carrots, scrubbed
    and cubed
3 cups chicken stock
1/2 cup dry white wine (optional) or
    chicken broth
Salt and black pepper to taste

Wash the fennel and trim off the roots and any darkened portions. Roughly chop the bulbs. Chop the fronds and reserve for garnish.

Heat the oil over medium heat in a microwave-safe pan, add the onion and garlic and cook 1 minute. Stir in the fennel, potato and carrots and cook until fragrant and crispy, 4 or 5 minutes. Add the chicken broth, (optional) wine, salt and black pepper; cover and microwave on high for 10 minutes. Garnish with reserved fennel fronds.

Per serving: 135 calories, 5 grams fat, 5 milligrams cholesterol, 410 milligrams sodium.

THURSDAY

STUFFED PITA BREAD
WITH CHICKEN
SPINACH-APPLE SALAD*

Leftover couscous, of which you should have plenty, will fit quickly into pita breads for an easy dinner. Simple stir together the couscous grains and chicken stew, but keep the mixture dry rather than soupy, so that it will stay put in the pita breads. Look for the more nutritious whole-wheat pita breads; if they are unavailable, purchase pitas made from white bread.

Put together a simple salad of fresh spinach and chopped apple. Add sunflower seeds if you wish, and toss with a lemony vinaigrette.

STUFFED PITA BREAD
WITH CHICKEN

Makes 4 servings
Preparation time: 5 minutes
Cooking time: 5 minutes

3 cups leftover chicken stew,
    without broth
4 pita breads, split in half
1/4 cup cilantro, chopped

Turn the oven to 300 degrees. Heat the pita breads until warm and pliable, about 5 minutes.

Meanwhile, remove chicken from the bones and discard the bones. Heat the chicken stew, either in a heavy saucepan or in the microwave on High for 4 or 5 minutes or until thoroughly warmed. Fill each of the pita breads with the stew and garnish with cilantro.

Per serving: 416 calories, 20 grams fat, 101 milligrams cholesterol, 120 milligrams sodium.

FRIDAY

HOT RED PEPPER LINGUINI
WITH CHIVE BUTTER*
SPINACH-APPLE SALAD*
GINGERBREAD

Look to the refrigerator for tonight's meal. Leftover linguini with chive butter can be reheated, or even crisped in butter in a large shallow skillet. Add a salad of spinach with apple slices and pineapple chunks and more of the lemon vinaigrette. Serve gingerbread for dessert.

SATURDAY

GRILLED SALMON WITH
CREOLE MUSTARD
BAKED POTATOES*
GRILLED MUSHROOMS ON A
BED OF MUSTARD GREENS
POUND CAKE WITH
RASPBERRY SAUCE*

Both the salmon and vegetable dish will do well on the grill or under the broiler, one cooking right after the other.

Serve the fish with a platter of fragrant and flavorful grilled (or broiled) mushrooms served over just-wilted greens. Mustard greens are used here, as they cook quickly, yet hold their shape nicely. Their biting flavor accents the spicy salmon dish perfectly.

Choose the large, intensely-flavored, dark brown shiitake mushrooms that are now available, and, if you wish, add some large white cultivated mushrooms to hold down the cost. Some stores sell extra-long stems of rosemary, but any sprigs you find will add fragrance to your grilled dish. Even old stems of sage, oregano or thyme from the garden would make a fragrant grill. For dessert serve a purchased pound cake with pureed raspberry sauce, made from frozen raspberries.

GRILLED SALMON
WITH CREOLE
MUSTARD

Makes 4 servings
Preparation time: 5 minutes
Cooking time: 10 minutes

4 10-ounce salmon steaks
4 teaspoons olive oil
Salt and black pepper to taste

4 teaspoons Creole mustard

Preheat the grill or large cast iron skillet.

Brush the salmon steaks with olive oil and add salt and pepper; then grill or sear them in the hot skillet about 5 minutes per side. When the steaks are almost done, brush them with mustard. Place them back on the grill or in the skillet and cook just until the mustard coating turns brown and crisp.

Per serving: 416 calories, 20 grams fat, 101 milligrams cholesterol, 120 milligrams sodium.

GRILLED MUSHROOMS ON A BED OF MUSTARD GREENS

Makes 4 servings
Preparation time: 10 to 15 minutes
Cooking time: 15 minutes

1 pound mushrooms, combination of shiitake and white, washed, stemmed and halved if very large
1/2 cup walnut or olive oil or combination, divided
2 cloves garlic, minced
Several sprigs fresh thyme or 1 teaspoon dried
Several stems fresh rosemary (optional) or old sage stems
1/2 pound mustard greens, washed, stemmed and cut into strips
2 teaspoons cider vinegar

Arrange the mushrooms in a single layer in a large shallow bowl. Brush or sprinkle both sides with the oil, reserving 1 tablespoon; sprinkle with garlic and thyme. Cover loosely and refrigerate several hours or overnight. (The mushrooms will absorb the oil.)

Heat the grill or broiler and oil the grill or grill basket used for vegetables. Wet the sprigs of fresh rosemary or sage stems and toss them on the fire. Arrange the mushrooms on the grill or broiling pan, cover and cook until tender, 5 minutes per side.

When the mushrooms are just about done grilling, heat the reserved tablespoon of oil in a large skillet. Over medium-high heat, add the mustard greens and toss until wilted, 2 or 3 minutes. Sprinkle the greens with vinegar and put the greens on serving plates. If the mushrooms are very large, cut them into slices. Arrange mushrooms over the greens and serve.

Per serving: 149 calories, 14 grams fat, no cholesterol, 18 milligrams sodium.

WEEK 47

SHOPPING LIST

Meat, poultry, seafood

- 4 swordfish steaks, about 8 ounces each
- 1 pound fresh bratwurst
- 1 3- to 4-pound smoked turkey breast
- 1 pound lean ground beef

Produce

- 9 baking potatoes
- 2 cups snow peas
- 1 cup cherry tomatoes
- 2 heads lettuce, any type
- 1 bunch small mustard greens
- 2 medium yellow onions
- 2 medium red onions
- 1 medium red bell pepper (optional)
- 1 medium green bell pepper (optional)
- 4 ounces mushrooms
- 1 jicama, at least 7 ounces
- 1 large carrot

- 2 zucchini
- 1 4-pound spaghetti squash
- 3 tablespoons mixed herbs
- 1 12-ounce package fresh cranberries
- 1 navel orange
- $^{1}/_{4}$ cup parsley
- $^{1}/_{2}$ cup basil
- $^{1}/_{2}$ cup sage leaves
- 4 large cloves garlic

Dairy

- 13 tablespoons butter
- 3 cups milk
- 1 pint frozen lemon yogurt
- 5 ounces Gorgonzola cheese
- 4 ounces Fontina cheese
- 4 ounces Parmesan cheese
- $^{1}/_{2}$ cup cream
- 1 quart rum raisin ice cream

Deli

- 1 loaf crusty bread
- 4 brownies
- 8 flour tortillas

Miscellaneous

- 1 19-ounce can cannellini beans
- 1 14 $^{1}/_{2}$-ounce can stewed or crushed tomatoes
- 1 pound macaroni
- 1 5-ounce package cornbread mix (optional)
- 3 pastry rounds
- $^{1}/_{2}$ cup pine nuts
- 1 15 $^{1}/_{4}$-ounce can crushed pineapple
- 2 tablespoons orange juice
- $^{1}/_{2}$ cup walnuts
- 8 slices whole wheat bread
- 18-ounce bottle 97% fat-free blue cheese salad

dressing
- $^{1}/_{2}$ cup slivered almonds

Staples

- All-purpose flour
- Brown sugar
- Cider vinegar
- Cinnamon
- Cumin seed
- Ground cloves
- Minced garlic in olive oil
- Nutmeg
- Olive oil
- Peppercorns, black, green or both
- Raisins
- Rosemary
- Salt
- Sugar
- Thyme leaves
- Unseasoned chili powder
- Vegetable oil
- Whole fennel seeds

*Suggested accompaniments

SUNDAY

SWORDFISH STEAKS WITH PEPPERCORNS
BAKED POTATOES*
SAUTEED SNOW PEAS AND CHERRY TOMATOES

Start the week with swordfish steaks baked under a crust of crushed pepper and herbs. Bake 4 extra potatoes to use later in the week.

SWORDFISH STEAKS WITH PEPPERCORNS

Makes 4 servings
Preparation time: 5 minutes
Cooking time: 6 to 10 minutes

3 tablespoons unsalted butter, softened
1 tablespoon chopped mixed herbs (fresh parsley, thyme, tarragon, chives or basil)
4 swordfish steaks, about ³/4-inch thick
Salt to taste
2 tablespoons crushed peppercorns (use all black or a mixture of black and green)

Preheat the broiler. In a small bowl, combine the butter and herbs. Set aside.

Sprinkle the fish with salt. With the heel of your hand, press the peppercorns into the fish, or roll with a rolling pin. Broil 4 or 5 minutes on each side. Serve the steaks topped with a dollop of herb butter.

SAUTEED SNOW PEAS AND CHERRY TOMATOES

Makes 4 servings
Preparation time: 10 minutes
Cooking time: 5 minutes

1 tablespoon olive oil
2 cups snow peas, ends trimmed
1 cup cherry tomatoes, stems removed and halved
2 tablespoons chopped herbs (dill, basil or tarragon)

Heat the olive oil in a skillet, add the snow peas and cook, stirring for 2 or 3 minutes, until snow peas are bright green, yet still crisp. Add the cherry tomatoes and stir gently, just to warm them. Turn off the heat and sprinkle with fresh herbs.

Per serving: 252 calories, 7 grams fat, no cholesterol, 506 milligrams sodium.

MONDAY

WHITE BEAN AND GARLIC SOUP
GREEN SALAD*
CRUSTY BREAD*

The past couple of years have brought wonderful vegetarian cookbooks. The recently released *Sundays at Moosewood Restaurant*, by the Moosewood Collective (Fireside Books, $16.95), is one of the best. Don't miss this comfy soup perfect for an autumn evening. Don't leave out the fennel; it adds a wonderful anise flavor and fragrance that will make your kitchen a welcoming place.

WHITE BEAN AND GARLIC SOUP

Makes 4 servings
Preparation time: 10 minutes
Cooking time: 20 minutes

2 tablespoons olive oil
1 medium onion, chopped
1 large carrot, finely chopped
¹/2 fennel bulb, cleaned and inner pieces chopped
Salt and black pepper to taste
1 19-ounce can cannellini beans, undrained
1 quart water
4 large garlic cloves, flattened and peeled
¹/2 teaspoon fresh or dried rosemary
1 large white potato, unpeeled and cubed
¹/4 cup fresh parsley, chopped

In a deep-sided skillet or heavy saucepan, add the olive oil and saute the onion until soft and fragrant, about 5 minutes. Add the carrot and fennel and saute a couple of minutes. Add the beans and their liquid, the water, garlic cloves, rosemary and the potato. Cover and simmer 15 minutes.

Puree half the soup in the food processor or blender and stir back into the soup. Add salt and black pepper to taste. Garnish with parsley and serve.

Per serving: (without milk) 252 calories, 7 grams fat, no cholesterol, 506 milligrams sodium.

TUESDAY

MASHED POTATOES WITH ZUCCHINI AND BASIL
GRILLED BRATWURST*
FROZEN LEMON YOGURT*

Mashed potatoes won't be the same once you taste this version. The baked potatoes add body and a more-intense potato flavor than do boiled potatoes, and the sauteed zucchini and basil add unexpected flavor. Look for freshly-made bratwurst at several local stores, and finish with a cooling dish of frozen yogurt.

Price: Sold in 12-ounce bags that range from $.85 to $1.50 a bag.

Nutrition: Unsweetened raw cranberries contain 44 calories per cup and are high in vitamins A and C.

Selection: Most years cranberries are available from October through December, but this year they will likely be gone by Thanksgiving. Look for firm, plump berries; pale or black areas on berries are fine and only indicate the variety. Avoid berries that look withered or are cracked open and leaky.

Storage: Bagged cranberries have been sorted, prewashed and dried and can be stored directly in the plastic bag in which they are packed. Refrigerate for 2 weeks or freeze up to a year.

Uses: A 12-ounce bag yields 3 cups of fruit. Use them in preserves, pies and breads or chutneys and relishes to serve with poultry or game dishes. Because of their extreme tartness they are best mixed with sugar or other fruits, such as apples, pineapple, oranges or dried apricots. It is not necessary to thaw frozen berries before using them; they can be stirred directly into batters or chopped in a food processor. Dried and sweetened cranberries, much like raisins, are currently available at farmers markets, or make your own to eat as a snack.

Cranberries are associated with our traditional feast day

dinner because native Americans taught the Pilgrims of their food value, flavor and many uses. Harvested from swampy bogs in autumn each year, their tart flavor is the perfect counterpoint to poultry and stronger-flavored game birds that are also in season in the autumn. The berries have a short 2-month season which usually ends after Christmas. Many recent seasons have ended shortly after Thanksgiving, due to bad weather and short supplies.

Four varieties make up the bulk of the cranberry crop. Some, like the Early Black, flourish as far south as New Jersey and sport a red color so dark they look black. The varieties are blended and packaged together; some berries will be round, others oblong, some light pink and others very dark red. They all have similar flavor and cook exactly the same.

Most cranberries are grown in large wetland areas in Massachusetts, Wisconsin, New Jersey and Washington state, where one acre of cranberries might be surrounded by as many as 10 acres of beautiful wetlands, water reservoirs, open space and wildlife. The open spaces help cranberry farmers intermittently dry the bogs for growing and flood the bogs for easy harvesting.

MASHED POTATOES WITH BASIL AND ZUCCHINI

Makes 4 servings
Preparation time: 5 minutes
Cooking time: 5 minutes

2 tablespoons butter
2 zucchini, chopped
4 potatoes, baked and peeled, leftover
    from Sunday dinner
$^1/_2$ cup basil leaves
2 tablespoons butter (optional)
Salt and black pepper to taste

In a skillet, melt the butter, add the zucchini and saute 5 minutes, but don't let it brown. Drain well on paper toweling and place in the work bowl of a food processor. Add the peeled baked potatoes and puree. Add the basil leaves and (optional) butter and process until the mixture is flecked with basil.

Per serving: (without optional butter) 176 calories, 6 grams fat, 15 milligrams cholesterol, 65 milligrams sodium.

WEDNESDAY

MACARONI AND THREE CHEESES MIXED GREEN SALAD* BROWNIES*

A classic macaroni and cheese that kids, grandparents and friends will love is a good choice for dinner the night before a holiday. Don't omit the Fontina cheese if possible, it has a wonderful nutty flavor and melts like velvet. The recipe is easily doubled and can sit in the oven or refrigerator to await guests. Add a green salad and purchased brownies for dessert.

MACARONI AND THREE CHEESES

Makes 4 servings
Preparation time: 10 minutes
Cooking time: 25 minutes

5 to 6 tablespoons butter
$^1/_4$ cup all-purpose flour
2 $^1/_2$ cups milk
5 ounces Gorgonzola cheese,
    crumbled
4 ounces Fontina, grated
$^1/_4$ teaspoon ground nutmeg
Salt and black pepper to taste
1 pound small macaroni
1 or 2 green onions, minced (optional)
2 to 3 ounces Parmesan cheese, grated

Preheat oven to 400 degrees. Grease a 2-quart baking dish.

Melt the butter in a medium-size saucepan over medium heat, stir in the flour and cook 1 minute. Gradually whisk in the milk. Cook, stirring constantly until thickened to the consistency of cream. Whisk in the Gorgonzola and Fontina, cook, whisking constantly until the cheeses are melted. Lower the heat if necessary to keep everything from scorching. Season with nutmeg and salt and pepper to taste. Remove from heat.

Meanwhile, cook the pasta and (optional) onion until al dente, about 5 minutes, and drain. Stir the pasta and onion into the cheese mixture, stir in the Parmesan and pour into a baking dish. Bake 15 minutes or until the top is crispy.

Per serving: 454 calories, 23 grams fat, 66 milligrams cholesterol, 623 milligrams sodium.

THURSDAY

SPAGHETTI SQUASH TART WITH PINE NUTS

SMOKED TURKEY*
BITTER GREENS SALAD*
ROSEMARY CORN
BREAD STICKS*
DAN'S CRANBERRY PIE WITH
RUM RAISIN ICE CREAM

With a few subtle changes, you can have a delicious Thanks-giving dinner that contains all the essential classic foods, yet tastes new. Start the meal with a nutty-sweet and lean squash tart, adapted from Michael Foley, executive chef of Printers Row Restaurant, Chicago, Illinois, and purchase a precooked smoked turkey for an effortless entree. Reserve some turkey slices for tomorrow night's dinner. Make the pie filling a day or two ahead if you wish; its tangy cranberry flavor will perk up any flagging appetites.

SPAGHETTI SQUASH TART WITH PINENUTS

Makes 6 servings
Preparation time: 10 minutes
Cooking time: 25 to 55 minutes

1 spaghetti squash, about 4 pounds,
    halved
1 pastry shell
$^1/_2$ cup pine nuts
$^1/_2$ cup cream
$^1/_2$ cup sage leaves, divided

Preheat the oven to 375 degrees. Cut the squash in half and remove the seeds and pulp. Place the squash pieces flesh-side down in a baking pan. Add 1/2 cup of water and cover loosely with foil. Bake for 45 minutes (or cook in the microwave, in a covered dish, for 15 minutes). When the squash is cooked, remove it from the oven and remove the flesh with a fork to produce long strands. Set the squash in a colander over a bowl to drain for 10 or more minutes. Set aside.

Meanwhile, place pastry shell in a 9-inch pie or tart pan and bake about 10 minutes, until lightly browned. Remove from the oven, fill with the reserved squash and sprinkle with pine nuts.

Meanwhile, place the cream and sage leaves in a small saucepan and simmer for 5 minutes to release the sage flavor into the cream. Remove and discard the sage leaves and serve a tablespoon of the cream over each tart slice. Garnish with reserved sage leaves.

Per serving: 371 calories, 19 grams fat, 22 milligrams cholesterol, 235 milligrams sodium.

DAN'S CRANBERRY PIE

Makes 8 servings
Preparation time: 10 minutes
Cooking time: 50 minutes

1 12-ounce package fresh cranberries
1 15 ¼-ounce can crushed
    pineapple with juice
2 tablespoons orange juice
1 ½ cups sugar
½ cup walnuts, roughly chopped
2 tablespoons all-purpose flour
2 pastry rounds
1 quart rum raisin ice cream

Place the cranberries, pineapple, orange juice and sugar in a medium-sized saucepan. Cook over medium heat until the sugar dissolves and the cranberries start to pop, 3 to 5 minutes. Turn off the heat and stir in walnuts. Allow the mixture to cool (this can be made a day or two ahead and refrigerated). When cool, stir in the flour.

Preheat the oven to 350 degrees. Fit one crust into a 9-inch pie pan, spoon in the filling

and top with the second crust. Crimp the edges. Bake the pie for 45 minutes. Cool and serve with ice cream.

Per serving: 392 calories, 19 grams fat, 29 milligrams cholesterol, 387 milligrams sodium.

FRIDAY

TURKEY AND BLUE
CHEESE SANDWICHES
RUM RAISIN ICE CREAM*

TURKEY AND BLUE CHEESE SANDWICHES

Makes 4 servings
Preparation time: 5 minutes
Cooking time: 10 to 15 minutes

Turn the reserved turkey into delicious sandwiches for tonight's dinner. Add a few crumbles of blue cheese if you wish, but the sandwich is fine without them. The brown cremini mushrooms, available at most grocery stores, are a meaty and flavorful addition to the dish.

8 slices thick-sliced whole wheat
    bread, toasted
4 tablespoons reduced calorie blue
    cheese dressing
1 tablespoon unsalted butter
1 medium red onion, thinly sliced
4 ounces fresh mushrooms
sliced lettuce leaves
12 ounces thinly sliced smoked
    turkey

Spread salad dressing on bread slices; set aside. In a medium skillet, melt butter, add onion and cook until soft and transparent, 5 minutes. Add the mushrooms and cook until tender, 5 to 8 minutes. Layer the bread slices with equal portions of onions, mushrooms, lettuce leaves and

turkey. Top with remaining bread slices, slice and serve.

Per serving: (with 2 tablespoons dressing per serving) 281 calories, 6 grams fat, 81 milligrams cholesterol, 499 milligrams sodium.

SATURDAY

PICADILLO WITH TORTILLAS
JICAMA AND ORANGE SALAD
FRESH SLICES OF PINEAPPLE*

An easy hamburger dish may be just what you need to feed the crowd tonight. Spicy picadillo, common in Spanish and Mexican homes, is a welcome relief from hamburger casseroles or standard taco fillings. Spoon it into hot flour tortillas and serve with a crunchy jicama salad. Both recipes are easily doubled and the picadillo can be refrigerated and frozen.

PICADILLO

Makes 4 servings
Preparation time: 10 minutes
Cooking time: 50 to 60 minutes

1 small onion, chopped
2 teaspoons minced garlic in olive oil
1 pound ground beef
1 cup chopped canned tomatoes
1 bell pepper, seeded and chopped
    (optional)
2 tablespoons vinegar
1 tablespoon brown sugar
½ teaspoon cumin
¼ teaspoon allspice
½ to ¾ teaspoon salt
½ cup raisins
½ cup blanched, slivered almonds
8 flour tortillas

Heat the garlic and onions in a 10-inch skillet and cook about 5 minutes. Add the ground beef and saute until it begins to brown. Add the (optional) bell pepper, vinegar, brown sugar, cumin, allspice, and salt, and simmer, covered for 30 minutes, stirring occasionally. Add the raisins and almonds and cook a few more minutes uncovered, until the excess liquid has evaporated.

Meanwhile heat the tortillas in a dry skillet or 4 or 5 minutes in a hot oven. Serve the picadillo with the hot tortillas.

Per serving: 300 calories, 15 grams fat, 47 milligrams cholesterol, 223 milligrams sodium.

JICAMA AND ORANGE SALAD

Makes 4 servings
Preparation time: 15 minutes

7 ounces jicama, peeled and cut into
    ¹/₄-inch dice
1 navel orange, peeled and pith
    removed and sliced
6 or 8 slices red or sweet onion
1 kiwi fruit, peeled and sliced
    (optional)
2 tablespoons poppy seed dressing

In a mixing bowl, blend the jicama, orange, onion and (optional) kiwi fruit. Toss with the dressing and serve.

WEEK

48

SHOPPING LIST

Meat, poultry, seafood

- ❑ 2 ¹/₂-to ³/₄-pound pork tenderloins
- ❑ 1 ¹/₄ pounds smoked ham or turkey (purchased or leftover)
- ❑ 1 turkey carcass (left-over)

Produce

- ❑ 1 medium onion
- ❑ 2 leeks
- ❑ 3 carrots
- ❑ 2 celery ribs
- ❑ 1 bunch parsley
- ❑ 1 bunch basil
- ❑ 1 medium zucchini
- ❑ ¹/₂ pound green beans
- ❑ 1 pound baby carrots
- ❑ 1 ¹/₂ to 2 cups fresh cran-berries
- ❑ 1 knob fresh ginger
- ❑ 1 bulb fresh garlic
- ❑ 3 bunches green onions

- ❑ 8 ounces mushrooms
- ❑ 3 large Granny Smith apples
- ❑ 2 large red peppers
- ❑ 1 10-ounce package spinach
- ❑ 4 pears
- ❑ 7 oranges

Dairy

- ❑ ¹/₂ cup skim milk
- ❑ 4 ounces grated Parmesan cheese
- ❑ 1 16-ounce container ricotta cheese
- ❑ 1 tablespoon butter
- ❑ 6 ounces shredded Monterey Jack cheese
- ❑ 3 eggs

Deli

- ❑ 8 corn muffins
- ❑ 1 loaf crusty bread

Miscellaneous

- ❑ 1 ¹/₂ cups salsa or picante sauce
- ❑ 1 16-ounce can black beans
- ❑ 1 12-inch prepared pizza crust (or large Boboli)
- ❑ 1 15-ounce can black-eyed peas
- ❑ 1 ³/₄ cups unsweetened orange juice
- ❑ 3 cups bulgur wheat
- ❑ 15- to 16-ounce can Italian peeled tomatoes
- ❑ 1 box graham crackers

Staples

- ❑ All-purpose flour
- ❑ Baking powder
- ❑ Black pepper
- ❑ Cider vinegar
- ❑ Coarsely ground black pepper
- ❑ Cumin

- ❑ Dijon mustard
- ❑ Fennel seed
- ❑ Granulated sugar
- ❑ Homemade or bottled salad dressing
- ❑ Honey
- ❑ Honey mustard
- ❑ Marjoram
- ❑ Nutmeg
- ❑ Olive oil
- ❑ Reduced-sodium soy sauce
- ❑ Safflower oil
- ❑ Salt
- ❑ Self-rising flour
- ❑ Sesame oil
- ❑ Vanilla
- ❑ Vegetable cooking spray
- ❑ Vegetable or peanut oil

* Suggested accompaniments

TURKEY SOUP WITH HERBED RICOTTA DUMPLINGS
CRUSTY BREAD *
FRESH PEARS *

Light, comforting, herb-flecked ricotta dumplings distinguish this turkey soup from the thousands of others simmering on stoves across America tonight. You'll easily have enough for two meals, so save half for later and add the dumplings to what's left. Half the dumpling batter should feed four, but they're so tasty you might want to add them all to this batch, and try a different twist with the next batch. If your carcass has already been tossed out, use about 8 cups of canned chicken stock for the broth base.

TURKEY-VEGETABLE SOUP WITH HERBED RICOTTA DUMPLINGS

Makes 8 servings
Preparation time: 20 minutes
Cooking time: 1 1/2 hours

1 turkey carcass, chopped into
    large pieces
2 leeks, chopped
3 carrots, cut into 1/2-inch slices
2 celery ribs, cut into 1/2-inch slices
Water to cover (about 12 cups)
5 or 6 sprigs parsley
Salt and pepper to taste
2 tablespoons olive oil
1 medium zucchini, scrubbed,
    halved lengthwise and cut into
    1/2-inch slices
1/2 pound green beans, trimmed
    and cut into 1-inch pieces
1 can (15-16 ounces) Italian peeled
    tomatoes, coarsely chopped
    (juice reserved)

1/2 teaspoon dried marjoram
Ricotta Dumplings
    (recipe follows)

For the broth: In a stockpot or large flameproof casserole, combine the turkey carcass, 1 onion, 1 carrot and 1 celery rib; add water to cover. Bring to a boil over moderately high heat; skim off any foam that rises to the surface. Add parsley, salt and pepper, reduce heat to low, and simmer for 1 hour. Set broth aside.

For the soup: In another pot, heat the oil. Add remaining chopped onion and cook over moderate heat, stirring until softened, 2 to 3 minutes. Add the remaining carrots and celery and the zucchini, green beans and chopped tomatoes.

Strain the broth into the saucepan and add the marjoram and reserved tomato juice. Bring to a boil, reduce the heat and simmer, partially covered, until the vegetables are tender, 20 minutes.

Make the dumplings (recipe follows) and drop into simmering soup. Simmer, partially covered, until the dumplings are cooked through, about 6 minutes.

Per serving, with dumplings: 211 calories, 11 grams fat, 61 milligrams cholesterol, 380 milligrams sodium.

HERBED RICOTTA DUMPLINGS

Makes 4 to 8 servings
Preparation time: 5 minutes
Cooking time: 6 minutes

1 cup grated Parmesan cheese
    (4 ounces)
1/2 cup ricotta cheese

1/2 cup all-purpose flour
1 large egg, lightly beaten
3 tablespoons minced fresh basil or
    parsley
Pinch of freshly grated nutmeg

Combine the Parmesan, ricotta, flour, egg, basil and nutmeg in the workbowl of a food processor or mixing bowl and pulse just until smooth. Drop heaping tablespoons of the mixture into the above simmering soup. Continue with the remaining dumpling dough. Simmer, partially covered, until the dumplings are cooked through, about 6 minutes.

Per serving (4 servings): 210 calories, 12 grams fat, 101 milligrams cholesterol, 515 milligrams sodium.

SWEET AND SOUR HAM SALAD WITH BLACK-EYED PEAS
CORN MUFFINS *

At many a Thanksgiving gathering the roast turkey is joined on the buffet table by a smoked turkey or ham. If that's the case at your house and you're still trying to use up those leftovers, try this tangy whole-meal salad adapted from *More Taste Than Time* by Abby Mandel (Simon & Schuster, $19.95). Serve corn muffins. Any extras will be great for tomorrow's lunch.

SWEET AND SOUR HAM SALAD WITH BLACK-EYED PEAS

Makes 6 servings
Preparation time: 20 minutes

Price: $1.29 to $1.89 for a bunch of three or four, which weighs about 1 ¹/₂ pounds. Some stores sell leeks by the pound, at about $.89 a pound, which averages out to the same price.

Nutrition: Three or four large stems have about 52 calories and are a fair source of potassium, calcium and vitamins and are rich in fiber.

Selection: While leeks are available throughout the year, they are most plentiful and at their best from October through May. Select leeks with crisp white bottoms and fresh-looking tops. Expect the bottoms to still have some dirt clinging to their roots since trimmed and washed leeks develop an unpleasant smell and lose their fresh flavor. Small to medium-size leeks (less than 1 ¹/₂ inches in diameter) are the most tender and have a mild, delicate flavor.

Storage: Store unwashed in several layers of plastic to prevent everything else in the refrigerator from smelling like leek. If the leaves are fresh and dry, the leeks should keep refrigerated for up to a week.

Uses: About 1 ¹/₂ pounds of untrimmed leeks will serve four as a grilled or braised vegetable. If using it chopped and cooked for its onion flavoring in a dish, one or two leeks will usually be adequate for a dish that serves four. To clean leeks, cut off the green tops no more than 2 inches above the white base and the root, then cut lengthwise halfway through the leek. Open the layers and wash under run-

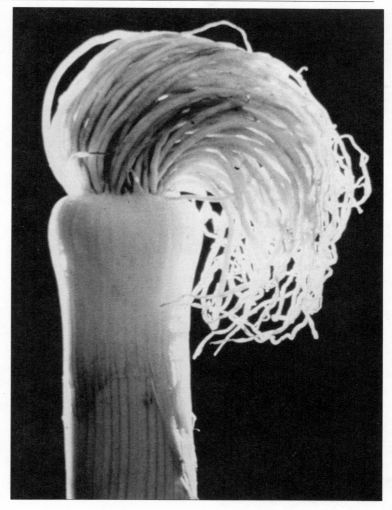

ning water to remove dirt and grit.

Leeks are a long, sleek member of the onion family. Related to both garlic and onion, they are a favorite winter vegetable for soups, prized for the deep flavors they add, as well as a great vegetable on the grill. They are widely available in grocery stores and farmers markets.

Summer supplies usually

come from New York or New Jersey and offer a large, long leek with a larger white portion. Later in the season, a smaller leek comes from Florida, says Case Lichtveld , produce manager at Harry's Farmers Market. Current supplies are coming from Central America and California and are of excellent quality.

DRESSING:

1/3 cup safflower oil
3 tablespoons cider vinegar
1 tablespoon Dijon mustard
2 teaspoons granulated sugar
2 teaspoons coarsely cracked black
    pepper (or less, if you prefer)
1/2 teaspoon salt

SALAD:

1 large Granny Smith apple,
    unpeeled, diced
1 large red pepper, cut in thin strips
6 green onions, cut in rings
1 1/4 pounds smoked ham (or
    smoked turkey), cubed
1 15-ounce can black-eyed peas,
    rinsed and drained

In a small bowl, whisk together the oil, vinegar, mustard, sugar, pepper and salt. In a large bowl, combine the apple, pepper, onions, ham and black eyed peas. Pour the dressing over the salad ingredients and mix gently. Serve immediately or cover tightly and refrigerate for several hours. Mix well and adjust the seasoning before serving if necessary.

Per serving: 361 calories, 21 grams fat, 56 milligrams cholesterol, 1,632 milligrams sodium.

TUESDAY

TURKEY-VEGETABLE SOUP *
**CORN MUFFINS WITH
HONEY MUSTARD AND
SMOKED
HAM (OR TURKEY)** *
**CRANBERRY PUDDING
MUFFINS**

Tonight, heat up that soup you saved and, if you ate all the dumplings Sunday, add 2 or 3 cubed, red-skinned potatoes to it as it simmers. Allow 10 or 15 minutes cooking time unless the potatoes are already cooked. Or beef up the protein with any cooked grain, pasta, corn or bean (lentils, chickpeas, kidney beans, etc.). Stuff those few remaining ham or smoked turkey slivers into leftover corn muffins. Then toss together this ultra-easy dessert, adapted from *Cooking Light* magazine, that tastes so rich, no one would ever guess it's fat-free. Serve it warm with its own sweet-tart sauce and, if you like, a scoop of frozen vanilla yogurt.

CRANBERRY PUDDING CAKE

Makes 8 servings
Preparation time: 10 minutes
Cooking time: 40-50 minutes

1 cup sugar, divided
1 1/2 to 2 cups fresh cranberries
2 teaspoons grated orange rind
1 3/4 cups unsweetened orange
    juice
1 cup self-rising flour
1/2 cup skim or 2 percent milk
1 teaspoon pure vanilla extract
Vegetable pan spray

Preheat the oven to 350 degrees.
    Combine 1/2 cup sugar, the cranberries, grated orange rind and orange juice in a large saucepan. Bring to a boil and cook 2 minutes or until the cranberries start to pop, stirring occasionally. Set aside.
    Stir together the remaining 1/2 cup sugar and flour in a medium bowl. Combine the milk and vanilla; then stir in the sugar and flour, stirring just until dry ingredients are moistened. Spoon into a shallow 2-quart casserole coated with cooking spray. Pour cranberry mixture evenly over batter. Bake at 350 degrees for 40-50 minutes or until golden.

Per serving: 189 calories, trace of fat, trace of cholesterol, 129 milligrams sodium.

WEDNESDAY

**MUSTARD PORK
TENDERLOIN
STEAMED BABY CARROTS** *
**SESAME-SEASONED
BULGUR WHEAT** *
CRANBERRY PUDDING CAKE *

This delicious tenderloin rubbed with mustard and fennel seeds comes from *Nathalie Dupree Cooks for Family and Friends* (Morrow, $21). While the meat cooks, steam baby carrots and cover nutty-tasting bulgur wheat (sometimes sold as tabouli mix) with boiling water; you'll have about 6 cups when the water is absorbed. Season half with a little sesame oil and soy sauce. Save the rest for tomorrow.

MUSTARD PORK TENDERLOIN

Makes 4 to 6 servings
Preparation time: 10 minutes
Cooking time: 20-30 minutes

3 garlic cloves, minced
2 tablespoons fennel seed
1/3 cup Dijon mustard
2 1/2- to 3/4-pound pork
    tenderloins
Coarsely ground black pepper

Preheat the oven to 400 degrees. Grease a baking pan just large enough to hold the two tenderloins.
    In a small bowl combine the

garlic, fennel seed and mustard. Rub the mixture over the tenderloins. Place them, side by side, in the baking pan and roast 20 to 30 minutes, or until a meat thermometer registers 160 degrees. Let them rest 5 minutes, then season with pepper. Slice the meat on the diagonal. Pour any juices over the meat.

Per serving (6 servings): 147 calories, 5 grams fat, 70 milligrams cholesterol, 233 milligrams sodium.

THURSDAY

BULGUR FRIED "RICE"
ORANGE SECTIONS

Fried rice is a classic catch-all for leftovers. It's even tastier, though, when you substitute nutty-tasting bulgur — which has a more interesting flavor and texture — for the rice, adapted from *Jane Brody's Good Food Book* (Norton, $19.95). Use leftover bulgur from last night for a quick meal. The following dish makes hearty servings.

BULGUR FRIED "RICE"

Makes 4 to 6 servings
Preparation time: 15 minutes
Cooking time: 15 minutes

3 cups cooked bulgur wheat
4 teaspoons peanut or sesame oil, divided
1 egg white plus 1 whole egg, slightly beaten
1 clove minced garlic
1 tablespoon minced fresh ginger
2 or 3 green onions, thinly sliced
1/2 cup sliced mushrooms
1 cup diced cooked leftover turkey, pork, ham or tofu
2 tablespoons soy sauce

1/2 teaspoon sugar
Freshly ground black pepper

Heat 2 teaspoons of the oil in a large non-stick skillet. Add the eggs as an omelet: swirl the pan and cook, stirring some, until the eggs are just set. Transfer them to a plate and, when cool, cut in shreds.

Heat the remaining 2 teaspoons of oil in the skillet; add garlic, ginger, green onions and mushrooms. Cook, stirring, for about 1 minute. Add poultry, meat, or tofu and cooked bulgur. Saute the mixture over high heat until hot.

Combine soy sauce, sugar and pepper; add sauce and shredded eggs to the rice mixture, tossing the ingredients to combine well.

Per serving, with turkey: 261 calories, 8 grams fat, 95 milligrams cholesterol, 369 milligrams sodium.

FRIDAY

BRUNSWICK STEW *
CRACKERS *
APPLES AND ORANGES*

In Georgia, Brunswick stew typically turns up at summertime barbecues. But it's probably better appreciated as a wintertime warm-up. Look for it anywhere that sells barbecue and you're likely to find a tasty version. Add crackers and fresh fruit and your meal is complete.

SATURDAY

SOUTHWEST BLACK
BEAN PIZZA

SPINACH AND
MUSHROOM SALAD *
GRAHAM CRACKERS SPREAD
WITH HONEY-SWEETENED
RICOTTA *

Who says pizza has to be Italian? A Boboli or other premade pizza crust provides the perfect vehicle for myriad toppings, including the one below, with a Southwest flavor. Add a salad and — for something sweet but not too sinful afterward — graham crackers spread with ricotta cheese, sweetened to taste with honey.

SOUTHWEST BLACK BEAN PIZZA

Makes 4 servings
Preparation time: 15 minutes
Cooking time: 15 minutes

1 medium onion, chopped
2 garlic cloves, minced
1 tablespoon olive oil
3/4 cup salsa or picante sauce
1 16-ounce can black beans, rinsed and drained
1 teaspoon ground cumin
1 12-inch prepared pizza crust (or large Boboli)
1 large red or green bell pepper, sliced into thin rings
1 1/2 cups (6 ounces) shredded Monterey Jack or Pepper Jack cheese
Extra salsa or picante sauce for serving

Preheat oven to 425 degrees. In a 10-inch skillet, saute onion and garlic in olive oil, stirring occasionally, until tender, about 4 minutes. Stir in salsa or picante sauce, beans and cumin. Simmer 2 minutes. Spread evenly over crust. Overlap pepper rings over bean mixture. Sprinkle with cheese. Bake in preheated oven 15 minutes or until cheese is bubbly. Cut into wedges to serve. Serve with additional salsa or picante sauce.

Per serving: 572 calories, 18 grams fat, 41 milligrams cholesterol, 848 milligrams sodium.

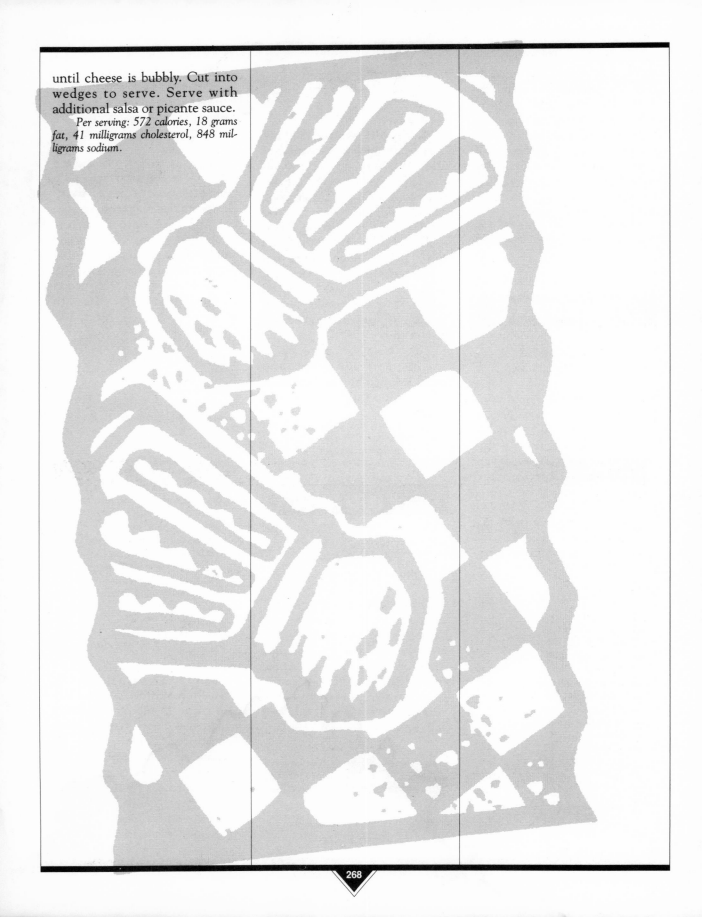

WEEK

49

SHOPPING LIST

Meat, poultry, seafood

- ❏ 1 4-pound chicken, cut into 8 pieces
- ❏ 1 to 1 1/2 pounds sausage patties or bulk sausage

Produce

- ❏ 8 medium to large onions
- ❏ 3 garlic cloves
- ❏ 1 bulb fennel
- ❏ 2 stalks celery (optional)
- ❏ 1 pound carrots
- ❏ 2 green bell peppers
- ❏ 1 red bell pepper
- ❏ 1 yellow bell pepper
- ❏ 10 small potatoes
- ❏ 1 small head cabbage
- ❏ 1 head iceberg or romaine lettuce
- ❏ 7 sweet potatoes
- ❏ 1 bunch Swiss chard
- ❏ 1 small knob ginger
- ❏ 3 1/2 to 4 pounds tart spicy apples

- ❏ 1 bunch rosemary (optional)
- ❏ 1 bunch thyme (optional)
- ❏ 1 bunch Italian parsley

Dairy

- ❏ 6 tablespoons unsalted butter
- ❏ 2 eggs

Deli

- ❏ 2 tablespoons Roquefort cheese
- ❏ 1 8-ounce package dry herb pasta
- ❏ 1 loaf rye bread
- ❏ 1 loaf crusty bread
- ❏ 1 package Cheddar bread sticks (6 to 8)
- ❏ 8 ounces shredded extra-sharp Cheddar cheese
- ❏ 3/4 cup grated Parmesan cheese

Miscellaneous

- ❏ 2 ounces dried Italian mushrooms
- ❏ 3/4 cup dry white wine
- ❏ 3 28-ounce cans whole tomatoes
- ❏ 1 15-ounce can kidney beans
- ❏ 1/4 cup candied peel or candied pineapple
- ❏ 1/4 cup pecans
- ❏ Pastry for 2 9-inch pie shells (not preformed)
- ❏ 1 unbaked pie shell
- ❏ 1 14 1/2-ounce can black olives
- ❏ 1 cup quinoa
- ❏ 2 14 1/2-ounce cans chicken broth
- ❏ 1 cup Georgia cane syrup, dark corn syrup or honey

Staples

- ❏ All-purpose flour

- ❏ Black pepper
- ❏ Bread crumbs
- ❏ Cinnamon
- ❏ Cornmeal
- ❏ Dried rosemary
- ❏ Dry mustard
- ❏ Granulated sugar
- ❏ Lemon juice
- ❏ Minced garlic in oil
- ❏ Olive oil
- ❏ Paprika (optional)
- ❏ Red pepper flakes
- ❏ Salt
- ❏ Soy or tamari sauce
- ❏ Thyme leaves
- ❏ Vegetable oil
- ❏ Worcestershire sauce

* Suggested accompaniments

ITALIAN BRAISED CHICKEN AND VEGETABLES
APPLE-NUT TURNOVERS

A roasting chicken or larger, cheaper hen could be used in this luscious braised dish, adapted from *Pleasures of the Good Earth* by Edward Giobbi (Knopf, $23). The older hen would also offer more flavor, but take several hours to cook; you will likely find it frozen, so plan on defrosting time. Save the leftovers, but store the chicken and vegetables separately. Substitute celery for the fennel if you wish a more subtle flavor. Porcini are a good choice for dried mushrooms, available at many grocery and specialty stores.

ITALIAN BRAISED CHICKEN AND VEGETABLES

Makes 8 servings
Preparation time 15 minutes
Cooking time 85 minutes

1 4-pound chicken, cut into 8 pieces, washed
2 tablespoons olive oil
Salt and black pepper to taste
2 tablespoons chopped fresh or dried rosemary
2 medium onions, coarsely chopped
2 ounces dried Italian mushrooms, covered with warm water for 15 minutes
1/2 cup dry white wine
3 garlic cloves, unpeeled
1 28-ounce can whole tomatoes
1 cup warm water
1/2 fennel bulb, chopped
1 pound vegetables — combination of red, green and yellow bell peppers, carrots or cabbage and frozen peas
10 small potatoes, sliced

Heat the olive oil in a large skillet and add the chicken, skin side down. Season with salt, pepper and rosemary, and cook, uncovered, over moderate heat, turning the chicken often, about 10 minutes.

When the chicken begins to brown, add the onions, mushrooms and mushroom liquid. Continue to cook until the onions become translucent, about 5 minutes. Add the wine and garlic, and cook, covered, for 10 minutes. Stir in the tomatoes, water, fennel and vegetables. Cover and simmer the chicken at least 45 minutes or until tender. Add the potatoes and cook 15 minutes more.

Per serving: 495 calories, 20 grams fat, 100 milligrams cholesterol, 481 milligrams sodium.

APPLE-NUT TURNOVERS

Makes 8 small turnovers
Preparation time: 20 minutes
Cooking time: 15 minutes

1 1/2 pounds spicy tart cooking apples, peeled and finely sliced
Granulated sugar, to taste
3 tablespoons unsalted butter
1/4 cup candied peel or candied pineapple
1/2 teaspoon cinnamon
1/4 cup pecans, chopped and toasted
Pastry for 2 9-inch pie shells (not pre-formed)

Preheat oven to 400 degrees.

Place the apple slices and a few tablespoons of water and sugar in a skillet and cook about 10 minutes, until mushy. Stir in the butter, candied peel and cinnamon. Stir in the nuts. Set aside.

Roll out the pastry on a pastry cloth until it is quite thin and cut it into eight squares. Put 2 tablespoons of the apple mixture in the center, then fold the pastry over to make a triangle. Moisten the edges, press together (crimp) with a fork. Put the turnovers on a baking sheet and bake for 12 to 15 minutes until puffed. Cool a few minutes before serving.

Per serving 339 calories, 22 grams fat, 25 milligrams cholesterol, 275 milligrams sodium.

HERB PASTA TOSSED WITH BLACK OLIVES *
LETTUCE WEDGES *
PAPRIKA ROQUEFORT DRESSING

A substantial pasta dinner complements this salad with an equally hearty dressing. If you omit the paprika the dressing will taste the same, it just won't have the traditional orange coloring. Use big wedges of iceberg, just like your mother did.

PAPRIKA ROQUEFORT DRESSING

Makes 4 servings
Preparation time: 10 minutes

1/3 cup vegetable oil
1/4 teaspoon paprika (optional)
1 teaspoon dry mustard
1/2 teaspoon granulated sugar
2 tablespoons lemon juice
3 tablespoons dry white wine
1 teaspoon Worcestershire sauce
2 tablespoons Roquefort cheese, crumbled
Salt and pepper to taste

Combine the oil, (optional) paprika, mustard, sugar, lemon juice, wine, Worcestershire sauce, cheese and pepper and blend well. It's fine to leave crumbles of Roquefort cheese throughout the dressing.

Per serving: 195 calories, 20 grams fat, 6 milligrams cholesterol, 141 milligrams sodium.

TUESDAY

STIR-FRY CABBAGE
BAKED SWEET POTATOES *
GRILLED SAUSAGE PATTIES *

Add this quick vegetable stir-fry, adapted from John Pinderhughes book, *Family of the Spirit Cookbook* (Simon & Schuster, $24.95), to a dinner of baked sweet potatoes and grilled sausage. Cook enough sausage to have ¹/₂ pound leftover to use Saturday, and keep it very cold or frozen until then.

STIR-FRY CABBAGE

Makes 4 servings
Preparation time: 10 minutes
Cooking time: 10 minutes

1 tablespoon minced garlic in oil
2 cups coarsely shredded cabbage
1 small green pepper, cut in thin
    strips
1 medium onion, cut in thin slices
1 to 2 tablespoons fresh Italian
    parsley leaves, roughly chopped
Pinch red pepper flakes
¹/₂ teaspoon granulated sugar
1 teaspoon soy or tamari sauce

Heat the oil in a wok or large frying pan over a medium-high flame. When the oil is hot, add the cabbage. Stir to coat the cabbage with oil. Add the green pepper and onion, and cook for 3 to 5 minutes, tossing constantly. Sprinkle with the parsley, red

DECEMBER

White onions are still scarce and high-priced, but pearl onions are widely available. The harvest of Florida carrots has started, and in the coming weeks may drive down the prices of California carrots. Fennel will be available through the holidays, and collards and other greens should be in good supply unless a hard frost hits the harvests in North Georgia.

In general, vegetables are more expensive. With the end of the Florida season and the holidays here, corn, yellow and zucchini squash, tomatoes, okra, cucumbers, and green beans are higher in price. Greens are still reasonable and asparagus is coming down in price. California Haas avocados are in season now and quite inexpensive; other avocados are also in season: the Florida Fuerte, a green avocado, is shaped like Haas but has a higher fat content than the more watery Florida green avocados. Broccoli is slowly going up in price but spinach is still reasonable. Winter squashes are still widely available and well-priced.

Bartlett pears, both green and red, are finished, and Seckels are almost finished, but green and red D'Anjou are still available. Butter-soft Comice pears will be available through the holidays.

Smaller sizes of red and white grapefruit are a better bargain than the larger sizes. Strawberries are coming from Columbia, California and Florida, but the quality of all of them is variable. The quality of cantaloupe and honeydew melons from Guatemala and Honduras is also variable and prices high. Soft fruit from Chili is in many stores now — particularly grapes — and the quality is good. Prices on acorn and butternut squash are steady, but prices on spaghetti squash are going up. Don't expect to find fresh black-eyed peas for New Year's Day, but collard greens will be plentiful and of good quality.

There is lots of variety in citrus: the pineapple, Parson Brown and Hamlin, and all juice oranges are available. Look for the first two extra-flavorful varieties at health food stores and farmers markets and the Hamlin at grocery stores, while others are available at health food stores. Florida Valencias have been cheap and are staying cheap; the sweeter and less acidic California Valencias are getting tight as their season ends. Tangerines are everywhere; the early Robinson is gone, but Dancy and Sunburst and the sweeter Fairchild mandarin are in. Late season apples are still cheap and wonderful-tasting. Georgia apples are gone, but some North Carolina and plenty of eastern apples — Empire, Spartan, McIntosh, Fugi, Winesap and Idared — are available. Bosc and D'Anjou pears are reasonable; Seckle and Asian pears are still available. Look at cranberries carefully to be sure they are solid and not rotting; prices are holding through the holiday. New Mexico cantaloupes are high, and off-shore grapes and stone fruit are in, but are expensive. Pineapples are a good buy now.

pepper, ginger and sugar. Fry 3 minutes more or until the cabbage is tender-crisp. Toss cabbage with soy or tamari sauce.

Per serving: 63 calories, 4 grams fat, no cholesterol, 102 milligrams sodium.

WEDNESDAY

NUBBLY QUINOA WITH VEGETABLES
TOASTED RYE BREAD *

Purchase quinoa (KEEN-wha) at health-food stores or farmers markets. This ancient grain is small and much lighter and more delicate than rice, but power-packed with nutrition. It is a complete protein, possessing all the essential amino acids, just like meat, milk and eggs. Be sure to rinse it under cold running water to rid it of any bitter saponin residue. Save leftovers from this great dish for later in the week; use again in a savory dish or top with maple syrup and milk for breakfast.

NUBBLY QUINOA WITH VEGETABLES

Makes 8 servings
Preparation time: 5 minutes
Cooking time: 23 minutes

1 cup quinoa
2 tablespoons vegetable or olive oil
2 onions, finely diced
2 carrots, finely diced
1/2 bulb fennel, chopped
1 tablespoon fresh rosemary leaves, crushed to release fragrance
2 14 1/2-ounce cans chicken broth or water
1 teaspoon salt
Freshly ground black pepper
1/2 cup grated Parmesan cheese

Place the quinoa in a sieve and rinse under cold running water for about 1 minute.

Heat the oil in a medium-size saucepan over medium heat. Add the onions, carrots, fennel and rosemary and saute, stirring frequently, until the onions are soft and fragrant, 5 to 8 minutes. Add a tablespoon of water if the vegetables stick to the bottom of the pan, and continue to cook.

Add the quinoa to the vegetables and saute for another minute. Add the broth, salt and pepper to taste. Cover and simmer over low heat for 10 minutes. Remove the pot from the heat and stir in the cheese; let it stand covered 5 minutes longer. Add salt and pepper to taste and fluff up the grain with a fork before serving.

Per serving 159 calories, 5 grams fat, 4 milligrams cholesterol, 396 milligrams sodium.

THURSDAY

TOMATO VEGETABLE SOUP
CHEDDAR BREAD STICKS *

A refrigerator of leftovers provides great fodder for this hearty soup. Add or subtract vegetables, beans and grains that you may have. Serve Cheddar bread sticks, available at many grocery deli counters.

TOMATO VEGETABLE SOUP

Makes 10 servings
Preparation time 10 minutes
Cooking time 20-30 minutes

2 tablespoons vegetable oil

1 medium onion, chopped
2 stalks celery, diced (optional)
1/2 cup cooked sweet potato, spooned out of the shell
1 to 2 cups cooked potatoes, carrots, and peas from Sunday's dinner
2 28-ounce cans tomatoes, undrained
1 15-ounce can kidney beans, undrained
Salt and black pepper to taste
1 cup coarsely chopped Swiss chard
1/4 cup grated Parmesan cheese

In a Dutch oven or large saucepan, heat the oil. Add the onion and (optional) celery and saute for 5 minutes. Add the sweet potato and other vegetables, and toss with the onions. Add the tomatoes and juice, beans and juice, and salt and pepper to taste. Add more water to make a thinner soup, if you wish.

Simmer the soup 10 to 20 minutes, until heated through and the vegetables cooked. Just before serving, add the Swiss chard and cook 2 to 3 minutes until it is wilted. Serve in soup bowls and sprinkle with Parmesan cheese.

Per serving: 174 calories, 5 grams fat, 2 milligrams cholesterol, 584 milligrams sodium.

FRIDAY

NUBBLY QUINOA WITH VEGETABLES *
TOMATO VEGETABLE SOUP *
CRUSTY BREAD *

Leftover soup and quinoa can be stirred together to produce a thick porridge. Serve it over thick slices of crusty bread for a hearty and easy dinner.

In Season ❋ Sugar Cane Syrup

Price: Stalks (6 feet long) will range from $.79 to $.99 in local farmers markets and health food stores. Many stores also sell it in 12-inch "batons."

Nutrition: Cane syrup has 50 calories per tablespoon and negligible amounts of iron and calcium, which sorghum molasses has in abundance. Sugar cane is high in carbohydrates but has only trace amounts of other nutrients.

Selection: The stalks are very tough and fibrous, with sweet juice nestled between the fibers. Choose batons that are firm with no wrinkles, and the top of the stalks should be green and not dried out. To eat, peel off the outer bark and cut the interior into fine strips for chewing.

Storage: Refrigerate up to 6 months.

Uses: Chewed raw, one long stalk will keep 12 children busy for a day.

The fresh stalks are sold to chew raw, almost as a licorice stick. They are a favorite fall treat for children all over the deep South.

For Southern cooks, the autumn harvest of sugar cane brings a new supply of the favored and intensely flavored cane syrup. Most of the Georgia cane has now been harvested; through the end of November, farmers in South Georgia will be holding "cane grinding parties" to press the cane and boil the juice into syrup.

The Georgia Agrirama, a 19th Century Living History Museum in Tifton, Georgia will hold nighttime cane grinding parties, complete with pressing the juice the traditional way with mule teams, syrup cooking, bonfires and candy pulling on November 14, 21, and 28 from 7 to 10 pm. For information call 912-386-3344.

For much of the past 250 years, Southerners grew the labor-intensive sugar cane; then, the major end product was rum. Originally it was grown along the coastline, but after an 1824 hurricane damaged the plantations, it was moved inland to the area around Tifton. Today, cane cultivation centers in this area, southward through Florida.

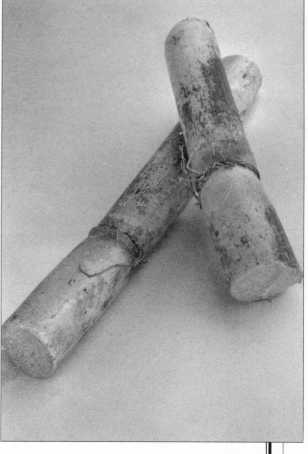

Today cane harvests are dwindling and supplies of pure "blue ribbon" are harder to find. Look for supplies at Atlanta area farmers markets or roadside stands in the Tifton area of Georgia. "The flavor of cane has more presence than the cheaper corn syrup," said Eugene Walter, a Southern food historian located in Mobile, Alabama. "It tastes slightly wild."

Cane syrup has a heavier taste, is thicker and darker next to corn syrup, says John Johnson, director of interpretation and education at the Georgia Agrirama Museum in Tifton, Ga.

Sorghum syrup, made from sorghum grain grown in north Georgia, has an even more intense flavor, bordering on bitter, Mr. Johnson says.

Corn syrup is great for dipping flaky Southern biscuits, and can be used in baking, from jam cakes to cornbread.

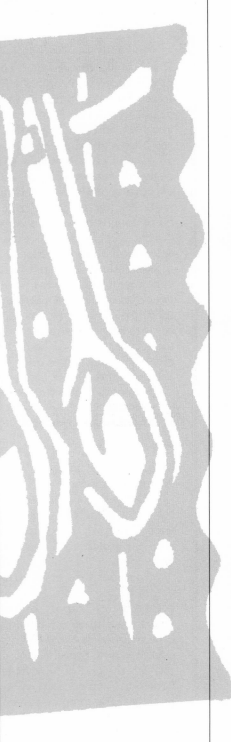

SWEET POTATO, SAUSAGE
AND APPLE GRATIN
A SOUTHERN CUSTARD PIE
WITH CANE SYRUP

Serve this autumn menu after a day of outdoor chores. The gratin is similar to an onion pie, and if you use a food processor for the chopping chores, it will cut 10 minutes from the preparation time. The syrup custard pie is a Southern classic. Add pecans to the mix before baking, or keep it simple as in the delicious pie below.

SWEET POTATO, SAUSAGE AND APPLE GRATIN

Makes 6 servings
Preparation time: 20 minutes
Cooking time: 45 minutes

2 tablespoons vegetable oil
2 large onions, sliced
1 teaspoon fresh or dried thyme leaves
2 1/2 cups thinly sliced very spicy
    apples
1 tablespoon all-purpose flour
2 cups shredded Cheddar cheese
1/2 cup bread crumbs
2 large sweet potatoes, cooked and
    lightly mashed
Salt and black pepper to taste
1/2 pound cooked sausage, crumbled

Preheat the oven to 350 degrees. Grease a deep 8-by-8-inch baking dish or pie pan with pan spray or oil.

    Heat the oil in a medium skillet. Add the onions and thyme and gently saute until the onions are soft, fragrant and golden, at least 10 minutes. Meanwhile, toss the apple slices with flour, cheese and bread crumbs and set aside.

    In a separate small skillet, brown the sausage and blot dry with paper towels.

    Layer the ingredients into the baking dish. First put in a layer of sweet potatoes, add salt and pepper, then add the onions, the sausage and the apple-cheese mixture. Bake, covered, for 30 minutes, then uncovered for 15 minutes. The apples should be tender and the topping bubbly and golden brown.

    Per serving: 559 calories, 38 grams fat, 93 milligrams cholesterol, 816 milligrams sodium.

A SOUTHERN CUSTARD PIE WITH CANE SYRUP

Makes 8 servings
Preparation time: 10 minutes
Cooking time: 40 minutes

2 eggs
1 cup granulated sugar
1 cup Georgia cane syrup
1 tablespoon flour
1 tablespoon cornmeal
3 tablespoons butter, melted
1 9-inch unbaked pie shell

Preheat oven to 450 degrees.

    Break the eggs into a bowl and beat well. Add the sugar, syrup, flour and cornmeal. Mix well. Add the melted butter and blend.

    Pour the mixture into a pastry shell and bake for 10 minutes. Reduce oven heat to 350 degrees and bake for about 30 minutes or until custard is firm and the pastry golden brown.

    Per serving: 378 calories, 13 grams fat, 72 milligrams cholesterol, 199 milligrams sodium.

WEEK

50

SHOPPING LIST

Meat, poultry, seafood

- [ ] 1 4- to 7-pound smoked turkey breast
- [ ] 5 strips bacon
- [ ] 1 1-pound ham steak
- [ ] 2 dozen Apalachicola oysters

Produce

- [ ] 1 head romaine lettuce (for Caesar salad)
- [ ] 1 head chicory or endive lettuce
- [ ] 1 bunch watercress
- [ ] 3 or 4 heads Belgian endive
- [ ] 2 medium yellow onions
- [ ] 5 cloves garlic
- [ ] 1 shallot
- [ ] 1 pound carrots
- [ ] 1 head celery with leaves
- [ ] 6 large russet potatoes
- [ ] 2 pounds green beans
- [ ] 2 Granny Smith apples
- [ ] 1 eating apple

- [ ] 1 large bunch fresh rosemary
- [ ] $1/4$ cup apple cider
- [ ] 1 cup blue cheese salad dressing

Dairy

- [ ] 3 sticks plus 2 tablespoons unsalted butter
- [ ] 2 cups milk
- [ ] 1 cup half-and-half
- [ ] 1 cup whipping cream
- [ ] 7 eggs (2 go in Caesar salad)
- [ ] $1/4$ cup plain non-fat yogurt

Deli

- [ ] 1 baguette French bread
- [ ] 1 loaf Cheddar cheese bread
- [ ] 4 slices rye bread
- [ ] 4 corn muffins
- [ ] 2 ounces gorgonzola or other blue cheese

- [ ] 6 ounces Italian fontina cheese

Miscellaneous

- [ ] 1 16-ounce bag frozen baby lima beans
- [ ] 1 8-ounce bag egg noodles
- [ ] 1 6.5-ounce bag fresh peeled chestnuts
- [ ] 2 tablespoons Bailey's Irish Cream
- [ ] 1 tablespoon Grand Marnier or other orange liqueur
- [ ] 4 14 $1/2$-ounce cans low-sodium chicken broth (or 8 chicken boullion cubes)
- [ ] 2 ounces pecans
- [ ] $1/2$ cup almonds
- [ ] 1 4-ounce bag garlic-sesame pita chips
- [ ] 1 $1/2$ cups dried yellow split peas
- [ ] 2 cups bottled spaghetti

sauce
- [ ] $3/4$ cup regular grits
- [ ] 2 12-ounce packages cranberry-raspberry sauce

Staples

- [ ] All-purpose flour
- [ ] Black pepper
- [ ] Cider vinegar
- [ ] Coffee
- [ ] Coarsely cracked black pepper
- [ ] Curry powder
- [ ] Dijon mustard
- [ ] Dried dill weed
- [ ] Granulated sugar
- [ ] Lemon juice
- [ ] Olive oil
- [ ] Pure almond extract
- [ ] Pure orange extract
- [ ] Salt

* Suggested accompaniments

SMOKED TURKEY BREAST *
BUTTERED EGG NOODLES *
LIMA BEANS WITH
CHESTNUTS AND FRESH
ROSEMARY
COFFEE BREAD PUDDING
WITH IRISH CREAM

Make an easy dinner with smoked turkey breast, heated through in the oven if desired. Ready-to-use fresh and peeled chestnuts turn a simple vegetable dish into a holiday treat. Frozen chestnuts are available at the Dekalb Farmers Market or by mail order by calling 800-745-3279. Use a baguette for the luscious bread pudding, adapted from *Coffee and Tea 1992* by Shannon Jeter Gridley (Culinary Collections, $10.25). The baguette's slender size will fit in a bread pan with no further cutting. Add a couple tablespoons of Bailey's Irish Cream to the whipping cream to serve alongside.

LIMA BEANS WITH CHESTNUTS AND FRESH ROSEMARY

Makes 8 servings
Preparation time: 5 minutes
Cooking time: 10 minutes

4 tablespoons butter
1 6.5-ounce bag peeled chestnuts, cut in half
1 16-ounce package frozen baby lima beans, thawed
4 tablespoons fresh rosemary

In a large skillet, melt the butter. Add chestnuts and saute 5 minutes. Add the lima beans and rosemary and continue to saute another 5 minutes. Serve immediately.

Per serving: 148 calories, 6 grams fat, 15 milligrams cholesterol, 82 milligrams sodium.

COFFEE BREAD PUDDING WITH IRISH CREAM

Makes 8 servings
Preparation time: 10 minutes
Cooking time: 1 hour

2 cups milk
1 cup half-and-half
1 cup strong coffee (a flavored coffee, French or Italian roast or espresso is nice)
2 to 3 tablespoons unsalted butter, softened
8 to 10 slices stale French bread (baguette works best), 1/2-inch thick
1/2 cup granulated sugar
2 eggs, slightly beaten
1/2 teaspoon salt
1 teaspoon orange extract
Whipped cream with Irish cream liqueur (optional)

Preheat oven to 350 degrees. Grease a 9-by-5-inch loaf pan and set aside. Butter the bread slices and place them in the bread pan slightly overlapping to make a shingled effect. Set aside.

Place the milk, half-and-half and coffee in a large microwave-safe bowl and heat on high (100 percent power) in the microwave until hot, about 2 minutes, then cool slightly. Stir the sugar, eggs, salt and orange extract into the milk mixture; pour over the bread. Bake 1 hour.

Per serving, with 1 tablespoon each of whipped cream and liqueur: 313 calories, 14 grams fat, 112 milligrams cholesterol, 381 milligrams sodium.

BAVARIAN POTATO SOUP
WITH LIMA BEANS
CAESAR SALAD *
COFFEE BREAD PUDDING *

Serve this different potato soup with dill-flavored croutons. The soup would be delicious with the easy addition of one diced bulb of anise-flavored fennel — fennel is at its best and cheapest during the winter months. Add a Caesar salad and reheat any remaining Coffee Bread Pudding.

BAVARIAN POTATO SOUP WITH LIMA BEANS

Makes 6 servings
Preparation time: 10 minutes
Cooking time: 30 minutes

5 bacon strips, cut into 1/2-inch pieces
1 medium yellow onion
2 large carrots, coarsely chopped
Handful celery leaves and upper stems, coarsely chopped
1 tablespoon rosemary leaves, crushed
4 large russet potatoes, peeled and cut into 1-inch cubes
4 14 1/2-ounce cans low-sodium chicken broth (or 8 chicken boullion cubes and 8 cups water)
1/2 cup cooked lima beans with rosemary
1/4 cup unsalted butter
4 slices rye bread, 1/2-inch thick, cut into cubes
Salt to taste

Heat the bacon in a heavy, large saucepan over medium heat until the fat is rendered. Add the onion, carrots and celery leaves to the pan

Price: Oysters in the shell will average $3.99 a dozen or $.69 a pound for 3 to 4 oysters.

Nutrition: A 3 ½-ounce serving has 69 calories, 2.5 grams fat, 55 milligrams cholesterol, 112 milligrams sodium and is an excellent source of iron and zinc.

Selection: Oysters are sold live in the shell and fresh-shucked, packed in bulk or in containers. Oysters must be alive when purchased in the shell, indicated by shells that close tightly when handled. Live oysters are usually sold by the dozen.

In shucked oysters, two sizes are available: the larger select and smaller sized standard. A pint of select will have 26 to 38 oysters, while a pint of standard will have 38 to 63 oysters. Whether they are offered in bulk or pre-packed, check the date and choose oysters that have 4 days to a week left before the pull date. Oysters are safe to eat year round, although summer oysters may be milky-looking, mushier and less tasty.

Storage: Oysters will remain alive from seven to ten days if stored un-iced in the coldest part of the refrigerator, at about 35 to 40 degrees.

Uses: Purchase 6 oysters in the shell per serving. Oysters may be eaten raw, poached in their own liquor or other liquid, baked or fried.

After a devastating hurricane and drought and a hard climb back into production, the delicious Apalachicola Bay oysters are back in stock for the first time since 1985. They are available live, in the shell, now through early spring, and served raw on the half shell or cooked make great holiday party food.

Look for plenty of supplies in December and January, when the smaller oysters begin to reach market size. Look for them at area grocery stores.

Most of the oysters harvested from Apalachicola Bay are destined for "half-shell" oyster bars around the country. They have a distinctive taste, texture and size that are especially savored in the raw form.

From one part of the country to another, oysters taste different according to the food they eat and the water in which they live — northern oysters from colder waters and most eastern oysters are saltier with more of an ocean flavor, while western oysters taste milder. American oysters, especially Eastern, are among the best-tasting in the world, says A. J. McClane in his book *Fish*.

As with other raw foods

and mollusks, don't eat oysters raw if you suffer from immune-deficiency diseases or chronic illness of the liver, stomach or blood since they could be contaminated.

"Eating raw molluscan shellfish (oysters, mussels and clams) is one of the more common problems we have with food safety today," says Mildred Cody, associate professor of nutrition and dietetics at Georgia State University.

and cook over medium heat, stirring, about 5 minutes. Add potatoes and stock and continue to simmer 20 minutes or until the potatoes are cooked through. Add limas with 5 minutes cooking time remaining.

Meanwhile, make the croutons, melt butter in a skillet. Add bread cubes and salt and toss to coat. Cook until golden brown, tossing frequently, 5 to 7 minutes. To serve, ladle the soup into bowls and sprinkle with croutons.

Per serving: 297 calories, 12 grams fat, 26 milligrams cholesterol, 930 milligrams sodium.

TUESDAY

SMOKED TURKEY, APPLE AND PECAN SALAD
CORN MUFFINS *

Use leftover smoked turkey in this easy winter salad. Add purchased or homemade corn muffins.

SMOKED TURKEY, APPLE AND PECAN SALAD

Makes 4 servings
Preparation time: 10 minutes

4 cups chicory lettuce, rinsed, dried, torn into pieces
1 cup watercress leaves
2 cups Belgian endive leaves, separated, cut lengthwise into thin strips
12 ounces smoked turkey, cut into strips
1 apple, cored, cut into 1/4-inch slices
3 or 4 tablespoons pecans
2 ounces gorgonzola or blue cheese, crumbled
1/4 cup olive oil
3 tablespoons cider vinegar

1 teaspoon Dijon mustard
Salt and pepper to taste

Heat the oven to 300 degrees. Put the pecans on a baking sheet and place in the oven. Toast, stirring, for 8 to 10 minutes, until the pecans turn browner and fragrant.

In a large bowl, combine the chicory, watercress, endive, turkey, apple, pecans and cheese. In a small bowl whisk together the oil, vinegar, mustard, salt and pepper. Pour vinaigrette over the salad, tossing to combine. Serve immediately.

Per serving, with no added salt: 393 calories, 28 grams fat, 65 milligrams cholesterol, 91 milligrams sodium.

WEDNESDAY

SPLIT-PEA CURRIED STEW
GARLIC-SESAME PITA CHIPS *

This homey winter stew comes from Atlantan Susan Mack. She prepares this in a crockpot, allowing it to simmer all day while she's at work. If you want to do the same, simply add all the ingredients to the pot and cook for 6 to 8 hours. Ms. Mack also makes her own curry mixture for the dish, but I have used commercial curry powder for convenience.

SPLIT-PEA CURRIED STEW

Makes 8 servings
Preparation time: 10 minutes
Cooking time: 30 to 45 minutes

1 tablespoon vegetable or olive oil
1 medium yellow onion, finely chopped

4 to 5 cloves garlic, finely minced
1 1/2 cups dried yellow split peas
2 cups bottled spaghetti sauce
2 medium potatoes, cubed
Water to cover (3 to 4 cups)
1 tablespoon curry powder
Salt to taste
1/4 cup plain non-fat yogurt

In a Dutch oven or other large saucepan, heat the oil. Add onion and garlic and saute 5 minutes. Add the peas, spaghetti sauce, potatoes, water, curry powder and salt. Cover and cook 30 minutes on medium-low heat.

Ladle soup into bowls; swirl a tablespoon of yogurt into each serving.

Per serving: 212 calories, 2 grams fat, trace of cholesterol, 29 milligrams sodium.

THURSDAY

PAN-FRIED HAM STEAK *
FONTINA GRITS
STEAMED GREEN BEANS WITH LEMON*

This creamy grits dish, adapted from *Around the Southern Table* by Sarah Belk (Simon & Schuster, $24.95), is as at home at the dinner table or as a bedtime snack in front of the TV. Use regular grits for a fuller flavor, but instant grits will cook more quickly. Danish fontina is available in most grocery stores; the creamier and more flavorful Italian can be found in cheese shops. Stone-ground grits have a fuller corn flavor and the nutrition of the whole grain. Look for them at local farmers markets and specialty stores, as well as some grocery stores. Save leftover grits for another meal.

FONTINA GRITS

Makes 8 servings
Preparation time: 5 minutes
Cooking time: 20 minutes

4 cups water
1 1/4 cups grits (not instant if
    possible)
2 or 3 slices bacon (optional)
4 or 5 tablespoons unsalted butter
    (or more to taste)
6 ounces Italian fontina cheese,
    grated (about 1/2 cup)
Salt and ground black pepper to
    taste

Bring salted water to a boil in a
heavy saucepan. Add grits slowly
while stirring to prevent lump-
ing. Cover and simmer 18 to 20
minutes or until water has been
absorbed. Meanwhile, fry the
(optional) bacon in a skillet;
drain and crumble and set aside.

Stir in the butter and cheese
until they melt. Stir in the
bacon and season to taste with
salt and pepper and serve hot.
Per serving without bacon: 179
calories, 12 grams fat, 38 milligrams
cholesterol, 285 milligrams sodium.

FRIDAY

SPLIT-PEA CURRIED STEW *
FRIED GRITS*
CARROT AND STICKS

Reheat the week's leftovers for
tonight's dinner, split-pea stew
and fried slices of cheese grits.
Add carrots for some raw fiber.

SATURDAY

OYSTERS ON THE HALF SHELL

WITH APPLE CIDER
MIGNONETTE
VEGETABLE AND CHEESE
TRAY WITH BLUE CHEESE
DIPPING SAUCE *
CRANBERRY TARTLETS

Delicious, raw oysters make
perfect holiday party food. Serve
them simply, with an update of a
classic vinegar and black pepper
sauce called mignonette, adapted from *Cold Weather Cooking* by
Sarah Leah Chase (Workman,
$13.95). Apalachicola oysters
from Florida are smallish, just
right for eating raw, and are
among the tastiest available this
season. Look for them at area
grocery stores.

Cranberries, almonds and
orange go together to make a
great holiday dessert. Make the
tartlets small, as in the following
recipe, for a buffet-style party;
for a sit-down dinner with six or
eight people, make the tarts in
larger muffin or tartlet pans.

OYSTERS ON THE
HALF SHELL WITH
APPLE CIDER
MIGNONETTE

Makes 3/4 cup sauce, enough for
*   6 servings*
Preparation time: 15 minutes
Standing time: 1 hour

1 shallot, trimmed and finely minced
2 Granny Smith apples, peeled,
    cored and finely diced
1/2 cup cider vinegar
1 tablespoon balsamic vinegar
1 teaspoon coarsely cracked black
    pepper
2 dozen raw oysters, chilled

Mix together the shallot, apples,
vinegars and black pepper and let
sit for 1 hour to mellow. Open
oysters. Spoon sauce over freshly

chilled raw oysters on the half
shell.
Per serving: 67 calories, 2 grams
fat, 47 milligrams cholesterol, 96 mil-
ligrams sodium.

CRANBERRY
TARTLETS

Makes 10 tartlets
Preparation time: 25 minutes
Cooking time: 10 minutes

1/2 cup almonds
1 1/2 cups all-purpose flour
1 stick butter, chilled, cut into
    small pieces
2 tablespoons granulated sugar
Pinch salt
1 egg
1 teaspoon almond extract
2 12-ounce packages cranberry-
    raspberry sauce
1/4 cup granulated sugar
2 large egg yolks
1/4 cup unsalted butter
1 tablespoon Grand Marnier or
    other orange liqueur

Heat the oven to 400 degrees.
Put the almonds on a baking
sheet and toast until golden,
about 8 minutes.

To prepare the almond
crust: Place the almonds and
flour in a food processor and
process until the nuts are finely
ground. Add the butter, sugar
and salt; process until the mixture resembles coarse meal. Add
the egg and almond extract and
continue to pulse a few times
just until the dough holds
together.

Press the dough into 24
mini-muffin cups. Bake about 8
minutes, until the crusts are
starting to brown. Remove from
the oven and cool.

To prepare the cranberry
filling: Place the cranberry sauce
and sugar in a medium saucepan
and heat until warm. Stir in the

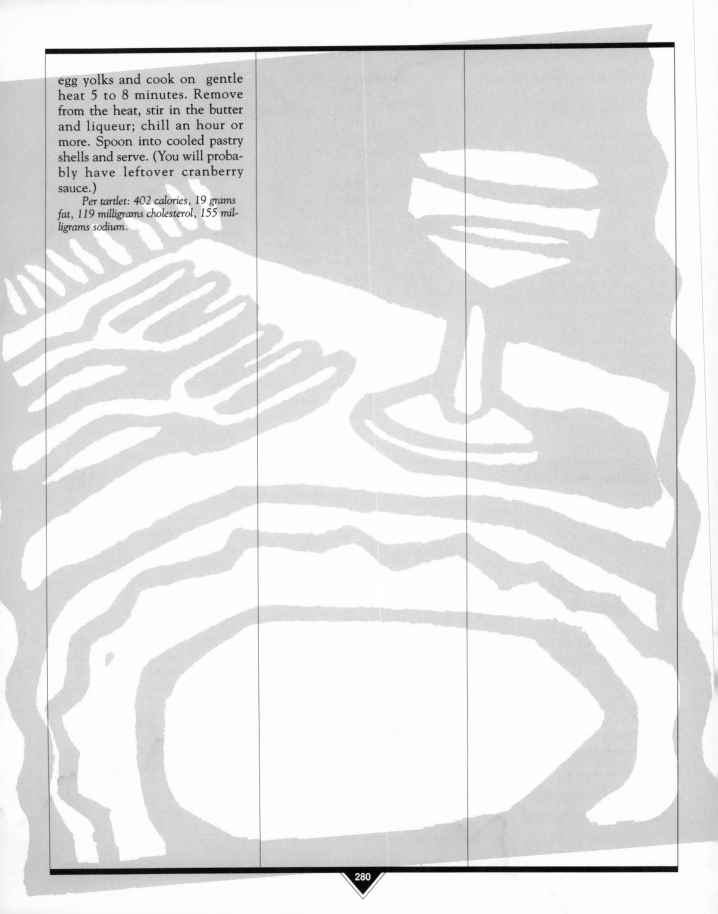

egg yolks and cook on gentle heat 5 to 8 minutes. Remove from the heat, stir in the butter and liqueur; chill an hour or more. Spoon into cooled pastry shells and serve. (You will probably have leftover cranberry sauce.)

Per tartlet: 402 calories, 19 grams fat, 119 milligrams cholesterol, 155 milligrams sodium.

WEEK

51

SHOPPING LIST

Meat, poultry, seafood

- ❑ 1 4-pound roasting chicken
- ❑ 2 ounces salt pork (or bacon)
- ❑ 1 5-pound honey-baked ham
- ❑ 1 $1/4$ pounds catfish fillets

Produce

- ❑ 1 3-pound bag new red potatoes
- ❑ 1 head lettuce
- ❑ 2 bunches spinach
- ❑ 30 large mushrooms
- ❑ 2 stalks celery
- ❑ 3 or 4 carrots
- ❑ 2 pints brussels sprouts
- ❑ 9 sweet potatoes
- ❑ 2 yellow onions
- ❑ 2 leeks
- ❑ 4 garlic cloves
- ❑ 1 12-ounce bag cranberries
- ❑ 4 ripe figs

- ❑ 4 Comice pears
- ❑ 2 medium navel oranges
- ❑ 1 red grapefruit
- ❑ 3 tangerines
- ❑ 4 kumquats
- ❑ 3 lemons
- ❑ 1 bunch parsley
- ❑ 1 bunch mint
- ❑ 1 red or green bell pepper

Dairy

- ❑ $1/2$ cup (4 ounces) low-fat lemon yogurt
- ❑ 4 ounces feta cheese
- ❑ 1 stick plus 2 tablespoons unsalted butter
- ❑ 3 eggs
- ❑ 1 cup grated Cheddar cheese
- ❑ $1/3$ cup milk
- ❑ 1 cup whipping cream

Deli

- ❑ 1 banana bread
- ❑ 1 quart oyster stew

- ❑ 1 pint coleslaw

Miscellaneous

- ❑ $1/4$ cup apricot nectar
- ❑ 8 1-ounce squares semi-sweet chocolate
- ❑ 1 32-ounce box vanilla wafers
- ❑ 1 cup pecans
- ❑ 1 cup walnuts
- ❑ $1/2$ cup plus 1 tablespoon bourbon
- ❑ $1/4$ cup port
- ❑ 1 cup rice
- ❑ $1/2$ cup barley
- ❑ 1 cup cornmeal
- ❑ 4 14 $1/2$-ounce cans chicken broth
- ❑ 1 14 $1/2$-ounce can tomato wedges
- ❑ 1 to 2 cups frozen sliced okra
- ❑ 2 tablespoons orange juice
- ❑ Whole-wheat crackers
- ❑ 1 9-inch pastry shell

- ❑ Christmas cookies

Staples

- ❑ Black pepper
- ❑ Bread crumbs (fresh is best)
- ❑ Brown sugar
- ❑ Cane syrup
- ❑ Cayenne pepper
- ❑ Granulated sugar
- ❑ Ground nutmeg
- ❑ Herbs de Provence
- ❑ Honey
- ❑ Olive oil
- ❑ Pure vanilla extract
- ❑ Salt
- ❑ Vegetable shortening

* Suggested accompaniments

SUNDAY

ROAST CHICKEN AND NEW RED POTATOES *
CITRUS SALAD WITH APRICOT-LEMON SAUCE
KENTUCKY BOURBON BALLS

Choose a chicken large enough to supply leftovers for later in the week. A 3-pound bag of new red potatoes should also supply enough to serve in a later dish. Add a delicious fruit salad with lemon sauce, and prepare a Southern Christmas specialty, Kentucky Bourbon Balls, adapted from *American Cooking Southern Style* (Time-Life Books, $12.95). Of course, any good-quality whiskey, not only bourbon, can be used. This dessert will yield enough to serve during the holiday week.

CITRUS SALAD WITH APRICOT-LEMON SAUCE

Makes 4 servings
Preparation time: 25 minutes

1 medium navel orange, peeled and sectioned
1 red grapefruit, peeled, seeded and sectioned
3 tangerines, peeled, seeded and sectioned
4 kumquats, unpeeled and thinly sliced

APRICOT-LEMON SAUCE:
1 tablespoon honey
1/4 teaspoon ground nutmeg
1/2 cup low-fat lemon yogurt
1/4 cup apricot nectar
Fresh mint sprigs for garnish

Divide and arrange fruit on 6 plates. Set aside.
To make the sauce, stir honey and nutmeg into the lemon yogurt. Add apricot nectar. Stir until smooth. (May be stored in the refrigerator for up to 2 weeks.) Drizzle dressing over fruit. Garnish with lemon slices and fresh mint sprigs.

Per serving: 122 calories, less than 1 gram fat, 1 milligrams cholesterol, 20 milligrams sodium.

KENTUCKY BOURBON BALLS

Makes 60 1-inch candies
Cooking time: 4 minutes
Preparation time: 30 minutes

8 1-ounce squares semisweet chocolate, coarsely chopped
60 vanilla wafers, pulverized in food processor (to make 3 cups)
1 cup finely chopped pecans
1 2/3 cups granulated sugar
1/2 cup bourbon
1/4 light corn syrup or honey

Put the chocolate in a microwave-safe dish. Partially cover and melt in microwave on medium (50 percent power) for 3 to 4 minutes. Let the chocolate cool slightly.
Pulverize the vanilla wafers in a food processor, then move them to a large bowl. Finely chop the pecans in the food processor and add to the vanilla wafers. Add 2/3 cup of sugar to the bowl. Pour in the chocolate, bourbon and corn syrup and mix vigorously with a wooden spoon or your hands until the ingredients are well combined.
To shape each bourbon ball, scoop up about a tablespoon of the mixture and pat it into a 1-inch ball. Roll the balls in the remaining cup of sugar and when they're lightly coated on all sides, place them in a wide-mouth 1-quart jar with a tight-fitting lid.

Cut two rounds from paper towels to fit inside the lid of the jar. Moisten the paper rounds with a little additional bourbon and press them tightly into the lid. Seal the jar with the paper-lined lid and set the bourbon balls aside at room temperature for 3 or 4 days before serving. Tightly covered, they will keep 3 to 4 weeks.

Per piece: 78 calories, 3 grams fat, 2 milligrams cholesterol, 11 milligrams sodium.

MONDAY

LIMPING SUSAN
MIXED GREEN SALAD *
BANANA BREAD *

No one seems to know how this dish got it's name, but it's a wonderful Southern dish to serve simply with a green salad and dessert. The baking step takes a bit longer to get the dish to the table, but it produces a drier rice and perfectly cooked okra, adapted from *Gulf Coast Cooking* by Virginia Elverson (Shearer, $34.95). Use leftover chicken, turkey, or shrimp if you prefer. Make or purchase banana bread tonight to serve as a late Christmas Eve snack or for Christmas morning breakfast.

LIMPING SUSAN

Makes 10 servings
Preparation time: 10 minutes
Cooking time: 45 minutes

1/4 cup salt pork (or bacon), finely chopped
1 cup uncooked rice
1 yellow onion, finely chopped
3 cups chicken broth
2 cups mashed canned tomatoes

Price: Will range from $1.99 to $4.99 a pound.

Nutrition: 1 kumquat has 12 calories, a trace of fat, is high in potassium, low in sodium and a good source of vitamin C.

Selection: In season from November through Christmas and through January in some stores. Press individual fruits to make sure they are firm, not soft. Two Japanese varieties are available — the more common oblong Nagami and harder-to-find, rounder and sweeter Meiwa.

Storage: If you plan to use them within a few days, they may be stored at room temperature, otherwise, refrigerate them up to 2 weeks. Wash before serving to remove any fungicides.

Uses: Serve kumquats as you would fresh grapes — whole on a fruit platter or sliced in a fruit salad. They can also be candied whole. Use them interchangeably with oranges in cooked dishes with pork or poultry. Add to stuffings, steamed puddings, cakes and sweet breads. The whole fruits can be pureed into a thick sauce.

This miniature Japanese fruit looks like any ordinary citrus, but its flavors are turned upside down. Unlike other fruits that fall under the citrus classification, the sweetness of kumquats is found in its thick skin, and the flesh is decidedly sour. They are commonly eaten whole, and the combination of intense sweetness and sourness is a flavorful surprise. The flavor is similar to lemongrass, says Case Lichtveld, produce manager at Harry's Farmers Market.

Kumquats don't ship or store as well as other citrus, as the high sugar content causes the peel to soften quickly. Kumquats are sweeter at picking time, but the fruits lose the sweetness within one week.

2 tablespoons parsley (optional)
1 to 2 cups frozen cut okra, frozen
1 cup slivered cooked chicken
Salt and pepper to taste

Preheat oven to 325 degrees.

In a heavy saucepan fry salt pork until crisp. Add rice and onions and stir until onions are golden brown and soft, then add broth. Reduce heat, cover and cook about 15 minutes.

Stir in the tomatoes, parsley, okra, chicken and salt and pepper to taste. Bake, uncovered, for 30 minutes.

Per serving: 160 calories, 4 grams fat, 20 milligrams cholesterol, 416 milligrams sodium.

TUESDAY

MUSHROOMS ROASTED
WITH WALNUTS
OYSTER STEW *
SPINACH SALAD WITH
FETA CHEESE *
RIPE COMICE PEARS,
CHRISTMAS COOKIES AND
KENTUCKY BOURBON BALLS

Prepare this dish in the morning if you wish, and refrigerate, then bake just before serving time. Add a traditional pot of oyster stew, a big salad with feta cheese and ripe Comice pears and Christmas cookies and candies for a simple, but elegant Christmas Eve dinner.

MUSHROOMS ROASTED WITH WALNUTS

Makes 8 servings
Preparation time: 15 minutes
Cooking time: 15 minutes

30 large mushrooms, cleaned,

stemmed and thickly sliced
$1/2$ cup olive oil
Juice of 1 lemon
4 large garlic cloves, crushed and peeled
1 cup walnut pieces
1 cup fresh bread crumbs
1 tablespoon herbs de Provence
Salt, to taste

Preheat the oven to 400 degrees. Coat a 10-inch pie plate or other shallow baking dish with some of the olive oil.

Put the lemon juice in a shallow dish and roll the mushrooms around in it, then place them in a baking dish.

Dice the mushroom stems and saute them in the rest of the olive oil in a medium skillet. Add the garlic and saute until it turns golden, about 30 seconds. Add the walnuts, bread crumbs, herbs de Provence and salt and blend. Spoon the mixture over the mushrooms and bake uncovered for 15 minutes.

Per serving: 282 calories, 26 grams fat, no cholesterol, 32 milligrams sodium.

WEDNESDAY

HONEY-BAKED HAM *
LEMON-SCENTED
SWEET POTATOES
STEAMED BRUSSELS SPROUTS *
CRANBERRIES BAKED
WITH PORT
DRIED FIGS SAUTEED
IN BUTTER *

A Christmas ham dinner wouldn't be complete without the requisite side dishes of sweet potatoes and cranberries. Lemon sweet potatoes are a refreshing change from heavier versions of this dish, and cranberries baked

in port make a good side dish as well as great Christmas presents, compliments of my talented friend and cook, Emily Cassady . Keep dessert simple with halved dried figs, plumped in brandy and quickly sauteed in butter. Drizzle them with a flavored cream, slightly whipped, if you wish.

LEMON-SCENTED SWEET POTATOES

Makes 6 servings
Preparation time: 10 minutes
Cooking time: 30 to 40 minutes

5 medium sweet potatoes, about $2 1/2$ pounds
2 lemons, 1 juiced, 1 thinly sliced
2 tablespoons butter

Preheat the oven to 350 degrees. Grease a baking pan with pan spray or oil.

Cook the unpeeled potatoes in the microwave oven on High for 8 to 10 minutes. (Or bring a large pot of water to a boil. Add the potatoes and cook for 10 to 12 minutes, until you can just pierce them with a fork.) The potatoes should be slightly underdone. Peel and cut in 1-inch thick slices. Let cool, then cut the slices in large dice.

Put the potatoes in the prepared baking pan. Mix in the lemon slices and sprinkle with the juice; dot with butter. Bake for about 20 minutes, stirring once or twice, until the potatoes are soft and crispy-brown.

Per serving: 235 calories, 4 grams fat, 10 milligrams cholesterol, 59 milligrams sodium.

CRANBERRIES BAKED WITH PORT

Makes 10 servings
Preparation time: 5 minutes
Cooking time: 1 hour

1 12-ounce bag fresh cranberries
1 cup brown sugar
2 tablespoons orange juice
Grated rind of 1 orange
1/4 cup port

Preheat the oven to 300 degrees. In a large baking dish combine the cranberries, brown sugar, orange juice and grated orange rind, cover and bake 1 hour. Stir in the port, cover and allow to cool. Serve warm or at room temperature.

Per serving: 108 calories, trace of fat, no cholesterol, 7 milligrams sodium.

THURSDAY

LIMPING SUSAN WITH ROASTED MUSHROOMS *
SPINACH SALAD *
CORN BREAD *

With plenty of leftovers in the refrigerator, treat yourself to a night out of the kitchen. Limping Susan with roasted mushrooms tossed in, fresh spinach, even ham sandwiches would be welcomed tonight. Bake a pan of corn bread as a great accompaniment to the rice dish if you wish.

FRIDAY

HAM AND BARLEY SOUP
RAW VEGETABLES *
WHOLE-WHEAT CRACKERS *

Use leftover ham and roasted potatoes for this warming soup. Serve a tray of raw vegetables, such as celery, carrots or zucchini, and crackers to round out the meal.

HAM AND BARLEY SOUP

Makes 6 servings
Preparation time: 10 minutes
Cooking time: 20 minutes

1/4 cup unsalted butter
1 cup baked ham, cut into 1-to
    2-inch pieces
2 leeks, white part only, cleaned and
    sliced
2 cups roasted potatoes, quartered
2 14 1/2-ounce cans chicken broth
1/2 cup barley
Salt and black pepper to taste

Melt the butter or margarine in a Dutch oven or large pan and add the ham; let it cook and release some fat into the pan. Add the leeks and cook until they are soft, about 5 minutes. Add the potatoes, broth, barley and salt and pepper. Cover and cook 10 to 15 minutes, until the barley has doubled in size and the broth is slightly thickened. Season with more salt and black pepper if necessary.

Per serving: 286 calories, 12 grams fat, 35 milligrams cholesterol, 758 milligrams sodium.

SATURDAY

FRIED CATFISH *
DELTA DOGS
COLESLAW *
SWEET POTATO PIE

Keep it casual this Saturday night, with fried catfish, extra-spicy hush puppies, adapted from *Gourmet* magazine, and sweet potato pie, made with Southern-made bourbon and cane syrup (see In Season, page 273). Cut back on the cayenne and black pepper for milder hush puppies.

(The batter tastes spicier than the finished hush puppies.)

If you make the Delta Dogs in the summer, use sweet or hot banana peppers for a wonderful spicy addition.

DELTA DOGS

Makes about 16
Preparation time: 5 minutes
Cooking time: 15 minutes

Vegetable shortening, vegetable oil
    or lard for deep frying
1 large onion, grated
1 cup grated sharp Cheddar cheese
2 tablespoons chopped red or green
    bell pepper
1 cup cornmeal plus additional if
    necessary
1 teaspoon cayenne pepper
1 teaspoon black pepper
3/4 teaspoon salt
Boiling water

Heat the shortening to 350 degrees in a deep saucepan. To grate the onion quickly, pulse quartered sections several times in a food processor.

In a bowl, toss together well the onion, cheese, bell pepper, 1 cup of cornmeal, cayenne, black pepper and salt. Stir in 3/4 cup boiling water and combine the batter well.

Test the batter by frying a heaping teaspoon of it in 2 inches of 350-degree shortening for 2 to 3 minutes, or until it is golden brown. If the fritter disintegrates in the fat, stir some additional cornmeal into the batter. Fry heaping teaspoons of the batter in batches in the hot shortening for 2 minutes, or until the Delta Dogs are golden brown. Transfer them as they are cooked to brown paper or paper towels to drain, and serve immediately.

Per dog, using vegetable fat: 79 calories, 5 grams fat, 7 milligrams cholesterol, 144 milligrams sodium.

SWEET POTATO PIE

Makes 8 servings
Preparation time: 20 minutes
Cooking time: 45 minutes

4 medium sweet potatoes, peeled and
    quartered
4 tablespoons butter, softened
³/4 cup brown sugar
3 eggs, lightly beaten
¹/3 cup cane syrup
¹/3 cup milk
2 teaspoons grated lemon peel
1 tablespoon bourbon
¹/4 teaspoon ground nutmeg,
    preferably freshly grated
¹/2 teaspoon salt (optional)
1 9-inch pastry pie shell, baked and
    cooled
Whipped cream (optional)

Preheat oven to 425 degrees.

Cook the sweet potatoes in the microwave on high (100 percent power) for 10 to 12 minutes, or until completely soft. Peel and puree them in the workbowl of a food processor. Transfer them to another bowl and cool to room temperature.

In the food processor, cream the butter and brown sugar until light and fluffy. Add pureed sweet potatoes back in, then eggs one at a time, beating well after each addition. Add the cane syrup, milk, lemon peel, bourbon, nutmeg and salt and continue to process until the filling is smooth.

Pour the filling into the pie shell, spreading it evenly with a rubber spatula. Bake in the middle of the oven for 10 minutes, then reduce oven temperature to 325 degrees and bake for 35 minutes longer, or until a knife inserted in the center comes out clean. Serve warm or at room temperature with whipped cream.

Per serving, without bourbon and with 1 tablespoon whipped cream: 304 calories, 15 grams fat, 122 milligrams cholesterol, 405 milligrams sodium.

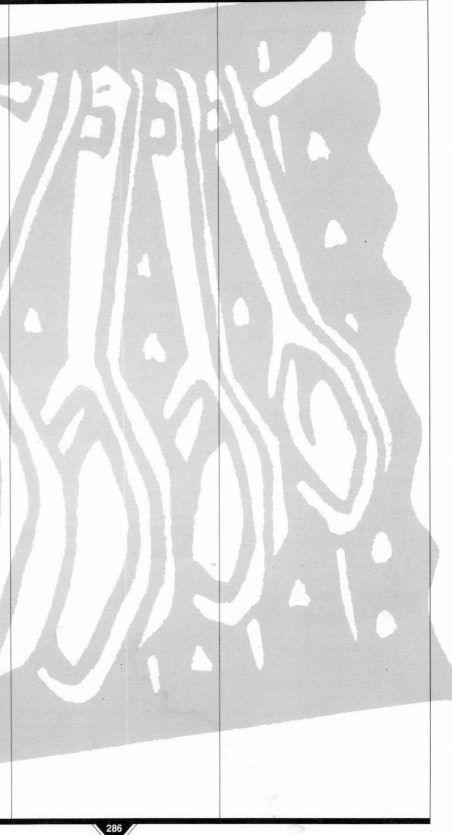

WEEK

52

SHOPPING LIST

Meat, poultry, seafood

- ❏ 2 pounds pork tenderloin
- ❏ 12 ounces sirloin steak, pounded thin
- ❏ 6 fresh, precooked Dungeness crabs

Produce

- ❏ 1 pound Brussels sprouts
- ❏ 3 large sweet potatoes
- ❏ 1 head curly endive
- ❏ 1 or 2 heads Belgium endive
- ❏ 1 head lettuce, any type
- ❏ 1 large onion
- ❏ 1 bell pepper
- ❏ 1/2 small red onion
- ❏ 1 clove garlic
- ❏ 3 cups fresh spinach
- ❏ 1 pound green beans
- ❏ 2 tangerines
- ❏ 1 orange
- ❏ 2 pears
- ❏ 4 firm apples, such as Granny Smith or York

- ❏ 13 lemons

Dairy

- ❏ 1 stick plus 4 table-spoons butter
- ❏ 1 1/2 cups milk
- ❏ 1 1/2 cups half-and-half or cream
- ❏ 8 eggs
- ❏ 18-ounce package cream cheese
- ❏ 1/2 cup freshly grated Parmesan cheese

Deli

- ❏ 2 loaves crusty bread
- ❏ 6 ounces Stilton or other blue cheese
- ❏ 4 ounces provolone cheese
- ❏ 4 sourdough rolls

Miscellaneous

- ❏ 1 cup wild rice

- ❏ 2 tablespoons apricot jam
- ❏ 1/4 cup orange juice
- ❏ 8 frozen tart shells (or homemade pastry dough)
- ❏ 2 16-ounce cans black-eyed peas
- ❏ 2 14 1/2-ounce cans low-sodium chicken broth
- ❏ 19-ounce package cinna-mon red hots
- ❏ 1/2 cup broken pecans
- ❏ 1 cup frozen peas
- ❏ 1/3 cup dried tomatoes

Staples

- ❏ Black pepper
- ❏ Brown sugar
- ❏ Dijon-style mustard
- ❏ Dried oregano
- ❏ Dried rosemary
- ❏ Grated nutmeg
- ❏ Ground cinnamon
- ❏ Minced garlic in oil
- ❏ Paprika
- ❏ Red wine vinegar
- ❏ Salt

- ❏ Soy sauce
- ❏ Sugar
- ❏ Tabasco sauce
- ❏ Vegetable oil
- ❏ Worcestershire sauce

GLAZED PORK TENDERLOIN
STEAMED WILD RICE*
BRUSSELS SPROUTS IN
BUTTER SAUCE*
NORTH CAROLINA SWEET
POTATO PUDDING

Pork tenderloin makes an easy Sunday meal and offers leftovers to use in a salad later in the week. Add steamed wild rice and Brussels sprouts and, for dessert, a sweet potato pudding.

GLAZED PORK TENDERLOIN

Makes 8 servings
Preparation time: 5 minutes
Marinating time: several hours
Cooking time: 30 minutes

1/4 cup vegetable oil
2 tablespoons soy sauce
2 tablespoons apricot jam
1 teaspoon dried rosemary
1 teaspoon minced garlic in oil
1 teaspoon grated orange rind
1/4 cup orange juice
1 teaspoon Dijon-style mustard
2 pounds pork tenderloin
1/4 cup red wine vinegar

Make a marinade by combining in a food processor the oil, soy sauce, jam, rosemary, orange rind and juice and mustard. Place the tenderloins in a glass or enamel dish large enough to contain them compactly and cover with marinade. Cover with plastic wrap and refrigerate for several hours. Bring to room temperature before cooking.

Preheat oven to 450 degrees. Remove tenderloins from the marinade and place them in a roasting pan. Roast 30 minutes turning twice during cooking, or until a meat thermometer registers 155 degrees. Transfer to a heated platter.

Over medium heat, add the vinegar to the roasting pan juices and deglaze, scraping up any particles clinging to the pan. Add reserved marinade and stir constantly until very hot. Slice the tenderloins and serve with accompanying sauce.

NORTH CAROLINA SWEET POTATO PUDDING

Makes 8 servings
Preparation time: 10 minutes
Cooking time: 50 minutes

5 cups peeled and grated raw sweet potatoes (about 3 potatoes)
3/4 cup brown sugar, packed
1 1/2 cups milk
1 stick unsalted butter, melted
3 eggs, beaten
1 teaspoon grated orange rind
1/2 teaspoon ground cinnamon
1/2 cup raisins
1/2 cup shredded coconut
1/2 cup chopped pecans

Preheat oven to 400 degrees. Grease a 1 1/2-quart baking dish or ovenproof skillet.

Combine the sweet potatoes, brown sugar, milk, butter, eggs, orange rind, cinnamon, raisins, coconut and pecans in a large mixing bowl, then pour into the prepared baking dish. Bake for 50 minutes. As a crust forms around the edges, remove from the oven and stir pudding well to mix in the crust; repeat several times during baking. Serve warm or cold, plain or topped with ice cream.

MINIATURE STILTON AND
PEAR QUICHES
DUNGENESS CRAB
ITALIAN STYLE
CURLY ENDIVE AND BELGIUM
ENDIVE SALAD*
CRUSTY BREAD*

New Year's Eve calls for a memorable and slightly extravagant meal and this informal crab dinner is just the dish to get the year started right. The crab dish comes courtesy of the August Sebastiani wine-making family. Dungeness crab is only available in Atlanta for a couple of weeks a year, right around Christmas, and it hasn't been available in local grocery stores for a few years. Precooked fresh crab, as it is sold in Atlanta, makes an effortless meal with only a minimum of ingredients. Preparing dinner will be easier if you have your seafood clerk crack and clean the crabs; just be sure to retain the flavorful crab juices to add to the vinaigrette.

Start your dinner with tarts made with Stilton and pears, adapted from Dallas, Texas chef, Margaret Bracken. Add a green salad and lots of crusty bread for dipping in the vinaigrette that covers the crab.

MINIATURE STILTON AND PEAR QUICHES

Makes 12 to 14 tarts
Preparation time: 20 minutes
Cooking time: 15 minutes

4 ounces Stilton or other blue cheese, crumbled
1 pear, cored and diced with peel

Price: In the shell, will average $2.99 a pound and $6.99 a pound for organic nuts.

Nutrition: A 3-ounce serving of shelled nuts has 160 calories, 1.1 grams fat, 6.7 milligrams sodium and no cholesterol.

Selection: Chestnuts can be spoiled on the inside without showing any sign of it on the shell. Look for glossy, unblemished nuts that are firm, solid and heavy for their size. Check with the produce manager that the nuts are fresh, not last year's supply. Some stores also carry peeled and flash-frozen nuts and chestnut flour for cakes and breads.

Storage: Fresh, unshelled nuts will keep up to a week in a cool place. If chestnuts are stored at 33 to 35 degrees with 70 percent humidity, they will last 6 to 8 weeks. In a refrigerator, chestnuts will keep 4 weeks. Frozen, peeled nuts will keep up to two years.

Uses: One pound of unshelled nuts will yield bout $3/4$ pound of shelled nuts, enough for 2 to 3 servings. The peeled nuts can be sauteed in olive oil or butter, alone or with other vegetables, added to turkey dressing or pureed for a creamy dessert. The chestnut meal can be dried and used as a flour in cakes and breads.

Along with dark evenings and damp weather comes the season for roasting chestnuts, whether you buy them on a street corner or do it yourself. Peeling and eating the fragrant hot nuts is probably the very best way to enjoy them, although the roasted nuts can be used in cakes, breads and desserts. With the holiday looming, take an opportunity to roast your own.

The holiday season is chestnut season. Fresh nuts in the shell from Italy are in grocery stores now through Christmas. This year's harvest was a good one, so quality and supplies are the best they have been in years.

The peeled nuts are sweet and starchy and add richness to many wintry dishes. Add them to the turkey dressing or saute them in browned butter with lima beans for an easy holiday dish. In France the finest quality chestnuts are called marrons and are used for making candied or glaced chestnuts.

left on
1 1/2 cups half-and-half or cream
3 large eggs
Salt and pepper to taste
12 to 14 tart shells
1 to 2 pears, cored, sliced and dipped
   in lemon water for garnish

Preheat oven to 375 degrees. Make pastry or use preformed tart shells found in the freezer section of the grocery store; bake for 8 to 10 minutes; cool slightly.

Distribute equal amounts of crumbled cheese and diced pears into the shells. Whisk eggs and cream together, add salt and pepper to taste. Spoon the egg-cream mixture into shells until almost filled. Bake on ungreased cookie sheets 10 to 15 minutes. To serve, garnish with pear slices.

DUNGENESS CRAB ITALIAN STYLE

Makes 4 servings
Preparation time: 20 minutes
Marinating time: 2 hours or more

6 2- to 2 1/2-pound cooked crabs
Juice of 12 lemons
1/2 cup wine vinegar
1/2 cup olive oil
1/2 teaspoon paprika
1 teaspoon Tabasco sauce
1 teaspoon Worcestershire sauce
2 long loaves French or other crusty
   bread

Break off the legs and claws from the crab and crack them, retaining any juices. Pull off the crab backs and remove spongy gills. Remove the small tapered "apron" from the underside of the crabs, then cut the bodies into six pieces. Place all the parts in a large bowl and set aside.

Combine the lemon juice, vinegar, olive oil, paprika, Tabasco sauce and Worcestershire sauce and pour the mixture over the crab. Refrigerate and marinate 2 hours or more, turning occasionally. Offer nutcrackers and small forks to each person and serve with big chunks of French bread to dunk in the marinade.

TUESDAY

BLACK-EYED PEA SALAD
WITH PORK
CORNBREAD SLICES*
MIXED GREEN AND
TANGERINE SALAD*
CINNAMON APPLES

Start the new year with good luck with this tasty black-eyed pea salad. Add slices of leftover pork from Sunday's meal and your favorite cornbread recipe. Add a salad and for dessert serve cinnamon apples, a Christmas family favorite from a great gardener and friend, Atlantan Jean Givens. The kids will enjoy melting cinnamon red hots to make this dish. It's helpful to use an apple corer to core the apples without splitting them in half.

BLACK-EYED PEA SALAD WITH PORK

Makes 5 to 6 servings
Preparation time: 10 minutes
Marinating time: several hours

2 16-ounce cans black-eyed peas,
   drained and rinsed (or 6 cups
   cooked)
1/2 small red onion, thinly sliced
1 garlic clove, flattened and peeled

1/3 cup olive oil
2 tablespoons herbed red wine
   vinegar
1/2 teaspoon dried (or 1 teaspoon
   fresh) oregano
Salt and black pepper to taste
4 to 8 lettuce leaves
6 to 8 ounces sliced and slivered pork
   tenderloin
The grated peel of 1 lemon
   (optional)

In a medium bowl, combine the peas, onion, garlic, oil, vinegar, oregano, salt and pepper. Cover and chill several hours or overnight; remove garlic.

Arrange lettuce leaves and pork tenderloin slices on plates and spoon pea salad over. Garnish with (optional) grated lemon peel.

CINNAMON APPLES

Makes 4 servings
Preparation time: 15 minutes
Cooking time: 10 to 15 minutes

4 firm apples, such as York or Granny
   Smith, cored and peeled
1 cup sugar
1 cup water
19-ounce package cinnamon
   red hots
18-ounce package cream cheese,
   softened
1/2 cup broken pecans
Lettuce for the plates

Core and peel as many apples as you have people to serve; set aside. Heat the sugar and water together to make a sugar syrup; add the package of cinnamon red hots and allow them to melt.

Cook the apples in the syrup, turning and basting them until they are tender and turn a rose color, 10 to 15 minutes. Don't let them cook until they turn mushy (cooking time will depend on the softness of the apples and how many you are cooking at one time).

Meanwhile, mix together the cream cheese and pecans; set aside.

When the apples are tender, remove them from the syrup and fill the cores with the cream cheese mixture. To serve, place each on a lettuce-lined plate.

WEDNESDAY

STRACCIATELLA WITH FRESH SPINACH AND PEAS
CRUSTY BREAD*

This comforting Italian soup goes together in minutes. Little meat-balls are sometimes added, but the meatless version is very satisfying, adapted from *Cold Weather Cooking* by Sarah Leah Chase (Workman Publishing, $13.95).

STRACCIATELLA WITH FRESH SPINACH AND PEAS

Makes 4 servings
Preparation time: 5 minutes
Cooking time: 5 to 8 minutes

1 to 2 tablespoons Italian parsley
2 large eggs
$1/4$ cup freshly grated Parmesan cheese
1 tablespoon fresh lemon juice
Pinch of grated nutmeg
2 14 $1/2$-ounce cans or 4 cups low-sodium chicken broth or beef broth
Salt and black pepper to taste
2 to 3 cups fresh spinach, washed, and cut in thin shreds
1 cup frozen peas, thawed and patted dry
Several tablespoons grated Parmesan cheese for garnish

Put the parsley in the workbowl of a food processor and pulse until minced. Add the eggs, cheese, lemon juice and nutmeg and pulse to blend.

Put the chicken broth in a large saucepan and bring to a boil over medium heat. Whisk in the egg mixture, stirring gently. Cook, stirring constantly, until tiny flakes of the cooked egg appear in the stock, 1 to 2 minutes. Add salt and pepper to taste; remove from the heat.

Place the spinach and peas in the bottom of a soup tureen or serving bowls and ladle the hot soup over the vegetables. Serve at once, passing a bowl of grated Parmesan cheese.

THURSDAY

PHILADELPHIA CHEESE STEAK
STEAMED GREEN BEANS*

Try this easy family dinner when you don't have a lot of time but want a hearty meal.

PHILADELPHIA CHEESE STEAK

Makes 4 servings
Preparation time: 10 minutes
Cooking time: 20 minutes

4 sourdough rolls, cut in half lengthwise
2 tablespoons butter
2 tablespoons olive oil
1 large onion, thinly sliced
1 bell pepper, seeded and diced
$1/2$ teaspoon oregano
Salt and pepper to taste
$3/4$ pound sliced sirloin steak or eye of round, pounded thin, or Steak-Umms

4 ounces provolone cheese, sliced

Preheat oven to 350 degrees.

Wrap bread in aluminum foil and heat 15 minutes.

In a large skillet, melt the butter and oil over medium heat. Add the onion and green pepper and saute until soft and fragrant, 5 to 10 minutes. Season with oregano, salt and pepper. Remove the vegetables from the pan and keep warm.

In the same skillet saute the beef slices on both sides over medium-high heat to desired doneness (add more olive oil to the skillet if necessary). During the last minute of cooking, top the meat with the cheese and let it melt. Fill the breads with onion and pepper mixture, beef and cheese slices and serve.

FRIDAY

BLACK OLIVES AND SWEET PEPPERS IN VINAIGRETTE*
CHICKEN LASAGNA*
CRUSTY BREAD*

Look no further than your neighborhood deli for good take-out food for tonight's dinner. Many such spots, such as the Pharr Road Cheese Shop, sells lasagna by the slice and it reheats quickly for a sturdy Friday night dinner.

SATURDAY

WINTER BREAD
SALAD

RAVIOLI WITH
GORGONZOLA SAUCE*
PECAN PIE*

Winter bread salad was devised to make a meal out of leftovers, and this one adds the hearty winter flavor of dried tomatoes. The smoky flavor of the grilled bread adds a wonderful flavor to this salad, adapted from a recipe from Nathalie Dupree, cookbook author and host of public television's "Matters of Taste." Purchase ready-made ravioli and gorgonzola or other blue-cheese sauce in the deli section. Leftover pecan pie from the holidays can finish the meal.

WINTER BREAD SALAD

Makes 4 servings
Preparation time: 15 minutes
Cooking time: 5 minutes
Marinating time: at least 30 minutes

8 slices day-old, thick-sliced French
      or Italian bread
$^1/_4$ cup olive oil
$^3/_4$ cup vinaigrette, divided
$^1/_3$ cup dried tomatoes, cut in shreds,
      with some of the oil from the jar
4 cups mixed greens
1 cucumber, peeled and sliced
$^1/_2$ cup finely diced red onion

Preheat the broiler. Cut the bread into large croutons, about 3 or 4 inches in diameter. Sprinkle the bread with olive oil, then place the bread under the broiler and lightly toast. Toss the bread with $^1/_2$ cup vinaigrette and dried tomatoes and let stand 30 minutes, until it has soaked up most of the vinaigrette — as long as a day if necessary. Sprinkle the bread with a few tablespoons water to make it more moist, if necessary.
      Meanwhile, toss the mixed greens, cucumber and red onion with any remaining vinaigrette, add the croutons and serve.

BIBLIOGRAPHY

Adams, Marcia. *Heartland.* Clarkson Potter.

Aken, Norman Van. *Feast of Sunlight.* Ballantine.

American Cancer Society. *Look What's Cooking Now!* Minnesota Division.

Ballister, Barry. *Barry Ballister's Fruit and Vegetable Stand.* The Overlook Press.

Barnard, Melanie and Brooke Dojny. *Parties!* HarperCollins.

Belk, Sarah. *Around the Southern Table.* Simon & Schuster.

Better Homes and Gardens. *The New Cookbook.* Meredith Corp.

Bon Appetit Magazine. March 1991.

Boteler, Alison. *What Should I Bring?* Barron's.

Brody, Jane. *Jane Brody's Good Food Book.* Bantam.

———. *Jane Brody's Good Food Gourmet.* Norton.

Brown, Edward and Deborah Madison. *The Greens Cookbook: Extraordinary Vegetarian Cuisine from the Celebrated Restaurant.* Bantam.

Brown, Ellen. *Gourmet Gazelle.* Bantam.

Bugialli, Giuliano. *Giuliano Bugialli's Foods of Italy.* Stewart, Tabori & Chang.

Burgess, Linda and Rosamond Richardson. *Alfresco.* Clarkson Potter.

Burros, Marian. *20 Minute Menus.* Simon & Schuster.

Burt, Lizzie and Nelda Mercer. *High Fit–Low Fat.* University of Michigan Medical Center.

Caggiano, Biba. *Modern Italian Cooking.* Simon & Schuster.

———. *Trattoria Cooking.* MacMillan.

Carpenter, Hugh. *Pacific Flavors.* Stewart, Tabori & Chang.

Carper, Jean. *The Food Pharmacy Guide to Good Eating.* Bantam.

Chase, Sarah Leah. *Cold Weather Cooking.* Workman.

———. *Nantucket Open House Cookbook.* Workman.

Choate, Judith. *Hot.* Crown.

Cooking Light Magazine. *Cooking Light: Fish and Shellfish.* Warner.

Cooking Light Magazine. *Cooking Light Desserts.* Warner.

Cooper, Leslie L. *America's New Low-Fat Cuisine.* Houghton Mifflin.

———. *Best Recipes for Weekend Breakfasts.* Prentice Hall.

———. *Betty Crocker's Easy Entertaining.* Prentice Hall.

———. *Betty Crocker's Eat and Lose Weight.* Prentice Hall.

———. *Betty Crocker's Cookbook.* Golden Press.

Cunningham, Marion. *The Supper Book.*

De Medici, Lorenza. *Italy: The Beautiful Cookbook.* Collins Publishers.

Dent, Huntley. *Feast of Santa Fe.* Simon & Schuster.

Dry, Jeri and Alex Engal. *Cookie Mania.* Contempory Books.

Dupree, Nathalie. *Nathalie Dupree Cooks for Family and Friends.* Morrow.

Elverson, Virginia. *Gulf Coast Cooking.* Shearer.

Emmerling, Mary. *American Country Cooking.* Clarkson Potter.

Escudier, Jean-Noel and Peta J. Fuller. *The Wonderful Food of Provence.* Harper & Row.

Ferrary, Jeannette and Louise Fiszer. *Sweet Onions & Sour Cherries.* Simon & Schuster.

Fields, Debbi. *Mrs. Field's Cookie Book.* Time-Life Books.

Fisher, Helen V. *Cookbook for the 90s.* Fisher.

Fox, Margaret S. and John Bear. *Cafe Beaujolais*. Ten Speed.
——. *Morning Food*. Ten Speed.
Freiman, Jane. *Dinner Party*. Harper & Row.
Gibbons, Barbara. *Light & Spicy*. Harper & Row.
Giobbi, Edward. *Pleasures of the Good Earth*. Knopf.
Glen, Camille. *Heritage of Southern Cooking*. Workman.
Grausman, Richard. *At Home With the French Classics*. Workman.
Greene, Bert. *The Grains Cookbook*. Workman.
——. *Greene on Greens*. Workman.
Gridley, Shannon Jeter. *Coffee and Tea 1992*. Culinary.
Haedrich, Ken. *Home for the Holidays*. Bantam.
Hearty Soups. Bon Appetit Publishing.
Herbst, Sharon Tyler. *Cooking Smart*. HarperCollins.
Hirsch, David. *The Moosewood Restaurant Kitchen Garden*. Fireside.
Hom, Ken. *The Taste of China*. Simon & Schuster.
Hopping, Jane Watson. *The Country Mothers Cookbook*. Villard.
Hunter, Ethel Farmer. *Secrets of Southern Cooking*. Tudor.
Jaffrey, Madhur. *Madhur Jaffrey's Cookbook*. Harper & Row.
Johnson, Ronald. *Company Fare*. Simon and Schuster.
Junior League of Atlanta. *Atlanta Cooknotes*. Moran Printing.
Kafka, Barbara. *Microwave Gourmet*. William Morrow.
——. *Party Food*. William Morrow.
Katzen, Mollie. *Still Life With Menu*. Ten Speed Press.
Khasla, Baba S. *Great Vegetables*. Perigee.
——. *Vegetables From the Great Chefs*. Perigee.
Kinderlehrer, Jane. *Smart Cookies*. Newmarket.
Leach, Robin. *Lifestyles of the Rich and Famous*. Viking Studio Books.
Lindsay, Anne. *Low-Cholesterol Cuisine*. Hearst Books.
——. *The American Cancer Society Cookbook*. Hearst Books.
London, Sheryl and Mel. *Fresh Fruit Desserts*. Prentice Hall.
Loomis, Susan Herrmann. *The Great American Seafood Cookbook*. Workman.
Lundy, Ronni. *Shuck Beans, Stack Cakes and Honest Fried Chicken*. Atlantic Monthly Press.
Madison, Deborah. *The Savory Way*. Bantam.
Mandel, Abby. *More Taste Than Time*. Simon & Schuster.
Mangum, Karen. *Life's Simple Pleasures*. Pacific Press.
McLaughlin, Michael. *An American Kitchen*. Simon & Schuster.
——. *The New American Kitchen*. Simon & Schuster.
Metropolitan Home. July 1992.
Meyers, Perla. *Art of Seasonal Cooking*. Simon & Schuster.
——. *Perla Meyers' Art of Seasonal Cooking*. Simon & Schuster.
Miller, Mark. *Coyote Cafe*. Ten Speed Press.
Moosewood Collective. *Sundays at Moosewood Restaurant*. Simon & Schuster.
Olney, Richard. *Simple French Food*. Atheneum.
Papas, Lou Seibert and Jane Horn. *The New Harvest*. 101 Productions.
Parker, Courtney. *How to Eat Like a Southerner and Live to Tell the Tale*. Clarkson Potter.
Payne, Rolce Redard and Dorrit Speyer Senior. *Cooking With Fruit*. Crown.
Pepin, Jacques. *The Short-Cut Cook*. William Morrow.
Pickarski, Brother Ron. *Friendly Foods*. Ten Speed Press.
Pinderhughes, John. *Family of the Spirit Cookbook*. Simon & Schuster.

Pressman, Thelma. *365 Quick and Easy Microwave Recipes*. Harper & Row.
Puckett, Susan. *A Cook's Tour of Iowa*. University of Iowa Press.
Robinson, Kathleen and Pete Luckett. *Fresh Fruits and Vegetables*. Fisher.
Rodgers, Rick. *The Turkey Cookbook*. HarperCollins.
Rogers, Ford. *Citrus*. Simon & Schuster.
Rosbottom, Betty. *First Impressions*. William Morrow.
Ross, Larry. *Nanny's Texas Table*. Simon & Schuster.
Rosso, Julee and Sheila Lukins. *The Silver Palate Good Times Cookbook*. Workman Publishing.
——. *The New Basics Cookbook*. Workman Publishing.
Rozin, Elizabeth. *Blue Corn and Chocolate*. Knopf.
Sass, Lorna. *Recipes From an Ecological Kitchen*. Morrow.
Schlesinger, Sarah and Barbara Earnest. *The Low-Cholesterol Olive Oil Cookbook*. Villard Books.
Schlesinger, Chris and John Willoughby. *Thrill of the Grill*. William Morrow.
Schneider, Elizabeth. *Uncommon Fruits and Vegetables*. Harper & Row.
Schneider, Sally. *The Art of Low-Calorie Cooking*. Stewart, Tabori, & Chang.
Schult, Phillip Stephen. *As American as Apple Pie*. Simon & Schuster.
Schur, Sylvia and Vivian Schulte. *365 Easy Low Calorie Recipes*. Harper & Row.
Scicolone, Michele. *Fish Steaks and Fillets*.
Seed, Diane. *Favorite Indian Food*. Ten Speed Press.
Shaw, Diane. *Sweet Basil, Garlic, Tomatoes and Chives*. Harmony Books.
Shepherd, Renee and Fran Raboff. *Recipes From a Kitchen Garden, Volume Two*. Shepherd's Garden Publishing.
Simmons, Marie. *The Light Touch*. Chapters.
Simon, Susan. *Visual Vegetables*. Clarkson Potter.
Sorosky, Marlene. *Easy Entertaining With Marlene Sorosky*. Harper & Row.
Stapley, Patricia. *The Little Bean Cookbook*. Crown.
Stone, Sally and Martin. *The Essential Root Vegetable Cookbook*. Clarkson Potter.
Stovel, Edith. *Picnic!*. Garden Way Publishing.
Styler, Christopher. *Primi Piatti*. Harper & Row.
Tolley, Emelie and Chris Mead. *Cooking With Herbs*. Clarkson Potter.
Ungerer, Miriam. *Summertime Food*. Random House.
Urvater, Michele. *Monday-to-Friday Recipes*. Workman.
Walter, Eugene. *American Cooking Southern Style*. Time-Life Books.
Waters, Alice, Patricia Curtain and Martine Labro. *Chez Panisse Pasta Pizza and Calzone*. Random House.
Waters, Alice. *Chez Panisse Menu Cookbook*. Random House.
White, Jasper. *Jasper White's Cooking from New England*. Harper & Row.
Wilson, Jane Weston. *Eating Well When You Just Can't Eat the Way You Used To*. Workman.
Wise, Victoria and Susanna Hoffman. *Good & Plenty*. Harper & Row.
Young, Joyce LaFray. *Tropic Cooking*. Ten Speed Press.
Zimmerman, Linda and Peggy Mellody. *Cobblers, Crumbles & Crisps*. Clarkson Potter.